# International Copyright Law

## by Lionel S. Sobel

**Professor, Southwestern Law School**

**Chair (2007-2009), American Bar Association
Forum Committee on the Entertainment & Sports Industries**

**Professor Lionel S. Sobel**
**Southwestern Law School**
**3050 Wilshire Boulevard**
**Los Angeles, California 90010-1106**
**lsobel@swlaw.edu**

# International Copyright Law
## Table of Contents

# Chapter 1

# Introduction to International Copyright

## A. Copyright's role in the intellectual property "family"

You're about to begin the study of the fascinating subject of international *copyright* law. I emphasize the word "copyright," because copyright is just one member of an entire family of doctrines known as "intellectual property law" (often called "IP law" for short). Copyright's siblings are: patent, trademark and trade secret law; and relatively new laws that protect Internet domain names. Copyright has cousins too: the right of publicity, and privacy and defamation law.

International copyright is too big a field to cover all of intellectual property law in a single course. But before we dig into the details of international copyright, it's important for you to be able to recognize what is covered by *copyright*, and what is covered by *other* members of the IP family. It's important, because in actual practice, the *differences* between copyright and other IP doctrines are more significant than their similarities. It's also important, because a client's legal problem could easily involve several different IP doctrines, all at once. To see how this is so, imagine that you have a client named Leonora da Vinci.

Leonora is highly accomplished in both the arts and the sciences. She is national of Italy and a resident of Florence. Indeed, she may be a descendant of her namesake, the great 16th century Italian artist and inventor, Leonardo da Vinci. From her office in Florence, Leonora runs a world-wide art and technology business, selling her own creations.

As an artist, Leonora creates spectacular works of visual art, which she sells as digital downloads.

As a scientist, she invented a digital display device, called a TabulaArtistica. It is similar to a Kindle or Sony eBook Reader, but it has a much larger screen; it displays works of visual art in color (as well as text); it is thinner and lighter than a Kindle or Sony; and it connects to directly to the web (no computer is necessary). Leonora holds a patent on TabulaArtistica's display screen, and a separate patent on the file format in which she encodes the digital images of the art works she sells to TabulaArtistica owners.

Leonora also holds a registered trademark in the "TabulaArtistica" name of her invention.

She sells digital downloads of her artwork to TabulaArtistica owners, directly from the website for which she is the registered owner of the domain name www.tabula-aesthetica.com.

Leonora is well known by art lovers and technology buffs all around the world. Her face and her name are immediately recognized, because photographs of her appear frequently in art, technology and general news periodicals, in connection with articles about her accomplishments.

Not everything about Leonora is well known, however. Until very recently, the public did *not* know any of these things about her: she has been married and divorced three times; she has had several lovers, before, after, between and even during her marriages; she has one child, a young son, born shortly before she divorced husband number three; and her son is not the child of that husband.

The public *now* knows about Leonora's divorces, lovers and child, because of a man named Dominique Voleur.

Voleur is a French national who used to reside in Florence. While living there, Voleur was Leonora's most trusted employee and confidant, but was never one of her lovers, much to his chagrin. Two years ago, in a jealous fit, Voleur quit and moved to Montreal, Quebec, Canada. When he moved, he took with him two things Leonora had kept secret from all outsiders: the plans and specifications necessary to manufacture TabulaAristicas, and the names and addresses of the companies that manufactured TabulaAristica's many components.

Now living in Montreal, Voleur is doing several things, without Leonora's consent: He

a. manufactures a device that he calls an "eArtTablet," which is an exact knock-off of Leonora's TabulaArtistica, built using the plans and specifications he took from her,

b. using components he purchases from Leonora's suppliers,

c. which he sells to customers in the United States, as well as Canada and elsewhere in the world,

d. from a website for which he registered the domain name www.LeonoraDaVinci.com,

e. which features Leonora's name and likeness on its home page, and

f. from which he also sells digital versions of Leonora's art works.

Leonora responded by sending him a stern email in which she demanded that he stop doing all of these things, and threatened to sue him if he didn't stop. Voleur, however, has not stopped. Instead, on his website, which is hosted by a web-hosting company on a server in Virginia, he posted:

g. photos of her, taken with telephoto lens through the windows of her home and over the fence surrounding her back yard, in the company of men that Voleur's website said are her lovers, which in fact they are, and

h. articles that said that Leonora's artworks are not created by her, but instead are created by abused children in factories in Myanmar, which is totally false.

Imagine that Leonora has just retained you to sue Voleur. Your first task will be to determine which legal doctrines may provide Leonora with protection. Below are thumbnail descriptions of the doctrines that may be helpful. As you read the thumbnails, watch for (and make note of) the answers to the following question.

*Question:*

Which IP legal doctrine applies to each of Voleur's activities ("a" through "h" above)? (The following thumbnails will not give you enough knowledge to fully assess whether Leonora will prevail on each claim. But they will give you enough knowledge so that you will know what legal materials you'd have to read in order to do a full and proper analysis.)

---

### 1. Patent law

Patent law protects inventions. Many inventions are physical devices, or individual parts of devices. But intangible procedures and methods may be patentable inventions too. In order for an invention to be eligible for patent protection, it must have three characteristics. It must be novel, nonobvious and useful.

To be "novel," it must be different from anything that's already been patented, or sold, or written about. To be "nonobvious," it must be so groundbreaking that the invention would not be obvious to other people who are knowledgeable in the invention's field. To be "useful," the invention must actually do something.

Inventions that are novel, nonobvious and useful are *eligible* for patent protection. But in order to actually be protected, the inventor must apply for and obtain a patent from a government agency. In the United States, that agency is the U.S. Patent & Trademark Office. An invention is not protected, unless and until a patent is issued.

Once a patent is issued, it gives its owner the exclusive right to make, sell or use the invention, for a period of 20 years (in the U.S. and most other countries). Making, selling or using a patented invention without the patent owner's permission is an infringement. And the patent owner may sue infringers for damages and injunctive relief to prevent further infringements.

### 2. Trade secret law

Trade secret law protects private information that enables businesses to earn money. Protectable information can be of almost anything, including formulas (like the formula for Coca-Cola), procedures, methods, pricing information, and customer and supplier lists.

However, in order to be protectable, the information must be kept private. Once a business discloses information, it is no longer a "trade secret." Also, trade secret law does not protect once-secret information that others have figured out for themselves, even by using techniques that techies call "reverse engineering."

Typically, trade secret law is what enables businesses to protect their private (but non-patentable) information from being taken by employees, when employees leave to go to work for, or to start their own, competing businesses.

Trade secrets do not have to be registered with the government, or anyone, to be protected. They are protected automatically, assuming of course they are eligible for protection. And they remain protected, for as long as they remain secret which can be forever. (The Coca-Cola formula is still a protected trade secret even though the current Coke® formula reportedly dates back to the 1920s.)

## 3. Trademark law

Trademark law protects words and logos (and even sounds or colors) that
- distinguish the trademark owner's goods or services from those manufactured or sold by others, and thus
- indicate to consumers that the trademark owner is the source of goods or services to which the trademark is attached.

In order to do these things, a trademark must be distinctive. Some marks are naturally distinctive, because they are fanciful (like "Clorox" for bleach), or arbitrary (like "Shell" for gasoline), or suggestive (like "Coppertone" for suntan lotion). Other marks are not naturally distinctive, but become distinctive over time, because they acquire secondary meaning in the minds of consumers (like "Chap Stick" for lip balm). Generic words, like "bread" or "cola" are not distinctive are not eligible for trademark protection, ever.

As a general rule, eligible marks have to be used in commerce before they are protected by law. Trademarks may be registered with a government agency. (Indeed, in the U.S. and in many other countries, it is possible to register a mark that one intends to use in the future, even before it has been used; and the utility of doing so will be explained below.) In the U.S., trademarks are registered in the U.S. Patent & Trademark Office. Trademark owners obtain several valuable benefits from registering their marks, but – in the United States, at least – registration is not *required* for protection.

A trademark is protected for as long as it continues to be used in commerce, which means trademarks can be protected forever.

## 4. Domain name protection law

Website owners obtain the exclusive *ability* – not "right," but "ability" – to use domain names, worldwide, by registering their desired names with non-governmental bodies known as "domain name registrars."

The process for registering Internet domain names is simple, fast and cheap. It may be done by anyone, anywhere in the world, using nothing more than an Internet-connected computer and a credit card. Neither ownership of the name being registered, nor authorization to register it, have to be shown in advance – not even if the name being registered is a trademark belonging to someone else, or is the name of a famous personality.

The ease with which domain names may be registered has led to some unintended consequences. In the mid-1990s – before most people realized that the World Wide Web would become a global marketplace and mass communications medium – several forward-thinking folks began registering other people's trademarks and celebrity names. In earlier times and other settings, these folks might have been called "homesteaders" or even "entrepreneurs." But before the '90s were over, they were in fact called something else: "cybersquatters."

The personal names of dozens of entertainers were registered by cybersquatters. Among them were: recording artists Celine Dion, Eminem, Peter Frampton, Madonna, Bruce Springsteen, Sting, and Jethro Tull; actors Pamela Anderson, Pierce Brosnan, Tom Cruise, Robert Downey Jr., Carmen Electra, Nicole Kidman, Julia Roberts, and Kevin Spacey; television personalities Larry King and Martha Stewart; athletes Dan Marino, and Venus and Serena Williams; and authors Jeffrey Archer, Michael Crichton, J.K. Rowlings and Tom Stoppard.

The question – for companies whose trademarks had been registered by cybersquatters, as well as for celebrities – was whether they could do anything about it. The answer turned out to be "yes," though until 1999, the legal tool for doing so was plain old trademark law. Companies sometimes succeeded with these tools against trademark cybersquatters. (See, e.g., *Panavision International v. Toeppen*, 141 F.3d 1316 (9th Cir. 1998).) But celebrities (such as Reverand Jerry Falwell) often did not. (See, e.g., *Lamparello v. Falwell*, 420 F.3d 309 (4th Cir. 2005), cert.denied, 126 S.Ct. 1772 (2006).

In 1999, the United States Congress enacted the Anticybersquatting Consumer Protection Act (commonly referred to as the "ACPA") – a statute that deals specifically with cybersquatting. ACPA prohibits the unauthorized use of trademarks and celebrity names as domain names.

Also in 1999, another major "law" was adopted by the Internet Corporation for Assigned Names and Numbers (commonly referred to as "ICANN"). ICANN is the world-wide manager of the Internet domain name system, and in 1999 it adopted its own procedure for resolving domain name disputes. That policy is kknown as the Uniform Dispute Resolution Policy (commonly referred to as the "UDRP").

The UDRP is not a treaty or even a statute. Instead, it is a provision that has been incorporated into the domain registration agreements between most domain-name registrars and people who register domain names. The reason the UDRP is so useful against cybersquatters is that the phrase "most domain-name registrars" really means "most." The UDRP has been adopted by all domain-name registrars for domain names ending in .com, .net, and .org, as well as the managers of country-code top-level domains (such as .uk, .nu, .tv, .ws and .ir). It is, in other words, impossible for cybersquatters to avoid agreeing to the UDRP, because if a person declines to consent to be bound by its provisions, the domain name will not be registered.

The UDRP enables a trademark owner, or a celebrity, to get back a domain name registered by a cybersquatter, if:

- the domain name is confusingly similar to the trademark or celebrity's name;
- the cybersquatter has no right to or legitimate interest in the domain name; and
- the cybersquatter registered and used the domain name in bad faith.

## 5. Right of publicity law

The right of publicity is the right to control the use of one's own name and likeness for commercial purposes such as advertising and merchandising (though *not* the right to control their use in news, biography, or docudrama, even when those things are done for profit).

Protection against the unauthorized use of a person's name or likeness lasts at least as long as the person is alive, and in some jurisdictions even after the person has died.

Protection usually does not require registration, though some jurisdictions permit registration and may require it for post-mortem (i.e., after-death) protection.

## 6. Privacy law

The doctrine known as the "right to privacy" is closely related to the right of publicity. In the United States, privacy is the older doctrine and is the doctrine that gave birth to the right of publicity, in the sense that the right of publicity was viewed, at first, as an aspect of privacy. The reason that the right of publicity developed into a conceptually separate doctrine from privacy is that the two doctrines protect somewhat different interests.

The right of publicity protects the financial interest that celebrities (and others) have in preventing, or being compensated for, the use of their names and likenesses for commercial purposes. By contrast, the right to privacy protects a personal and psychological interest – the interest that celebrities (and others) have in protecting themselves against the emotional distress that can be caused by the disclosure of private information.

In a nutshell, the right to privacy is the right to prevent (or be compensated in damages for) the disclosure of personal, previously unknown information of a kind the disclosure of which would offend a person of reasonable sensibilities.

## 7. Defamation law

A defamatory statement is a *false* statement of *fact* that damages the reputation of the person about whom it is made. (The statement must be false, because if the statement is true, it is not defamatory, even if it damages the reputation of the person about whom it is made. And the statement must be one of fact, because if the statement is an opinion, it is not defamatory, even if it damages the reputation of the person about whom it is made.)

Protection against defamation is provided by compensating those who are defamed with damages in money. (In the United States, at least, anticipated defamatory statements cannot be enjoined in advance.) A person's right to protection against defamation lasts only as long as that person is alive. As Jonathan Turley once put it: "you cannot defame the dead (which, in practical terms, means you can)." Professor Turley explained the reason for this legal principle by quoting English jurist Sir James Stephen who, back in 1887, said "The dead have no rights and can suffer no wrongs." That seems harsh, I know, but insofar as defamation is concerned, it's the law.

It isn't necessary to register one's good reputation in order to receive legal protection against defamation (and that's good, because it isn't at all obvious how one would go about registering his or her good reputation, if that were necessary). A defamation lawsuit is all that's necessary to get damages. But defamation lawsuits are rarely simple, because defamation claims clash with free speech principles (in the United States and even in the European Union).

## 8. Copyright law

Copyright protects literary, dramatic, musical and artistic works, including paintings, sculptures, movies, recordings, and video games. Copyright even protects television broadcasts of live sporting events.

There are some conditions that must be satisfied for works to be eligible for copyright protection. Works must be original (which simply means they must not copied from someone else), and they must be at least minimally creative (a great deal of creativity isn't necessary, but a single word or a straight line is not sufficient). In the United States (but not in all countries), works also must be fixed in a tangible medium, such as recorded on tape, or written on paper.

Copyright "protection" means that the copyright owner has the exclusive right to reproduce, distribute, perform, display and make other versions of the work, and the right to authorize others to do any of these things. Doing any of these things without authorization from the copyright owner is an infringement. There are lots of limitations on these exclusive rights, and even outright exceptions to them. But for present purposes, this definition of copyright "protection" will work just fine.

Copyright protection does not require compliance with formalities, so neither copyright notices nor registration are required for protection. Nor does copyright protection require actual use – not even in countries where protection is sought (so, as you will see in later chapters of this book, German novels are protected in the U.S., even if they haven't been published in the U.S.).

---

## B. Overview of international copyright principles

The analysis of international copyright law questions is always a fascinating, and sometimes convoluted, exercise. Indeed, it's a lot like playing three-dimensional tick-tack-toe. To reach a conclusion about any particular question, it's necessary to consider

- whether a foreign work will be protected at all, and if so,
- which country's law provides protection, and finally,
- what sort of protection that country's law actually provides.

Each step is a full and complete exercise in itself. The first step – whether a work will be protected at all – as you'll soon read, is unique to international *copyright* law; it has no counterpart in other areas of the law, not even in trademark or patent law. The second step – which country's law applies – is a *conflicts of law* question, applied in an especially interesting context. And the third step – what protection is provided – is pure *copyright* law, involving the laws of other countries (sometimes the laws of more than one other country).

If you're comfortable with the "game" analogy, then think of this book as a statement and explanation of the rules of the game, and in some sections, a strategy guide as well.

We begin with a quick overview of the subject – one that will enable you to put the following chapters in context and to see what the significance is of the topics that follow.

### 1. International copyright protection available internationally only if required by treaty, proclamation or domestic law

Copyright protection is available internationally – that is, in one country for a work from another country – only if international protection is required by: (1) a treaty; (2) a proclamation of reciprocal protection; or (3) domestic law.

United States law provides protection to works from other countries in all three of these ways, under slightly different – but legally significant – circumstances.

#### a. Treaty

**United States Copyright Act §104(b)**

Published Works . . . are subject to protection under this title if –

(1) on the date of first publication, one or more of the authors is a national or domiciliary of the United States, or is a national, domiciliary, or sovereign authority *of a treaty party* . . . ; or

(2) the work is first published in the United States or in a foreign nation that, on the date of first publication, *is a treaty party*; or

(3) the work is a sound recording that was first fixed in *a treaty party*; or

(4) the work is a pictorial, graphic, or sculptural work that is incorporated in a building or other structure, or an architectural work that is embodied in a building and the building or structure is located in the United States or *a treaty party*. . . .

[Emphasis added.]

Thus, in *Rano v. Sipa Press, Inc.*, 987 F.2d 580 (9th Cir. 1993), the court noted – though only in a footnote – that "Although Rano is not a citizen of the

United States [he is a citizen of the United Kingdom], his work is protected under the Copyright Act. A work is subject to copyright if on the date of first publication the author was a national of a foreign nation that is a party to a *copyright treaty* to which the United States is also a party. . . . [The] United Kingdom and the United States have been treaty partners since 1887." (Emphasis added.) The court got the date wrong; the United Kingdom and the United States have been treaty partners only since 1891. But the court was nevertheless correct that Rano's work is protected in the United States, because the two countries are parties to a copyright treaty.

### b. Proclamation of reciprocal protection

#### United States Copyright Act §104(b)

Published Works . . . are subject to protection under this title if − . . .

(5) the work comes within the scope of a Presidential proclamation. Whenever the President finds that a particular foreign nation extends, to works by authors who are nationals or domiciliaries of the United States or to works that are first published in the United States, copyright protection on substantially the same basis as that on which the foreign nation extends protection to works of its own nationals and domiciliaries and works first published in that nation, the President may by proclamation extend protection under this title to works of which one or more of the authors is, on the date of first publication, a national, domiciliary, or sovereign authority of that nation, or which was first published in that nation. . . .

### c. Domestic copyright law

#### United States Copyright Act §104(b)(1)

Published Works . . . are subject to protection under this title if . . . on the date of first publication, one or more of the authors is a . . . domiciliary of the United States, . . . or is a stateless person, wherever that person may be domiciled. . . .

#### United States Copyright Act §104(a)

Unpublished Works . . . are subject to protection under this title without regard to the nationality or domicile of the author.

### 2. Difference between copyright and other laws in this regard

Copyright differs from other areas of the law, because international protection of other kinds of intellectual property rights does *not* depend on treaties or proclamations. Below are thumbnail descriptions of the requirements (or the lack of requirements) for international protection of IP rights other than copyright. The point of these descriptions − including the details about international patent and trademark protection − is simply to give you a sense of how different international copyright protection is from international protection for other IP rights. This book is for a course in international *copyright* law, so the following thumbnails are for background only.

### a. Defamation, right of publicity, and domain name protection

For example, in *Sharon v. Time*, 575 F.Supp. 1162, 599 F.Supp. 538 (S.D.N.Y. 1984), American law was applied (in denying defense motions to dismiss and for summary judgment) in a defamation lawsuit filed by Israeli General Ariel Sharon against *Time* magazine. (An article in *Time* had suggested that General Sharon had "instigated, encouraged, or condoned" the massacre of Palestinians in refuge centers in Lebanon, and that an Israeli government investigating commission found that Sharon had lied during his testimony before it.) There is no treaty between Israel and the United States providing for the protection of the reputations of their citizens. Yet, the absence of a treaty or other basis for applying American law to defamation claims by an Israeli citizen was *not* even discussed in either opinion in that case.

Similarly, in *Bi-Rite Enterprises, Inc. v. Bruce Miner Co.*, 757 F.2d 440 (1st Cir. 1985), American right of publicity law was applied to enjoin the unauthorized distribution in the United States of posters of popular British music performers, despite the absence of any treaty or statutory basis for doing so, and despite the fact that British law did not recognize a right to control the commercial exploitation of names and likenesses. The absence of a treaty or other basis for applying American law to provide publicity rights to British performers was not discussed. The court's rationale for applying American, rather than British, law was that "any rule basing publicity rights on the nationality of the performer would give rise to unnecessary confusion," would be "anomalous and unworkable," and "would create tremendous uncertainty for foreign performers . . . who seek to do business in this country."

Insofar as domain names are concerned, the United States' Anticybersquatting Consumer Protection Act (ACPA) provides protection to people and companies regardless of their nationality or residence, even though the United States does not belong to any domain-name treaty (because there is none). Of course, in order for U.S. courts to be able to decide an ACPA case, it must have personal jurisdiction over the alleged cybersquatter (for reasons you learned in your first-year Civil Procedure course) or over the domain name registrar (15 USC §1125(d)(2)(C)). That's why the Uniform Domain Name Dispute Resolution Policy (UDRP) is so important. Protection under the UDRP does not depend on a treaty, because those who register domain names – no matter where in the world they may reside – agree to bound by the UDRP when the register domain names.

### b. Patent protection

International patent protection does not depend on the existence of a treaty between the inventor's country and the country where a patent, or enforcement of a patent, is sought. Instead, nations automatically provide patent protection to inventions from other countries, on the same terms and conditions as they provide patent protection to local inventions. Those terms and conditions involve compliance with a lot of formalities; and those formalities may be easier, as a practical matter, for local inventors to comply with than foreign inventors. But the key point is that international patent law practice is largely a matter of dealing with the national patent statute of one country on behalf of an inventor from another country.

Patent protection requires an inventor to file an application with the proper office in the exact form required by the law of the country in which a patent is sought. In most of the world, the "proper" office for filing patent applications is the patent office of each country where a patent is sought. That is, an application filed in the patent office of one country will not suffice to obtain a patent in another country. As a result, it usually is necessary to file patent applications in the patent offices of all of the countries where a patent is desired.

The European Patent Convention created a notable exception to this need-to-file-everywhere principle. Now, it is possible to obtain patent protection in all nations of the European Union by filing just one patent application, though inventors still may choose to file separate applications in individual EU countries. Non-EU inventors may take advantage of the European Patent Convention; its benefits are not limited to EU inventors.

The Patent Cooperation Treaty (PCT) is worldwide treaty that makes it easier than it used to be to file patent applications in many countries. But it does not do for the whole world what the European Patent Convention does for the EU. That is, the PCT does not provide a procedure for filing a single application that results in a worldwide patent. Instead, the PCT provides a uniform application form that will be accepted by the patent offices of all adhering countries. It also gives inventors who file a PCT application in one country a 30-month "priority" in all other PCT countries. This priority can be critically important in obtaining patents in other countries; but separate applications still must be filed in all PCT countries, to actually get patents in those countries.

The patent laws of all countries require applications to be filed before the invention is disclosed to the public, or shortly thereafter. In the United States, applications must be filed not later than one year after disclosure. In the European Union and Japan, applications must be filed within six months. And the patent laws of other countries have no "grace period," so applications must be filed before inventions are disclosed to the public.

If an application is not filed on time, the invention will not be eligible for patent protection. The filing deadline in each country is determined by that country's own patent law.

In the day-to-day practice of patent law, lawyers must advise their clients about the deadlines for each country in which they may want to seek patents. An American inventor who waits 11 months after disclosing the invention to the America public to file an application in the United States Patent and Trademark Office (USPTO) will be on time for a U.S. patent. But the inventor will be too late to file an application in many countries of the world, including Europe and Japan, if the inventor waited 11 months to file there too.

What's more, activities that amount to "public disclosure" of an invention also vary from country to country. As a result, activity that does not amount to disclosure in one country may amount to disclosure in another, even if the inventor engages in that activity only in the country where it is not a public disclosure!

Because filing deadlines and public disclosure definitions vary from country to country, it isn't uncommon for inventors to lose their patent rights in many countries, accidentally. To avoid this, at least two kinds of things have been done.

First, in 1994, the United States Patent Act was amended to permit the filing of "provisional applications" that are easier (and less expensive) to file than regular applications, while being adequate to satisfy the requirement that an application be filed within a year of public disclosure.

Second, efforts have been made to negotiate an international patent treaty (or an amendment to an existing treaty) that would: (1) create a uniform filing deadline in all adhering countries (including a grace period); and (2) a uniform definition of public disclosure. But these efforts haven't produced such a treaty provision, yet.

A patent application must have "priority" over any other application to patent the same invention. It is not uncommon for unrelated inventors, working separately, to invent the same invention and apply for a patent for it, at about the same time. If two inventors file separate applications for the same invention, a patent will be issued only to the application that has "priority," and the other will not receive a patent.

There are two different ways to decide which application has priority: the "First-to-Invent" method, and the "First-to-File" method. The United States and the Philippines use the "First-to-Invent" method. As a result, patents in those countries are given to the inventor who invented first, even if another inventor files an application first. Other countries use the "First-to-File" method. Patents in those countries are given to the inventor who files an application first, even if another inventor actually invented first.

Because most of the world uses the "First-to-File" method, something has been done to help first-filers claim priority in many countries at once. Paris Convention Article 4 provides that if an inventor files a patent application in a Paris Convention member, the date of that filing will be the inventor's priority date in other Paris Convention members, so long as the inventor actually files in those other countries within 12 months. In other words, the first inventor to file in a Paris Convention country has a 12-month priority against competing inventors in other Paris Convention countries. The Patent Cooperation Treaty gives inventors an even longer priority. Inventors who file a PCT application in one country have a 30-month "priority" in all other PCT countries. (The priorities that come from the Paris Convention and the Patent Cooperation Treaty are another reason that an American inventor may choose to file a "provisional application." If a provisional application is filed before anyone else files an application anywhere for the same invention, that provisional application will give the American inventor priority over other inventors, in first-to-file countries.)

### c. Trademark protection

In its early years – before 1883 – international trademark protection was available without treaties, though it usually depended on "reciprocity." This meant that the owner of a mark in one nation would receive protection for that mark in another nation only if the owner of a mark in that other nation would receive similar protection for its mark in the first nation.

I mention the year 1883, because that is the year the Paris Convention was adopted; and the Paris Convention requires adhering nations to protect the trademarks of all other adhering nations. The Paris Convention replaced reciprocity with "national treatment." And it reduced the probability of non-reciprocal protection between countries by requiring each member to register any mark that was registered in another member.

Though the Paris Convention did do a little to harmonize trademark protection among its members, it left room for significant differences between nations: concerning what types of marks were eligible for protection; how trademark protection was obtained; how priority of use was determined; how registration was accomplished; and how a long registration lasted before it had to be renewed.

A number of subsequent treaties (subsequent, that is, to the Paris Convention) were adopted to deal with these differences – especially with differences in registration procedures, and the need to register separately in each country in which protection was sought. The most significant of these treaties are:

- TRIPs (in 1994), which requires protection for designated subject matters, at least some of which were not previously protected in all countries, though even TRIPs does not require protection for all types of marks including some (like sounds and fragrances) that are protected in the United States;
- the European Community Trademark system (in 1996), which harmonized the substantive trademark laws of EC members, and provides for a single EC trademark registration application process – a process that may be used by non-EC as well as EC trademark owners – that results in a single registration good throughout the EC; and
- the Trademark Law Treaty (in 1998) that further harmonizes trademark registration procedures throughout the world, and requires adhering countries to provide service mark protection on par with Paris-type trademark protection.

Although treaty-adherence is not required for trademark protection, adherence to the Paris Convention makes it possible for some trademark owners to claim protection in other countries, under circumstances where their marks would not have been protected if the Paris Convention had not been adhered to by their countries.

It is not at all unusual for two companies to use the same mark, without either company being aware of the other at the time each began to use the mark. In cases like this, the first company to use the mark is said to have "priority." The result is that the company with priority gets to use the mark, and the other company must stop. (There are some exceptions to this very general statement; but those exceptions are the subject matter of a Trademark Law course, rather than this course.)

Here's how the priority issue works: Suppose that

- Company A used a mark first in the United States,
- then Company B used the same mark in Italy, and
- then Company A used the mark in Italy.

In the absence of a treaty providing otherwise, priority of use would be determined country-by-country. This would mean that Company B would have priority in Italy because B used the mark first *there*, and Company A would not be able to use its mark in Italy, even though, on a worldwide basis, A used the mark before B did. The Paris Convention might change this result, and give A priority in Italy, even though B was the first to use the mark *there*. Here's how.

The United States and Italy both have adhered to the Paris Convention. Although first use in Italy usually is required to get priority there, Company A will have priority in Italy *if*:

- Company A files an application to register the mark in the United States before anyone used the mark in Italy, and
- within 6 months of the filing in the United States, Company A files an application to register the mark Italy,
- even if Company B begins using the mark in Italy *after* A filed an application in the U.S. but *before* A filed an application to register the mark in Italy.

This 6-month priority "window" is available by virtue of Paris Convention Article 4; and it works in both directions, of course. That is, if Company B filed an application to use the mark in Italy before Company A used the mark in the United States, and within 6 months of the filing in Italy, Company B filed an application to register the mark in the United States, Company B would be the owner of the mark in the U.S., even if Company A began using the mark in the U.S. after B used the mark in Italy but before B began using the mark in the U.S.

It used to be the law that an application to register a mark in the U.S. required the mark to have been used in the U.S. or a registration application to have been filed in another Paris Convention country. Since other countries permitted applications to be filed there, even by those who had not used the mark there, companies in other countries could get priority in the U.S. by filing in other countries without using the mark there or in the U.S. This gave companies in other countries an advantage in the U.S. over American companies, because American companies had to use a mark in the U.S. before they could file a registration application in the U.S. As a result, the U.S. amended its law in 1988 to permit trademark owners to file an application register a mark based on their intent to use it, before they actually use it. That intent-to-use application gives the applicant a priority filing date as well as a period of time within which to actually use the mark, during which period the applicant has priority over others who may use the mark after the intent-to-use application is filed.

Where copyright is concerned, the absence of a treaty (or proclamation or statutory provision) means that foreign works receive no copyright protection at all in the United States, despite the "tremendous uncertainty" this sometimes causes for foreign copyright owners.

One copyright case, in fact, went all the way to the United States Supreme Court (which declined to hear it) on the surprisingly uncertain question of whether the United States has a copyright treaty with Taiwan. The plaintiff in that case, *N.Y. Chinese TV Programs v. U.E. Enterprises*, 954 F.2d 847 (2d Cir. 1992), cert. denied, 113 S.Ct. 86 (1992), was the licensee of copyrights to television programs produced in Taiwan (*not* the Peoples Republic of China). The defendant asserted that there is no treaty between the United States and Taiwan entitling the plaintiff to copyright protection in the United States. Taiwan was *not* a member of the Berne Convention or the Universal Copyright Convention, so the question became whether there was a bilateral copyright treaty between Taiwan and the United States. At one time there was. In 1946, the two countries entered into a Treaty of Friendship, Commerce and Navigation which did include a provision concerning copyright. But in 1978, the United States terminated relations with Taiwan and recognized the Peoples Republic of China as the sole China. Shortly thereafter, the United States enacted the Taiwan Relations Act which had the effect of transferring to Taiwan the benefits of the 1946 treaty. The Taiwan Relations Act thus made the 1946 Treaty the "treaty" requiring copyright protection in the U.S. for Taiwanese television programs, *unless* the Taiwan Relations Act was unconstitutional. In an effort to avoid copyright infringement liability, the defendant argued that the Act was unconstitutional. But the court ruled otherwise and held that it is constitutional. As a result, the plaintiff was entitled to copyright protection for the Taiwanese television programs in the United States. But in order to get to that point, the case had to make a lengthy inquiry into the history of U.S.-China relations and had to resolve a difficult issue concerning the constitutionality of an Act that deals with much more than copyright.

### 3. Characteristics of international copyright protection, when provided

When international copyright protection is provided, it *usually* is provided pursuant to the national copyright law of the country where protection is sought. This form of protection is known as "national treatment."

### a. National treatment

National treatment is required, for example, by the Berne Convention – a requirement that is honored in the United States by its Copyright Act.

## Berne Convention Article 5(1)

Authors shall enjoy, in respect of works for which they are protected under this Convention, in countries of the Union other than the country of origin, *the rights which their respective laws do now or may hereafter grant to their nationals*, as well as the rights specially granted by this Convention. [Emphasis added.]

## United States Copyright Act §104

(a) Unpublished works . . . are subject to protection *under this title* [i.e., Title 17 of the United States Code, the Copyright Act of 1976; emphasis added] . . . .

(b) Published works . . . are subject to protection *under this title* [i.e., Title 17 of the United States Code, the Copyright Act of 1976; emphasis added]. . . .

### b. Not uniform or centralized

Because "national treatment" requires protection pursuant to the national law of the country where protection is sought, it necessarily follows that when international protection is provided, it is not uniform throughout the world, nor is the administration of international copyright law centralized in any way.

### c. Formalities not required

Unlike international trademark and patent protection – which *do* require compliance with formalities – international copyright protection does *not*. In fact, formalities are prohibited by the Berne Convention – a prohibition that is honored in the United States by its Copyright Act.

## Berne Convention Article 5(2)

The enjoyment and the exercise of these rights shall not be subject to any formality. . .

## United States Copyright Act §411(a)

. . . no action for infringement of the copyright *in any United States work* shall be instituted until registration of the copyright claim has been made in accordance with this title. . . . [Emphasis added.]

## Pepe (U.K.) Ltd. v. Ocean View Factory Outlet Corp.
### 770 F.Supp. 754 (D.P.R. 1991)

United States District Judge Jose Antonio Fuste:

On June 12 and 13, 1991, plaintiffs Pepe (U.K.) Ltd. ("Pepe (U.K.)") and Pepe Clothing (U.S.A.) Inc. ("Pepe (U.S.A.)") made ex parte applications for a seizure of T-shirts bearing the trademark PEPE. The items to be seized duplicated the appearance of various designs on T-shirts sold by plaintiffs. These were manufactured and/or sold by the defendants Ocean View Factory Outlet Corp. [and] Puerto Rico Blantor, Inc., [and others] . . . (collectively "Blantor defendants"). On June 13, 1991, such orders were granted. Seizures were conducted on June 15, 1991. On June 27, 1991 a hearing was held with regard to the propriety of such ex parte seizures and to ascertain whether the facts supporting the findings of fact and conclusions of law which gave rise to the original issuance of the orders were still valid.

At the hearing, the Blantor defendants appeared through counsel. They expressly did not contest the facts as set forth by plaintiffs in their original declarations or at the hearing, or the propriety of the conduct of the seizure, nor did they offer any evidence contrary to that offered by plaintiffs. The Blantor defendants, however, did contest whether the facts set forth in the original declarations and at the hearing were sufficient to legally justify the seizure. . . .

## I. Background

Pepe Group PLC is a British Holding Company, which through subsidiaries and related companies is in the business of designing, licensing, sourcing, wholesaling, and marketing coordinated ranges of casual clothing and related accessories under the trademark PEPE throughout a large part of the world, including the United States and the Commonwealth of Puerto Rico. . . .

. . . Pepe (U.K.)'s exclusive distributor and licensee in the United States is Pepe Clothing (U.S.A.). . . .

Pepe T-shirts come with a number of different designs imprinted on the shirt. . . . Each of these designs was created by employees of Pepe (U.K.), and was first published in the United Kingdom after March 1, 1989, and more than thirty days thereafter in the United States. Pepe (U.K.)'s copyright in the Pepe World Service logo had been asserted both in the United Kingdom and in Hong Kong, where a seizure based on this copyright was obtained.

Defendant Puerto Rico Blantor, Inc. is in the business of printing T-shirts and selling the same at wholesale and retail. Many of the designs imprinted by the Blantor defendants on T-shirts bear the trademarks of well-known companies. Among other T-shirts, they print T-shirts bearing the Pepe Co London and World Service logo designs. . . .

On June 15, 1991, over 2,000 T-shirts bearing the PEPE mark as described above, along with various screens and acetates used in the production of such T-shirts were seized from the Blantor defendants. In addition, a limited number of business records dealing with the sale of T-shirts bearing the PEPE mark were also seized.

## II. Discussion

The order of seizure of June 13, 1991 issued on three bases [including] . . . with regard to certain of the designs, for copyright infringement pursuant to 17 U.S.C. §503. . . .

### C. The Right of Ex Parte Seizure for Infringement of Copyright

To establish a prima facie case of copyright infringement and thus show proper probable success in the merits of the claim, plaintiffs must show that (i) they own valid copyrights in the Pepe World Services design, the Pepe Co London design and the Pepe Special Design, and (ii) defendants violated one of the exclusive rights granted plaintiffs in 17 U.S.C. §106 by copying or distributing plaintiffs' copyrighted works without authorization.

Prior to March 1, 1989, it was necessary to obtain a registration prior to filing an action for copyright infringement. However, as of that date the copyright law was amended to allow foreign copyright owners to sue under their copyrights in the United States without fulfilling formalities such as registration, provided the work in question was a Berne Convention work as defined in 17 U.S.C. §101. . .

Here, the copyright owner is a foreign corporation, Pepe (U.K.). The testimony of Pepe (U.K.)'s secretary, Richard Cooper, indicated that each of the works was developed and first published in the United Kingdom after March 1, 1989, and more than thirty days thereafter was first published in the United States. Although Mr. Cooper was not able from his own personal knowledge to indicate the exact dates of publication in the United States, his testimony was clear that Pepe (U.K.) was a British company; that designs were first developed in Britain and then some substantial time later (always far in excess of thirty days) published by the various subsidiaries outside the United Kingdom, including the United States. His testimony was based upon the business records of his company and his knowledge as to how the company operated. Mr. Cooper further testified as a British barrister with regard to British copyright law. He indicated that under British law, no formalities were required to perfect the copyright. There was no contradictory evidence offered. Such testimony is, at least, sufficient for the purposes of this hearing to establish that the works in question were non-U.S. Berne works. Thus, as noted in 17 U.S.C. §411, plaintiffs have the right to bring the present action for copyright infringement without first complying with U.S. formalities.

The seizure itself has established that defendants have manufactured and distributed T-shirts bearing the Pepe designs in question without authorization. On the basis of these facts, there can be little doubt that plaintiffs shall likely prevail on the merits of their copyright infringement claim.

One of the rights granted under the Berne Convention is that of seizure. Thus plaintiff Pepe (U.K.) has the same right to seizure in the United States as any other copyright owner. See Article 16, Berne Convention (Paris Text, July 24, 1971).

Since defendants have not argued nor have they introduced any evidence which indicates that plaintiffs have failed in any way to conform to the requirements of the Rules of Practice and Procedures for Copyright Cases promulgated by the United States Supreme Court, the ex parte seizure of those T-shirts and means of production which bore duplication of plaintiffs' designs in the Pepe World Service, Pepe Co London, and Pepe Special designs was proper.

*III. Conclusion*

After hearing on the seizures, we confirm that the original order of seizure . . . was proper and the conditions which gave rise to the order are still in effect, and, accordingly, the seizure orders remain for the duration of the present litigation.

Although copyright *protection* does not depend on registration, or on compliance with any other formality, obtaining some of the *benefits* of copyright ownership *may* depend on compliance with certain formalities. These benefits include certain remedies like statutory damages and attorneys fees, and even the receipt of certain types of collectively administered royalties. Compliance with these formalities will be covered later.

### 4. Three basic steps in international copyright analysis

There are three basic steps in the analysis of an international copyright question:

1. Is there a treaty (or proclamation or domestic law) that requires protection? If so. . .
2. Does national treatment apply? If not, what law does?
3. How is the copyright issue resolved under the applicable law?

### 5. "Rule of Thumb" and circumstances when it may not be accurate

Although international copyright law analysis can become quite complicated, there is a simple Rule of Thumb that works in most cases.

#### a. The Rule of Thumb

Copyright protection for *most* recently-authored (and older but recently-published) works is provided in *most* countries pursuant to the law of the country where protection is sought, just as though they were authored by nationals of that country and had first been published there. The reason this is the rule in *most* cases is that *usually* there is a treaty (or proclamation or domestic law) that requires protection; and *usually*, national treatment does apply.

#### b. Sample cases illustrating application of the Rule of Thumb

##### i. Protection of foreign works in the United States

The next two decisions illustrate the application of the Rule of Thumb, in cases where foreign works were protected in the United States. These decisions are not included here for the legal doctrines used to decide them; they are included simply to show the Rule of Thumb "in action." In the first opinion, *Benny v. Loew's*, the court devoted just one sentence to a simple assertion that the plaintiff's British play was protected by U.S. copyright law. In the second opinion, *Hospital for Sick Children v. Melody Faire Dinner Theatre*, the court didn't do even that; it merely applied U.S. copyright law, as though the plaintiff's British play was an American play. As a result, you should read these next two decisions for what is *not* discussed – why the two British plays were protected in the United States – rather than for what they do discuss. The *Hospital for Sick Children* decision is included for an additional reason too: the plaintiff's play, "Peter Pan," has been given unique copyright treatment in the United Kingdom, and therefore will be considered again, later in the course, for that reason.

**Benny v. Loew's**
**239 F.2d 532 (9th Cir. 1956)**
**aff'd by an equally divided Supreme Court sub nom.**
**CBS v. Loew's, 356 U.S. 43 (1958)**

Circuit Judge McAllister:

Patrick Hamilton, an English author and a British subject, some time prior to December, 1938, conceived and wrote an original play entitled, "Gas Light." It was published and protected by copyright in February, 1939. Shortly thereafter, it was publicly performed in England, first in Richmond, and later, in London. On December 5, 1941, it was produced as a play in New York under the name, "Angel Street," and had a successful run of 1,295 consecutive performances, extending over a period of more than 37 months.

On October 7, 1942, the exclusive motion picture rights for "Gas Light" were acquired by Loew's, Inc., better known under its trade name of Metro-Goldwyn-Mayer. . . .

*There is no question of the right of the dramatic work to protection under the copyright laws of both Great Britain and the United States.* [Emphasis added.] . . .

[The court held that Jack Benny infringed the copyright to "Gas Light" in 1952 by performing half-hour "burlesque" of it on the CBS television network.]

## Hospital for Sick Children v. Melody Faire Dinner Theatre
## 516 F.Supp. 67 (E.D.Va. 1980)

District Judge Bryan, Jr.

This action is brought by the alleged owners of a copyright to a play or dramatic composition entitled "Peter Pan or The Boy Who Would Not Grow Up." The plaintiffs assert copyright infringement . . . on the part of the defendants for their producing and presenting a musical play entitled "Peter Pan The Magical Musical" and advertisements in connection with that production. . . .

*Ownership*

As a first issue, the defendants contend that there is not only insufficient proof that the plaintiffs own the copyrighted work, but that the evidence shows that the ownership of the work is vested in one Charles Frohman (Frohman), for whom James Matthew Barrie (Barrie), the plaintiff's predecessor, was to write the work under a commission for hire.

The court will discuss the latter contention first. The evidence to support this contention is as follows: First, a statement on the back of a record jacket for a recording of "Jean Arthur and Boris Karloff in J. M. Barrie's Peter Pan," with song and lyrics by Leonard Bernstein; and second, a passage in "Charles Frohman: Manager and Man" which is quoted in "J. M. Barrie and the Lost Boys," and a passage in "Barrie: The Story of a Genius." These items of evidence refer to the work as having been written by Barrie on commission from Frohman. Opposed to these are the voluminous credits over the years attributing the work to Barrie without reference to Frohman and culminating in the copyright grant in 1928. It is true that the copyright was obtained after Frohman's death, albeit thirteen years hardly an indecent interval after that event. The court, however, has an insufficient basis, at this late date, to ascribe, as suggested by counsel, any theft of Frohman's work or other perfidy to Barrie. Apparently, it has not occurred to any successor to Frohman to challenge Barrie's claim to rights in the work. The court is satisfied that ownership of the work is legitimately vested in Barrie and his successors.

The question of the chain of title to Barrie's interest in the work centered around the authenticity of foreign documents, namely, the document vesting assent of the executors of Barrie's estate, the will of Barrie and the assignment to The Hospital for Sick Children. The court admitted into evidence all of these documents over the objection of defendants. No serious basis for believing the documents are not what they purport to be has been advanced; and despite defendants' assertions to the contrary, the court is persuaded that a reasonable opportunity has been given to all parties to investigate the authenticity and accuracy of the documents and therefore that they should be admitted.

Certain facts are pertinent to the ownership of the copyright in question and they are these:

1. The play "Peter Pan" was written in 1904 by Barrie, was first produced in England in 1905, and was first published[3] in the United States in 1928. [Fn.3 The word "published" as used here means the publication as referred to in Section 10 of the Copyright Act of 1909, and the securing of the statutory copyright. The work was apparently shown in the United States well prior to 1928; and the plaintiffs rely on their common law right of representation prior to that time.]

2. In 1928, the United States Copyright Office issued certificate of copyright registration D 85173 for the play "Peter Pan or The Boy Who Would Not Grow Up" in the name of James Matthew Barrie.

3. By instrument dated August 14, 1929, Barrie assigned to The Hospital for Sick Children the copyright for the play "Peter Pan."

4. Barrie died in 1937.

5. In his last will and testament, proved on September 15, 1937, Barrie bequeathed all of his copyright interest in and to the play "Peter Pan," among other literary properties, to The Hospital for Sick Children. By his will, Barrie named as his executors and trustees Peter Llewelyn Davies and Lady Cynthia Asquith.

6. By instrument dated January 20, 1942, Peter Llewelyn Davies and Lady Cynthia Asquith, as executors of the last will and testament of Barrie, assented to the vesting in The Hospital for Sick Children of all rights to the copyright of the play "Peter Pan" as well as other literary properties referred to in the assignment dated August 14, 1929.

7. The reference to "Peter Pan" in the above documents and elsewhere is a reference to "Peter Pan or The Boy Who Would Not Grow Up." The court is not persuaded that the omission of the words "or The Boy Who Would Not Grow Up" or the various forms of the title listed in the Catalog of Plays of Samuel French warrants a contrary finding.

8. The United States Copyright Office issued a certificate of registration to renewal copyright for the play "Peter Pan or The Boy Who Would Not Grow Up," No. R 171R21, in the names of Peter Llewelyn Davies, Lady Cynthia Asquith and Barclay's Bank Ltd., as executors of Barrie.

9. The play "Peter Pan or The Boy Who Would Not Grow Up" consists of material wholly original with Barrie, and constitutes copyrightable subject matter under the laws of the United States.

From the foregoing the court concludes that The Hospital for Sick Children is the owner of all rights and interest in the copyright of the play "Peter Pan or

The Boy Who Would Not Grow Up." It further finds that plaintiff Samuel French, Inc., is the owner of the exclusive right to license the play in the United States.

*What Was Copyrighted?*

During the presentation of the defendants' evidence it was revealed that the copy or copies of the copyrighted work which were deposited in the Copyright Office in 1928 could not be found by that office. Accordingly the court has to resolve the factual issue whether plaintiffs' exhibit 3 entitled "Peter Pan, a Fantasy in Five Acts" by J. M. Barrie, is the same as the copy which was originally filed with the Copyright Office. The court finds that it is. While of course the legend and notice appearing at page 2 of the publication is not conclusive, it is entitled to some weight. Moreover the testimony convinces the court that the contents of exhibit 3 constitute the only work which has been licensed in the United States for the over 1500 productions and 8500 performances of the play "Peter Pan" presented since 1928; and is the only publication of what was copyrighted of which any party has any knowledge. Apparently there has been no question concerning this until now.

*Infringement*

In determining the merits of the case the court's first task is that of comparison of the works involved, which are plaintiffs' exhibit 3 and the play of the defendants, "Peter Pan The Magical Musical."

There are slight differences and variations, but the cast of characters in both includes Peter Pan, Michael, Mr. and Mrs. Darling, John, Wendy, Tinker Bell (Tinkerbell in defendants' work), Slightly Soiled (Slightly Damp in defendants' work), Nibs (Nip in defendants' work), Captain Hook, and Smee (Shmee in defendants' work). Each work begins with Mrs. Darling putting her children to bed at night. The theme and plot of both includes the following elements: Peter Pan, the boy who flies, appears at the window after Mrs. Darling has left; his shadow is a detachable thing; his saying he will never grow up; Never Land; the lagoon; the crocodile who had swallowed the clock and who had eaten the hand of Captain Hook, the pirate; the lost boys; fairies and mermaids; the fairy Tinker Bell; Wendy as the pretend mother; sewing on Peter's shadow; Captain Hook's desire for revenge against Peter Pan for causing the loss of his hand to the crocodile; the pirates poisoning the medicine (a cake in defendants' work) which Tinker Bell drinks (eats); the kidnapping of the children by the pirates; the fight between Peter Pan and Captain Hook; the rescue of the children; and the return of the children to the nursery where the story began. More specific similarities have been cataloged by the plaintiffs; that catalog is attached as part of the court's findings of fact.

The plaintiffs of course must prove that its work was copied. One need do no more than read the two works to find striking and substantial similarities.[5] [Fn.5 Once the works are read it is clear why the defendants spent so much of their case contesting ownership and what was copyrighted. The plaintiffs' evidence on the merits is overwhelming.] The work of the defendants is manifestly a "piratical composition" as to plot, theme, setting and characters.

If defendants' access to the copyrighted work need be shown, it can hardly be denied in the face of the wide dissemination of plaintiffs' work. The play "Peter Pan" has acquired considerable fame and popularity as a result of many performances on stage and in motion pictures and television over a period of 75 years in the United States and throughout the world. In the last eleven years, Samuel French has licensed some 700 separate productions of the play throughout the United States. In addition, it has licensed over 400 productions of the musical version of "Peter Pan" in that period. Between 1968 and 1979, stock and amateur performances of the musical version of "Peter Pan" have grossed over $3 million. Famous Broadway performances of "Peter Pan" have been presented, including the production starring Mary Martin, and the current production starring Sandy Duncan. Prior to opening on Broadway, the Sandy Duncan production played in Dallas, Washington, D.C., and Atlanta in 1979, where it grossed over $900,000. The National Broadcasting Company presented the play on television starring Mary Martin in 1955, 1956, 1960, 1963, 1966 and 1973. Many thousands of copies of the play have been sold by Samuel French, Inc. Moreover the defendant Ardith Cavallo testified as to her access to two and perhaps three recordings of other arrangements of the musical play "Peter Pan."

The court concludes that the defendants' work is a copy of the plaintiffs' work entitled "Peter Pan or The Boy Who Would Not Grow Up," as copyrighted since 1928.

### Infringing Activities of Defendants

In March, April, May and June, 1979, defendants Melody Fare Dinner Theatre, Real Corporation and Lawrence Cavallo presented "Peter Pan The Magical Musical," authored by defendant Ardith Cavallo, at the Melody Fare Dinner Theatre, before paying audiences. No license was sought or acquired by any defendant from either plaintiff with respect to the production of the play at the Melody Fare Dinner Theatre.

### Defenses

The defendants argue that Peter Pan is merely an amalgam of characters from earlier works of Barrie, principally The Little White Bird; that these characters were in the public domain; and that therefore there is no copyrightable material to sustain the validity of the 1928 copyright. First, while characters alone may not be copyrightable, the "amalgamation" of the characters into the theme of "Peter Pan" was done by Barrie. Second, The Little White Bird, while containing a Peter Pan, contains no Tinker Bell, Captain Hook (or other character who is a pirate), Mr. or Mrs. Darling, Michael, John, Wendy or Never Land. Insofar as the works "Peter and Wendy" and the "Boy Castaways of Black Island" are concerned, not enough is revealed in this record of the contents of those books to make any comparison. There is no suggestion that the theme or cast of characters in either work is the same as the theme or characters of "Peter Pan," although there may be some characters in "Peter Pan" who appear in the other works.

The defendants argue that their play is a libretto as distinguished from a narrative such as plaintiffs' exhibit 3. This distinction makes no difference. The defendants' work remains a material and substantial tracking of the pattern of plaintiffs' play.

### Damages

There is no evidence that the plaintiffs suffered any monetary damage; and the testimony concerning the defendants' profits is uncertain. While gross profits were approximately $38,000 for some 50 performances, this figure includes receipts for both dinner and the show, sold for a combination price of from $5.50 to $10.50. Of the $10.50 package ticket, $5.00 was allocated to the show; for a $5.50 ticket, $2.50 was allocated to the show. How many patrons at each price or the amount of overhead expenses incurred is not revealed by the evidence. In any event the plaintiffs elected, prior to judgment, pursuant to 17 U.S.C. §504(c), to recover an award of statutory damages. The court concludes that as basic statutory damages the sum of $2,500 is justified. This amounts to $50.00 per performance; and will be assessed against all the defendants jointly and severally.

In addition the court finds that the infringement was committed willfully on the part of the defendant Ardith Cavallo. She is the person who wrote the accused work and directed its performance. She applied for its copyright; and it is apparent to the court she was the guiding hand in the activities of the defendants insofar as the play was concerned. The court is not persuaded by the assertions of Ardith Cavallo that she felt she was entitled to publish this without license because of the "public domain" character of the theme. Her research which revealed the facts on which she relies for this characterization was conducted after she was sued here and in Richmond. Her attribution to "Peter Pan and Wendy" (sic) as the basis of her work in her March 2, 1979 application to the Copyright Office, while perhaps technically absolving her of plagiarism, does not excuse her copying. Licenses apparently had been obtained for prior productions at the Melody Fare Dinner Theatre, including "Oliver" and "Pal Joey." The damage award against Ardith Cavallo will be increased to $ 10,000. . . .

*Relief*

In addition to damages, plaintiffs are entitled to injunctive relief, and an award of attorneys' fees. 17 U.S.C. §505. The defendants against whom the relief is awarded are Melody Fare Dinner Theatre; Lawrence Cavallo who is the president of and owns all the stock in Real Corporation, which owned and operated the Melody Fare Dinner Theatre; and Ardith Cavallo.

### ii.  Protection of United States works in foreign countries

The following decision illustrates the application of the Rule of Thumb, in a case where an American work was protected in the United Kingdom. You should read this case too for what it does *not* discuss – why an American television program was protected in the United Kingdom – rather than for what it does discuss.

The background to the case is this. The plaintiff was Spelling-Goldberg, an American company that produced the "Starsky & Hutch" TV series. The defendant in the case, a British publisher, published individual frames from the TV series as photographs in a magazine and as a poster. Spelling-Goldberg's rights turned on the distinction made by British law between "films" and "photographs."

Prior to 1956, the rights of motion picture and television producers (as well as other copyright owners) in Britain were governed by the United Kingdom Copyright Act of 1911. That act provided that the owner of a copyright in a "cinematography film" owned a copyright in every individual frame on that film as a distinct photograph. In 1956, however, the British legislature enacted a new Copyright Act in which photographs and "cinematograph films" were distinguished and were dealt with separately, and in minor ways, differently. The Copyright Act of 1956 provides that cinematograph films may be copyrighted, and if they are, their owners have the exclusive rights to make copies of the films, to show them in public, and to broadcast them.

Because the British publisher in this case published photographs in a magazine and on a poster made from frames of "Starsky & Hutch," Spelling Goldberg contended that the publisher had made copies of its "cinematograph films" in violation of the United Kingdom Copyright Act. Spelling Goldberg made this argument in the lawsuit it filed in England against the publisher. The publisher argued otherwise, however. The United Kingdom Copyright Act defines "cinematograph film" to mean "any sequence of visual images . . . capable . . . of being shown as a moving picture." The British publisher thus argued that since the single frames it had copied were not capable of being shown as a moving picture, it had not made copies of the "Starsky & Hutch" "cinematograph films," and thus had not violated any of Spelling Goldberg's exclusive rights.

The trial court agreed with the British publisher. On appeal, however, the United Kingdom's Supreme Court of Judicature reversed. In a lengthy decision excerpted below, all four judges of that court agreed with Spelling Goldberg that under the United Kingdom Copyright Act of 1956, a single frame of a film is a part of that film, and thus, a copy of a single frame is a copy of the film as well. The issue was analyzed just as though Spelling Goldberg had been a British company and "Starsky & Hutch" a British program. The applicability of United Kingdom law, and Spelling Goldberg's rights under that law, were apparently without controversy. The only mention made of either issue is in the italicized portions of the following opinions of two of the four judges.

### Aaron-Spelling Productions Inc. v. B.P.C. Publishing Limited
### [1979] FSR 494, [1981] RPC 283 (U.K.Ct.App. 1980)

*Judge Mervyn Davies Q.C.*

This is a copyright action. The plaintiffs are Aaron Spelling Productions Inc. and Leonard Goldberg Productions Inc. Both are incorporated under the laws of the State of California. They trade as a limited partnership under California law, using the name Spelling Goldberg Productions. The defendant company is an English limited company trading as Phoebus Publishing Co. The dispute between the parties concerns some photographs published by the defendant company in what has been called a magazine and a poster. The photographs show some of the characters in a well-known B.B.C. television programme entitled "Starsky and Hutch".

The relief claimed in the statement of claim includes (1) a claim for an injunction to restrain the defendants from reproducing or publishing certain films and photographs, being films and photographs the copyright in which is owned by the plaintiffs; (2) an enquiry as to damages for infringement of copyright . . . ; and (5) delivery up of infringing material. The . . . action came before me as an action for infringement of copyright in films and photographs. However, the action then proceeded as an action for infringement of film copyright only, that is, not for infringement of copyright in photographs. . . .

I turn to the facts of the case. There is little dispute here. The plaintiffs are the producers of a series of television films called "Starsky and Hutch". *United Kingdom copyrights exist in this film: Copyright Act 1956, section 13(1) to (5)(b) and the Copyright (International Conventions) Order 1972 made under section 32 of the 1956 Act. The plaintiffs are the owners of the United Kingdom copyright in the film: Copyright Act 1956, section 13(4).* [Emphasis added.]

The defendants are well-known publishers. They conduct a very large business and publish multi-volume reference works on a weekly basis and are the sole publishers throughout the world of the Cordon Bleu Cookery Course and publishers of such works as A. Liddell Hart's *History of the Second World War*, and A. J. P. Taylor's *History of the Twentieth Century*. As well, they publish hard-back books of illustrated matter and also magazines, and what were called one-off titles. As may be supposed, they make great use of photographic agencies. I was told that they are in daily communication with one agency or another.

In the course of this business the defendants, at the end of 1976, put out two publications; the first is a Starsky and Hutch pin-up poster priced at 35p; and the second is a magazine-type publication of 30 pages priced at 45p. The front cover has photographs of Starsky and Hutch below the words "Starsky and Hutch, packed with facts and colour pictures". The plaintiffs' complaint is that eight of these colour pictures were printed and published in breach of their copyright. Seven of the pictures show Starsky and Hutch and the others show two other characters in the series. . . .

*Buckley L.J.*

. . . The plaintiffs were the makers and producers of a series of films intended for television broadcasting and well known under the designation of Starsky and Hutch, relating to the adventures of a pair of American policemen. *The United Kingdom copyright in those films is vested in the plaintiffs.* . . . [Emphasis added.]

### c. Circumstances when the Rule of Thumb may not be accurate

Like all rules of thumb, this one is not always accurate. Here are examples of *some* of the instances when the Rule of Thumb may not be accurate:

- When the work is not recently-authored or recently-published. The older the work, the less likely it is that Rule of Thumb analysis will be sufficient. This is so because the older the work, the more likely it is that there was no copyright treaty between the two countries *when the work was first published*; and that could have put the work in the public domain. Though the copyrights to many public domain works were restored, as required by the Berne Convention (an issue to be covered later), copyright-restoration is complicated and not always effective. Also, the older the work, the more likely its copyright expired in its country of origin, which may have caused its copyright to expire elsewhere under the Rule of the Shorter Term (which also will be covered later).

- When the work is a kind that was recently-invented, such as computer programs and mask works (i.e., computer chip designs), because even if recently-invented works are protected by copyright in their countries of origin, they may not be protected by copyright elsewhere.
- When the right claimed is not protected by the Berne Convention, and therefore not universally recognized, such as the right to resale royalties, library-lending royalties, blank-tape royalties, and public performance rights for recording artists and record companies.

Do not despair that the Rule of Thumb is not always accurate. If it were, there wouldn't be reason to study or practice *international* copyright law. One of the objectives of this course is to enable you to recognize when the Rule of Thumb is *not* accurate, and to know what the actual rule is in those cases.

# Chapter 2

# International Copyright Treaties

Although international copyright protection is sometimes available on the basis of proclamations or provisions of domestic law, international treaties are the most common and important basis for such protection.

## A. Three roles of international copyright treaties

International copyright treaties play three distinct roles:
- As "pipelines" from one country to another, "through" which works from one country obtain copyright protection in other countries.
- As influences on the substance of national copyright laws.
- As direct sources of substantive principles.

The importance of each of these roles varies from country to country. In some countries, treaties play all three roles, but in others they play only one or two.

### 1. As "pipelines" from one country to another

#### a. To the United States from other countries

In the United States, treaties are "pipelines" through which works from other countries receive copyright protection in the U.S. as a result of Copyright Act section 104(b) which provides protection for any published work from "a treaty partner." (You read the exact language of that section in Chapter 1.)

#### b. To other countries from the United States

Treaties also are "pipelines" through which United States works receive protection in other countries, because copyright laws of other countries contain provisions comparable to U.S. Copyright Act section 104(b) – provisions, in other words, that have the effect of granting protection to U.S. works.

Here is just one example:

### Copyright Act of Canada §5(1)

Subject to this Act, copyright shall subsist in Canada, for the term hereinafter mentioned, in every original literary, dramatic, musical and artistic work if any one of the following conditions is met:

(a) in the case of any work, whether published or unpublished, including a cinematographic work, the author was, at the date of the making of the work, a citizen or subject of, or a person ordinarily resident in, *a treaty country*;

(b) in the case of a cinematographic work, whether published or unpublished, the maker, at the date of the making of the cinematographic work,

   (i) if a corporation, had its headquarters *in a treaty country*, or

   (ii) if a natural person, was a citizen or subject of, or a person ordinarily resident in, *a treaty country*;

or

(c) in the case of a published work, including a cinematographic work, . . . the first publication occurred *in a treaty country*.

[Emphasis added.]

### 2. As influences on domestic copyright laws

Treaties also have a significant influence on the substance of national copyright laws, because in order to adhere to a treaty, countries must conform their national copyright laws to the requirements of the treaty. These requirements may be thought of as "minimum standards."

The reason that multi-national treaties impose minimum standards is that "national treatment" without minimum standards may not result in reciprocally equivalent protection for copyright owners from two countries. That is, if Country A's copyright law provided extensive protection while Country B's law provided very little protection, works from Country A would receive very little protection in Country B, while works from Country B would receive extensive protection in Country A. If a treaty permitted this result, countries with laws that provide extensive protection would have no incentive to adhere that treaty.

Thus, minimum standards are designed to bring national copyright laws into conformity with one another, as a condition of treaty adherence, and thus as a condition to relying on the treaty as a basis for claiming national treatment in other countries. In practice, minimum treaty standards have tended to increase and make uniform the level of copyright protection provided to foreign works. The United States' adherence to multi-national treaties certainly has had the effect of increasing the level of copyright protection offered in the U.S. – not only to foreign works but to U.S. works too.

The United States was not able to adhere to the Berne Convention prior to 1989, because U.S. copyright law did not then satisfy Berne's minimum standards, as required by Article 36.

### Berne Convention Article 36

(1) Any country party to this Convention undertakes to adopt, in accordance with its constitution, the measures necessary to ensure the application of this Convention.

(2) It is understood that, at the time a country becomes bound by this Convention, it will be in a position under its domestic law to give effect to the provisions of this Convention.

In the Copyright Act of 1976 – enacted in anticipation of the United States' eventual adherence to Berne – Congress extended the duration of copyright from 28-years-from-publication (plus a 28-year-renewal) to life-of-the-author-plus-50 years, in order to "give effect" to this provision of Berne:

### Berne Convention Article 7

(1) The term of protection granted by this Convention shall be the life of the author and fifty years after his death.

When the United States was finally ready to join Berne in 1989, Congress amended the Copyright Act further to:
- eliminate the requirement that a copyright notice be affixed to all published works (though affixing notice is still advantageous)
- eliminate the requirement that copyrights to works of foreign (Berne country) origin be registered with the U.S. Copyright Office before infringement lawsuits are filed (though registration of the copyrights to works of U.S. origin is still required), and
- eliminate the requirement that transfers of copyrights be recorded in the U.S. Copyright Office before infringement lawsuits are filed (though recordation is still very important for other purposes).

The United States made these changes in order to "give effect" to this provision of Berne:

### Berne Convention Article 5(2)

The enjoyment and the exercise of [the] rights [protected by the national laws of Berne countries] shall not be subject to any formality. . . .

In 1989, Congress also amended the Copyright Act to:
- provide copyright protection for architectural structures (in addition to plans which already were protected)

in order to "give effect" to this provision of Berne:

### Berne Convention Article 2(1)

The expression "literary and artistic works" shall include . . . three-dimensional works relative to . . . architecture. . . .

At the time Congress made these changes, no one doubted that Congress had the constitutional power to do so. It is possible that no one doubted Congress' power to do so simply because these changes seem perfectly compatible with Congress' power under Article I Section 8 of the Constitution "to promote the Progress of Science and useful Arts, by securing for limited Times to Authors and Inventors the exclusive Right to their respective Writings and Discoveries."

To adhere to Berne, the U.S. should have made one more change to the Copyright Act, and it eventually did (in 1994). It had to restore copyright protection to certain foreign works that had gone into the public domain in the U.S. (even though those works were still protected by copyright in their countries of origin and elsewhere). In order to induce countries to join Berne, the Berne Convention contains a provision that is intended to provide retroactive protection for works from newly-joining countries. The provision was necessary to overcome the general principle that publication *anywhere* in the world prior to the effective dates of a treaty in *both* the work's country-of-origin *and* the country where protection is sought means that the work went into the publication domain in the country where protection is sought. This general principle will be discussed more closely later. But first, here is the Berne provision that requires retroactive protection and that required the United States to retroactively restore the copyrights to certain foreign works:

### Berne Convention Article 18

(1) This Convention shall apply to all works which, at the moment of its coming into force, have not yet fallen into the public domain in the country of origin through the expiry of the term of protection. . . .

(4) The preceding provisions shall also apply in the case of new accessions to the Union [which is the organization of all countries that have adhered to the Berne Convention]. . . .

Congress finally did amend the U.S. Copyright Act, in 1994, to comply with Article 18 of the Berne Convention as required by its Article 36. (The reason for the delay, and the reason Congress finally amended the Copyright Act, will be covered later.) Congress amended the Copyright Act by adding section 104A. That section also will be covered later, in detail. In a nutshell, though, it restored U.S. copyright protection to many foreign works that had been in the public domain in the United States; and it did so over the objections of some people and companies that wanted those works to remain in the public domain. Those who objected challenged Congress' constitutional *power* to restore the copyrights of foreign works.

### Luck's Music Library, Inc. v. Gonzales
### 407 F.3d 1262 (D.C.Cir. 2005)
### rehearing en banc denied, 2005 U.S.App.LEXIS 18268 (D.C.Cir. 2005)

Williams, Senior Circuit Judge:

Plaintiffs challenge the constitutionality of §514 of the Uruguay Round Agreements Act ("URAA"), codified at 17 U.S.C. §104A, which implements Article 18 of the Berne Convention for the Protection of Literary and Artistic Works. The section establishes copyright in various kinds of works that had previously entered the public domain, and plaintiffs argue that any such provision violates the Copyright and Patent Clause of the U.S. Constitution. U.S. Const. art. I, §8, cl. 8. Finding no such bar in the Constitution, the district court dismissed plaintiffs' claims. (A district court in Colorado has recently agreed. *Golan v. Gonzalez*, 2005 U.S.Dist.LEXIS 6800, 2005 WL 914754 (D.Colo. Apr. 20, 2005).) We review the district court's order de novo. . . , and affirm.

Section 514 of the URAA establishes copyrights of foreign holders whose works, though protected under the law where initially published, fell into the public domain in the United States for a variety of reasons – the U.S. failed to recognize copyrights of a particular nation, the copyright owner failed to comply with formalities of U.S. copyright law, or, in the case of sound recordings "fixed" before February 15, 1972, federal copyright protection had been unavailable. See 17 U.S.C. §104A(h)(6). Plaintiff Luck's Music Library is a corporation that rents and sells classical orchestral sheet music. Moviecraft is a commercial film archive that preserves, restores, and sells old footage and films. Both plaintiffs allege that because of the URAA they may no longer freely distribute certain works in their portfolios.

The Copyright and Patent Clause provides that Congress shall have the power "to promote the Progress of Science and useful Arts, by securing for limited Times to Authors and Inventors the exclusive Right to their respective Writings and Discoveries." U.S. Const., art. I, §8, cl. 8. The Clause authorizes the granting of a temporary monopoly over created works, in order to motivate authors and inventors while assuring the public free access at the end of the monopoly. . . . Plaintiffs are correct that the Clause "contains both a grant of power and certain limitations upon the exercise of that power." . . . But they are wrong that the Clause creates any categorical ban on Congress's removing works from the public domain.

Plaintiffs first suggest that to pass muster under the Clause a statute must create an incentive for authors to create new works: legislation must "promote the progress of science." In their view, copyright laws that remove works from the public domain "do not provide significant incentives for new creations" because "rewarding prior works will not provide any significant incentive to create new works because it will not change the costs and benefits of doing so." . . . This of course was the core argument advanced against the Copyright Term Extension Act in *Eldred v. Ashcroft*, 537 U.S. 186, 154 L. Ed. 2d 683, 123 S. Ct. 769 (2003). There it was argued that extensions for works already in existence could not possibly affect authors' incentives to create those works. As a result, the *Eldred* plaintiffs urged, Congress utterly lacked the power to grant such extensions, . . . the extension was an irrational exercise of the power . . . , it failed to promote the progress of science . . . , and it failed to comply with a quid pro quo requirement embedded in the Clause. . . . In all of these variations the argument lost.

It is true, of course, that changes in the law of copyright cannot affect the structure of incentives for works already created. But the knowledge that Congress may pass laws like the URAA in the future does affect the returns from investing time and effort in producing works. All else equal, the expected benefits of creating new works are greater if Congress can remedy the loss of copyright protection for works that have fallen accidentally into the public domain. The *Eldred* Court made a parallel point in rejecting plaintiffs' quid pro quo theory, noting that any author of a work "in the last 170 years would reasonably comprehend, as the 'this' [i.e., quid] offered her, a copyright not only for the time in place when protection is gained, but also for any renewal or extension legislated during that time." . . .

To be sure, the extra incentive afforded by §514 is meager. But to the extent that *Eldred* requires *any* direct incentive, it plainly need not be great. Justice Breyer argued in dissent that the extension upheld there would, assuming a 1% chance that a work would yield $100 a year in years 55-75 of the work's life, have a total present value of seven cents. . . . The majority did not contest his figures . . . , so we may assume it regarded such a low value as direct incentive enough.

Perhaps more than enough. It is by no means clear that *Eldred* requires a direct incentive at all. The majority expressly relied on its understanding that adoption of the 20-year term extension enhanced the United States' position in negotiating with European Union countries for benefits for

American authors. . . . Here, similarly, the Senate argued in support of § 514 that its adoption helped secure better foreign protection for US intellectual property and was "a significant opportunity to reduce the impact of copyright piracy on our world trade position." S. Rep. No. 100-352, at 2 (1988). Plaintiffs do not gainsay the value of the rule in § 514 as a bargaining chip.

On a pragmatic plane, plaintiffs argue that a bright line rule against laws that remove works from the public domain would assure a sound balance between the founders' desire to allow proper incentives for creative effort and their anxiety about political establishment of unjustifiable monopolies. Here they make a public choice argument:

> Just as the English Crown could not be trusted to grant socially beneficial monopolies over existing goods and industries, Congress cannot be trusted to issue patents and copyrights over existing goods and services because there is a "persistent asymmetry" in the legislative process. [William M.] Landes & [Richard A.] Posner, *The Economic Structure of Intellectual Property Law* 408 [(2003)].

. . . . They go on to argue that "authors and large entertainment companies" have a clear and focused interest in obtaining exclusive rights of works in the public domain, whereas those likely to be adversely affected are a diffuse group who at the time of legislation will lack an adequate interest to justify any lobbying effort (or, plaintiffs might add, even much effort at becoming informed on the matter). . . .

The picture is a bit overdrawn; authors and the large entertainment companies are themselves users of copyrightable works, as literature is itself a source of literature (think of Shakespeare and Holinshed). Further, the principled and rigorous application of plaintiffs' public choice analysis would radically tilt the relations among the three branches of government. But the key flaw in the argument is that the *Eldred* plaintiffs were similarly arguing for a bright line rule (no extension of copyright terms for already completed works), in a context with a closely parallel lobbying imbalance, and *Eldred* rejected their claims.

Plaintiffs completely fail to adduce any substantive distinction between the imbalance (if it be that) in tacking 20 years onto a copyright term about to expire in (say) a year, and extending protection to material that has fallen into the public domain. One can imagine that creation of copyright ex nihilo would entail special practical difficulties for parties that have relied on the apparent availability of works in the public domain only to find free access snatched away, but §514 protects those who have relied without notice . . . , and plaintiffs don't challenge these provisions' adequacy.

Unable to offer a material distinction between this case and *Eldred* in terms of the language of the Copyright and Patent Clause or the proper roles of Congress and the judiciary, plaintiffs turn to a historical distinction. They say that taking works out of the public domain is without precedent, in contrast with the congressional pattern of extensions of copyright for completed works on which the Court relied in *Eldred*. Especially lacking, they say, is a practice of the First Congress, whose action bears the imprimatur of the founders themselves. . . .

In fact, evidence from the First Congress points toward constitutionality. The Copyright Act of 1790 granted copyright protection to certain books already printed in the United States at the time of the statute's enactment. . . . If such works were unprotected by common law copyright, that statute would necessarily have granted protection to works previously unprotected –

that is, works in the public domain. The historical evidence on this point is contested, but as early as 1834 the Supreme Court was of the view that the Act of 1790 created new copyright protection rather than simply recognizing existing protections, relying on the statutory language (the author "shall have the sole right," etc.) in reaching that conclusion. See *Wheaton v. Peters,* 33 U.S. (8 Pet.) 591, 661, 8 L. Ed. 1055 (1834) ("Congress, then, by this act, instead of sanctioning an existing right, as contended for, created it.").

Apart from the Act of 1790, plaintiffs insist that no federal statute has ever authorized removing work from the public domain. But the government and the district court point to other statutes that seemingly have done just that. The Act of Dec. 8, 1919, Pub. L. No. 66-102, 41 Stat. 368, gave the President authority to give authors publishing works abroad during World War I time to comply with procedural formalities in the United States after the war's end. Similarly, the Act of Sept. 25, 1941, Pub. L. No. 77-258, 55 Stat. 732, gave the President authority to make copyright protection available to authors who might have been temporarily unable to comply with required formalities because of disruption or suspension of needed facilities. Plaintiffs urge that these acts simply extended the time limits for filing and that they do not purport to modify the prohibition on removing works from the public domain. But to the extent that potential copyright holders failed to satisfy procedural requirements, such works would necessarily have already entered the public domain at the time the statutes were passed.

Plaintiffs also invoke a dictum in *Graham v. John Deere Co.,* 383 U.S. 1, 15 L. Ed. 2d 545, 86 S. Ct. 684 (1966): "Congress may not authorize the issuance of patents whose effects are to remove existent knowledge from the public domain, or to restrict free access to materials already available." . . . Several factors weaken the dictum's force. First, the case dealt with patents rather than copyright, and ideas applicable to one don't automatically apply to the other. For example, the *Eldred* Court saw the "quid pro quo" idea as having a special force in patent law, where the patentee, in exchange for exclusive rights, must disclose his "discoveries" against his presumed will. . . . In contrast, the author is eager to disclose her work. . . .

Second, the *Eldred* Court itself weakened any inference that might be drawn from the *Graham* dictum, using patent cases as a basis for upholding the extension of existing copyrights. Discussing *McClurg v. Kingsland,* 42 U.S. 202, 11 L. Ed. 102 (1843), the Court said that the

> patentee in that case was unprotected under the law in force when the patent issued because he had allowed his employer briefly to practice the invention before he obtained the patent. Only upon enactment, two years later, of an exemption for such allowances did the patent become valid, retroactive to the time it issued.

. . . On this view, *McClurg* upheld the creation of patent protection for an invention that had lapsed into the public domain at least two years earlier. Plaintiffs insist that the *Eldred* Court misread *McClurg,* and that its characterization was mere dictum anyway. . . . While *McClurg* strikes us as one of the most opaque decisions ever crafted, so that we can hardly rule out the possibility of a Supreme Court misreading, we do not see the sort of smoking gun that might embolden us, as an "inferior" federal court (U.S. Const., art. III, §1), to substitute our judgment for the Court's discussion, now but two years old. Certainly we are not persuaded that *McClurg* "implicitly" agrees with plaintiffs "that Congress may not grant patents over matters in the public domain." . . .

The decision of the district court is *Affirmed.*

In order to become a member of the World Trade Organization (WTO), and in order to adhere to the WIPO Performances and Phonograms Treaty, Congress also had to amend the U.S. Copyright Act to prohibit the unauthorized recording of live musical performances, a practice that is commonly referred to as "bootlegging." Here are the provisions of the WTO TRIPs Agreement and of the WIPO Performances and Phonograms Treaty that required Congress to do so:

### World Trade Organization TRIPs Agreement Article 14(1)

. . . [P]erformers shall have the possibility of preventing the following acts when undertaken without their authorization: the fixation of their unfixed performance and the reproduction of such fixation. . . .

### WIPO Performances and Phonograms Treaty Articles 3(1) and 6

3(1) Contracting Parties shall accord the protection provided under this Treaty to the performers and producers of phonograms who are nationals of other Contracting Parties.

6      Performers shall enjoy the exclusive right of authorizing, as regards their performances: . . . (ii) the fixation of their unfixed performances.

Congress did amend U.S. law by adding section 1101 to Title 17 of the United States Code (the same Title that contains the Copyright Act) and by adding section 2319A to Title 18 of the United States Code (the Title that contains federal criminal law). In a nutshell, both sections prohibit bootlegging: 15 U.S.C. §1101 makes bootlegging a civil infringement; 18 U.S.C. §2319A makes bootlegging a federal crime. Again, Congress' constitutional *power* to prohibit bootlegging was challenged.

### United States of America v. Martignon
### 492 F.3d 140 (2d Cir. 2007)

Pooler, Circuit Judge:
     This appeal presents a recurring issue in constitutional law: the extent to which Congress can use one of its powers to enact a statute that it could not enact under another of its arguably relevant powers. See, e.g., *Ry. Labor Executives' Ass'n v. Gibbons*, 455 U.S. 457, 102 S. Ct. 1169, 71 L. Ed. 2d 335 (1982); *Heart of Atlanta Motel, Inc. v. United States*, 379 U.S. 241, 85 S. Ct. 348, 13 L. Ed. 2d 258 (1964); *In re Trade-Mark Cases*, 100 U.S. 82, 25 L. Ed. 550, 619 (1879). Here the statute involved is Section 2319A of Title 18, which prohibits the unauthorized recording of performances as well as the copying, distribution, sale, rental, and trafficking of these bootlegged phonorecords. The constitutional grants of congressional power at issue are the Commerce Clause, Art. I § 8, cl. 3, which permits Congress "[t]o regulate Commerce with foreign Nations, and among the several States, and with the Indian Tribes," and the Copyright Clause, Art. I, § 8, cl. 8, which empowers Congress "[t]o promote the Progress of Science and useful Arts, by securing for limited Times to Authors and Inventors the exclusive Right to their respective Writings and Discoveries."

The district court held that Section 2319A was not validly enacted under the Copyright Clause because it gives rights to performers that are unlimited in time without requiring that the performer have reduced his or her performance to a fixed form. The court also held that Congress could "not enact [such] copyright-like legislation . . . under the [C]ommerce [C]lause (or any other clause), when the legislation conflicts with the limitation[s] imposed by the Copyright Clause."

After examining the statute, its background, the two relevant constitutional clauses, and applicable precedent, we conclude that Congress was free to act under the Commerce Clause to enact Section 2319A(a)(1) and (3). . . .

*Background*

*The Statute*

The URAA was passed after the Uruguay Round of negotiations respecting the General Agreement on Tariffs and Trade ("GATT"). The Uruguay Round produced, in addition to other agreements, the Agreement on Trade-Related Aspects of Intellectual Property Rights ("TRIPS"). TRIPS art. 14(1) provides: "In respect of a fixation of their performance on a phonogram, performers shall have the possibility of preventing the following acts when undertaken without their authorization: the fixation of their unfixed performances and the reproduction of such fixation." These rights must persist for at least fifty years from the end of the calendar year in which the fixing or performance took place. The state parties to TRIPS are "free to determine the appropriate method of implementing the provisions of [TRIPS] within their own legal system and practice."

On December 15, 1993, President Clinton notified the House and Senate of his intent to enter into the Uruguay Round Trade Agreements including TRIPS. The URAA contains two sections aimed at preventing bootlegging of records. Section 512, codified at 17 U.S.C. § 1101, provides a civil cause of action for a performer whose performance was recorded without her consent, while Section 513, codified at 18 U.S.C. § 2319A, provides criminal remedies to the government.

Section 2319A(a) provides that a person who, without the consent of the performer or performers, "knowingly" and for "commercial advantage or private financial gain"

(1) fixes the sounds or sounds and images of a live musical performance in a copy or phonorecord, or reproduces copies or phonorecords of such a performance from an unauthorized fixation;

(2) transmits or otherwise communicates to the public the sounds or sounds and images of a live musical performance; or

(3) distributes or offers to distribute, sells or offers to sell, rents or offers to rent, or traffics in any copy or phonorecord fixed as described in paragraph (1)

may be imprisoned for up to five years and for up to ten years for a second offense.

*District Court Proceedings*

On October 27, 2004, a grand jury charged Martignon, the proprietor of Midnight Records in Manhattan, with one count of violating Section 2319A by reproducing an unauthorized phonorecord and by distributing and selling and offering to distribute and sell phonorecords of performances which had been recorded or fixed without the consent of the performer or performers.

Martignon moved to dismiss the indictment, arguing that Section 2319A violated the Copyright Clause because live performances are not "Writings" within the meaning of the clause and because live performances were given protection for perpetuity rather than for a "limited Time[]". Martignon also claimed that the statute violated the First Amendment. The government responded that Congress had authority to enact Section 2319A under the Commerce and Necessary and Proper Clauses. [2] [n2 The Necessary and Proper Clause, which does not figure in our disposition of this case, allows Congress "[t]o make all Laws which shall be necessary and proper for carrying into Execution the foregoing Powers, and all other Powers vested by this Constitution in the Government of the United States, or in any Department or Officer thereof." U.S. Const., art. I, § 8, cl. 18.]

The district court granted the motion to dismiss.

[T]he government filed a timely notice of appeal.

*The Government's Contentions on Appeal*

The government argues that the district court's order is erroneous for two principal reasons. First, they claim that the Copyright Clause is solely an affirmative grant of power and does not limit Congress's power to act under other clauses of the Constitution. Second, even assuming that the Copyright Clause has some limitations, the government contends that these limitations can only apply to matters within its scope, that is, fixed creative works or "Writings."

*Discussion*

Because the government concedes Congress could not have enacted Section 2319A pursuant to the Copyright Clause, we must determine whether the Copyright Clause's limitations also limit Congress's power to regulate creative works under the Commerce Clause. On its face, Article I, § 8, simply grants powers to Congress. No Section 8 clause, including the Copyright Clause, states that Congress can make certain laws only pursuant to that particular clause or that any limitations on the power granted by that clause carry over to Congress's power to act in a related area under a different Section 8 clause. Nevertheless, in limited instances, the expressed limitations of one clause do apply externally to another clause. To determine whether Section 2319A is invalid because it violates limitations of the Copyright Clause, we must analyze the extent to which the Copyright Clause can be read to limit Congress's power to enact legislation under the Commerce Clause. Because a central focus of the parties' argument on external limitations is whether "Writings" in the Copyright Clause is part of that clause's grant of power or its limitations, we first consider whether the grant of power in the Copyright Clause can be separated with any clarity from constitutionally created limitations on that power. We conclude that another word in the Copyright Clause --"securing"-- may more easily be read to be at least a part of the Clause's grant of power, rather than a limitation; we thus need not determine on which side of the line "Writings" falls. Primarily focusing on a trio of cases -- the *Trademark Cases*, *Heart of Atlanta*, and *Gibbons* -- in which the Supreme Court has considered issues similar to the one that confronts us, we conclude that the Commerce Clause suffices as authority for Section 2319A.

## Scope and Limits of the Copyright Clause

. . . The Copyright Clause provides that Congress has the power "[t]o promote the Progress of Science and useful Arts, by securing for limited Times to Authors and Inventors the exclusive Right to their respective Writings and Discoveries." U.S. Const. art. 1, § 8, cl. 8. The government argues that this clause means that the government has the power to regulate creative and fixed works by granting their creators exclusive rights for a limited time. Martignon, on the other hand, contends that the clause gives the government the power to regulate creative works by granting authors and inventors exclusive rights in written works for a limited time. Under the government's interpretation of the clause, performances are completely outside the scope of the Copyright Clause because they are not fixed. Under Martignon's interpretation, performances are within the scope of the Copyright Clause because they are creative works but violate its limits because the performances are not fixed and the protection is granted for an unlimited time. In an alternative argument, Martignon claims that the subsections underlying the charge against him violate the "limited Times" provision --regardless of whether the fixation requirement is considered as part of the grant of power or as a limitation --because he could only have sold, copied or distributed fixed works. Martignon further argues that once we determine original works are within the scope of the Copyright Clause, we must necessarily conclude that Congress cannot regulate original works under any other grant of power.

. . . The Supreme Court has indicated that Congress can sometimes enact legislation under one constitutional provision that it could not have enacted under another. See, e.g., *Heart of Atlanta*, 379 U.S. at 260-61 (upholding a civil rights statute as a permissible exercise of Commerce Clause power, although a similar statute previously had been declared unconstitutional as beyond the power of Congress under the Thirteenth and Fourteenth Amendments, see *The Civil Rights Cases*, 109 U.S. 3, 10-25, 3 S. Ct. 18, 27 L. Ed. 835 (1883)). However, this power is not unlimited. See *Gibbons*, 455 U.S. at 465-66 (holding that a statute was repugnant to the Bankruptcy Clause and could not be considered a legitimate exercise of Commerce Clause power even though bankruptcy and commerce are "intimately connected"). Because the parties attach different import to these cases and to the Trade-Mark Cases, we examine them to determine where to draw the line between (1) a law which, while related to one constitutional provision and unauthorized by it, can be validly enacted under a different provision; and (2) legislative action that is prohibited under one provision and cannot be enacted under another even though it is seemingly within the purview of the second provision. We find no absolute answers because none of the cases cited by the parties is directly on point. However, we do find strong indicators of the lines along which our analysis must proceed.

. . . We believe that the Supreme Court's cases allow the regulation of matters that could not be regulated under the Copyright Clause in a manner arguably inconsistent with that clause unless the statute at issue is a copyright law. We draw this lesson from *Heart of Atlanta* and from *Gibbons*. In *Heart of Atlanta*, the Court found authority for Congress to enact a statute that prohibited race discrimination in public accommodations affecting interstate commerce, even though the prohibition ran to discrimination not involving "state action," under the Commerce Clause although the Fourteenth Amendment did not allow Congress to enact a similar statute.

The *Gibbons* Court found that RITA was actually a bankruptcy law, not that it was very close to a bankruptcy law or that it was bankruptcy-like. Because *Gibbons* is the only case called to our attention by the parties or the amici in which the Supreme Court struck down a statute that violated the limitation of one constitutional provision despite its clear nexus to another provision, we conclude that Congress exceeds its power under the Commerce Clause by transgressing limitations of the Copyright Clause only when (1) the law it enacts is an exercise of the power granted Congress by the Copyright Clause and (2) the resulting law violates one or more specific limits of the Copyright Clause. . . .

Section 2319A does not create and bestow property rights upon authors or inventors, or allocate those rights among claimants to them. It is a criminal statute, falling in its codification (along with Section 2319B about bootlegged films) between the law criminalizing certain copyright infringement and the law criminalizing "trafficking in counterfeit goods or services." It is, perhaps, analogous to the law of criminal trespass. Rather than creating a right in the performer him- or herself, it creates a power in the government to protect the interest of performers from commercial predations. Section 2319A does not grant the performer the right to exclude others from the performance -- only the government can do that. Neither may the performer transfer his or her interests under Section 2319A to another. Section 2319A only prevents others from doing something without the authorization of the protected person. It may therefore protect the property interests an individual holds by virtue of other laws, but it does not itself allocate those interests. Section 2319A is not a law "secur[ing] . . . rights," nor is it a copyright law.

Thus . . . Section 2319A is not subject to the limitations of Article I, Section 8, cl. 8. . . .

Section 2319A might be read to give the artist at least one right -- the right to allow the fixation of his or her performance -- but the Copyright Act gives the author an extensive bundle of rights in his fixed work. Unlike a performer under Section 2319A, an author enjoying Copyright Act protection may prevent others from performing, copying, or preparing derivative works from the author's copyrighted work. Further, the Copyright Act, but not Section 2319A, gives the author of a work the right to transfer his rights in the work to another person or entity. See 17 U.S.C. § 106. Because "the princip[al] purpose of the [Copyright Act] is to encourage the origination of creative works by attaching enforceable property rights to them," the contrast between the very limited right given to a performer by Section 2319A and the extensive rights given by Section 106 is significant.

> In sum, Section 2319A does not create, bestow, or allocate property rights in expression, it does not share the defining characteristics of other laws that are concededly "copyright laws," and it differs significantly from the Copyright Act that was passed pursuant to the Copyright Clause (and that is valid under it). We therefore conclude that it was not enacted under the Copyright Clause. We have no need to examine whether it violates limits of the Copyright Clause and proceed instead to an examination of its sustainability under the Commerce Clause.

*Commerce Clause Authority*

. . . Section 2319A has substantial commercial and economic aspects. Indeed, regulation of bootlegging is necessary at the federal level because of its interstate and international commercial aspects. . . . Given the nexus between bootlegging and commerce, it is clear that absent any limitations stemming from the Copyright Clause, Congress would have had the power to enact Section 2319A(a)(1) & (3) under the Commerce Clause. Further, Section 2319A regulates only fixing, selling, distributing, and copying with a commercial motive, activities at the core of the Commerce Clause.[8] [n8 This commercial purpose distinguishes Section 2319A from Section 1101. A person who recorded a concert for her personal enjoyment would not violate Section 2319A. Further, because no commercial motive is required for a Section 1101 violation, we specifically limit today's holding to Section 2319A and express no opinion on Section 1101's constitutionality.] It would have been eminently reasonable for Congress to conclude that the sale and distribution of bootleg phonorecords will have a substantial interstate effect on the sale and distribution of legitimate phonorecords. Because Section 2319A is not a copyright law and its enactment was well within the scope of Congress's Commerce Clause authority, it is constitutionally permissible unless some other constitutional provision prevents its enforcement.

*First Amendment*

Martignon argued below and amici Twenty-Nine Intellectual Property and Constitutional Law Professors argue here that Section 2319A violates the First Amendment because it is unconstitutionally overbroad, containing no fair use exception or durational limitation. The district court did not reach this argument because it found a violation of the Copyright Clause. We therefore remand to allow the district court to consider the First Amendment argument.

. . .

*Martignon* concerned only the *criminal* anti-bootlegging statute. Indeed, in footnote 8 (just above), Judge Pooler noted that she expressed "no opinion" on the constitutionality of the *civil* anti-bootlegging provision. Is there any reason that Congress may have had the authority to enact the criminal provision but not the civil provision? The constitutionality of the civil provision has been litigated. The following (pre-*Martignon*) decision expresses the opinion of one District Court judge that the civil provision is constitutional too. Does the following decision seem sound to you, especially given the basis for the Court of Appeals' ruling in *Martignon*?

## KISS Catalog, Ltd. v. Passport Int'l Prod.
### 405 F.Supp.2d 1169 (C.D.Cal. 2005)

Dale S. Fischer, United States District Judge.
*Introduction and Procedural Background*

On December 21, 2004, the Honorable William J. Rea, to whom this case was originally assigned, granted Defendants' motion to dismiss the Seventh Claim for Relief for violation of 17 U.S.C. § 1101, the anti-bootlegging statute, finding that § 1101(a)(3) violated the "for limited Times" requirement of the Copyright Clause and was therefore unconstitutional. *KISS Catalog, Ltd. v. Passport Int'l Prods.*, 350 F.Supp.2d 823, 837 (C.D. Cal. 2004) ("Order").

The United States learned of this finding only after the Order was entered, and sought leave to intervene in the action. On June 7, 2005, Judge Rea granted that request. On August 5, 2005, due to Judge Rea's death, the action was transferred to this Court for all further proceedings. This matter is now before the Court on the motion of the United States to reconsider the finding that § 1101(a)(3) ("Statute") is unconstitutional. Plaintiffs have joined in the motion; Defendants have opposed it.

*I. The Motion to Reconsider is Granted. . . .*

*II. Section 1101(a)(3) is a Constitutional Exercise of Congress' Commerce Clause Power*

. . . Until Judge Rea's Order, no published decision had yet addressed the constitutionality of 17 U.S.C. § 1101(a)(3). Only two, *United States v. Moghadam*, 175 F.3d 1269 (11th Cir. 1999), cert. denied, 529 U.S. 1036, 120 S. Ct. 1529, 146 L. Ed. 2d 344 (2000), and *United States v. Martignon*, 346 F.Supp.2d 413 (S.D.N.Y. 2004), discuss a related criminal statute, 18 U.S.C. § 2319A.[4] [n4 All three decisions are thoroughly and impressively researched. This Court relies on their discussion of the history of the anti-bootlegging legislation.] *Moghadam* and *Martignon*, after a careful consideration of whether the anti-bootlegging legislation is a constitutional exercise of congressional power under the Copyright Clause or the Commerce Clause, reached opposite conclusions.

This analysis of the constitutionality of the Statute addresses two separate considerations: (a) did Congress have the power to enact the legislation? and (b) if so, is the legislation "fundamentally inconsistent" with the Copyright Clause?

This Court agrees with the analysis of *Moghadam*: the Statute is constitutional.

*A. The Commerce Clause Empowers Congress to Enact the Statute*

Because Congress may exercise only those powers granted to it by the Constitution . . . , the Court must determine whether Congress had the power to enact the Statute in the first instance. The Copyright Clause, U.S. Const. art. I, § 8, cl. 8, the Commerce Clause, id. cl. 3, and the Necessary and Proper Clause, id. cl. 18, are the generally suggested sources of such power. Congress may have believed that it was acting pursuant to the Copyright Clause, which provides that Congress has the power to "promote the Progress of Science and useful Arts, by securing for limited Times to Authors and Inventors the exclusive Right to their respective Writings and Discoveries." . . . The Statute was placed within Title 17, and incorporates the statutory remedies for copyright infringement.[7] [n7. . . . At least one author has touted incorporating that durational limit into the Statute as an approach to preserving constitutionality. Angela T. Howe, *United States v. Martignon and Kiss Catalog v. Passport International Products: The Anti-Bootlegging Statute and the Collision of International Intellectual Property Law and the United States Constitution*, 20 Berkeley Tech. L.J. 829, 851 (2005). . . .]

It appears unlikely, however, that Congress could have derived the power to enact the Statute from the Copyright Clause. . . .

This does not end the analysis, however, as Congress' intent is not dispositive. . . . There is a "presumption of constitutionality." Therefore, it is the Court's obligation to look elsewhere for a source of congressional power to enact the Statute.

The United States argues that the Commerce Clause grants such authority. This Court agrees with the United States and with the Eleventh Circuit's analysis in *Moghadam*, 175 F.3d at 1274-77. Indeed, Judge Rea believed the Statute could be enacted under the Commerce Clause if not for the conflict with the Copyright Clause. . . .

Though *Martignon* criticized *Moghadam*'s "swift conclusion" that the legislation is authorized under the Commerce Clause (potential Copyright Clause limitations aside), this Court agrees that the Statute is well within Congress' Commerce Clause powers as broadly defined by, inter alia, *Gonzales v. Raich*, 125 S. Ct. 2195, 162 L. Ed. 2d 1 (2005), and *Lopez*. As the United States Supreme Court most recently made clear in these cases, Congress' authority to enact legislation pursuant to the Commerce Clause has been interpreted broadly in the modern era. Indeed, Supreme Court "case law firmly establishes Congress' power to regulate [even] purely local activities that are part of an economic class of activities' that have a substantial effect on interstate commerce.". . . .

*Moghadam* assumed, without deciding, that the anti-bootlegging legislation could not stand under the Copyright Clause. It simply turned to an alternate source, the Commerce Clause, noting that the test of constitutionality under that clause is "'whether a rational basis existed for concluding that a regulated activity sufficiently affected interstate commerce.'" . . . . Even in the absence of legislative findings of an interstate commerce nexus, the court easily concluded: "The link between bootleg compact discs and interstate commerce and commerce with foreign nations is self-evident." "Bootleggers depress the legitimate markets because demand is satisfied through unauthorized channels." In addition, that § 1101 was enacted in connection with an international treaty called for by the World Trade Organization establishes its connection with – if not its reliance on – interstate and international commerce. [A]ccord Howe, supra, at 846 (citing, inter alia, Office of United States Trade Representative, at http://www.ustr.gov. (last visited March 19, 2005)).

This Court finds that the Commerce Clause grants Congress the power to enact the Statute.[9] [n9 Because the Court finds § 1101(a)(3) valid under the Commerce Clause, the Court need not consider whether it might alternatively be authorized under the Necessary and Proper Clause. There has been some suggestion that the Necessary and Proper Clause would even more clearly provide a constitutional source for the Statute. Howe, supra, at 847-50.]

*B. The Statute Is Not "Fundamentally Inconsistent" With the Copyright Clause*

Though Judge Rea and the court in *Martignon* next considered whether the anti-bootlegging law was fundamentally inconsistent with the Copyright Clause, that step is not necessarily mandated. Arguably, a determination that the Statute does not fall within the ambit of the Copyright Clause ends the analysis.

In general, the various grants of legislative authority contained in the Constitution stand alone and must be independently analyzed. In other words, each of the powers of Congress is alternative to all of the other powers, and what cannot be done under one of them may very well be doable under another.

In contrast, *Martignon*, concluded:

In order to give meaning to the express limitations provided in the Copyright Clause, when enacting copyright-like legislation, such as the anti-bootlegging statute, . . . Congress may not, if the Copyright Clause does not allow for such legislation, enact the law under a separate grant of power, even when that separate grant provides proper authority.

The court provides no authority for this conclusion, however. Instead, as discussed below, it reads the Copyright Clause too broadly, and circumscribes Congress' power under other constitutional grants of authority too narrowly.

Judge Rea, following *Martignon*, deemed the Statute "copyright-like," and then proceeded to the conclusion that the power to regulate a subject matter that admittedly does not fall within the parameters of the Copyright Clause is nevertheless subject to the limitations imposed by that clause. This characterization, even if valid, is not particularly helpful. As the United States points out, nothing prohibits Congress from protecting similar things in different ways – so long as some provision of the United States Constitution allows it to do so. *Railway Labor Executives' Association v. Gibbons*, 455 U.S. 457, 102 S. Ct. 1169, 71 L. Ed. 2d 335 (1982) is not to the contrary. There the Supreme Court examined the definition of "bankruptcy," the language of the challenged legislation, the events surrounding its passage, and its legislative history, and concluded that "Congress was exercising its powers under the Bankruptcy Clause." In other words, it was a bankruptcy statute – not a "bankruptcy-like" statute. Neither the appellant nor the United States argued that Congress could have enacted the law pursuant to the Commerce Clause. The Supreme Court noted that the Commerce Clause does not require uniformity of regulation; therefore, if it held that the Commerce Clause did provide authority for nonuniform bankruptcy laws, the Court "would eradicate from the Constitution a limitation on the power of Congress to enact bankruptcy laws."

The analysis here is different. All parties, and all authorities cited, agree that Congress does not have the authority to legislate concerning live performances under the Copyright Clause. Finding that Congress does have the authority to do so under the Commerce Clause does not negate any of the purposes of, protections afforded by, or limitations established by, the Copyright Clause. Thus the *Railway Labor* analysis does not apply. . . .

The Court again agrees with the United States (and *Moghadam*) that the analysis of *The Trade-Mark Cases* is more to the point. There, the Supreme Court noted that legislation that could not be permitted under the Copyright Clause could nevertheless pass muster under the Commerce Clause – if the independent requirements of that clause were met. Under the more restrictive view of the Commerce Clause that prevailed at the time, those requirements were not met. As noted above, modern case law has expanded the interpretation of the Commerce Clause and modem cases upholding trademark protection are based on the Commerce Clause. Therefore, once the Court concludes that the Statute does not fall within the purview of the Copyright Clause, it need no longer consider whether it complies with the limitations of the Copyright Clause. To do so imports into the Commerce Clause limits that clause does not have. That the Statute might provide "copyright-like" or "copyright-related" protection to matters clearly not covered by the Copyright Clause is not important. One need only find an alternative source of constitutional authority. This Court finds such authority in the Commerce Clause.

Neither the court in *Martignon* nor Judge Rea gave sufficient deference to the fundamental premise that legislation is presumed to be constitutional. Rather, they seemed to feel compelled to choose between the several enumerated powers that might apply – and to choose in a way that rendered the Statute unconstitutional (at least in their view) for failure to meet the "for limited Times" limitation. The *Martignon* court concluded: "That the anti-bootlegging statute has its roots in an inter-country initiative cannot save the statute; it does not serve to transform what appears on its face to be an intellectual property statute into one whose primary purpose is to regulate commerce." But nowhere does the court explain why only a statute's "primary purpose" can be considered in determining its constitutionality.

As noted, the Copyright Clause allows Congress to protect a narrowly defined subject matter within defined parameters. The Statute addresses a similar, but different, subject matter. This Court agrees with *Moghadam*:

> We hold that the Copyright Clause does not envision that Congress is positively forbidden from extending copyright-like protection under other constitutional clauses, such as the Commerce Clause, to works of authorship that may not meet the fixation requirement inherent in the term "Writings." The grant itself is stated in positive terms, and does not imply any negative pregnant that suggests that the term "Writings" operates as a ceiling on Congress' ability to legislate pursuant to other grants. Extending quasi-copyright protection to unfixed live musical performances is in no way inconsistent with the Copyright Clause, even if that Clause itself does not directly authorize such protection.

At least one author opined that Judge Rea "wrongly ignor[ed] the basic tenet that courts should when possible protect the constitutionality of statutes through their interpretive judgments." 1 Raymond T. Nimmer, INFORMATION LAW § 6:30 (2005).

> The "fundamental conflict" standard gives deference to the separate, co-equal character of constitutional grants, creating preemptive conflict only where the separate enactment conflicts with a core and explicit, broad limitation of the other constitutional power. In this respect, the Copyright Clause speaks only to the creation of a separate, limited constitutional grant and, unlike concepts such as are in Due Process and Fourth Amendment rules, does not place broad limitations on any and all exercises of congressional power. Thus the [*Moghadam*] court's analysis was clearly correct.

As Nimmer goes on to state:

> An important aspect of the *Kiss Catalog*[] result was its further conclusion that, while the statute could have been enacted under the Commerce Clause (which contains no time limitation), Commerce Clause powers could not be invoked to subvert an express limitation in the Copyright Clause. This conclusion creates an unwarranted hierarchy among otherwise seemingly co-equal constitutional grants and is particularly suspect in a modern era in which Commerce Clause authority is broadly construed. It hinges entirely on the court's belief that, in some fashion, this statute was a "copyright-like" enactment and, thus, governed entirely and solely by the Copyright Clause.

With regard to *Martignon*'s holding that the criminal version of the statute also violates the "Writings" provision (an issue not addressed by Judge Rea), Nimmer comments:

> This . . . analysis . . . only holds if one assumes that the limitations of the Copyright Clause dominate other provisions of the Constitution, a conclusion that is conducive in this instance to a restrictive view of Congressional power to provide for rights in

information products, but that has little grounding in constitutional history or the purpose of a clause that was intended to create a power, rather than comprehensively limit governmental conduct.

Even if a "fundamental conflict" with the Copyright Clause would invalidate the Statute, none exists here. Considering whether the Copyright Clause prevents Congress from exercising its Commerce Clause power perpetually to prohibit bootlegging – or more specifically, the dissemination of bootlegged recordings – the Court concludes it does not. As indicated previously, the Statute merely proscribes conduct not otherwise addressed, prohibited or protected by the Copyright Clause: the non-consensual recording of a live performance. Stated differently, what Congress regulates here is an unauthorized and (by this statute) unlawful recording of a live performance, not an authorized, protected, and constitutionally-encouraged fixation of an author's original work. Thus, the Statute complements, rather than violates, the Copyright Clause by addressing similar subject matter, not previously protected – or protectible – under the Copyright Clause. . . .

In contrast to *Railway Labor*, the question is not whether legislation empowered by the Copyright Clause – but invalid under it – can otherwise be empowered by the Commerce Clause. The question is whether matters not encompassed within the Copyright Clause can be addressed by the Commerce Clause free of the restrictions of the Copyright Clause. The answer to that question is, clearly, yes.

One does not have to stretch the presumption of constitutionality to conclude that legislation that prevents dissemination in perpetuity of an unauthorized videotape by a third-party of a live performance does not conflict with a clause that protects, "for limited Times," the voluntarily disseminated "Writings" of authors. That portion of the Order that holds the Statute unconstitutional is hereby vacated.

*Conclusion*

For the reasons stated above, the motion to reconsider is granted, the portion of the Order holding 17 U.S.C. § 1101(a)(3) unconstitutional is vacated, and Defendants' motion to dismiss the Seventh Claim for Relief on the grounds that 17 U.S.C. § 1101(a)(3) is unconstitutional is DENIED.

So (as of 2009) three separate decisions have upheld the constitutionality of the anti-bootlegging statutes – both criminal and civil (*Martignon*, *KISS Catalog*, and the 11th Circuit's *Moghadam* decision, cited in *KISS Catalog*).

The possibility – however remote it now seems – that Congress does *not* have the *power* to enact copyright legislation required by treaty obligations is remarkable. What's more, because Congress enacted the anti-bootlegging statute to comply with *treaty* obligations, it is surprising that so much emphasis has been placed on Congress' powers under the *Commerce* Clause, and so little attention has been give to Congress' power under the Necessary and Proper Clause. In *Martignon*, Judge Pooler simply stated that the government's Necessary and Proper Clause argument played no part in her analysis (footnote 2); and in *KISS Catalog*, Judge Fischer did the same (footnote 9).

The Necessary and Property Clause is the source of Congressional power to enact legislation to comply with treaties. The Supreme Court has held – though not in a copyright case – that the clause does give Congress the power to enact federal legislation that otherwise would have been beyond

Congress' power, even in cases where Congress' power was limited by another provision of the Constitution. *Missouri v. Holland*, 252 U.S. 416 (1920).

It is important to know whether Congress does have the power to enact copyright legislation under the Necessary and Proper Clause, because if Congress does not – so the anti-bootlegging statute really is unconstitutional – serious consequences are possible and even likely. Assume the anti-bootlegging statute is unconstitutional, and consider these questions:

- KISS is an American band. Suppose its live performances in United States had been bootlegged, and that bootleg recordings were then sold in, say, Germany – a country which also has anti-bootlegging legislation. Do you suppose that KISS would be able to assert anti-bootlegging rights in Germany? This question will be answered later, in connection with two German cases, one involving an unnamed American recording artist and the other involving British recording artists Phil Collins and Cliff Richard. (*Re Copyright in an Unauthorized U.S. Recording* and *Collins v. Imtrat Handelsgesellschaft*.) Both cases were decided before the United States enacted its anti-bootlegging statute, and they indicate what the consequences would be for American artists abroad, if the U.S. anti-bootlegging statute is unconstitutional.

- Suppose KISS's bootlegging lawsuit had not been filed by KISS but instead had been filed by U2, an Irish band, because its performances were bootlegged. If U2's lawsuit were dismissed because the U.S. anti-bootlegging statute is unconstitutional, what consequences could follow for American recording artists and indeed for Americans who aren't even in the music business? This question too will be answered later in connection with a case that involved a different section of the U.S. Copyright Act (titled *Report of WTO Panel on United States Section 110(5) of the US Copyright Act*).

- Is there any way to amend the anti-bootlegging statute so it would be constitutional, even in the eyes of the *District* Court judge in the *Martignon* case?

The question of Congress' power to enact copyright (or copyright-like) legislation in response to treaty obligations is not limited to the single-industry problem of whether bootlegging may be prohibited by federal law. It is a critical issue that affects the United States' ability to participate in international copyright policy making.

Congress enacted the entire Digital Millennium Copyright Act (which prohibits the circumvention of technological measures used to protect the rights of copyright owners and prohibits the removal or alteration of copyright management information, 15 U.S.C. §§1201-1205) to satisfy obligations the U.S. assumed when it adhered to the WIPO Copyright Treaty and the WIPO Performances and Phonogram Treaty.

The World Intellectual Property Organization has been considering proposed treaties that, if adopted, will extend intellectual property protection to databases (see, e.g., http://www.wipo.int/meetings/ n/topic.jsp?group _id=62) and to the traditional knowledge, genetic resources and folklore of

Indigenous People. (See, e.g., http://www.wipo.int/tk/en/studies/cultural/minding-culture/studies/finalstudy.pdf) Databases and most (perhaps all) traditional knowledge, genetic resources and folklore would *not* be eligible for protection under current U.S. copyright or patent laws. Assuming the United States has the political desire to adhere to such treaties, its ability to do so may depend on Congress having the power to enact necessary legislation under the Necessary and Proper Clause of the Constitution.

The power of Congress to enact copyright legislation under the Necessary and Proper Clause has been considered, thoughtfully, in only one opinion:

## Bridgeman Art Library, Ltd. v. Corel Corp.
### 36 F. Supp. 2d 191 (S.D.N.Y. 1999)

Lewis A. Kaplan, District Judge

On November 13, 1998, this Court granted defendant's motion for summary judgment dismissing plaintiff's copyright infringement claim on the alternative grounds that the allegedly infringed works – color transparencies of paintings which themselves are in the public domain – were not original and therefore not permissible subjects of valid copyright and, in any case, were not infringed. It applied United Kingdom law in determining whether plaintiff's transparencies were copyrightable. The Court noted, however, that it would have reached the same result under United States law.

Following the entry of final judgment, the Court was bombarded with additional submissions. On November 23, 1998, plaintiff moved for reargument and reconsideration, arguing that the Court erred on the issue of originality. . . . At about the same time, the Court received an unsolicited letter from Professor William Patry, author of a copyright law treatise, which argued that the Court erred in applying the law of the United Kingdom to the issue of copyrightability. Plaintiff then moved for an order permitting the filing of an *amicus* brief by one of its associates, The Wallace Collection, to address the United Kingdom law issue. The Court granted leave for the submission of the *amicus* brief and invited the parties to respond to Professor Patry's letter. The matter now is ripe for decision. . . .

Professor Patry argues principally that there can be no choice of law issue with respect to copyrightability because the Copyright Clause of the Constitution permits Congress to enact legislation protecting only original works of authorship. In consequence, he contends, only original works, with originality determined in accordance with the meaning of the Copyright Clause, are susceptible of protection in United States courts.

Of course, the ability of Congress to extend the protection of copyright is limited by the Copyright Clause. Nevertheless, the constitutional issue is not as straightforward as Professor Patry suggests. Bridgeman claims that the infringed works are protected by United Kingdom copyrights and that the United States, by acceding to the Convention for the Protection of Literary and Artistic Works, popularly known as the Berne Convention, and the Universal Copyright Convention and by enacting the Berne Convention Implementation Act of 1988 (the "BCIA"), agreed to give effect to its United Kingdom copyrights.

The fact that plaintiff's rights allegedly derive from its claimed British copyrights arguably is material. Granting Professor Patry's point that Congress, in light of the originality requirement of the Copyright Clause, in ordinary circumstances may not extend copyright protection to works that are not original, the questions remain whether (1) the United States constitutionally may obligate itself by treaty to permit enforcement of a foreign copyright where that copyright originates under the law of a signatory nation which does not limit copyright protection to works that are original in the sense required by the United States Constitution and, if so, (2) the United States in fact has done so. Thus, Professor Patry's contention that the United States may not apply foreign law less restrictive than its own with respect to originality may be too narrow because it rests exclusively on the Copyright Clause. The legal effect and constitutionality of treaties also is implicated.

Article II, Section 2, of the Constitution provides that the President "shall have Power, by and with the Advice and Consent of the Senate, to make Treaties, provided two thirds of the Senators present concur." Treaties, by virtue of the Supremacy Clause, join the Constitution and federal statutes as "supreme law of the land." As the Supreme Court wrote in *Geofroy v. Riggs:*

> "The treaty power, as expressed in the Constitution, is in terms unlimited except by those restraints which are found in that instrument against the action of the government . . . , and those arising from the nature of the government itself and the States. It would not be contended that it extends so far as to authorize what the Constitution forbids, or a change in the character of the government or in that of one of the States, or a cession of any portion of the territory of the latter, without its consent . . . But with these exceptions, it is not perceived that there is any limit to the questions which can be adjusted touching any matter which is properly the subject of negotiation with a foreign country."

And while it now is clear that the treaty power is "subject to the constitutional limitations that apply to all exercises of federal power, principally the prohibitions of the Bill of Rights," the treaty power retains considerable scope.

The Copyright Clause and the Copyright Act both recognize that the United States has an important interest in protecting the intellectual property of its citizens and of those whose creative efforts enrich our lives. In this increasingly interconnected world, securing appropriate protection abroad also is important. Hence, it cannot seriously be denied that international copyright protection is "properly the subject of negotiation with" foreign countries.

Decades ago, the Supreme Court held in *Missouri v. Holland* that Congress could enact legislation necessary and proper to the implementation of a treaty which, absent the treaty, would have been beyond its powers. Although the case arose in a different context,[16] it suggests that the Conventions, if their purported effect actually is to permit enforcement in the United States of foreign copyrights which do not meet U.S. standards of originality – in other words, if they require enforcement here of any copyright valid under the law of the signatory nation in which copyright attached, even if that copyright does not meet U.S. standards of validity – would not be obviously invalid. [n16 The issue [in *Missouri v. Holland*] was whether a statute regulating the hunting of migratory birds, enacted to implement a U.S.-Canadian treaty, violated the Tenth Amendment by invading a province reserved to the states. Here, on the other hand, the question would be whether the Copyright Clause, in limiting copyright protection to original works, prohibits the United States from agreeing to extend protection to foreign works which do not meet that requirement.]

In view of these considerations, the proposition advanced by Professor Patry – that the Copyright Clause forecloses any choice of law issue with respect to the validity of a foreign Berne Convention work, is not free from doubt. It is necessary to decide that question, however, only if the Conventions require application of foreign law in determining the existence of copyright and, if so, whether there is any true conflict of law in this case on that point.

[Judge Kaplan then went on – in a portion of the opinion excerpted later – to decide that Berne and the Universal Copyright Convention do *not* require the United States to apply foreign law to decide whether a work is protected by copyright in the U.S. Instead, both conventions require the U.S. to apply its own law for that purpose.]

Section 102(a) limits copyright protection in relevant part to "original works of authorship . . . ." Accordingly, there is no need to decide whether the Berne Convention adopts any rule regarding the law governing copyrightability or whether the treaty power constitutionally might be used to extend copyright protection to foreign works which are not "original" within the meaning of the Copyright Clause. Congress has made it quite clear that the United States' adherence to the Berne Convention has no such effect in the courts of this country. And while there is no comparable legislation with respect to the Universal Copyright Convention, the question whether that treaty is self-executing is of no real significance here because the substantive provisions of the UCC are "of very limited practical import . . ."

Judge Kaplan's opinion suggests that Congress *does* have the authority to enact copyright legislation under the Necessary and Proper Clause; but his opinion on this point is merely *dicta*. What's more, there is authority to the contrary – not authority dealing with copyright legislation in particular, but authority questioning whether Congress does have the power to enact legislation that it would not otherwise have the power to enact, under that Clause. See *Reid v. Covert*, 354 U.S. 1 (1957) (plurality opinion holding that treaties are subject to constitutional limitations); and Nicholas Quinn Rosenkranz, *Executing the Treaty Power*, 118 Harv.L.Rev. 1867 (2005) (arguing that *Missouri v. Holland* was incorrectly decided in the first place).

### 3. As sources of substantive principles

It also *appears* that treaties are themselves sources of substantive copyright law principles that might be relied on, for example, in international copyright litigation.

**Berne Convention Article 5(1)**

Authors *shall enjoy* . . . the rights [provided by national treatment] . . . as well as *the rights specially granted by this Convention*. [Emphasis added.]

In fact, in some countries – but not all – treaties are treated as sources of substantive copyright law.

### a. In countries *other than* the United States

In many civil law countries, treaties are incorporated directly into national law, and thus in those countries the provisions of the Berne Convention may by applied directly by national courts in cases involving international copyright disputes. Belgium, Spain and Switzerland are "[p]rominent Berne Union countries where this is so. . . ." Sam Ricketson, *The Berne Convention for the Protection of Literary and Artistic Works: 1886-1986* at 826 n. 470 (1987). Germany is such a country too; but Israel is not. Paul Edward Geller, *International Copyright: An Introduction* §3[2][a] in *International Copyright Law and Practice* (2000).

In some countries, treaty provisions may be relied on even in purely domestic copyright disputes between parties who are nationals of that country. In Belgium, for example, "the provisions of the Berne Convention apply between Belgians if they are more favorable than national copyright provisions." Alain Strowel, *Belgium* §1[4] in Paul Edward Geller, *International Copyright Law and Practice* (2000).

### b. In the United States

In the United States, it *appears* as though treaties are themselves sources of law. The Constitution seems to say so:

### United States Constitution Article VI, Clause 2

This Constitution, and the Laws of the United States which shall be made in Pursuance thereof; and *all Treaties made, or which shall be made, under the Authority of the United States, shall be the supreme Law of the Land*; and the Judges in every State shall be bound thereby, any Thing in the Constitution or Laws of any State to the Contrary notwithstanding. [Emphasis added.]

Nevertheless, in the United States, international copyright treaties are *not* a direct source of law, not even in international disputes. This is so for three reasons.

First, prior to the United States' adherence to the Berne Convention in 1989, no other copyright treaty to which the U.S. adhered granted greater or different rights than U.S. domestic copyright law.

Second, some treaties – such as the Phonograms Convention – provide by their own terms that they are not to be considered sources of law in themselves.

### Phonograms Convention Article 3

The means by which this Convention is implemented shall be a matter for the domestic law of each contracting State and shall be include one or more of the following: protection by means of the grant of a copyright or other specific right; protection by means of the law relating to unfair competition; protection by means of penal sanctions.

As a result, until the U.S. adhered to the Berne Convention, there was no reason to look to copyright treaties as sources of copyright law in the United States.

Things appeared to change when the U.S. adhered to Berne, because the Berne Convention does grant certain rights not found in U.S. domestic copyright law (e.g., moral rights). But – and this is the third reason copyright treaties are not a direct source of law in the U.S. – when the U.S. adhered to the Berne Convention and Congress amended the U.S. Copyright Act to comply with Berne's Article 36 (above), Congress also inserted into the Copyright Act this provision:

### United States Copyright Act §104(c)

Effect of Berne Convention. – No right or interest in a work eligible for protection under this title may be claimed by virtue of, or in reliance upon, the provisions of the Berne Convention, or the adherence of the United States thereto. Any rights in a work eligible for protection under this title that derive from this title, other Federal or State statutes, or the common law, shall not be expanded or reduced by virtue of, or in reliance upon, the provisions of the Berne Convention, or the adherence of the United States thereto.

It could be argued, and has been, that section 104(c) of the Copyright Act improperly conflicts with Article 5(1) of the Berne Convention (above), and thus with Article 36 of Berne (above). But those arguments have not been successful.

### In re AEG Acquisition Corp.
### 127 Bankr. 34, 1991 Bankr.LEXIS 638 (C.D.Cal.Bankr.Ct. 1991)

United States Bankruptcy Judge Samuel L. Bufford: . . .

Article VI of the United States Constitution provides: "This Constitution, and the Laws of the United States which shall be made in Pursuance thereof; and all Treaties made, or which shall be made, under the Authority of the United States, shall be the supreme Law of the Land . . . ." It is presumably under this constitutional provision that Zenith argues that [it had certain rights under] the Berne Convention. . . . However, United States law on treaties is more complex.

Some treaties are self-executing, under United States treaty law, and some are not. A self-executing treaty creates rights for the nationals of a country that is a party to the convention without the need for any implementing domestic legislation. A treaty that is not self-executing, on the other hand, requires implementing domestic legislation to create rights thereunder for the citizens of the state party to the treaty. Whether a particular treaty is self-executing or not normally turns on the domestic law of the particular state party, and may vary from one state party to another.

At the time that it ratified the Berne Convention, the United States Senate determined that the treaty should not be self-executing in the United States, and Congress enacted implementing legislation to give it effect in the United States. Thus the Berne Convention creates rights in United States law only to the extent that it is implemented through domestic legislation. . . .

**Edison v. BMI**
**954 F.2d 1419 (8th Cir.)**
**cert. denied, 112 S.Ct. 1995 (1992)**

Circuit Judge Bowman: . . .

Finally, BMI argues that the District Court's decision . . . conflicts with this country's international treaty obligations. . . .

BMI's argument that this decision interferes with the international treaty obligations of the United States also fails. The treaty in question is the international copyright agreement known as the Berne Convention. The Convention . . . entered into force for the United States on March 1, 1989. Congress then revised the Copyright Act (although section 110(5) [the "homestyle receiver" public performance exemption] was unaffected) and declared that the Act as amended "satisfies the obligations of the United States in adhering to the Berne Convention and no further rights or interests shall be recognized or created for that purpose."

BMI asserts that the District Court's interpretation of section 110(5) to provide shelter for Edison under the homestyle exemption expands the scope of the exemption to such a degree that it renders section 110(5) in violation of the United States' treaty obligations under Article 11*bis* of the Berne Convention. Under that article, authors of artistic works have exclusive rights to authorize "the public communication by loudspeaker or any other analogous instrument transmitting, by signs, sounds or images, the broadcast of the work." The flaw in BMI's argument is that the District Court's interpretation of section 110(5) does not expand the homestyle exemption, but merely declares that the statutory language means what it says. We cannot presume that Congress, in enacting this language, intended something else, and we know that Congress declared its handiwork to be consistent with the Berne Convention. Congress thus declared the public policy of the United States and, for us, that is the end of the matter.

Congress was emphatic that the United States' participation in the Berne Convention should not give rise to an expanded claim of copyright protection. . . . In view of this unmistakably clear congressional directive, BMI's claim to a "right or interest . . . by virtue of . . . the adherence of the United States" to the Berne Convention cannot be sustained.

The judgment of the District Court is affirmed.

## B. U.S. copyright treaty relations with other countries

### 1. A brief history

The history of U.S.-international copyright relations is divided into five phases.

#### a. From 1790 to 1891

From 1790 (when the first copyright law was enacted in the United States) to 1891, the United States had no copyright treaties (or proclamations) with other countries. In fact, the first Copyright Act specifically *permitted* the reprinting of books published by those who were not citizens of the United States. Paul Goldstein, *Copyright's Highway: From Gutenberg's Bible to the Celestial Jukebox* 184 (1994).

During this phase of our history, the United States was the world's leading copyright "pirate"!

### b.  From 1891 to 1955

From 1891 to 1955, the United States entered into several bilateral treaties (and reciprocal proclamations) with other countries, and one multi-national treaty with other Western Hemisphere countries (the Buenos Aires Convention). During this phase, the United States stopped being an international pirate, but it didn't fully join the international copyright community, because that community had formed around the Berne Convention whose minimum standards were not satisfied by the then-existing U.S. Copyright Act.

### c.  From 1955 to 1989

In 1955, the United States adhered to the Universal Copyright Convention (UCC), a multi-national convention whose minimum standards were crafted to accommodate the then-existing U.S. Copyright Act.

In 1974, the U.S. adhered to the Convention for the Protection of Producers of Phonograms Against Unauthorized Duplication of Their Phonograms (commonly known as the "Phonograms Convention").

In 1985, the U.S. adhered to the Convention Relating to the Distribution of Programme-Carrying Signals Transmitted by Satellite (commonly known as the "Satellite Convention").

### d.  From 1989 to 1995

In 1989, the United States finally adhered to the Berne Convention, after amending its Copyright Act in several required ways.

### e.  From 1995 to date

In 1995, the United States joined the World Trade Organization whose central document – the General Agreement on Tariffs and Trade (GATT) – was amended (by the Uruguay Round Agreement) to include very significant provisions relating to intellectual property, including copyright. Those provisions are set forth in the Agreement on Trade-Related Aspects of Intellectual Property Rights, known as "TRIPs" for short.

In 1998, the United States adhered to the WIPO Copyright Treaty and the WIPO Performances and Phonograms Treaty.

### 2.  Copyright treaties to which U.S. adheres

As a result of this activity, the United States now adheres to eight multi-national treaties:

- WIPO Performances and Phonograms Treaty
- WIPO Copyright Treaty
- WTO TRIPs Agreement
- Berne Convention
- Satellite Convention
- Phonograms Convention
- Universal Copyright Convention
- Buenos Aires Convention

The bilateral treaties and proclamations to which the United States is a party are identified (along with the multi-national treaties to which the U.S. adheres) in *Copyright Office Circular 38a: International Copyright Relations of the United States* (available at http://www.copyright.gov/circs/circ38a.pdf).

The reason that several copyright treaties exist simultaneously, and the reason that most countries (including the U.S.) adhere to several, is that treaties differ from one another with respect to:
- the works they cover
- the rights they protect, and
- the countries that adhere to them.

No one treaty requires protection for all types of works or rights or is adhered to by all copyright-protecting countries. Thus, adherence to several treaties is necessary in order for a country to obtain (for its own works) as much international protection as it desires (and is willing to give to works from other countries).

### 3. Important multi-national treaties to which U.S. is not a party

There are two important multi-national copyright treaties to which the United States is *not* a party:
- International Convention for the Protection of Performers, Phonograms and Broadcasts
- Treaty on the International Registration of Audiovisual Works

The International Convention for the Protection of Performers, Phonograms and Broadcasts – which is commonly referred to by copyright lawyers as "the Rome Convention," though there are other unrelated treaties that are known by that name too – is separate from, has different provisions than, and thus should not be confused with the WIPO Performances and Phonograms Treaty, to which the U.S. does adhere. The Rome Convention requires, among other things, adhering countries to protect the rights of performers to prevent or be compensated for the public performance and broadcasts of recordings of their performances. The consequences to U.S. performers of the failure of the U.S. to adhere to this treaty are shown in a decision of the Supreme Court of Germany in the *Bob Dylan* case (which will be covered later).

The Treaty on the International Registration of Audiovisual Works creates a central international register of copyright ownership and transfers for audiovisual works, including movies and television programs. The contents of the register are considered "true" (in countries adhering to the treaty), unless the contrary is proved. The treaty does not contain substantive copyright provisions, nor does it provide an international forum for resolving disputes. It merely creates prima facie evidence of current copyright ownership.

Why do you suppose the United States has failed to adhere to these two treaties? (There are two entirely different reasons that explain why the U.S. hasn't adhered to either treaty.)

## C. Deciding which treaty is the appropriate "pipeline"

Recall (from Chapter 1) that the first basic step in the analysis of an international copyright question is to determine whether there is a treaty (or proclamation or domestic law) that requires protection in one country for a work whose country-of-origin is another country. Since there are several separate copyright treaties, it's essential – even in cases where the two countries do have a treaties with one another – to determine whether any of those treaties provide the necessary "pipeline" for protection.

### 1.  Importance of "connecting factors"

In order for a treaty to be a "pipeline" requiring protection in one country for a work whose country-of-origin is another country, two types of "connecting factors" *must* exist:

1.   The treaty must require protection for
     a.  *works* of the kind in question, and for *rights* of the kind in question, and
     b.  the treaty must require such protection between the two countries *as of the date the work was first published* anywhere in the world; and

2.   One of the following geographic connections must exist between the work and some country which has a treaty relationship with the country where protection is sought:
     a.  the author of the work is a national or resident of such a country, *or*
     b.  the work was first published in such a country.

These factors will be examined in detail in Chapter 3, but, first, one more preliminary point needs to be made.

### 2.  Hierarchy of copyright treaties

In many cases, more than one treaty between two countries will satisfy both the works/rights and geographic connecting factors. For example, both countries may have adhered to both Berne and the UCC, or the countries may have a bilateral treaty with one another and adhered to the UCC. In those cases, if the question is whether the country where protection is sought has satisfied its treaty obligation to meet minimum standards, the order in which those treaties are considered is this: first, Berne; then the UCC or the bilateral, whichever (as between the UCC and the bilateral) requires the *greatest* protection for the work.

The reason this "hierarchy" was necessary is that many countries already were members of Berne – and thus provided Berne-level protection – when the UCC came into existence in the mid-1950s. The UCC had lower minimum standards than did Berne; in other words, the UCC required less copyright protection than Berne did. For that reason, the Berne Union was afraid that countries would drop out of Berne and adhere to the UCC *instead of*, rather than in addition to, Berne. In order to prevent that from happening, the UCC itself provides that it does not apply to works from countries that dropped out of Berne after January 1, 1951. (UCC Declaration to Article XVII.)

Then, to resolve the question of which minimum standards apply as between countries that adhere to both Berne and the UCC, the UCC itself provides that Berne standards apply. (UCC Article XVII and Declaration thereto.) As between the UCC and a bilateral, however, the bilateral applies if it provides greater protection for the work than the UCC would. (UCC Article XIX.)

This hierarchy would be important to legislators who wonder whether (and if so, how) they must amend their national copyright statute upon joining Berne or the UCC. And it could be important in an international dispute among countries over whether one of them is satisfying its treaty obligations. However, as between individual copyright owners and users, the hierarchy would be important only if the country in which protection is sought is a country whose treaties are incorporated directly into its national law, and thus may by applied directly by national courts in cases involving international copyright disputes.

## Chapter 3

# Circumstances Necessary for International Protection:
# Essential "Connecting Factors"

Determining whether a treaty applies to a particular work is much like playing three-dimensional tick-tack-toe. It is necessary to look for *works* along one dimension, *rights* along another, and the *nationality or residence* of the author, or the *country* of first publication, along the third; and then it is necessary to see whether all three converge in a single treaty.

To do this, it is necessary to look at the language of specific treaties. Excerpts from five treaties are reproduced below: the Berne Convention; the UCC; the Satellite Convention; the Phonograms Convention; and the Rome Convention. The Berne Convention neatly separates those of its provisions (called "Articles") that identify protected *works* from those that identify *rights* conferred; but the other four conventions identify protected works and rights conferred together in a single provision.

Treaties (like statutes and contracts) make for dull reading. So, to focus your attention on the following excerpts, assume that you have been asked to determine whether

- the owner of the copyright to an American *sound recording* or perhaps the recording artist, *and*
- the owner of the copyright to the recorded American *musical composition* (i.e., the music publisher) or perhaps the songwriter

are entitled to receive public performance royalties on account of the broadcast of that recording on radio stations in Canada.

In addition to the text of the treaties, here are some facts you'll need in order to answer this question:

- Canadian radio stations do pay royalties to Canadian record companies and Canadian artists, and to Canadian music publishers and songwriters.
- Canada has adhered to the Berne Convention, the UCC and the Rome Convention, but not to the Satellite convention or the Phonograms Convention.
- The United States has adhered to the Berne Convention, the UCC, the Satellite Convention and the Phonograms Convention, but not to the Rome Convention.

Do any of the following treaties obligate Canada to require Canadian radio stations to pay broadcast royalties to the:

- American record company
- American recording artist
- American music publisher, or
- American songwriter?

If so, which treaty? If none, why not? (These questions cannot be answered with just a quick scan of the following treaties. Look for the answers as you read the treaties slowly and carefully. Also, as you do your analysis, keep in mind that the phrase "musical works" refers to musical *compositions*, not to recordings.)

## A. Works/rights connecting factors

### Berne Convention

*Article 2*

1. The expression "literary and artistic works" shall include every production in the literary, scientific and artistic domain, whatever may be the mode or form of its expression, such as books, pamphlets and other writings; lectures, addresses, sermons and other works of the same nature; dramatic or dramatico-musical works; choreographic works and entertainments in dumb show; musical compositions with or without words; cinematographic works to which are assimilated works expressed by a process analogous to cinematography; works of drawing, painting, architecture, sculpture, engraving and lithography; photographic works to which are assimilated works expressed by a process analogous to photography; works of applied art; illustrations, maps, plans, sketches and three-dimensional works relative to geography, topography, architecture or science.

2. It shall, however, be a matter for legislation in the countries of the Union to prescribe that works in general or any specified categories of works shall not be protected unless they have been fixed in some material form.

3. Translations, adaptations, arrangements of music and other alterations of a literary or artistic work shall be protected as original works without prejudice to the copyright in the original work.

4. It shall be a matter for legislation in the countries of the Union to determine the protection to be granted to official texts of a legislative, administrative and legal nature, and to official translations of such texts.

5. Collections of literary or artistic works such as encyclopaedias and anthologies which, by reason of the selection and arrangement of their contents, constitute intellectual creations shall be protected as such, without prejudice to the copyright in each of the works forming part of such collections.

6. The works mentioned in this article shall enjoy protection in all countries of the Union. This protection shall operate for the benefit of the author and his successors in title.

7. . . . [I]t shall be a matter for legislation in the countries of the Union to determine the extent of the application of their laws to works of applied art and industrial designs and models, as well as the conditions under which such works, designs and models shall be protected. Works protected in the country of origin solely as designs and models shall be entitled in another country of the Union only to such special protection as is granted in that country to designs and models; however, if no such special protection is granted in that country, such works shall be protected as artistic works.

8. The protection of this Convention shall not apply to news of the day or to miscellaneous facts having the character of mere items of press information.

*Article 2bis*

1. It shall be a matter for legislation in the countries of the Union to exclude, wholly or in part, from the protection provided by the preceding article political speeches and speeches delivered in the course of legal proceedings.

2. It shall also be a matter for legislation in the countries of the Union to determine the conditions under which lectures, addresses and other works of

the same nature which are delivered in public may be reproduced by the press, broadcast, communicated to the public by wire and made the subject of public communication . . . , when such use is justified by the informatory purpose.

3. Nevertheless, the author shall enjoy the exclusive right of making a collection of his works mentioned in the preceding paragraphs.

*Article 6bis*

1. Independently of the author's economic rights, and even after the transfer of the said rights, the author shall have the right to claim authorship of the work and to object to any distortion, mutilation or other modification of, or other derogatory action in relation to, the said work, which would be prejudicial to his honor or reputation.

2. The rights granted to the author in accordance with the preceding paragraph shall, after his death, be maintained, at least until the expiry of the economic rights, and shall be exercisable by the persons or institutions authorized by the legislation of the country where protection is claimed. However, those countries whose legislation, at the moment of their ratification of or accession to this Act, does not provide for the protection after the death of the author of all rights set out in the preceding paragraph may provide that some of these rights may, after his death, cease to be maintained.

3. The means of redress for safeguarding the rights granted by this article shall be governed by the legislation of the country where protection is claimed.

*Article 8*

Authors of literary and artistic works protected by this Convention shall enjoy the exclusive right of making and of authorizing the translation of their works throughout the term of protection of their rights in the original works.

*Article 9*

1. Authors of literary and artistic works protected by this Convention shall have the exclusive right of authorizing the reproduction of these works, in any manner or form.

2. It shall be a matter for legislation in the countries of the Union to permit the reproduction of such works in certain special cases, provided that such reproduction does not conflict with a normal exploitation of the work and does not unreasonably prejudice the legitimate interests of the author.

3. Any sound or visual recording shall be considered as a reproduction for the purposes of this Convention.

*Article 11*

1. Authors of dramatic, dramatico-musical and musical works shall enjoy the exclusive right of authorizing:

(i) public performance of their works, including such public performance by any means or process;

(ii) any communication to the public of the performance of their works.

2. Authors of dramatic or dramatico-musical works shall enjoy, during the full term of their rights in the original works, the same rights with respect to translations thereof.

*Article 11bis*

1.  Authors of literary and artistic works shall enjoy the exclusive right of authorizing:

>   (i)  the broadcasting of their works or the communication thereof to the public by any other means of wireless diffusion of signs, sounds or images;
>
>   (ii)  any communication to the public by wire or by rebroadcasting of the broadcast of the work, when this communication is made by an organization other than the original one;
>
>   (iii) the public communication by loudspeaker or any other analogous instrument transmitting, by signs, sounds or images, the broadcast of the work.

2.  It shall be a matter for legislation in the countries of the Union to determine the conditions under which the rights mentioned in the preceding paragraph may be exercised, but these conditions shall apply only in the countries where they have been prescribed. They shall not in any circumstances be prejudicial to the moral rights of the author, nor to his right to obtain equitable remuneration which, in the absence of agreement, shall be fixed by competent authority.

3.  In the absence of any contrary stipulation, permission granted in accordance with paragraph (1) of this article shall not imply permission to record, by means of instruments recording sounds or images, the work broadcast. It shall, however, be a matter for legislation in the countries of the Union to determine the regulations for ephemeral recordings made by a broadcasting organization by means of its own facilities and used for its own broadcasts. The preservation of these recordings in official archives may, on the ground of their exceptional documentary character, be authorized by such legislation.

*Article 11ter*

1.  Authors of literary works shall enjoy the exclusive right of authorizing:

>   (i)  the public recitation of their works, including such public recitation by any means or process;
>
>   (ii)  any communication to the public of the recitation of their works.

2.  Authors of literary works shall enjoy, during the full term of their rights in the original works, the same rights with respect to translations thereof.

*Article 12*

Authors of literary or artistic works shall enjoy the exclusive right of authorizing adaptations, arrangements and other alterations of their works.

*Article 13*

1.  Each country of the Union may impose for itself reservations and conditions on the exclusive right granted to the author of a musical work and to the author of any words, the recording of which together with the musical work has already been authorized by the latter, to authorize the sound recording of that musical work, together with such words, if any; but all such reservations and conditions shall apply only in the countries which have imposed them and shall not, in any circumstances, be prejudicial to the rights of these authors to

obtain equitable remuneration which, in the absence of agreement, shall be fixed by competent authority.

2. Recordings of musical works made in a country of the Union in accordance with Article 13(3) of the Conventions signed at Rome on June 2, 1928, and at Brussels on June 26, 1948, may be reproduced in that country without the permission of the author of the musical work until a date two years after that country becomes bound by this Act.

3. Recordings made in accordance with paragraphs (1) and (2) of this article and imported without permission from the parties concerned into a country where they are treated as infringing recordings shall be liable to seizure.

*Article 14*

1. Authors of literary or artistic works shall have the exclusive right of authorizing:
    (i) the cinematographic adaptation and reproduction of these works, and the distribution of the works thus adapted or reproduced;
    (ii) the public performance and communication to the public by wire of the works thus adapted or reproduced.

2. The adaptation into any other artistic form of a cinematographic production derived from literary or artistic works shall, without prejudice to the authorization of the author of the cinematographic production, remain subject to the authorization of the authors of the original works.

*Article 14ter*

1. The author, or after his death the persons or institutions authorized by national legislation, shall, with respect to original works of art and original manuscripts of writers and composers, enjoy the inalienable right to an interest in any sale of the work subsequent to the first transfer by the author of the work.

2. The protection provided by the preceding paragraph may be claimed in a country of the Union only if legislation in the country to which the author belongs so permits, and to the extent permitted by the country where this protection is claimed.

3. The procedure for collection and the amounts shall be matters for determination by national legislation.

## Universal Copyright Convention Article I

*Article I*

Each Contracting State undertakes to provide for the adequate and effective protection of the rights of authors and other copyright proprietors in literary, scientific and artistic works, including writings, musical, dramatic and cinematographic works, and paintings, engravings and sculpture.

*Article IVbis*

1. The rights referred to in Article I shall include the basic rights ensuring the author's economic interests, including the exclusive right to authorize reproduction by any means, public performance and broadcasting. The provisions of this article shall extend to works protected under this Convention either in their original form or in any form recognizably derived from the original.

2.    However, any Contracting State may, by its domestic legislation, make exceptions that do not conflict with the spirit and provisions of this Convention, to the rights mentioned in paragraph 1 of this article. Any State whose legislation so provides, shall nevertheless accord a reasonable degree of effective protection to each of the rights to which exception has been made.

*Article V*

1.    The rights referred to in Article I shall include the exclusive right of the author to make, publish and authorize the making and publication of translations of works protected under this Convention.

2.    However, any Contracting State may, by its domestic legislation, restrict the right of translation of writings, but only subject to the following provisions:

(a)  If, after the expiration of a period of seven years from the date of the first publication of a writing, a translation of such writing has not been published in a language in general use in the Contracting State, by the owner of the right of translation or with his authorization, any national of such Contracting State may obtain a non-exclusive license from the competent authority thereof to translate the work into that language and publish the work so translated.

(b)  Such national shall in accordance with the procedure of the State concerned, establish either that he has requested, and been denied, authorization by the proprietor of the right to make and publish the translation, or that, after due diligence on his part, he was unable to find the owner of the right. A license may also be granted on the same conditions if all previous editions of a translation in a language in general use in the Contracting State are out of print.

(c)  If the owner of the right of translation cannot be found, then the applicant for a license shall send copies of his application to the publisher whose name appears on the work and, if the nationality of the owner of the right of translation is known, to the diplomatic or consular representative of the State of which such owner is a national, or to the organization which may have been designated by the government of that State. The license shall not be granted before the expiration of a period of two months from the date of the dispatch of the copies of the application.

(d)  Due provision shall be made by domestic legislation to ensure to the owner of the right of translation a compensation which is just and conforms to international standards, to ensure payment and transmittal of such compensation, and to ensure a correct translation of the work.

(e)  The original title and the name of the author of the work shall be printed on all copies of the published translation. The license shall be valid only for publication of the translation in the territory of the Contracting State where it has been applied for. Copies so published may be imported and sold in another Contracting State if a language in general use in such other State is the same language as that into which the work has been so translated, and if the domestic law in such other State makes provision for such licenses and does not prohibit such importation and sale. Where the foregoing conditions do not exist, the importation and sale of such copies in a Contracting State shall be governed by its domestic law and its agreements. The license shall not be transferred by the licensee.

(f) The license shall not be granted when the author has withdrawn from circulation all copies of the work.

## Satellite Convention

*Article 1*

For the purposes of this Convention:

(i) "signal" is an electronically-generated carrier capable of transmitting programmes;

(ii) "programme" is a body of live or recorded material consisting of images, sounds or both, embodied in signals emitted for the purpose of ultimate distribution;

(iii) "satellite" is any device in extraterrestrial space capable of transmitting signals. . . .

*Article 2*

(1) Each Contracting State undertakes to take adequate measures to prevent the distribution on or from its territory of any programme-carrying signal by a distributor for whom the signal emitted to or passing through the satellite is not intended. This obligation shall apply where the originating organization is a national of another Contracting State. . . .

## Phonograms Convention

*Article 1*

For the purposes of this Convention:

(a) "phonogram" means any exclusively aural fixation of sounds of a performance or of other sounds;

(b) "producer of phonograms" means the person who, or the legal entity which, first fixes the sounds of a performance or other sounds;

(c) "duplicate" means an article which contains sounds taken directly or indirectly from a phonogram and which embodies all or a substantial part of the sounds fixed in that phonogram;

(d) "distribution to the public" means any act by which duplicates of a phonogram are offered, directly or indirectly, to the general public or any section thereof.

*Article 2*

Each Contracting State shall protect producers of phonograms who are nationals of other Contracting States against the making of duplicates without the consent of the producer and against the importation of such duplicates, provided that any such making or importation is for the purpose of distribution to the public, and against the distribution of such duplicates to the public.

# Rome Convention

*Article 3*

For the purposes of this Convention:
(a) "performers" means actors, singers, musicians, dancers, and other persons who act, sing, deliver, declaim, play in, or otherwise perform literary or artistic works;
(b) "phonogram" means any exclusively aural fixation of sounds of a performance or of other sounds;
(c) "producer of phonograms" means the person who, or the legal entity which, first fixes the sounds of a performance or other sounds;
(d) "publication" means the offering of copies of a phonogram to the public in reasonable quantity;
(e) "reproduction" means the making of a copy or copies of a fixation;
(f) "broadcasting" means the transmission by wireless means for public reception of sounds or of images and sounds;
(g) "rebroadcasting" means the simultaneous broadcasting by one broadcasting organisation of the broadcast of another broadcasting organisation.

*Article 12*

If a phonogram published for commercial purposes, or a reproduction of such phonogram, is used directly for broadcasting or for any communication to the public, a single equitable remuneration shall be paid by the user to the performers, or to the producers of the phonograms, or to both. Domestic law may, in the absence of agreement between these parties, lay down the conditions as to the sharing of this remuneration.

## B. Geographic connecting factors

The question you just analyzed asked you to consider the rights of the owners of the copyrights to an *American* sound recording and an *American* musical composition, but none of the facts you were given told you what made them "American." The nationality of a work – its country of origin – is determined by the country:

- of which the author is a national or resident, *or*
- in which the work was first published (or, possibly, first fixed).

Of course, it is possible (and frequently happens) that the author of a work is a national of one country, a resident of a second country, and the work is first published (or fixed) in a third country. In that case, for copyright purposes, the work has three countries of origin. What's more, any one of those countries may provide the necessary geographic connecting factor with the country where protection for the work is sought.

Each treaty has its own set of connecting factors. Immediately below are the connecting-factor provisions of the Berne Convention and the Rome Convention.

Suppose that the sound recording you considered in the prior question was an "American" recording in the sense that it was first released (i.e., first published) by an American record company (e.g., Warner Bros. Records) in the United States. But, suppose also that the recording artist is a British national and the recording was made in a recording studio in London. And suppose that a week after the recording was released in the United States, it was released in the United Kingdom as well. The United Kingdom – like Canada – has adhered to the Rome Convention.

Suppose too that the musical composition you considered in the prior question was "American" in the sense that it was written by British national who resides in the United States and was published by an American company (e.g., Warner Chappell Music).

Consider once again whether Canada is obligated to require Canadian radio stations to pay broadcast royalties to

- the American record company or artist, and
- the music publisher or songwriter.

## Berne Convention Article 3

(1) The protection of this Convention shall apply to:
   (a) authors who are nationals of one of the countries of the Union, for their works, whether published or not;
   (b) authors who are not nationals of one of the countries of the Union, for their works first published in one of those countries, or simultaneously in a country outside the Union and in a country of the Union.
(2) Authors who are not nationals of one of the countries of the Union but who have their habitual residence in one of them shall, for the purposes of this Convention, be assimilated to nationals of that country.
(3) The expression "published works" means works published with the consent of their authors, whatever may be the means of manufacture of the copies, provided that the availability of such copies has been such as to satisfy the reasonable requirements of the public, having regard to the nature of the work. The performance of a dramatic, dramatico-musical, cinematographic or musical work, the public recitation of a literary work, the communication by wire or the broadcasting of literary or artistic works, the exhibition of a work of art and the construction of a work of architecture shall not constitute publication.
(4) A work shall be considered as having been published simultaneously in several countries if it has been published in two or more countries within thirty days of its first publication.

## Rome Convention

*Article 4*

Each Contracting State shall grant national treatment to performers if any of the following conditions is met:
   (a) the performance takes place in another Contracting State;
   (b) the performance is incorporated in a phonogram which is protected under Article 5 of this Convention;…

*Article 5*

1. Each Contracting State shall grant national treatment to producers of phonograms if any of the following conditions is met:
   (a) the producer of the phonogram is a national of another Contracting State (criterion of nationality);
   (b) the first fixation of the sound was made in another Contracting State (criterion of fixation);

(c) the phonogram was first published in another Contracting State (criterion of publication).

2. If a phonogram was first published in a non-contracting State but if it was also published, within thirty days of its first publication, in a Contracting State (simultaneous publication), it shall be considered as first published in the Contracting State.

3. By means of a notification deposited with the Secretary-General of the United Nations, any Contracting State may declare that it will not apply the criterion of publication or, alternatively, the criterion of fixation. Such notification may be deposited at the time of ratification, acceptance or accession, or at any time thereafter; in the last case, it shall become effective six months after it has been deposited.

Here is what Canada actually has done, by statute, with respect to radio broadcast royalties:

### Canadian Copyright Act

2. *Definitions*
   In this Act . . .
   "maker" means . . . in relation to a sound recording, the person by whom the arrangements necessary for the first fixation of the sounds are undertaken. . . .
   "telecommunication" means any transmission of signs, signals, writing, images or sounds or intelligence of any nature by wire, radio, visual, optical or other electromagnetic system. . . .

19. *Right to remuneration*
   (1) Where a sound recording has been published, the performer and maker are entitled, subject to section 20, to be paid equitable remuneration for its performance in public or its communication to the public by telecommunication, except for any retransmission.
   (2) For the purpose of providing the remuneration mentioned in subsection (1), a person who performs a published sound recording in public or communicates it to the public by telecommunication is liable to pay royalties
      (a) in the case of a sound recording of a musical work, to the collective society authorized under Part VII to collect them; or
      (b) in the case of a sound recording of a literary work or dramatic work, to either the maker of the sound recording or the performer.
   (3) The royalties, once paid pursuant to paragraph (2)(a) or (b), shall be divided so that
      (a) the performer or performers receive in aggregate fifty per cent; and
      (b) the maker or makers receive in aggregate fifty per cent.

20. *Conditions*
   (1) The right to remuneration conferred by section 19 applies only if
      (a) the maker was, at the date of the first fixation, a Canadian citizen or permanent resident within the meaning of subsection 2(1) of the Immigration and Refugee Protection Act, or a citizen or permanent resident of a Rome Convention country, or, if a

corporation, had its headquarters in one of the foregoing countries; or

    (b)  all the fixations done for the sound recording occurred in Canada or in a Rome Convention country.

(2)  Notwithstanding subsection (1), if the Minister is of the opinion that a Rome Convention country does not grant a right to remuneration, similar in scope and duration to that provided by section 19, for the performance in public or the communication to the public of a sound recording whose maker, at the date of its first fixation, was a Canadian citizen or permanent resident within the meaning of subsection 2(1) of the Immigration and Refugee Protection Act or, if a corporation, had its headquarters in Canada, the Minister may, by a statement published in the Canada Gazette, limit the scope and duration of the protection for sound recordings whose first fixation is done by a maker who is a citizen or permanent resident of that country or, if a corporation, has its headquarters in that country.

(3)  If so requested by a country that is a party to the North American Free Trade Agreement, the Minister may, by a statement published in the Canada Gazette, grant the right to remuneration conferred by section 19 to performers or makers who are nationals of that country and whose sound recordings embody dramatic or literary works.

(4)  Where a statement is published under subsection (3), section 19 applies

    (a)  in respect of nationals of a country mentioned in that statement, as if they were citizens of Canada or, in the case of corporations, had their headquarters in Canada; and

    (b)  as if the fixations made for the purpose of their sound recordings had been made in Canada.

Does the Canadian Copyright Act satisfy Canada's treaty obligations?

Does the Canadian Copyright Act actually do *more* than is required by the Rome Convention? Suppose that a recording artist is a citizen or permanent resident of the United Kingdom (e.g., Madonna, who is now a U.K. resident), and she makes a recording in the United States (which has not adhered to Rome), and the recording is first released in the United States and not released in Canada or the U.K. (or any other Rome country) within 30 days of its release in the United States. In that case, would the artist and her record company be entitled to equitable remuneration, under the Canadian Copyright Act, if the recording is broadcast by Canadian radio stations? Does the Rome Convention obligate Canada to require its radio stations to pay royalties to the artist and her record company?

The United States, of course, has treaty obligations too, and the following section of the U.S. Copyright Act shows what it has done, with respect to geographic connecting factors. Has the U.S. done all that it is required to do, by treaty? More?

### U.S. Copyright Act

§ 104. Subject matter of copyright: National origin

    (a)  Unpublished works . . . are subject to protection under this title without regard to the nationality or domicile of the author.

    (b)  Published works . . . are subject to protection under this title if —

73

(1) on the date of first publication, one or more of the authors is a national or domiciliary of the United States, or is a national, domiciliary, or sovereign authority of a treaty party, or is a stateless person, wherever that person may be domiciled; or

(2) the work is first published in the United States or in a foreign nation that, on the date of first publication, is a treaty party; or

(3) the work is a sound recording that was first fixed in a treaty party; or

(4) the work is a pictorial, graphic, or sculptural work that is incorporated in a building or other structure, or an architectural work that is embodied in a building and the building or structure is located in the United States or a treaty party; or . . .

(6) the work comes within the scope of a Presidential proclamation.

. . .

For purposes of paragraph (2), a work that is published in the United States or a treaty party within 30 days after publication in a foreign nation that is not a treaty party shall be considered to be first published in the United States or such treaty party, as the case may be.

## C. Putting them all together: works, rights and geographic connecting factors

The similarity between international copyright analysis and three-dimensional tick-tack-toe is vividly illustrated by the following decision of the United States Supreme Court. In this case, the German owner of the copyright to a painting by a Peruvian artist – who the German owner thought was a Spanish artist – sought damages from an American company that made unauthorized copies of the painting. The case was decided almost a century ago, so the applicable statutes and treaties are different from those excerpted above. But the case nevertheless was centered on the concept of necessary "connecting factors," which turned out to be missing. Why wasn't the German copyright owner able to "connect the dots"? Would he have been able to do so, if the artist *had been* Spanish (as the German owner thought), rather than Peruvian?

### Bong v. Alfred S. Campbell Art Company
### 214 U.S. 236 (1909)

Mr. Justice McKenna delivered the opinion of the court.

This is an action under the copyright statutes to recover penalties and forfeitures for the infringement of a copyright of a painting.

The complaint shows the following facts: Plaintiff . . . was a citizen and subject of the German Empire and resident of the city of Berlin, that nation being one which permits to citizens of the United States the benefit of copyright on substantially the same basis as its own citizens. It is a party to an international agreement which provides for reciprocity in the granting of copyright, by the terms of which agreement the United States may at its pleasure become a party, the existence of which condition has been determined by the President of the United States by proclamation duly made. April 15, 1892, 27 Stat. 1021. The defendant is a New Jersey corporation doing business in New York under the laws of the latter State.

In 1899 one Daniel Hernandez painted and designed a painting called "Dolce far niente," he then being a citizen and subject of Spain, which nation permits the benefit of copyright to citizens of the United States on substantially the same basis as its own citizens, as has been determined by the proclamation of the President of the United States. July 10, 1895, 29 Stat. 871. Prior to November 8, 1902, plaintiff became the sole proprietor of said painting by due assignment pursuant to law. About said date plaintiff applied for a copyright, in conformity with the laws of the United States respecting copyrights, before the publication of the painting or any copy thereof. Plaintiff inscribed, and has kept inscribed, upon a visible portion of the painting the words "Copyright by Rich Bong," and also upon every copy thereof. By reason of the premises, it is alleged, plaintiff became and was entitled for the term of twenty-eight years to the sole liberty of printing, reprinting, publishing and vending the painting. A violation of the copyright by defendant is alleged by printing, exposing for sale and selling copies of the painting under the name of "Sunbeam," by Hernandez, and that defendant has in its possession over 1,000 copies. By reason of the premises, it is alleged [that under the then-current U.S. copyright law] . . . , defendant has [infringed plaintiff's copyright in the painting by Hernandez]. . . .

Defendant answered, admitting that it was a corporation as alleged, and was doing business in New York. It denied, either absolutely or upon information and belief, all other allegations.

The court directed a verdict for the defendant, counsel for the plaintiff having stated in his opening, as it is admitted, that he would offer no evidence to establish the citizenship of Hernandez, and would not controvert the statement made by the defense that he was a citizen of Peru (it was alleged in the complaint that he was a citizen of Spain), as to which country the President had issued no copyright proclamation. It is also admitted that plaintiff never owned the "physical painting." There was introduced in evidence a conveyance of the right to enter the painting for copyright protection in America and the exclusive right of reproduction. . . .

The ruling of the District Court, and that of the Court of Appeals sustaining it, were based on the ground that Hernandez, being a citizen of Peru and not having the right of copyright in the United States, could convey no right to plaintiff. Plaintiff attacks this ruling and contends that the act of March 3, 1891, "confers copyright where the person applying for the same as proprietor or assign of the author or proprietor is a subject of a country with which we have copyright relations, whether the author be a subject of one of those countries or not."

Whatever strength there is in the contention must turn upon the words of the statute conferring the copyright. [The then-current copyright act read] . . . as follows:

"The author, inventor, designer or proprietor of any book, map, chart, . . . painting . . . and the executors, administrators and assigns of any such person shall, upon complying with the provisions of this chapter, have the sole liberty of printing, reprinting, publishing, completing, copying, executing, finishing and vending the same," etc.

Other sections prescribe the proceedings to be taken to secure copyright, and §13 [of the then-current Copyright Act] provides as follows:

"That this act shall only apply to a citizen or subject of a foreign state or nation when such foreign state or nation permits to citizens of the United States of America the benefit of copyright on substantially the same basis as its own citizens, or when such foreign state or nation is a party to an international agreement which provides for reciprocity in the granting of copyright, by the terms of which agreement the United States of America may at its pleasure become a party to such agreement. The existence of either of the conditions aforesaid shall be determined by the President of the United States by proclamation made, from time to time, as the purposes of this act may require."

Plaintiff urges that he is "the 'assign' of the author and proprietor of the painting . . . and being himself a 'citizen or subject of a foreign nation' with which we have copyright relations," the condition of the statute is satisfied, and his copyright is valid, though Hernandez was not such citizen or subject. In other words, though the author of a painting has not the right to copyright, his assignee has if he is a citizen or subject of a foreign state with which we have copyright relations, these being, it is contended, the conditions expressed in §13.

Counsel's argument in support of this contention is able, but we are saved from a detailed consideration of it by the decision of this court in *American Tobacco Company v. Werckmeister*. . . . In that case we said that "the purpose of the copyright law is not so much the protection and control of the visible thing, as to secure a monopoly, having a limited time, of the right to publish the production, which is the result of the inventor's thought." In considering who was entitled to such right under the statute we defined the word "assigns," as used in the statute. We said: "It seems clear that the word 'assigns' in this section is not used as descriptive of the character of the estate which the 'author, inventor, designer or proprietor' may acquire under the statutes, for the 'assigns' of any such person, as well as the persons themselves, may, 'upon complying with the provisions of this chapter, have the sole liberty of printing, publishing and vending the same.' This would seem to demonstrate the intention of Congress to vest in 'assigns,' before copyright, the same privilege of subsequently acquiring complete statutory copyright as the original author, inventor, dealer or proprietor," and there was an explicit definition of the right transferred as follows: "While it is true that the property in copyright in this country is the creature of the statute, the nature and character of the property grows out of the recognition of the separate ownership of the right of copying from that which inheres in the mere physical control of the thing itself, and the statute must be read in the light of the intention of Congress to protect these intangible rights as a reward of the inventive genius that has produced the work." In other words, an assignee within the meaning of the statute is one who receives a transfer, not necessarily of the painting but of the right to multiply copies of it. And such right does not depend alone upon the statute, as contended by plaintiff, but is a right derived from the painter and secured by the statute to the assignee of the painter's right. Of this the opinion leaves no doubt, for it is further said: "We think every consideration of the nature of the property and the things to be accomplished support the conclusion that this statute means to give to the assignees of the *original owner of the right to copyright* an article [italics ours], the right to take out the copyright secured by the statute independently of the ownership of the article itself." The same idea was repeated when the court came to consider whether the exhibition of the painting, which was the subject matter of the case, in the Royal Gallery, constituted a general publication which deprived the painter, as the owner of the copyright, of the benefit of the statutory provision. It was said: "Considering this feature of the case, it is well to remember that the property of the author or painter in his intellectual creation is absolute until he voluntarily parts with the same." And the painter had the right of copyright, he being a subject of Great Britain, that country having copyright relations with the United States. His assignee, Werckmeister, was also a citizen of a country having copyright relations with us. But it was the right of the painter which was made prominent in the case and determined its decision.

It was not an abstract right the court passed on, one that arose simply from ownership of the painting. It was the right given by the statute, and which, when transferred, constituted the person to whom it was transferred an assignee under the statute and of the rights which the statute conferred on the assignor. "It is the physical thing created, or the right of printing, publishing, copying, etc., which is within the statutory protection." It is this right of multiplication of copies that is asserted in the case at bar, and it is not necessary to consider what right plaintiff might have had under the common law "before he sought his Federal copyright and published the painting."

It is next contended that Hernandez, as a subject of Peru, was entitled to a statutory copyright in his own right, because, as it is further contended, Peru belongs to the Montevideo International Union. This contention is based on the words of §13 which gives the right of copyright to a citizen or subject of a foreign state or nation when such state or nation "is a party to an international agreement which provides for reciprocity in the granting of copyright, by the terms of which agreement the United States of America may, at its pleasure, become a party to such agreement." If this were all there were in the statute, the contention of the plaintiff might have some foundation. The statute, however, provides that the existence of such condition "shall be determined by the President of the United States by proclamation, made from time to time, as the purposes" of the "act may require." It is insisted, however, that this provision is directory and a right is conferred independent of the action of the President, his proclamation being only a convenient mode of proving the fact. We cannot concur in this view. . .
.

It is admitted that the decision of the State Department is adverse to the contention, and, it is asserted by defendant and not denied by plaintiff, that the Librarian of Congress has always construed the statutes as denying to citizens of Peru copyright protection. We think, besides, the statute is clear and makes the President's proclamation a condition of the right. And there was reason for it. The statute contemplated a reciprocity of rights, and what officer is better able to determine the conditions upon which they might depend than the President?

On the record, we think there was no error in directing a verdict on the opening statement of counsel. . . . Judgment affirmed.

## D. The "Back Door" to Berne and other treaties

Though the facts of *Bong v. Alfred S. Campbell Art Company* were convoluted, they were not as complex as those of many other cases whose principal issue was whether necessary "connecting factors" existed. Three other cases – one from Switzerland and two from Germany – show how much effort may be necessary in a thorough search for connecting factors. By way of background to those three cases, recall that Article 3 of the Berne Convention provides that it protects even authors who are not nationals of an adhering country, if their works are first published, or simultaneously published, in a country that does adhere to Berne. (Berne Convention Article

3(1)(b)) This provision has been called the "Back Door to Berne," because it gives authors from non-Berne countries a way to get copyright protection in all Berne countries, simply by arranging first or simultaneous publication in any Berne country.

As you read the following case notes, make a checklist of the factors that ought to be considered when analyzing whether the "Back Door" to Berne provides protection for works that otherwise would be in the public domain in the country where protection is sought.

*The Gold Rush*, 2 IIC 315 (Switzerland S.Ct. 1970)

In this case, the Supreme Court of Switzerland relied on the "Back Door" to protect an American movie that was released many years (decades, actually) before the United States joined Berne. The issue in the case was whether Charlie Chaplin, then a resident of Switzerland and a British citizen, was entitled to copyright protection in Switzerland for the silent version of his film "The Gold Rush" which was first published in the United States in 1925.

Swiss copyright law protects works by Swiss nationals, which Chaplin was not, and works first published in Switzerland, which "The Gold Rush" was not. So that provision of Swiss law was not applicable.

Swiss copyright law also protects works whose protection is required by treaty. Switzerland and the United States are parties to a 1924 bilateral treaty. But that treaty applies only to works by nationals of the two countries, which Chaplin was not. So that treaty was not applicable.

Switzerland also is a member of Berne and has been since 1887. But the United States did not adhere to Berne until 1989, so publication of "The Gold Rush" back in 1925 did not make Berne applicable. Great Britain also has been a member of Berne since 1887, and Chaplin was a citizen of Britain. But the version of Berne that existed back in 1925 (the 1908 version) applied only to works first published in a Berne member country, which the U.S. was not, and to unpublished works which "The Gold Rush" was not. So Chaplin could not rely on his British citizenship to take advantage of Berne.

However, even if a work was first published in a non-Berne country, the 1908 version of Berne also applied to works "simultaneously" published in a Berne country. "The Gold Rush" was published in 1925 in Canada (as well as in the United States), and Canada was a Berne country even then. Thus, the issue in the case became whether the film's publication in Canada was "simultaneous" with its publication in the U.S. And the Swiss Supreme Court held that it was, even if it was not published at the same hour in both countries. (Berne has since been amended to define "simultaneous" publication as any publication that occurs within 30 days of first publication. Berne Article 3(4)) So, on that basis, the court held that "The Gold Rush" was protected in Switzerland.

*Atlas-Filmverleigh GmbH v. Roy Export Co.*, 4 IIC 245 (Germany S.Ct. 1972)

This case too involved "The Gold Rush." Atlas-Filmverleigh was the assignee of all rights in Germany to Chaplin's film, which Roy Export had exploited in Germany without authorization. Atlas-Filmverleigh relied on German copyright law and the Berne Convention for protection in Germany.

The primary issue in the case was whether a preview showing of "The Gold Rush" in Hollywood in *June* 1925 was the film's first publication, so that the film's release in Canada in *August* 1925 was *not* "simultaneous." The Supreme Court of Germany held that the June preview was not a "publication" so the first publication actually took place in August in Canada, so that Berne did apply to give the film protection in Germany.

A secondary issue in the case was whether there was any "publication" in Canada at all, because the film's distributor – an American company – did not maintain a "distribution center" in Canada. In an earlier case, a German court had ruled that the "publication" of *books* requires a distribution center in the country of publication. But in this case, the court held that films are sufficiently different in character from books that the distribution-center requirement did not apply. And thus the "publication" of films in Canada did not require a distribution center there, if distribution was being handled from the United States.

*Hermann Luchterhand Verlag v. Albert Langen-Georg Muller Verlag*, 17 IIC 134 (Germany S.Ct. 1975)

This case involved the question of whether the novel *August Fourteen* by Soviet author Alexander Solzhenitsyn was protected by copyright in Germany. The plaintiff, Hermann Luchterhand Verlag, had obtained a license from Solzhenitsyn's lawyer to publish the book in Germany. The defendant, Albert Langen-Georg Muller Verlag, published it without authorization.

Germany and the USSR had no copyright treaties at all between them at the time the novel was published in Germany. As a result, it apparently appeared to Albert Langen-Georg Muller Verlag that the novel was not protected in Germany.

However, Berne applies to works first published in any Berne country, regardless of the nationality of the author. The novel also had been published in France, which is a Berne country. Thus, the question in the case was whether the novel was "first" published in France, in which case the book would be protected in Germany, or whether instead a prior distribution of the novel in the USSR by "Samizdat" (i.e., secret "underground" distribution, because the book was censored in the USSR) was its first publication, in which case the book would not be protected in Germany.

The Supreme Court of Germany held that "Samizdat" is *not* "publication," so the novel's "first" publication was in France, and its copyright was protected in Germany via the "Back Door" to Berne.

"The Gold Rush" cases in Switzerland and Germany show how the owners of copyrights to American works obtained copyright protection in Berne countries, before the United States joined Berne in 1989. By the time the U.S. adhered to Berne in 1989, there were only 22 countries with which the United States did not then have copyright treaties (or proclamations). Few if any of those countries would be considered major markets for American works, and only one – Thailand – was considered a major copyright "pirate" nation. (The 22 countries were: Benin, Burkina Faso, Central African Republic, Chad, Congo, Cyprus, Egypt, Gabon, Ivory Coast, Libya, Madagascar, Mali, Mauritania, Niger, Rwanda, Surinam, Thailand, Togo, Turkey, Uruguay, Zaire, and Zimbabwe.)

Nevertheless, the "Back Door" to Berne remained significant, until the U.S. finally joined Berne in 1989, because it was the method by which U.S. copyright owners sought copyright protection in those countries with which the U.S. had treaties (or proclamations) for works that were first published *prior* to the dates those treaties took effect in both countries. The UCC, for example, didn't take effect between the U.S. and many other countries until the mid-1950s. And for all countries for which the UCC was the first copyright treaty with the U.S., pre-UCC (i.e., pre-1950s) American works were in the public domain in those countries, and works from those countries were in the public domain in the U.S. (for reasons explored in the very next section of this book).

Most "Back Door" publication by U.S. copyright owners was done in Canada or the United Kingdom. American book publishers, for example, routinely published books in Canada within 30 days of their publication in the United States (as can been seen on the copyright-notice pages of many pre-1989 books, where publication by the publisher's Canadian subsidiary was noted).

The "Back Door" to Berne is no longer necessary for Berne protection of *American* works first published since the United States adhered to Berne in 1989. However, the "Back Door" may still be necessary for protection of works from other countries that are not members of Berne.

For example, Saddam Hussein finished his fourth (and last) novel, *Ekhroj Minha Ya Mal'un* (i.e., *Get Out, Damned One*), the day before the U.S.-led war in Iraq began. Hussein, of course, was a national of Iraq. But Iraq is not a party to the Berne Convention (or any other copyright treaty). If the novel had been first published in Iraq, it would have been in the public domain everywhere else in the world. But Hussein's daughter arranged for the novel to be published in Jordan, which has adhered to the Berne Convention. Jordan reportedly banned the novel's publication "due to political concerns," though it's not clear whether the ban went into effect before, or only after, the book was published there. In any event, the novel has been published in Turkey which also is a Berne country. As a result, though Hussein himself was put on trial in Iraq – in a U.S.-funded court – for crimes that resulted in his being punished by death, his novel is protected by copyright in the United States (and in every other Berne country too).

The "Back Door" to Berne is the most famous of the back doors to copyright treaties, but it's not the only one. The Rome Convention has a back door as well, because its Article 5(2) provides that if a phonogram (i.e., a sound recording) is first published in a non-Rome country, but is also published in a Rome country within 30 days, it will be considered to have been first published in a Rome country, and thus entitled to Rome Convention protections.

## E. Importance of date of first publication in making the connection

The date of a work's first publication is enormously important. It's important, of course, to the work's author, for psychological reasons. And it is even more important for copyright reasons.

### 1. Public domain consequences of pre-effective date publication

The publication of a work anywhere in the world *before* the effective date of an applicable treaty (i.e., a treaty that covers that kind of work and the rights sought to be protected) in *both* countries (i.e., the work's country-of-origin and the country where protection is sought) means that the work probably went into the public domain in the country where protection is sought.

This principle is illustrated by both the Swiss and German "Gold Rush" cases, *The Gold Rush* and the *Atlas-Filmverleih* cases, discussed above. By the time those cases were filed, the U.S., Switzerland and Germany all were UCC countries. But at the time "The Gold Rush" was first released in 1925, the UCC didn't even exist. Thus, if "Back Door to Berne" protection had not been available, "The Gold Rush" would have been in the public domain in Switzerland and Germany.

This principle also can be seen in the *August Fourteen* case, *Luchterhand Verlag v. Muller Verlag*, discussed above. By the time that case was filed, the USSR and Germany both were UCC countries. But at the time Solzhenitsyn's novel was first published in Germany, there were no copyright treaties between the USSR and Germany. Thus, If "Back Door" protection had not been available, the novel would have been in the public domain in Germany.

### 2. Retroactive protection for foreign works in the public domain

As previously mentioned, in order to induce countries to join Berne, the Berne Convention contains a provision that is intended to provide retroactive protection for works from newly-joining countries. The provision was necessary to overcome the general principle that publication *anywhere* in the world prior to the effective dates of a treaty in *both* the work's country-of-origin *and* the country where protection is sought means that the work went into the publication domain in the country where protection is sought. Here is the language of that provision (some of which you read earlier):

## Berne Convention Article 18

(1) This Convention shall apply to all works which, at the moment of its coming into force, have not yet fallen into the public domain in the country of origin through the expiry of the term of protection.

(2) If, however, through the expiry of the term of protection which was previously granted, a work has fallen into the public domain of the country where protection is claimed, that work shall not be protected anew. . . .

(4) The preceding provisions shall also apply in the case of new accessions to the Union [which is the organization of all countries that have adhered to the Berne Convention]. . . .

This provision means that U.S. works (still protected by copyright in the U.S.) had to be given retroactive protection in all other Berne countries when the United States joined Berne in 1989, including those U.S. works that had previously fallen into the public domain in other Berne countries either because the U.S. previously had no copyright relations at all with those countries (like Thailand and Egypt) or because the works were first published in the U.S. before those countries joined the UCC (in the mid-1950s or later). This, no doubt, was why – after many years of opposing U.S. adherence to Berne – the American movie industry finally supported U.S. adherence to Berne in order to get retroactive copyright protection for movies first released before the mid-1950s which by 1989 were widely available on easily-copied homevideo tapes.

This provision also *should* have meant that works from other Berne countries (still protected by copyright in their countries-of-origin) that had fallen into the public domain in the United States would be given retroactive protection in the U.S. as soon as it joined Berne in 1989. Nevertheless, the United States expressly refused to give retroactive protection to works from other countries that were already in the public domain in the U.S.

## Berne Convention Implementation Act §12

Title 17, United States Code [i.e., the Copyright Act], as amended by this [Berne Convention Implementation] Act, does *not* provide copyright protection for any work that is in the public domain in the United States. [Emphasis added.]

On its face, section 12 of the Berne Convention Implementation Act appears to violate one of the United States' obligations of adherence to Berne, because (you'll recall) Berne provides:

## Berne Convention Article 36

(1) Any country party to this Convention undertakes to adopt, in accordance with its constitution, the measures necessary to ensure the application of this Convention.

(2) It is understood that, at the time a country becomes bound by this Convention, it will be in a position under its domestic law to give effect to the provisions of this Convention.

The reason that Congress thought – in 1989 – that retroactive protection was not necessary is this. As you read just above, Article 18 of Berne (the Article that requires retroactive protection) says that if a foreign work is in the public domain in another country because its copyright in that country *expired*, it is *not* necessary for that country to grant retroactive protection to that work. The U.S. Copyright Act provides copyright protection for all *un*published foreign works. Here again is that provision:

**U.S. Copyright Act**

§ 104. Subject matter of copyright: National origin
   (a) Unpublished works . . . are subject to protection under this title without regard to the nationality or domicile of the author.

Since all published works start out as unpublished works, this means that the U.S. has provided copyright protection to all foreign works for at least the period between the time they were created and the time they were published. Thus, when the U.S. joined Berne in 1989, the U.S. took the position that any foreign works that were then in the public domain in the U.S. were works whose copyrights had simply "expired" when they were published; and therefore, the U.S. did not have to grant retroactive protection to such works, because of Article 18(2) of Berne.

If this interpretation of Berne Article 18 seems a stretch, or even tortured, rest assured that others thought so too – especially because the U.S. also took the position that Article 18 did require other Berne countries to give retroactive protection to U.S. works even though the U.S. was not required to give retroactive protection to theirs! Russia and Thailand reportedly rejected the U.S. position out of hand. But the validity of the United States' denial of retroactive protection to works from other Berne countries was never tested in any legal forum. So for six years after the U.S. joined Berne in 1989 until the U.S. joined the World Trade Organization in 1995, the U.S. continued to deny retroactive protection to foreign works.

However, for reasons that will be examined later (in the section of this book dealing with "International trade law and its relation to copyright"), when the United States joined the World Trade Organization and thus was required to comply with the WTO's TRIPs agreement, the U.S. finally granted retroactive copyright protection to works from other countries. The U.S. did so by adding section 104A to its Copyright Act – a section titled "Copyright in restored works."

In addition to restoring the U.S. copyrights to works first published in countries with which the U.S. did not then have a copyright treaty (or proclamation), section 104A also restored U.S. copyrights to foreign works that had fallen into the public domain in the United States because the owners of those works had failed to comply with formalities previously required by the U.S. Copyright Act. And it restored the copyrights to foreign sound recordings published abroad before the U.S. Copyright first began protecting sound recordings in 1972.

The details of section 104A are important to the owners of pre-1989 works of foreign origin, many of which have commercial value in the United States. Those details also are important to American companies that had been publishing those works, royalty-free, in the U.S. before their copyrights were restored, and to Americans who would like to publish those works now, royalty-free, but are unable to do so because their copyrights have been restored. (Indeed, as you saw in an earlier section of this book, the constitutionality of section 104A was challenged, unsuccessfully, by some Americans who would like to continue to distribute those works, royalty-free.)

Section 104A is a long and complicated section that leaves many practical questions unanswered. Since it responded to issues that go beyond the specific issue addressed in this part of the book (publication before the effective date of a treaty), detailed consideration will be given to section 104A later in this book. One point, though, should be made now. Even though section 104A restored the copyrights to foreign works first published before the U.S. had copyright relations with those works' countries-of-origin, the manner in which restored works are treated by U.S. copyright law is somewhat different from the manner in which U.S. copyright law treats foreign works that never went into the public domain in the U.S. Therefore, it continues to matter, even now, whether a foreign work once was in the public domain in the U.S. The once-public-domain status of a foreign work is *not* a factor of merely historical interest.

# Chapter 4

# Applicable Law,
# When International Protection Is Provided:
# "National Treatment"

## A. National treatment: the general principle

The substantive principles of law for international copyright protection are provided by the *national* copyright laws of individual countries – *not* by international treaties (except in countries where treaties, by virtue of *national* law, are self-executing or have been made part of national copyright law). The phrase that describes this protection is "national treatment."

The concept that *international* protection is provided by *national* law is easy enough to understand and accept. But since, by definition, *international* copyright law involves works from *one* country seeking protection in *another* country, a decision must be made about *which* country's law is the law to be used. There are two possible laws that could be applied: the law of the country where protection is sought; or the law of the work's country of origin. And there are four possible sets of circumstances under which the choice between these two laws may have to be made.

- National treatment may be required by treaty, even if the laws of the two countries do *not* provide reciprocal – that is, equivalent – levels of protection to one another's works.
- National treatment may be required by treaty, if but *only if,* the laws of the two countries *do* provide reciprocal levels of protection to one another's works.
- National treatment may be granted unilaterally (that is, without being required to do so by treaty) by the national law of one country, even if the law of the other country does *not* provide reciprocal protection.
- National treatment may be granted unilaterally (that is, without being required to do so by treaty) by the national law of one country, if but *only if,* the law of the other country *does* provide reciprocal protection.

Thus, there are eight possible ways national copyright law could be applied, internationally.

| Source of the right to National Treatment | Reciprocity of treatment as a condition of National Treatment | Applicable national law | |
| --- | --- | --- | --- |
| | | Law of country where protection is sought | Law of country of origin |
| National treatment required by treaty | Reciprocity not required | 1 | 2 |
| | Reciprocity required | 3 | 4 |
| National treatment granted unilaterally by national law, without being required to do so by treaty | Reciprocity not required | 5 | 6 |
| | Reciprocity required | 7 | 8 |

Usually, the phrase "national treatment" is used to describe combination number 1: the law of the country where protection is sought is applied, because doing so is required by treaty, even if the laws of the two countries do not provide reciprocal treatment.

## 1. Protection for foreign works pursuant to domestic law

Here are samples of treaty provisions that require protection to be provided pursuant to the law of the country where protection is sought. Note that the Berne Convention makes it quite clear that such protection is required, even if the law of the work's country-of-origin does not provide reciprocal protection.

### Berne Convention Article 5

(1) Authors shall enjoy, in respect of works for which they are protected under this Convention, in countries of the Union other than the country of origin, the rights which their respective laws do now or may hereafter grant to their nationals, as well as the rights specially granted by this Convention.

(2) The enjoyment and the exercise of these rights . . . shall be independent of the existence of protection in the country of origin of the work. Consequently, . . . the extent of protection, as well as the means of redress afforded to the author to protect his rights, shall be governed exclusively by the laws of the country where protection is claimed.

### Universal Copyright Convention Article II

1. Published works of nationals of any Contracting State and works first published in that State shall enjoy in each other Contracting State the same protection as that other State accords to works of its nationals first published in its own territory, as well as the protection specially granted by this Convention.

The next case is an example of the UCC in action – a case in which copyright protection in France was provided for American musical compositions.

## SDRM v. Givaudan
## 12 IIC 413 (Paris District Court 1980)

As a result of a civil suit brought by the Societe pour l'Administration du droit de reproduction mecanique des auteurs, compositeurs et editeurs (SDRM) [the French mechanical rights society], Madame Beatrice de Bailencourt, married name Givaudan, was accused before this Court . . . of having reproduced, performed or disseminated works of human intellect, such works being musical compositions reproduced on phonographic records, in violation of the rights of the authors. The violation is alleged to have occurred . . . on French territory, more particularly, in Paris. . . .

It has been established and it is undisputed that Madame Givaudan, first as Director and later as President-Director General of the Société des Editions Claude Givaudan in Paris, . . . imported and distributed records, cartridges and cassettes of American manufacture in France between 1970 and June 13, 1974. The first seizure of July 29, 1970, revealed that certain of the seized records had been manufactured in the United States, purchased by Madame Givaudan in London and imported into France. They contained works in the repertoire of SDRM and no fee had been paid for their distribution in French territory. Two records, which contained works from this same repertoire and which had been manufactured in the United States, were purchased in New York and imported into France without the payment of a royalty to SDRM. Finally, a second seizure on June 13, 1974 and one following on December 17, 1974, revealed that a certain number of records, cartridges and cassettes which had likewise been manufactured in the United States, were imported by Madame Givaudan under the same circumstances for the purpose of distribution in France.

The defendant improperly argues that SDRM lacks standing to sue. A contract of July 10, 1972, between SDRM and the Harry Fox Agency, New York (representing the American publishers holding the copyrights) indicates that Harry Fox has assigned mechanical reproduction rights to SDRM. This gave SDRM the authority to sue for unlawful reproduction with respect to the works in question which were imported into France without authorization. A telegram from Harry Fox to SDRM on December 5, 1974 indicates that the licenses [that the Harry Fox Agency] granted for the manufacture of records and cassettes were only valid for the United States and Canada and that, in case of export, royalties were to be collected by the collecting society of the country of import on behalf of the holder of the rights of reproduction. . . .

On the merits, the defendant alleges that the problem at hand does not concern copyright law, but rather the simple purchase of physical objects (i.e. records) which may be freely circulated from one country to another. Even if the present activities partially concern the sale of a product, they must nevertheless be considered in light of international and domestic copyright law, especially under . . . the Law of March 11, 1957 on Literary and Artistic Property [the French copyright statute], dealing with the reproduction and distribution in another country (in the present case France) of an intellectual work whose physical form is a record.

The United States, where the records and other items involved in the litigation originated, is a compulsory licensing country, i.e. a country in which the mechanical reproduction of a work is permitted without the consent of the author upon payment of a fee. The fee is usually lower than in the case of a royalty paid under a contractual license and the system is limited in its applicability to the territory of that country. To the extent that contractual licenses have been granted in the United States for exploitation of the works in question, this has only occurred – according to the wording of the telegram – for the United States (and Canada). The royalties paid for these works in the United States, accordingly, only cover their exploitation in that particular country.

*In addition, Article II of the Universal Copyright Convention, to which both the United States and France are signatories, guarantees that works published in the United States shall enjoy the same protection in France as French law provides French citizens for works published in France. French law, i.e. the Law of March 11, 1957, is therefore applicable to the present case. A foreign author or his representative also enjoys the protection of French law, even if the exploitation of the work is free in the country of manufacture. . . .* [Emphasis added.]

The defendant was therefore obligated to pay the copyright owners, *i.e.* their representative in France, SDRM, the required royalties upon importing and distributing the works in question in France. The import and sale in France of the records involved in the litigation, as well as other products, even if permissibly manufactured abroad, constitutes a . . . distribution of intellectual works by the defendant. This was accompanied without the consent of the author or its representative and without payment of the fees which are due.

. . . The defendant has admitted that she has never concerned herself about her obligations in the field of copyright law since the start of her business activity to the present. The endorsement, "BIEM-Paid Directly UK," found on certain records imported through the United Kingdom, cannot exonerate the defendant. ["BIEM" – the Bureau International des Sociétés Gérant les Droits D'Enregistrement et de Reproduction Mécanique – is an organization of mechanical rights societies from many countries. The phrase "BIEM-Paid Directly UK," printed on records that Givaudan imported from the UK, may have meant that mechanical royalties for those records were paid to the British mechanical rights society.] Madame Givaudan knew thereafter that she was required to pay royalties to SDRM and did in fact pay such royalties for a long period of time, but then ceased these payments despite the fact that this caused her to be in default to this organization. . . .

For these reasons . . . , it is ordered that such amounts as correspond to the defendant's profits, derived from the illegal . . . distribution, be forfeited and that all the seized copies and other items be impounded. Upon application by SDRM (which has standing to sue, as a civil party), an expert opinion shall be prepared to determine the number of copies illegally imported by the defendant into France and to assess the damages sustained by SDRM. Madame Givaudan is further ordered to pay SDRM provisional damages of FF 10,000 [$2,350].

The *Givaudan* case shows that in many – perhaps most – instances, it is not difficult for courts to determine that the law of the country where protection is sought is the law to be applied. The Paris District Court had no trouble concluding that was so.

In the United States, the issue appears to be every bit as simple as it was in France. As you read in Chapter 1, the United States Copyright Act specifies that protection for qualifying foreign works is provided in the

United States "under this title" – meaning under Title 17 of the United States Code which is where the Copyright Act is codified. Copyright Act §§104(a) & (b). That seems clear enough, doesn't it? In all circumstances, though, it hasn't been, as the following case shows:

## Bridgeman Art Library, Ltd. v. Corel Corp.
## 36 F. Supp. 2d 191 (S.D.N.Y. 1999)

Lewis A. Kaplan, District Judge

On November 13, 1998, this Court granted defendant's motion for summary judgment dismissing plaintiff's copyright infringement claim on the alternative grounds that the allegedly infringed works – color transparencies of paintings which themselves are in the public domain – were not original and therefore not permissible subjects of valid copyright and, in any case, were not infringed. It applied United Kingdom law in determining whether plaintiff's transparencies were copyrightable. The Court noted, however, that it would have reached the same result under United States law.

Following the entry of final judgment, the Court was bombarded with additional submissions. On November 23, 1998, plaintiff moved for reargument and reconsideration, arguing that the Court erred on the issue of originality. It asserted that the Court had ignored the Register of Copyright's issuance of a certificate of registration for one of plaintiff's transparencies, which it takes as establishing copyrightability, and that the Court had misconstrued British copyright law in that it failed to follow *Graves' Case*, which was decided in the Court of Queens Bench in 1869.[5] [n5 The former argument, of course, is at least arguably inconsistent with plaintiff's position that its copyrights arose under British law.] At about the same time, the Court received an unsolicited letter from Professor William Patry, author of a copyright law treatise, which argued that the Court erred in applying the law of the United Kingdom to the issue of copyrightability. Plaintiff then moved for an order permitting the filing of an *amicus* brief . . . to address the United Kingdom law issue. The Court granted leave for the submission of the *amicus* brief and invited the parties to respond to Professor Patry's letter. The matter now is ripe for decision.

At the outset, it is worth noting that the post-judgment flurry was occasioned chiefly by the fact that the plaintiff failed competently to address most of the issues raised by this interesting case prior to the entry of final judgment. In particular, while plaintiff urged the application of U.K. law, it made no serious effort to address the choice of law issue and no effort at all (apart from citing the British copyright act) to bring pertinent U.K. authority to the Court's attention before plaintiff lost the case. Indeed, it did not even cite *Graves' Case*, the supposedly controlling authority that the Court is said to have overlooked.

Everything plaintiff has submitted on this motion should have been before the Court earlier, which is more than sufficient reason to deny its motion as an unwarranted imposition on the Court and, indeed, its adversary. The issues, however, are significant beyond the immediate interests of the parties. Accordingly, the Court will address them on the merits. . . .

In most circumstances, choice of law issues do not arise under the Berne and Universal Copyright Conventions. Each adopts a rule of national treatment. Article 5 of the Berne Convention, for example, provides that "authors shall enjoy, in respect of works for which they are protected under this Convention, in countries of the Union other than the country of origin, the rights which their respective laws do now or may hereafter grant to their nationals, as well as the rights specially granted by this convention" and that "the extent of protection, as well as the means of redress afforded to the author to protect his rights, shall be governed exclusively by the laws of the country where protection is claimed." Hence, the Conventions make clear that the holder of, for example, a British copyright who sues for infringement in a United States court is entitled to the same remedies as holders of United States copyrights and, as this Court previously held, to the determination of infringement under the same rule of law.

While the nature of the protection accorded to foreign copyrights in signatory countries thus is spelled out in the Conventions, the position of the subject matter of copyright thereunder is less certain. Do the Conventions purport to require signatory nations to extend national treatment with respect to such enforcement-related subjects as remedies for infringement only where the copyright for which protection is sought would be valid under the law of the nation in which enforcement is sought? Or do they purport to require also that a signatory nation in which enforcement is sought enforce a foreign copyright even if that copyright would not be valid under its own law?[19] [n19 *See Hasbro Bradley, Inc. v. Sparkle Toys, Inc.*, 780 F.2d 189, 192 (2d Cir. 1985) (applying U.S. copyright law "although the toys enjoyed no copyright protection under Japanese law").]. . .

Although the Supreme Court has not yet decided the point, it seems quite clear at this point that the Berne Convention is not self-executing. . . . Thus, while the Copyright Act . . . extends certain protection to the holders of copyright in Berne Convention works as there defined, the Copyright Act is the exclusive source of that protection. . . .

[Judge Kaplan then applied U.S. copyright law to the question of whether Bridgeman's photos and digital images of public domain art works were sufficiently original to be protected by copyright; and he again concluded that they are not. The critical point in this case was Bridgeman's "own admission [that it] has labored to create 'slavish copies' of public domain works of art." While the judge assumed that "this required both skill and effort, there was no spark of originality - indeed, the point of the exercise was to reproduce the underlying works with absolute fidelity." This was fatal to Bridgeman's copyright claim, because "Copyright is not available in these circumstances," Judge Kaplan held. Though U.S., not British, law determined this outcome, Judge Kaplan could not resist responding to Bridgeman's assertion that he had misapplied British law in his earlier ruling. Thus, the judge went on to reconsider that ruling too; and once again, he concluded that Bridgeman's photos and digital images would not be entitled to copyright under British law either.]

*Conclusion*

Plaintiff's motion for reargument and reconsideration of this Court's order granting summary judgment dismissing the complaint is granted. Nevertheless, on reargument and reconsideration, defendant Corel Corporation's motion for summary judgment dismissing the complaint is granted.

## 2. The rule that copyright law is "territorial"

"National treatment" could have been combination number 2 (in the chart at the beginning of this chapter). In that case, the rights of the author would have been governed by the law of the work's country-of-origin, even when protection was sought in other countries. This would have meant that works traveled around the world with their own copyright "DNA" – "DNA" supplied by the law of the country-of-origin of those works. In fact, the Montevideo Convention of 1889 (a Pan-American copyright treaty that made a brief and inconsequential appearance in *Bong v. Alfred S. Campbell Art Company* earlier in this book) did provide for copyright protection according to the law of the work's country of origin. But no other international treaty has done so. S.M. Stewart, *International Copyright and Neighbouring Rights* 37 (2d ed. 1989)

One reason that "national treatment" involves the application of the law of the country where protection is sought – rather than the law of a work's country-of-origin – is that, as a general rule, copyright laws are "territorial" in their application. This means that each country's copyright law operates only within its own boundaries, not in other countries. So most of the time, foreign copyright law is not applicable within the United States, and U.S. copyright law is not applicable abroad. These general rules are well-illustrated by several interesting cases.

### a. Foreign copyright law does not apply in U.S. or elsewhere

### Ferris v. Frohman
### 223 U.S. 424 (1912)

Mr. Justice Hughes delivered the opinion of the court.

This is a writ of error to the Supreme Court of Illinois.

The suit was brought by Charles Frohman, Charles Haddon Chambers, and Stephano Gatti . . . , to restrain the production of what was alleged to be a piratical copy of a play known as "The Fatal Card." Its authors were Charles Haddon Chambers and B.C. Stephenson, British subjects resident in London, who composed it there in 1894. The firm of A. & S. Gatti, theatrical managers of London, of which the complainant Gatti is the surviving partner, became interested with the authors and on September 6, 1894, the play was first performed in London. It was registered under the British Statutes on October 31, 1894, and again on November 8, 1894. Charles Frohman, of New York, by agreement of June 13, 1894, obtained the right of production in this country for five years. On March 25, 1895, Frohman acquired all the interest of Stephenson in the play in and for the United States, and it was extensively represented under his supervision. It was not copyrighted here.

George E. McFarlane made an adaptation of this play, called it by the same name, and transferred it to [the defendant], Richard Ferris, of Illinois, who . . . caused it to be performed in various places in this country. The adapted play differed from the original in various details, but not in its essential features.

The Superior Court of Cook County found that the complainants were the sole owners of the original play; that it had never been published or otherwise dedicated to the public in the United States or elsewhere; and that the Ferris play was substantially identical with it. Ferris was directed to account, and was perpetually restrained from producing the adaptation which he had copyrighted. The . . . Supreme Court of Illinois . . . affirmed. . . .

The substantial identity of the two plays was not disputed in the appellate courts of Illinois and must be deemed to be established. The contention was, and is, that after the public performance of the original play in London in 1894, the owners had no common-law right, but only the rights conferred by the British statutes; and that Frohman's interest (save the license which expired in 1899) was subsequently acquired. Hence, it is said, the play not being copyrighted in the United States was publici juris here and the adapter was entitled to use it as common material.

Performing right was not within the provisions of [the original British copyright act] 8 Anne, c. 19, which gave to authors the sole liberty of printing their books. The act of 1833, known as "Bulwer-Lytton's Act," conferred statutory playright [i.e., copyright] in perpetuity throughout the British dominions, in the case of dramatic pieces not printed and published; and for a stated term, if printed and published. By §20 of the Copyright Act of 1842, it was provided that the sole liberty of representing any dramatic piece should be the property of the author and his assigns for the term therein specified for the duration of copyright in books. The section continued: ". . . the first public . . . Performance of any Dramatic Piece . . . shall be deemed equivalent, in the Construction of this Act, to the first Publication of any Book." Mr. Scrutton, in his work on copyright (4th ed., p. 77), states that it is "probable, though there is no express decision to that effect, that the court, following *Donaldson v. Beckett*, would hold the common-law right destroyed by the statutory provisions after first performance in public." And it may be assumed, in this case, that after the play had been performed the right of the owners to protection against its unauthorized production in England was only that given by the statutes.

Further, in the absence of a copyright convention, there is no playright [i.e., copyright] in England in the case of a play, not printed and published, where the first public performance has taken place outside the British dominions. . . . In [the British case of] *Boucicault v. Delafield*, the author of the play known as "The Colleen Bawn" filed a bill to restrain a piratical production. It appeared that the play had first been represented in New York, and by reason of that fact – there being no copyright convention with the United States – it was held that, under the statute above quoted, there was no playright in England. To the same effect is [the British case] *Boucicault v. Chatterton*, where the author unsuccessfully sought to restrain an unauthorized performance of "The Shaughraun," an unprinted play which had first been represented here [in the United States].

The British Parliament, in thus fixing the limits and conditions of performing rights, was dealing with rights to be exercised within British territory. It is argued that the English authors in this case, by the law of their domicile, were without common-law right and in its stead secured the protection of the British statutes which cannot avail them here. But the British statutes did not purport to curtail any right of such authors with respect to the representation of plays outside the British dominions. They disclose no intention to destroy rights for which they provided no substitute. There is no indication of a purpose to incapacitate British citizens from holding their intellectual productions secure from interference in other jurisdictions according to the principles of the common law. Their right was not gone simpliciter, but only in a qualified sense for the purposes of the statutes, and there was no convention under which the authors' work became public property in the United States. When §20 of the [British copyright] act provided that the first public performance of a play should be deemed equivalent, in the construction of that act, to the first publication of a book, it simply defined its meaning with respect to the rights which the statutes conferred. The deprivation of the common-law right, by force of the statute, was plainly limited by the territorial bounds within which the operation of the statute was confined.

The present case is not one in which the owner of a play has printed and published it and thus, having lost his rights at common law, must depend upon statutory copyright in this country. The play in question has not been printed and published. It is not open to dispute that the authors of "The Fatal Card" had a common-law right of property in the play until it was publicly performed. And they were entitled to protection against its unauthorized use here as well as in England.

What effect, then, had the performance of the play in England upon the rights of the owners with respect to its use in the United States? There was no statute here by virtue of which the common-law right was lost through the performance of the unpublished play. . . . The fact that the [U.S.] act of March 3, 1891, was applicable to citizens of foreign countries, . . . and that proclamation to this effect was made by the President with respect to Great Britain, did not make the British statutes operative within the United States. Nor did that fact add to the provisions of the act of Congress so as to make the latter destructive of the common-law rights of English subjects in relation to the representation of plays in this country, which were not copyrighted under that act and which remained unpublished. These rights, like those of our own citizens in similar case, the act of 1891 did not disturb.

The public representation of a dramatic composition, not printed and published, does not deprive the owner of his common-law right, save by operation of statute. At common law, the public performance of the play is not an abandonment of it to the public use. Story states the rule as follows: "So, where a dramatic performance has been allowed by the author to be acted at a theatre, no person has a right to pirate such performance, and to publish copies of it surreptitiously; or to act it at another theatre without the consent of the author or proprietor; for his permission to act it at a public theatre does not amount to an abandonment of his title to it, or to a dedication of it to the public at large." It has been said that the owner of a play cannot complain if the piece is reproduced from memory. But the distinction is without sound basis and has been repudiated.

And, as the British statutes did not affect the common-law right of representation in this country, it is not material that the first performance of the play in question took place in England. In *Crowe v. Aiken* (1870), the play "Mary Warner" had been composed by a British subject. It was transferred to the plaintiff with the exclusive right to its representation on the stage in the United States for five years from June 1, 1869. It had not been printed with the consent either of the author or of the plaintiff. It was first publicly performed in London in June, 1869, and afterwards was represented here. The court (Drummond, J.), held that the plaintiff by virtue of his common-law right was entitled to an injunction restraining an unauthorized production. In *Palmer v. De Witt* (1872), the suit was brought to restrain the defendant from printing an unpublished drama called "Play," composed by a British citizen resident in

93

London. The plaintiff on February 1, 1868, had purchased the exclusive right of printing and performing the play in the United States. On February 15, 1868, it was first performed in London. It was held that the common-law right had not been destroyed by the public representation and the plaintiff had judgment. In the case last cited, and apparently in that of *Crowe v. Aiken*, the transfer to the plaintiff antedated the public performance, but neither decision was rested on that distinction. In *Tompkins v. Halleck* (1882), an unpublished play called "The World" had been written in England where, after being presented, it was assigned by the author to a purchaser in New York. It was acted in that city and then transferred to the plaintiffs with the exclusive right of representation in the New England States. The plaintiffs' common-law right was sustained and an unauthorized performance was enjoined.

Our conclusion is that the complainants were the owners of the original play and exclusively entitled to produce it. Their common-law right with respect to its representation in this country had not been lost. This being so, the play of the [defendant], which was substantially identical with that of the complainants, was simply a piratical composition. It was not the purpose or effect of the copyright law to render secure the fruits of piracy, and the [defendant] is not entitled to the protection of the statute. In other words, the claim of Federal right upon which he relies is without merit.

Judgment affirmed.

Is the following case in accord with *Ferris v. Frohman*, and the general rule that foreign copyright law does not apply within the United States?

## Leo Feist, Inc. v. Debmar Publishing Co.
## 232 F.Supp. 623 (E.D.Pa. 1964)

District Judge Kirkpatrick:

This action for copyright infringement is now before the court upon the defendants' motion for summary judgment. The defendants contend that the matter is res judicata, having been judicially determined in their favor in a proceeding in the English courts.

The plaintiff is the owner of a copyrighted musical composition entitled "In a Little Spanish Town." The defendants admit publication, reproduction, and performance of a musical composition entitled "Why," which two compositions were the basis of the suit in England.

No question is raised as to privity, but the plaintiff asserts that the principle of res judicata is not applicable because the present suit is brought under the copyright laws of the United States. I must agree that the principle of res judicata cannot be applied since this suit is brought under the United States statute for infringements which occurred in the United States, whereas the English suit was brought under the English statute for different infringements which occurred in England. However, there remains collateral estoppel.

Under the English law copying, either conscious or subconscious, is required to support an action for copyright infringement. The same is true of the American law. It is also true of the law of both countries that if no copying occurs there can be no recovery for a coincidental similarity even though substantial.

The evidence before the court as to the English law consists of the record of the case tried there together with the opinions rendered by the judges of the English Court of Appeals, and an affidavit submitted by a qualified expert in support of this motion for summary judgment. . . . The English court found as a fact that there was neither conscious nor subconscious copying. In making this finding the English court applied legal principles which, if different at all, are only very slightly different from those which would be applied in an American court. Unless the plaintiff can contest that fact finding in this court, the defendants must prevail here since without proof of copying, it cannot recover under the law of the United States.

Under the conditions set forth by the Supreme Court in the case of *Hilton v. Guyot*, the courts of the United States accord conclusive effect to matters litigated in foreign countries between the parties to a suit in America. It cannot be questioned that the courts of England meet these conditions.

An exception to this rule is that, if in any case there is a countervailing policy of the United States, such foreign judgments will not be recognized. However, I see no reason why the courts of this country in a case such as that before me should refuse to recognize the fact finding of an English court.

In the case of foreign judgment there is as much reason to apply the doctrine of collateral estoppel to a fact litigated as to apply the doctrine of res judicata. Both doctrines are designed to put an end to litigation and rest on the same foundation. Since in a hotly contested lawsuit in England it has been determined that there was neither conscious nor subconscious copying and since this fact would dispose of the litigation before me, I am compelled to enter summary judgment in favor of the defendants.

The defendants' motion is granted.

The principle that copyright laws are territorial is recognized in other countries too, and was in fact the basis for the outcome in the German case *Joseph Beuys' Works*, 24 IIC 139 (Germany Ct.App. 1992). In that case, the German Court of Appeals ruled that Germany's *droit de suite* – its resale royalties right –was *not* applicable to the sale of art works in the United Kingdom. By itself, this wasn't a remarkable ruling. What makes it remarkable is that the seller was a German art collector who issued sale instructions from Germany, delivered the art works in Germany for shipment to the U.K., and the seller was advised, and the sale was advertised, in Germany by a German subsidiary of the auction house that sold the art works in the U.K. In other words, the entire substance of the transaction took place in Germany, where Germany's *droit de suite* would have applied, except for the very final step – the actual sale – which took place in the United Kingdom, no doubt to avoid the obligation to pay resale royalties to the artist. (This case accurately illustrates the principle that copyright laws have no effect outside their own countries; but as of January 1, 2006, it no longer accurately illustrates the law of *droit de suite* within the European Union, for reasons that will be considered in Chapter 5.)

## b. U.S. copyright law does not apply abroad

### i. The general rule

**Beechwood Music Corp. v. Vee Jay Records, Inc.**
**328 F.2d 728 (2d Cir. 1964)**

Per Curiam

We affirm in open court an order of Judge Edelstein, in the District Court for the Southern District of New York, granting to the proprietor and the licensee of the copyrights of two musical compositions "Love Me Do" and "P.S. I Love You" a temporary injunction against the manufacture and sale of records embodying performances of them by The Beatles – whom we identify for posterity as four long-haired British "rock and roll" performers currently enjoying a *succes fou* [French for "wild success"]. Defendant Vee Jay Records, Inc. has been manufacturing the records from master recordings by The Beatles to which it was entitled under an agreement with Transglobal Music Co., Inc., admittedly not the copyright proprietor. Vee Jay's opposition to the grant of the injunction, below and here, rested on the . . . grounds . . . that it was entitled to manufacture and sell the records under the compulsory license provision of the Copyright Act. . . , because the copyright owner had licensed mechanical reproduction in Great Britain. . . .

It would be quite unreasonable to construe the condition of the compulsory license clause, "that whenever the owner of a musical copyright has used or permitted or knowingly acquiesced in the use of the copyrighted work upon the parts of instruments serving to reproduce mechanically the musical work," as being satisfied by the manufacture of records in a foreign country, at least when these have not been brought into the United States. "Rules of United States statutory law . . . apply only to conduct occurring within, or having effects within, the territory of the United States, unless the contrary is clearly indicated by the statute." American Law Institute, *Restatement of the Foreign Relations Law of the United States* (Proposed Official Draft), §38; *American Banana Co. v. United Fruit Co.*, 213 U.S. 347, 355, 29 S.Ct. 511, 53 L.Ed. 826 (1909); *Foley Bros., Inc. v. Filardo*, 336 U.S. 281, 69 S.Ct. 575, 93 L.Ed. 680 (1949).

Defendants' construction would lead to the absurd conclusion that a foreign copyright owner who licenses mechanical reproduction in his own country, without any intention of ever entering the United States market, must promptly file a notice in the copyright office in Washington or else lose even the 2 cent per record royalty given by the compulsory license clause. The discussion in the House report, H.R.Rep.No. 2222, 60th Cong.2d Sess. (1909), cited by defendants, is much too inconclusive to carry the day for them. Congress was concerned lest, as applied to the case at hand, any single record manufacturer should be able to monopolize the purveying of The Beatles' message to the American record buying public – not to accelerate the public's opportunity to hear their recordings of "musical compositions" with which the copyright proprietor has not yet chosen to favor us.

Although *Ferris v. Frohman*, 223 U.S. 424, 32 S.Ct. 263, 56 L.Ed. 492 (1912), dealt with a different claim of extraterritorial application of the Copyright Act, it points strongly against defendants' view.

. . . [T]he order is affirmed.

## ii. The special case of pre-1989 mandatory copyright notice

Before 1989, the U.S. Copyright Act required a copyright notice to be affixed to published copies of a work. If the required notice was omitted, the work could go into the public domain in the U.S. (unless the omission was cured in a prescribed time and fashion); and if a work was published without notice before 1978, it did go into the public domain in the U.S., automatically and irretrievably. The United States may have been the only country of the world to require copyright notices on published works, so authors and publishers in other countries often did not affix notices to works published in their own countries. In several cases involving such works, this raised the issue of whether publication outside the United States without the copyright notice then required by U.S. caused the works to fall into the public domain in the U.S., or whether, instead, their U.S. copyrights were saved by the general principle that U.S. does not apply to activity in other countries.

In a series of cases involving *pre-1955* foreign publications, courts applied the general principle that U.S. law does not apply abroad; and those courts held that the U.S. copyrights to those publications were not forfeited, even though they were published without copyright notices.

- In *Heim v. Universal Pictures Co.*, 154 F.2d 480 (2d Cir. 1946), the court ruled that the publication of a work in Hungary, without the copyright notice then required by U.S., law did not put the work into the public domain in the U.S., where it had never been published.
- Likewise, in *Mills Music, Inc. v. Cromwell Music, Inc.*, 126 F.Supp. 54 (S.D.N.Y. 1954), the court held that the distribution in Palestine (then under British law) of copies of the song "Tzena, Tzena" without the copyright notice then required by U.S. law (but not British law) did not put the song into the public domain in the U.S.
- And in *Eisen, Durwood and Co. v. Tolkein*, 794 F.Supp. 85 (S.D.N.Y. 1992), aff'd without opinion, 990 F.2d 623 (2d Cir. 1993), the court held that the British novel *The Lord of the Rings* by J.R.R. Tolkein had not forfeited its U.S. copyright, even though it was first published in the U.K. in 1952 without the copyright notice then required by U.S. copyright law.

In 1955, however, the United States adhered to the Universal Copyright Convention. That multi-national treaty permits countries to enforce a notice requirement if they wish to, even with respect to foreign-published works. As a result, in response to U.S. adherence to the UCC, the Copyright Office adopted a regulation that provided that in order for any work (U.S. or foreign) to acquire copyright protection under U.S. law, publication anywhere – even outside the United States – had to have been done with the copyright notice then required by U.S. law.

What's more, when Congress first enacted the Copyright Act of 1976, it too imposed extraterritorial notice requirements. Section 401(a) of that Act – as it read prior to 1989 – provided that "Whenever a work protected under this title is published in the United States *or elsewhere* [emphasis added] by authority of the copyright owner, a notice of copyright as provided by this section shall be placed on all publicly distributed copies. . . ."

Today, copyright notices are no longer required by U.S. law on works published anywhere (not even within the United States). The U.S. eliminated the notice requirement in 1989, when it adhered to the Berne Convention, in order to comply with Berne's ban on formalities. But for works published between 1955 and 1989, the notice requirement of the U.S. Copyright Act *did* apply abroad, and did result in many works of foreign origin going into the public domain in the U.S.

The fact that many works of foreign origin did go into the public domain in the U.S. is the reason that Congress was required to, and did, restore those copyrights (along with the copyrights of works published in countries with which the U.S. did not have copyright treaties before 1989) by enacting section 104A of the Copyright Act, when the U.S. joined the WTO in 1995. (The details of section 104A will be explored later.)

### c. Disputes about where the pertinent activity took place

In the cases you just read (and read about), there wasn't any doubt about where – that is, in which country – the pertinent activity took place. The only question was whether the copyright law of another country reached that activity. And as you saw, the answer (as a general rule) was "no." In some cases, though, there *is* a dispute about *where* the pertinent activity took place. These kinds of cases have become more common since the advent of satellite television and the Internet. Determining where the activity took place is especially critical in cases where the activity is infringing *if* it occurred in one country, but not *if* it occurred in the other. The following opinion is one such case. Under U.S. copyright law, satellite retransmissions of network TV broadcasts are permitted – that is, they are non-infringing – if the retransmissions are received only by households that cannot adequately receive those broadcasts over the air. (Satellite retransmissions are sold to subscribers, so another way to describe U.S. law is to say that satellite retransmission companies may only sell subscriptions to households that cannot adequately receive network TV broadcasts off the air.) In Canada, by contrast, the law permits satellite retransmissions of network broadcasts, without regard to whether households can adequately receive those broadcasts over the air. (Those retransmissions aren't royalty-free in Canada. Royalties are set by law and must be paid by satellite TV companies. But the retransmissions aren't infringing, as they would be in the U.S.)

### National Football League v. PrimeTime 24
### 211 F.3d 10 (2d Cir. 2000), cert. denied, 532 U.S. 941 (2001)

Van Graafeiland, Circuit Judge:
As almost every red-blooded American knows, the National Football League ("NFL") televises most of its weekly football games. Simultaneously with the broadcast, NFL makes videotape recordings of the games, which it registers with the United States Copyright Office.

PrimeTime 24 Joint Venture ("PrimeTime") is a satellite carrier that makes secondary transmissions of copyrighted television network programming to owners and renters of satellite dish antennae. PrimeTime has a statutorily granted license to make satellite transmissions to its subscribers in United

States households that do not have adequate over-the-air broadcast reception from primary television stations, i.e., "unserved" households. See generally 17 U.S.C. §119. However, PrimeTime has not limited its retransmissions to unserved households in the United States. Without securing permission from NFL, PrimeTime also makes secondary transmissions of football broadcasts to its satellite subscribers in Canada.

On several occasions in 1997, NFL officials wrote to PrimeTime demanding that this practice stop. The following excerpt from one of PrimeTime's replies explains why PrimeTime believes it has the right to continue this practice:

> Next, I would like to address your assertion that the provision of PrimeTime 24's service to subscribers in Canada infringes your copyright in the United States, notwithstanding the facts that all of the recipients in question are in Canada, and *PrimeTime 24's actions in this regard comport with applicable Canadian law* [emphasis added]. Under United States copyright law, the NFL is entitled to control the "public" display or performance of any audiovisual work for which it holds a valid copyright. Accordingly, there can be no infringement of the NFL's rights unless and until there has been a public display or performance. Because the copyright laws of the United States have no extraterritorial applicability, "public" performances that occur in other countries cannot trigger liability for copyright infringement under the laws of the United States. Instead, the law of the country in which the public performance does take place protects the copyright holder.

Letter from Sid Amira, Chairman and Chief Executive Officer of PrimeTime, to Frank Hawkins, Vice President of NFL (Aug. 8, 1997).

PrimeTime's continued retransmission of NFL programming into Canada resulted in the litigation now before us. By a memorandum and order dated March 23, 1999, the United States District Court for the Southern District of New York (McKenna, J.) denied PrimeTime's motion to dismiss NFL's complaint. By a decision dated September 24, 1999, the district court granted NFL's motion for summary judgment and referred the case to a magistrate judge for calculation of fees and damages. On October 18, 1999, the district court issued an order permanently enjoining PrimeTime from retransmitting telecasts of NFL football games outside the United States. PrimeTime asks us to reverse the final injunction.

Under the Copyright Act, the owner of a copyright has the exclusive right publicly to perform and display the copyrighted material. 17 U.S.C. §106(4) & (5). The Act explains that the right to perform copyrighted material publicly includes the right "to transmit or otherwise communicate a performance . . . of the work . . . to the public, by means of any device or process, whether the members of the public capable of receiving the performance . . . receive it in the same place or in separate places and at the same time or at different times." Id. §101. Congress stated that "each and every method by which . . . images or sounds comprising a performance or display are picked up and conveyed is a 'transmission,' and if the transmission reaches the public in [any] form, the case comes within the scope of [§106(4) or (5)]." H.R. Rep. No. 94-1476, at 64 (1976), reprinted in 1976 U.S.C.C.A.N. 5659, 5678.

The issue in this case is whether PrimeTime publicly performed or displayed NFL's copyrighted material. PrimeTime argues that capturing or uplinking copyrighted material and transmitting it to a satellite does not constitute a public display or performance of that material. PrimeTime argues that any public performance or display occurs during the downlink from the satellite to the home subscriber in Canada, which is in a foreign country where the Copyright Act does not apply. Although this Court has not squarely resolved the issue, several courts have rejected PrimeTime's reasoning.

In *WGN Continental Broad. Co. v. United Video, Inc.*, 693 F.2d 622, 624-25 (7th Cir. 1982), the Seventh Circuit considered whether an intermediate carrier had publicly performed copyrighted television signals by capturing broadcast signals, altering them and transmitting them to cable television systems. The court determined that "the Copyright Act defines 'perform or display . . . publicly' broadly enough to encompass indirect transmission to the ultimate public." Consequently, the *WGN* court concluded that an intermediate carrier is not immune from copyright liability simply because it does not retransmit a copyrighted signal to the public directly but instead routes the signal to cable systems, which then retransmit to the public.

Judge Posner, writing for the court in *WGN*, noted that a contrary result would render the passive carrier exemption in the Act superfluous. The passive carrier exemption provides that a secondary transmission is not copyright infringement if the transmitter has no control over the content or selection of the original signal or over the recipients of the secondary transmission and provides only the wires, cables, or communication channels for the use of others. See 17 U.S.C. §111(a)(3). In other words, if a copyrighted signal is publicly performed or displayed only when received by viewers, there would be no need for a passive carrier exemption because these passive intermediate carriers "do not transmit directly to the public." A district court in the Eighth Circuit has reached the same result. See *Hubbard Broad., Inc. v. Southern Satellite Sys., Inc.*, 593 F.Supp. 808, 813 (D. Minn. 1984), affirmed, 777 F.2d 393 (8th Cir. 1985) (finding secondary transmissions to be public performances whether made directly or indirectly to public).

District courts in this Circuit have agreed that a transmission need not be made directly to the public in order for there to be a public performance or display. For example, in *David v. Showtime/The Movie Channel, Inc.*, 697 F.Supp. 752, 759 (S.D.N.Y. 1988), Judge Tenney concluded that "Congress intended the definitions of 'public' and 'performance' to encompass each step in the process by which a protected work wends its way to its audience." Judge Tenney further stated that the definition of transmit "is broad enough to include all conceivable forms and combinations of wired or wireless communications media."

Other district courts have relied on *David* to reach the same conclusion. See *National Cable Television Ass'n, Inc. v. Broadcast Music, Inc.*, 772 F.Supp. 614, 650-51 (D.D.C. 1991) (citing analysis in *David* with approval); *Coleman v. ESPN, Inc.*, 764 F.Supp. 290, 294 (S.D.N.Y. 1991) ("Transmissions by a cable network or service to local cable companies who in turn transmit to individual cable subscribers constitute 'public performances' by the network."); *Broadcast Music, Inc. v. Hearst/ABC Viacom Entertainment Servs.*, 746 F.Supp. 320, 328-29 (S.D.N.Y. 1990) (finding public performance when cable supplier transmitted signal to cable operator that then relayed signal to viewers); see also *National Ass'n of Broadcasters v. Copyright Royalty Tribunal*, 809 F.2d 172, 179 n.9 (2d Cir. 1986) (noting that cable retransmissions are recognized as public performances under §106(4)).

The Court of Appeals for the Ninth Circuit has suggested a different result. When considering whether the Copyright Act preempted state law, that Court stated that copyright infringement does not occur until the signal is received by the viewing public. See *Allarcom Pay Television, Ltd. v. General Instrument Corp.*, 69 F.3d 381, 387 (9th Cir. 1995). This opinion has been subject to some non-judicial criticism, which we need not repeat. See Jane C. Ginsburg, *Extraterritoriality and Multiterritoriality in Copyright Infringement*, 37 Va.J.Int'l L. 587, 598 (1997); Andreas P. Reindl, *Choosing Law in Cyberspace: Copyright Conflicts on Global Networks*, 19 Mich.J.Int'l L. 799, 823 n.84 (1998). We accord the decision little weight largely because it contains no analysis of the Copyright Act.

We believe the most logical interpretation of the Copyright Act is to hold that a public performance or display includes "each step in the process by which a protected work wends its way to its audience." *David*, 697 F.Supp. at 759. Under that analysis, it is clear that PrimeTime's uplink transmission of signals captured in the United States is a step in the process by which NFL's protected work wends its way to a public audience. In short, PrimeTime publicly displayed or performed material in which the NFL owns the copyright. Because PrimeTime did not have authorization to make such a public performance, PrimeTime infringed the NFL's copyright. . . .

Using the court's "each step in the process" test for determining where copyright-relevant activity takes place, did PrimeTime 24 do anything in Canada that might have copyright significance under Canadian law? If PrimeTime 24 retransmitted a Canadian TV broadcast to its satellite subscribers in the United States, which country's copyright law would control PrimeTime's rights and obligations?

## B. National treatment as a two-edged sword

National treatment is a two-edged sword: it results in protection for some works that are not protected in their country-of-origin, and denial of protection for some works that are protected in their country-of-origin.

### 1. Protection for works not protected in country-of-origin

The principle that national treatment results in protection for some works not protected in their country-of-origin has been recognized in the United States, Germany and (no doubt) elsewhere too.

### Hasbro Bradley v. Sparkle Toys
### 780 F.2d 189 (2d Cir. 1985)

Circuit Judge Friendly:
The companies involved in this copyright case in the District Court for the Southern District of New York are Takara Co., Ltd. ("Takara"), a Japanese company that designed the toys here in question; plaintiff Hasbro Bradley, Inc. ("Hasbro"), a large American toy manufacturer and seller that acquired Takara's rights to United States copyrights for the toys; and defendant Sparkle Toys, Inc. ("Sparkle"), a smaller American toy manufacturer and seller that copied the toys in Asia from models manufactured by Takara which did not

carry the copyright notice required by §401 of the Copyright Act of 1976 (the "Act") and by Article III(1) of the Revised Universal Copyright Convention (U.C.C.), to which the United States and Japan are parties. The appeal, by Sparkle, is from an order of Judge Broderick entered April 29, 1985, granting Hasbro a preliminary injunction prohibiting Sparkle from "distributing, selling, marketing, promoting, advertising, imitating or exploiting, in this country, its toys, formerly denoted 'Trans Robot,' which are in violation of plaintiff's registered copyrights in the sculptural embodiments of its 'Topspin' and 'Twin Twist' toys."

"Topspin" and "Twin Twist" (the "toys") are part of Hasbro's "The Transformer" series of changeable robotic action figures. The sculptural expressions of the toys are original designs of Takara, which manufactures "The Transformers" for Hasbro. Takara authored the designs in the summer of 1983 and by the end of November had completed molds for manufacturing the toys. These molds did not contain a copyright notice. Takara avers that the omission was due to the facts that Japanese law does not recognize copyright in toy products and that Takara was unaware that American law does recognize copyright in such works but requires notice, even on copies of the work distributed outside the United States, for copyright protection to be claimed inside the United States. Production of the unmarked toys began in December 1983 and . . . approximately 213,000 of the unmarked toys were sold . . . [most if not all] in Asia. . . .

There is no dispute that the toys here at issue were originally designed by Takara in June 1983. Although the toys enjoyed no copyright protection under Japanese law,[3] they fell within the class of "pictorial, graphic, and sculptural works" covered by §102(a)(5) of the Act. See §101. [Fn.3 See 4 Z. Kitagawa, *Doing Business in Japan* §8.02[5][c] (1985) ("Models devised for the purpose of mass-producing practical goods are subject to the Design Act rather than the Copyright Act.").] Since the toys were authored by a Japanese national and first "published" (i.e. sold) in Japan, they enjoyed copyright protection under United States law from the moment they were created, see §302(a), by virtue of both §104(b) of the Act and Article II(1) of the U.C.C. . . .

This excerpt from *Hasbro* illustrates the point for which it is offered: namely, that the United States gives copyright protection to some foreign works that are not protected by copyright in their countries of origin. However, you may wonder whether this principle was of any practical benefit to Hasbro, because the toys were first published in Japan in 1983 or 1984. By that date, you'll recall, United States law required copyright notices on works published anywhere in the world. (If you don't recall this, re-read part A.2.b.ii. of this chapter.) Nevertheless, the absence of copyright notice was not fatal to Hasbro, because the U.S. Copyright Act then permitted copyright owners to cure the omission of necessary notices, and thereby preserve copyright protection, by following specified procedures; and Hasbro did.

Here, now, is an example from Germany of the principle that national treatment results in protection for some works not protected in their country-of-origin.

## Lounge Chair
## 13 IIC 777 (Frankfurt Court of Appeals 1981)

Plaintiff is the European licensee of Herman Miller, Inc., Zeeland, Michigan (USA), which, in 1947, acquired from the American Charles Eames the exclusive and worldwide rights for the manufacture and sale of furniture designed by the latter. . . . Among other creations Charles Eames designed the "Lounge Chair." This lounge chair has won several awards and is part of the permanent collection of the Museum of Modern Art in New York City. The artist Charles Eames died in 1978.

In May, 1978, plaintiff ascertained that defendant manufactures a chair, almost identical to Charles Eames' lounge chair, and that he distributes it in the German Federal Republic, including Frankfurt, as the "Eames 1000."

Defendant takes the position that the lounge chair is not copyrightable in the USA and is therefore not entitled to protection under the UCC.

In its decision of June 6, 1979, the District Court [in Germany] ruled against the defendant on the ground that the model at issue is indisputably protectable subject matter in its country of origin, the USA. Therefore, the Court went on to state, it is also protected in the Federal Republic of Germany, pursuant to the principle of . . . national treatment (Article II UCC), regardless of compliance with the formalities required by U.S. law. . . .

On July 17, 1979, defendant appealed from this decision.

Defendant contends that the District Court erroneously assumed that the model at issue is copyrightable subject matter in its country of origin (proof: expert opinion by the Max Planck Institute for Foreign and International Patent, Copyright, and Unfair Competition Law, Munich). According to defendant, plaintiff neither demonstrated nor proved the copyrightability, and since the lounge chair is in the public domain in the USA, it cannot be protected under the principles of the UCC in the German Federal Republic.

The appeal . . . is unsuccessful. Without error in result, the District Court ruled against defendant . . . since the copyright on the lounge chair which plaintiff is entitled to assert (Sec. 185 German Civil Code) has been infringed by defendant (Sees. 2, 97 and 121(4) Copyright Act).

Plaintiff, who is asserting the rights of the American designer, is entitled to this claim under Art. I of the Agreement Between Germany and the United States of America Concerning the Mutual Protection of Copyrights dated January 15, 1892, hereinafter referred to as the "Agreement." . . . According to Art. I of the aforementioned Agreement, citizens of the United States of America are to enjoy copyright protection on the same basis as is legally available to German citizens. Therefore, plaintiff was entitled to protection only if the lounge chair, had it been created and released in Germany, by a German citizen, would likewise have enjoyed copyright protection. In fact, it represents a work of applied art in the sense of Sec. 2(1)(4) [of the German] Copyright Act. Although it serves a practical use, the lounge chair must be considered a work of art due to its highly aesthetic structural composition.

That this chair, over and above its practical application, indeed constitutes an artistic creation is evident from the fact that the lounge chair has received several awards as a work of art, and is part of the permanent exhibit at the Museum of Modern Art in New York City. In this regard, it should be noted that defendant did not raise any significant objections against recognizing the chair as a work of art.

*Since the chair is considered a work of art in Germany, it is unnecessary for this Court to examine whether it is under copyright protection in the USA. . . . Neither the wording nor the intent of the Agreement justifies a different conclusion in this case, so that there is no need to discuss defendant's argument that the lounge chair does not qualify for copyright protection in the USA for lack of subject matter. . . .* [Emphasis added.]

Finally, the request for a decree is also admissible and justified. Defendant's infringement of plaintiff's asserted rights created a legal situation between the parties which justifies plaintiff's interest in obtaining, without delay, a decree establishing defendant's liability to pay damages.

The request for a decree is also justified due to the demonstrated probability that defendant's violation of the law will result in financial damage to the plaintiff, either through loss of sales or non-payment of royalties. . . .

## 2. Lack of protection for works protected in country-of-origin

The U.S. copyright status of the Italian film "The Bicycle Thief" presents a more complicated and dramatic example of the two-edged nature of national treatment. The film was first published in Italy in 1948. As a result of a 1993 European Council Directive that harmonized the term of protection within the European Union, the film's copyright will be protected in Italy until 70 years after the death of the film's director, screenwriter or music composer (whoever is the last to die). The film's director and composer have died, but some of its screenwriters (there were several) appear to be living still. This means the film's copyright will be protected in Italy (and throughout the EU) until late in the 21st century. Nevertheless, "The Bicycle Thief" went into the public domain in the United States in 1976, for the reasons explained in the following opinion.

### International Film Exchange v. Corinth Films
### 621 F.Supp. 631 (S.D.N.Y. 1985)

District Judge Sprizzo:

Plaintiffs International Film Exchange, Ltd. ("IFEX") and others brought an action seeking damages for copyright infringement with respect to the foreign film classic, "Ladri Di Biciclette" ("The Bicycle Thief," hereinafter the "Film"). Defendants Corinth Films, Inc. ("Corinth") and others counterclaimed for infringement, alleging that they, and not plaintiffs, are entitled to the exclusive United States distribution rights to the Film. Both sides have moved for summary judgment . . . .

It is undisputed that the date of publication of the Film was December 6, 1948. Under the 1909 Act, statutory copyright protection attached and endured for twenty-eight years from the date of first publication with notice. See 17 U.S.C. §24 (1909 Act) (superseded). Thereafter, an application for renewal of copyright would have had to have been filed with the Copyright Office within one year prior to the expiration of the original term of copyright in order to extend the copyright protection afforded by the statute. Thus, the initial term of copyright in the Film expired December 6, 1976, and an application for a valid renewal would have had to have been filed between December 6, 1975 and December 6, 1976.

It is undisputed that neither of the defendants ever filed for a renewal of copyright for the Film during that period. Plaintiff IFEX applied for and received a renewal certificate from the Copyright Office on November 29, 1976. However, since this renewal application was made in the name of IFEX, it was not effective to validly extend the copyright term. A mere licensee, as opposed to an assignee, cannot validly renew a copyright in its own name. As a consequence, the Film *irrevocably* entered the public domain upon the expiration of the initial term of copyright. . . . [Emphasis added.]

As things turned out, Judge Sprizzo was wrong – for reasons he could not have anticipated when he decided the case in 1985 – when he said the film "irrevocably" went into the public domain. As a result of the enactment of section 104A of the U.S. Copyright Act in 1994, the U.S. copyright to "The Bicycle Thief" was restored on January 1, 1996. The film's U.S. copyright will have a duration of 75 years from its first publication, which means it will be protected in the U.S. until 2023 when it will go into the public domain in the U.S. for a second time – once again, before its copyright expires in Italy (or the EU).

## C. Potential ineligibility for national treatment

Though national treatment is the *general* rule, there are circumstances under which national treatment is not required by treaty and is not provided. Indeed, there are other circumstances under which national treatment actually is prohibited by overriding legal principles in the country where protection is sought.

### 1. Reciprocity requirements not satisfied

The following opinion illustrates one set of circumstances under which national treatment was not available in Germany to bootleg recordings of performances by American artist Bob Dylan. As you read the decision, you will see that the court goes through four (or perhaps five) independent analytical steps, before it concludes that Dylan did not have a right to prevent the unauthorized sale of those bootleg albums. Make a note of what those steps were, so we can discuss them in class.

**Bob Dylan**
**18 IIC 418 (German Federal Supreme Court 1985)**

The second plaintiff [Bob Dylan], an American citizen, is a musician. He is under contract to CBS, Inc., New York. The first plaintiff is the German subsidiary of CBS, Inc., New York; both companies are engaged in the recording, production, and distribution of phonograph records and audio tapes. The first plaintiff has released numerous sound recordings of performances by [Dylan].

Defendant, a German wholesale distributor of sound recordings, distributes an album set containing three long-playing records of performances by [Dylan]. The cover of the album, which bears the title "Bob Dylan," shows a photograph of [Dylan].

The album set containing the three records was released by the Italian firm SAAR s.r.l., which intervened in the proceeding on the defendant's side. . . .

In this action, plaintiffs demand that defendant discontinue distribution in the Federal Republic of Germany, including West Berlin, of the long-playing record set "Bob Dylan" bearing the artist's photo on the cover, as well as of the individual audio recordings. . . . Plaintiffs stated that they had not authorized either the production or the distribution of the audio recordings at issue, which are based on covert recordings of concert performances. They therefore claimed the right to prohibit the defendant's distribution of the sound recordings. In this regard, they claimed rights arising . . . from [German] copyright law. . . . The first plaintiff derives its rights from its parent company which, based on its contract with [Dylan], has the exclusive right to produce sound recordings of [Dylan]'s performances, to distribute them world-wide, and to transfer its rights to its subsidiaries as exclusive rights of exploitation. [Dylan] sought national treatment for protection under German law and invoked the rights of the performing artist deriving from Secs. 73 *et seq.,* [German] Copyright Act. . . .

In an interlocutory decision, the trial court . . . ruled in favor of [Dylan]'s demand for an injunction. . . . The appellate court . . . revised the trial court's decision and ordered defendant, as requested by [Dylan], to discontinue distribution of the album set at issue if a photograph of [Dylan] were reproduced on its front cover. Otherwise the appellate court dismissed [Dylan]'s further request for injunction. . . .

The plaintiffs' objections to this judgment, in their appeals on the law, are unsuccessful.

The appellate court's rejection of plaintiffs' demands for injunction and damages under Sec. 97(1), Copyright Act, was the legally correct result. In this connection we need not decide the question . . . whether or not the distribution in the Federal Republic of Germany of the sound recordings at issue represent a violation of the law. Any claims based on copyright law fail precisely because [Dylan], an American citizen, cannot claim national treatment as a performing artist for protection against the distribution of unauthorized, foreign-made recordings. In the case before the Court, [Dylan] is asserting his rights only as a performing artist and not as an author [i.e., not as a songwriter]. . . .

The provisions of the German copyright law concerning foreigners . . . do not grant [Dylan] national treatment.

. . . [S]uch protection cannot be derived from Sec. 125(2), Copyright Act. According to that provision, foreign citizens are protected as performing artists only for domestic performances; this is not the case here. . . .

Nor can [Dylan] obtain national treatment for protection on the basis of treaties (Sec. 125(5), Copyright Act). . . . [T]he International Convention for the Protection of Performers, Producers of Phonograms and Broadcasting Organisations . . . ("the Rome Convention") is not applicable since the United States of America, in contrast to the Federal Republic of Germany, is not a signatory to this Convention. Similarly, in the present case, national treatment for protection cannot be derived from the Universal Copyright Convention . . . which was signed by the United States, because this Convention deals solely with the rights of authors and not with those of performing artists.

In addition, the Convention between the German Reich and the United States of America Concerning the Reciprocal Protection of Copyrights of January 15, 1892, which is invoked by the appellants, cannot justify domestic standing for protection in this case. . . . [T]his Convention guarantees national treatment only for the author and not for the performing artist as well. By its very wording, the Convention refers only to copyrighted works. At the time, protection for the performing artist was not an issue any more than protection for producers of sound recordings or broadcasting organizations. This protection became necessary only as a consequence of the technological development of copying and communication capabilities for artistic performances. For a long period it was uncertain whether the rights of protection would be considered copyrights or whether they dealt with a mere protection of the performance. In German legislation, the rights or performing artists and producers of mechanical music recordings were covered for the first time in the Copyright Act Concerning Literary Works, amendments of 1910 [the predecessor of the present German Copyright Act]. In the newly introduced Sec. 2(2), Copyright Act Concerning Literary Works, they were granted to a limited extent a copyright based on the legal fiction that the performance was an adaptation of the underlying work. Legal recognition and detailed formulation of a special performance protection right did not follow until the Copyright Act of 1965. . . .

It is true that the agreement of 1892 with the United States grants domestic standing for protection according to the current legal formulation of national rights, so that revisions, as a matter of principle, are covered as well. This applies, however, only to the current legal definitions of copyright itself, and not also to the essentially different neighboring rights, even though they are both governed by the same unified statute.

It should be noted that the above interpretation is confirmed by the international evolution of copyright on the one hand, and neighboring rights on the other. These developments always progressed along separate lines. Both the Berne Convention of 1886 and the Universal Copyright Convention of 1952 regulate only the protection of authors. The long standing lack of international safeguards for the neighboring rights of performing artists, producers of sound recordings, and broadcast organizations was corrected only in 1961 with the Rome Convention. This was not signed by the United States which does not recognize a corresponding neighboring right for performing artists. Subsequently, the 1971 Convention for the Protection of Producers of Phonograms Against Unauthorized Duplication of their Phonograms came into effect.

In accordance with the above, [Dylan] does not enjoy national treatment for protection as a performing artist with regard to the right to prohibit distribution under [the] Copyright Act. This simultaneously precludes any claims under copyright law on the part of the first plaintiff which derives its rights . . . from [Dylan]. . . .

Do you think the result in the *Bob Dylan* case would have been the same, *if* the case had arisen in 1995, *after* the United States (and Germany) joined the World Trade Organization, instead of in 1985 when bootlegging was *not* prohibited by federal law in the U.S.? The WTO TRIPs Agreement requires anti-bootlegging protection, which is why the U.S. added an anti-bootlegging provision to Title 17 of the United States Code in 1994 (just before joining the WTO). Would the result would have been the same, *if* the *Martignon* case had been decided differently – that is, *if Martignon* had held that the U.S. anti-bootlegging statutes are unconstitutional?

## 2. Necessary (and permitted) formalities not satisfied

The Berne Convention prohibits formalities, using the following language:

### Berne Convention Article 5

(1) Authors shall enjoy, in respect of works for which they are protected under this Convention, in countries of the Union other than the country of origin, the *rights* which their respective laws do now or may hereafter grant to their nationals. . . .

(2) The enjoyment and the *exercise of these rights* shall not be subject to any formality. . . .

[Emphasis added.]

Do the "rights" granted to foreigners include all of the "remedies" and other benefits of copyright ownership that are granted to nationals? Suppose that a country's law offers its nationals a variety of remedies, but some of those remedies are made available only to those nationals who comply with certain formalities. May that country also limit the availability of those remedies to foreigners who comply with the required formalities?

Here are two opinions (trial and appellate) in a single U.S. case that suggests the answer is "yes" – a country *may* limit the availability of certain remedies to those who comply with required formalities, even with respect to works of foreign Berne country origin.

### In re AEG Acquisition Corp.
### 127 Bankr. 34 , 1991 Bankr.LEXIS 638 (C.D.Cal.Bankr.Ct. 1991)

Samuel L. Bufford, United States Bankruptcy Judge

*I. Introduction*

This preference and fraudulent conveyance action presents the issue of whether the contract between the parties, relating to distribution rights in three motion picture films, is an option contract or a conditional sales contract. If it is a conditional sales contract, the Court must determine whether the creditor has duly perfected its security interest in the three films at issue.

The Court finds that the agreement is a conditional sales contract, and that the creditor has duly perfected its interest in only one of the three films. The Court further finds that the two foreign films must be registered as a condition of perfecting a security interest in them. . . .

*II. Facts*

AEG Acquisition Corp. ("AEG") is a Chapter 11 debtor whose principal asset is a library of copyrights, distribution rights and licenses to more than 100 motion picture films.

In 1987 Atlantic Entertainment Group, Inc. ("Atlantic"), predecessor to the debtor, entered into three distribution agreements with Zenith Productions, Ltd. ("Zenith"). These distribution agreements relate to three motion pictures entitled "Patty Hearst," "For Queen and Country," and "The Wolves of Willoughby Chase." Zenith delivered the films to Atlantic in 1987.

Atlantic failed to pay the guaranteed minimum advances under the original agreements. . . .

[Subsequent] . . . negotiations resulted in a . . . Restructuring Agreement dated February 7, 1989 ("the Agreement"). . . .

The Agreement provided for AEG to reacquire the distribution rights to the three motion pictures for $6 million. . . .

AEG also gave Zenith a security agreement that granted a security interest in the motion pictures, and a UCC-1 financing statement, which Zenith filed in California, Indiana and New York. Zenith additionally recorded a copyright mortgage for each of the films with the United States Copyright Office on March 29, 1989. Shortly thereafter, on April 12, 1989, Zenith filed a certificate of copyright registration with respect to "Patty Hearst." Zenith claims that it was unnecessary to register the other two films, because they are foreign works exempt from registration pursuant to the "Berne Convention Act."

AEG made two payments to Zenith under the agreement: $250,000 on April 12 and $1.81 million on May 10, 1989. On July 28, 1989 AEG filed its chapter 11 petition. AEG subsequently filed this adversary proceeding to recover the $2,060,000 from Zenith as both preferences and fraudulent transfers pursuant to Bankruptcy Code §§ 547 and 548. . . .

### III. Analysis

#### A. Preferential Transfer

AEG seeks to recover, as avoidable preferential transfers, the April and May payments to Zenith by AEG. Bankruptcy Code § 547(b) authorizes the avoidance of a preferential transfer. . . .

Zenith . . . contends that it is secured, at least to the extent of the payments. . . .

#### 3. Perfection

Because the Agreement is a conditional sales contract, it is necessary to determine whether Zenith has a perfected security interest in each of the three films.[4] [n4 Zenith argues that its security interest is not limited to the copyright in the three films, but extends also to the prints of the films, contract and distribution rights, and to accounts relating thereto. The Court has not been made aware of any such interests that are not integral to the copyrights themselves. . . . ] The Debtor's hypothetical lien creditor status entitles it to prevail over the holder of an unperfected security interest under Bankruptcy Code § 544(a). The Court finds that Zenith perfected its interest in "Patty Hearst," but not in the two foreign works, "For Queen and Country" and "The Wolves of Willoughby Chase."

A security interest in a film is perfected under the United States Copyright Act, and not under the Uniform Commercial Code. . . . The Copyright Act preempts the UCC for security interests in films. Thus Zenith's filing of its UCC-1 gave it no assistance in perfecting its security interest in these motion pictures.

Perfection of a security interest in a motion picture, as in any copyright, requires two steps: the film must be registered with the United States Copyright Office, and the security interest must be recorded in the same office. Registration of a copyright is accomplished by the submission of an application to the copyright office together with a nominal filing fee and one or two copies of the work to be copyrighted.

Recordation of a security interest is also accomplished through the Copyright Office. The Copyright Act states, "any transfer of copyright ownership or other document pertaining to a copyright" may be recorded in the United States Copyright Office. Section 205(c) further provides that recordation acts as constructive notice of the facts stated in the document if the document specifies the work and if registration has been made for the work. The first to execute in compliance with § 205(c) prevails when conflicting transfers arise. The filing of a copyright mortgage with the United States Copyright Office constitutes perfection of the security interest as long as an underlying registration is also filed with the Office.

### a. "Patty Hearst"

It is undisputed that Zenith registered the film "Patty Hearst" on April 12, 1989, which was more than 90 days before the filing of this bankruptcy case.

. . .

AEG has not attacked this registration and recordation as a preference to an insider. Thus the Court assumes that Zenith's security interest in "Patty Hearst" is valid.

### b. Foreign films. . .

Zenith argues that the two foreign films are governed by the "Berne Convention Act," and that registration of the underlying works is not a prerequisite to perfection of its security interests. Presumably Zenith intends to refer to the Berne Convention for the Protection of Literary and Artistic Works (Paris Text, 1971) ("Berne Convention"). The Court disagrees and concludes that registration is required to perfect a security interest in a foreign film.

One of the principal substantive provisions of the Berne Convention is its provision that authors enjoy the same protection in any member country as the nationals of that country. The Convention provides certain rights superior to national law, however, which notably include the right to copyright protection without complying with any formalities. If this provision were applicable without restriction in the United States, Zenith might prevail in its argument that registration is not required as a condition for the perfection of a security interest in a foreign work.

Article VI of the United States Constitution provides: "This Constitution, and the Laws of the United States which shall be made in Pursuance thereof; and all Treaties made, or which shall be made, under the Authority of the United States, shall be the supreme Law of the Land . . . ." It is presumably under this constitutional provision that Zenith argues that the Berne Convention excuses it from registering its copyrights in the foreign films as a condition of perfecting its security interests. However, United States law on treaties is more complex.

Some treaties are self-executing, under United States treaty law, and some are not. A self-executing treaty creates rights for the nationals of a country that is a party to the convention without the need for any implementing domestic legislation. A treaty that is not self-executing, on the other hand, requires implementing domestic legislation to create rights thereunder for the citizens of the state party to the treaty. Whether a particular treaty is self-executing or not normally turns on the domestic law of the particular state party, and may vary from one state party to another.

At the time that it ratified the Berne Convention, the United States Senate determined that the treaty should not be self-executing in the United

States, and Congress enacted implementing legislation to give it effect in the United States. Thus the Berne Convention creates rights in United States law only to the extent that it is implemented through domestic legislation. The language of the convention alone does not excuse Zenith from complying with United States law to preserve its rights as a secured creditor in the foreign films here at issue, except to the extent that internal United States law so provides.

Section 411 is specific in providing rights under the Berne Convention without further compliance with United States law. It permits "actions of infringement of copyright in Berne Convention works" without registration. United States copyright law provides no other Berne Convention exemption, however, from complying with the registration provisions. Thus Zenith is required to comply with domestic United States law to perfect its security interest in these films. Additionally, section 205, which deals specifically with transfers, does not distinguish between foreign and domestic works. Since Zenith did not register the underlying foreign films, third parties were not put on notice of the copyright mortgages for the foreign films, and Zenith's interests remained unperfected. . . .

### In re AEG Acquisition Corp.
### 161 Bankr. 50 (BAP 9th Cir. 1993)

Jones, Bankruptcy Judge: . . .

*. . . Improper Perfection of Foreign Films*

The trial court determined that Zenith had failed to perfect its security interests in the foreign Films because the Films had not been registered with the United States Copyright Office. Zenith argues that the court erred because, under the Berne Convention for the Protection of Literary and Artistic Works (Paris Text 1971) ("Berne Convention"), registration is a prohibited formality.

Under United States law, recording a document in the Copyright Office gives all persons constructive notice of the information contained in the document only if the document identifies the work to which it relates and the work is registered. The Berne Convention provides that authors of foreign works enjoy the same protections of any member country as do nationals of that country. In addition, authors of Berne Convention works are entitled to copyright protections without complying with formalities.

Zenith argues that requiring registration is a "formality" which may not be imposed on a Berne Convention work. Zenith points out that registration is not a prerequisite to the bringing of an infringement action for a Berne Convention work, while it is a prerequisite for a work not covered by the Berne Convention. Zenith asserts that registration as a prerequisite to perfecting a security interest in a foreign film is a similarly prohibited formality.

As the trial court here noted, however, United States law provides no other exemptions for Berne Convention works. Moreover, 17 U.S.C. § 205, which deals with recordation of transfers of copyrights, makes no distinction between foreign and domestic works. We therefore hold that Zenith's failure to register the two foreign Films before AEG filed bankruptcy defeats its attempt to perfect its security interest in the copyrights. . . .

Based upon the foregoing, we affirm the trial court's decision.

The *AEG Acquisition* case is not the definitive word on whether remedies may be restricted to those who comply with formalities. It isn't, for two reasons. First, since the Berne Convention is not self-executing in the United States, these opinions were based on what the U.S. Copyright Act actually says, but they did not analyze whether the Act says what the Berne Convention actually requires it to say. Second, the use of copyrights as collateral for secured loans may not be a "right." It certainly isn't one of the rights identified in the U.S. Copyright Act, nor is it a right identified in the Berne Convention. If the use of copyrights as collateral for secured loans is not a "right," then requiring compliance with formalities in order to do so does not violate Berne's ban on requiring compliance with formalities in order to "exercise . . . rights."

Consider, though, a different – and probably more common – question: may the remedies of statutory damages and attorney's fees be conditioned on copyright registration, in cases where the infringed work is a foreign Berne country work?

Earlier (in Chapter 1) you read *Pepe (U.K.) Ltd. v. Ocean View Factory Outlet Corp.* That case, you will recall, held that a British company was not required to register its copyright to a British work before *filing* an infringement lawsuit in a U.S. court or before obtaining an order allowing the *seizure* of allegedly infringing goods. The decision was certainly correct on both points. The U.S. Copyright Act requires a copyright to be registered before an infringement lawsuit is filed, only if the work is a U.S. work:

### United States Copyright Act §411(a)

. . . no action for infringement of the copyright in any *United States work* shall be instituted until registration of the copyright claim has been made in accordance with this title. . . . [Emphasis added.]

Also, the section of the U.S. Copyright Act that authorizes seizures of allegedly infringing works does *not* require plaintiffs to register their copyrights before seizure orders are issued:

### United States Copyright Act §503(a)

At any time while an action under this title is pending, the court may order the impounding, on such terms as it may deem reasonable, of all copies or phonorecords claimed to have been made or used in violation of the copyright owner's exclusive rights, and of all plates, molds, matrices, masters, tapes, film negatives, or other articles by means of which such copies or phonorecords may be reproduced.

By contrast, the U.S. Copyright Act *does* limit the remedies of *statutory damages* and *attorney's fees* to plaintiffs who registered their copyrights:

### United States Copyright Act §412

In any action under this title, . . . no award of statutory damages or of attorney's fees, as provided by sections 504 and 505, shall be made for —

(1) any infringement of copyright in an unpublished work commenced before the effective date of its registration; or

(2) any infringement of copyright commenced after first publication of the work and before the effective date of its registration, unless such registration is made within three months after the first publication of the work.

Suppose that the plaintiff in the *Pepe (U.K.)* case won the case, but couldn't prove its damages or the defendant's profits, so it asked for statutory damages instead, and for attorney's fees. Would it be able to recover statutory damages and attorney's fees? Congress, apparently, thought not:

## House Statement on the Berne Convention Implementation Act of 1988
### 134 Cong. Rec. H10097 (daily ed. Oct. 12, 1988)

There is no real discrimination against American authors [in requiring them to register their copyrights, but not requiring foreign Berne country authors to do so] because foreign authors must also register in order to obtain the important benefits of the presumption of validity and statutory damages. In essence, all authors are treated equally.

If the plaintiff in the *Pepe (U.K.)* case could not prove (and thus could not recover) its own damages or the defendant's profits, and it could not recover statutory damages or even its attorney's fees, simply because it did not register its copyright, has the United States complied with Berne's requirement that "The enjoyment and the exercise of [the] rights [protected by national copyright laws] shall not be subject to any formality. . . " ?

## Football Ass'n Premier League v. Youtube
### 633 F.Supp 2d 159 (S.D.N.Y. 2009)

District Judge Louis L. Stanton

In this . . . action for copyright infringement . . . , defendants move for judgment on the pleadings dismissing plaintiffs' claims under the Act for . . . statutory damages on foreign works that have not been registered with the U.S. Copyright Office. . . .

Section 412 has no exception excusing foreign works from its mandate: it requires registration to obtain statutory damages for both domestic and foreign works. . . .

Plaintiffs contend that unless Section 412 is construed to exempt all foreign works from its directive it would violate two international agreements to which the U.S. is bound: the Berne Convention for the Protection of Literary and Artistic Works, an international copyright treaty which the U.S. joined in 1989, and the Agreement on Trade-Related Aspects of Intellectual Property Rights ("TRIPs"), a trade agreement the President made in 1994. . . .

None of the materials on which plaintiffs rely so alters Section 412's terms.

*1. The Berne Convention*

Plaintiffs assume that if Section 412 denied statutory damages on a foreign work for failure to register, it would violate "one of the most fundamental tenets of Berne, that 'the enjoyment and the exercise of [copyright] shall not be subject to any formality.'"

Congress rejected that assumption when it passed the Berne Convention Implementation Act of 1988 "to make the changes to the U.S. copyright law that are necessary for the United States to adhere to the Berne Convention." The Senate Judiciary Committee . . . "concluded that section 411(a) in its current form is incompatible" with Berne. Although the House of Representatives disagreed, Congress as a whole ultimately exempted foreign "Berne Convention works" from Section 411(a)'s registration requirement, while leaving it intact as to U.S. and other works. Thus, pursuant to that exemption, one could bring an infringement suit (although not obtain statutory damages) based on an unregistered foreign Berne Convention work.

Neither the House nor the Senate found that Section 412, which denies statutory damages for both foreign and domestic unregistered works, violated the Berne Convention. The Senate Judiciary Committee concluded that Section 412 and other provisions of the Copyright Act "do not condition the availability of all meaningful relief on registration, and therefore are not inconsistent with Berne."

Even if Section 412 were in conflict with the Berne Convention, Section 412 would be binding. The Berne Convention has no effect on U.S. law unless Congress so provides, and Congress left Section 412 "unaffected" by the Berne Convention Implementation Act.

*2. Agreement on Trade-Related Aspects of Intellectual Property Rights ("TRIPs")*

Nor would Section 412 be altered by TRIPs, one of the Uruguay Round Agreements on trade entered into by the President in 1994, even if applying it to foreign works conflicted with TRIPS. "TRIPs is plainly not a self-executing treaty", and Congress has mandated that U.S. laws such as Section 412 prevail if they conflict with . . . .

Thus, Section 412 must be construed according to its terms: subject to specified exceptions, it bars statutory damages for all foreign and domestic works not timely registered.

Plaintiffs' Copyright Act claims for statutory damages are dismissed with respect to all unregistered foreign works that do not fall within any such exception. . . .

Judge Stanton did a thorough job of determining what Congress *actually did* when it required registration, even of foreign works from Berne Convention countries, in order for successful copyright owners to recover statutory damages (and attorneys fees). But how thorough a job did he do in responding to the plaintiffs' argument that Congress didn't do what it *had to*, in order to comply with the United States' obligations under Berne and TRIPs? If the Football Association and its fellow plaintiffs were correct when they argued that Congress didn't do what it *had to*, is there anything they can do about that now? This question will be explored in Chapter 5, where we will look at a case in which Irish songwriters (and other Europeans) successfully contended that Congress did something that Berne and TRIPs prohibited it from doing.

### 3. Limitations on exclusive rights that may be imposed by free trade treaties

In some countries, national treatment – or at least treatment pursuant to their national copyright laws – actually is prohibited by overriding legal principles. These overriding legal principles are imposed by free trade treaties. This issue has arisen in cases within the European Union. It is an important issue that affects common copyright transactions, even transactions involving U.S. copyright owners, and it will be considered in Chapter 5.

## D. Potential eligibility for treatment more favorable than national treatment

In order to comply with the minimum standards required by certain copyright treaties, including the Berne Convention, some countries occasionally grant *greater* protection to foreign works than to works from their own country. They are able to do so, because the minimum standards required by treaties are applicable only to foreign works, not to domestic works. This is how the Berne Convention does this:

### Berne Convention Article 5(1)

Authors shall enjoy, in respect of works for which they are protected under this Convention, *in countries of the Union other than the country of origin*, the rights which their respective laws do now or may hereafter grant to their nationals, as well as the rights specially granted by this Convention. [Emphasis added.]

The United States is one of the countries that has taken advantage of this leeway to provide less protection to American works than to works from other Berne countries. The U.S. has done so in two important ways.

First, as you read above, it continues to require registration of copyrights for American works, though not for foreign works. Copyright Act §411(a).

Second, the United States restored the copyrights of certain foreign works that were in the public domain in the U.S. But it did not restore the copyrights of any American works that were in the public domain.

### Copyright Act §104A(h)(8)(a)

[To be eligible for restoration] [t]he "source country" of a restored work [must be] . . . a nation other than the United States. . . .

Copyright restoration will be considered in detail in Chapter 6.

## E. Potential applicability of law of country-of-origin or country where transaction occurred

Although the general rule is that international copyright matters are decided under the law of the country where protection is sought, that is not always the case. As to certain issues, the applicable law may be the law of the work's country-of-origin. And as to other issues, it may be the law of the country where a transaction was entered into. These issues include the duration of copyright, and ownership of copyright. In some countries, duration is affected by the Rule of the Shorter Term; and ownership, especially following a transfer, may be a contract law – rather than copyright law – issue.

## 1. Duration of copyright issue: Rule of the Shorter Term

The duration of copyright for works of foreign origin is treated in a unique way, in some countries. All countries apply their own law (as you would expect from the usual rule of national treatment), *if* their own duration is *shorter* than the duration in the work's country-of-origin. However, *some* countries apply the law of the work's country-of-origin, rather than their own, *if* the duration in the work's country-of-origin is *shorter* than their own. Countries that do this apply what is known as the "Rule of the Shorter Term."

The "Rule of the Shorter Term" provides that the duration of copyright is the term in the country where protection is sought, *or* the term in the work's country-of-origin, *whichever is shorter*. Countries that choose to apply this Rule – despite the usual rule that national treatment must be provided to foreign works – are permitted to do so by both Berne and the UCC.

The Rule of the Shorter Term will be covered in some detail in Chapter 6. Until then, it is sufficient to note that in countries that apply that Rule, the law applied to determine the duration of copyright for a foreign work may be the law of that work's country-of-origin, rather than the law of the country where protection for that work is sought.

## 2. Ownership of copyright issues

So far you've read authority for the proposition that whether a work of a particular type is protected by copyright is determined by the law of the country where protection is sought and for the proposition that whether a particular use is infringing (or requires the payment of royalties) also is determined by the law of the country where protection is sought. What law, however, should be applied to determine *who owns* the copyright to the work for which protection is sought? The answer to this question is important in at least two different contexts (both, common):

- Someone in the United States may want to obtain a license to use a work of foreign origin in the U.S. If two different people or companies both claim to be the owner of the work's copyright, which country's law determines who the actual owner is in the United States?
- If someone in the United States is sued for infringing the copyright to a work of foreign origin, which country's law determines whether the plaintiff is the actual owner of the copyright to the allegedly infringed work?

Neither Berne nor the UCC is explicit about which country's law should be applied.

### Berne Convention Article 5

(1) *Authors shall enjoy*, . . . in countries of the Union other than the country of origin, *the rights* which their respective laws do now or may hereafter grant to their nationals. . . .

(2) The enjoyment and the *exercise* of these rights . . . , . . . the *extent of protection*, as well as the *means of redress* afforded to the author to protect his rights, shall be governed exclusively by the laws of the country where protection is claimed. [Emphasis added.]

### Universal Copyright Convention Article II (1)

Published works of nationals of any Contracting State and works first published in that State shall enjoy in each other Contracting State the *same protection* as that other State accords to works of its nationals first published in its own territory. . . . [Emphasis added.]

Even in the United States (where copyright case law is abundant), the question of which country's law should be applied to determine who owns a copyright wasn't answered definitively until 1998 – and it was answered "definitively" at that time only if you agree that the opinion of one federal appellate court panel definitively determines the law.

### Itar-Tass Russian News Agency v. Russian Kurier, Inc.
### 153 F.3d 82 (2nd Cir. 1998)

Jon O. Newman, Circuit Judge:

This appeal primarily presents issues concerning the choice of law in international copyright cases and the substantive meaning of Russian copyright law as to the respective rights of newspaper reporters and newspaper publishers. The conflicts issue is which country's law applies to issues of copyright ownership and to issues of infringement. The primary substantive issue under Russian copyright law is whether a newspaper publishing company has an interest sufficient to give it standing to sue for copying the text of individual articles appearing in its newspapers, or whether complaint about such copying may be made only by the reporters who authored the articles. Defendants-appellants Russian Kurier, Inc. ("Kurier") and Oleg Pogrebnoy (collectively "the Kurier defendants") appeal from the March 25, 1997, judgment of the District Court for the Southern District of New York (John G. Koeltl, Judge) enjoining them from copying articles that have appeared or will appear in publications of the plaintiffs-appellees, mainly Russian newspapers and a Russian news agency, and awarding the appellees substantial damages for copyright infringement.

On the conflicts issue, we conclude that, with respect to the Russian plaintiffs, Russian law determines the ownership and essential nature of the copyrights alleged to have been infringed and that United States law determines whether those copyrights have been infringed in the United States and, if so, what remedies are available. We also conclude that Russian law, which explicitly excludes newspapers from a work-for-hire doctrine, vests exclusive ownership interests in newspaper articles in the journalists who wrote the articles, not in the newspaper employers who compile their writings. We further conclude that to the extent that Russian law accords newspaper publishers an interest distinct from the copyright of the newspaper reporters, the publishers' interest, like the usual ownership interest in a compilation, extends to the publishers' original selection and arrangement of the articles, and does not entitle the publishers to damages for copying the texts of articles contained in a newspaper compilation. We therefore reverse the judgment to the extent that it granted the newspapers relief for copying the texts of the articles. However, because one non-newspaper plaintiff-appellee is entitled to some injunctive relief and damages and other plaintiffs-appellees may be entitled to some, perhaps considerable, relief, we also remand for further consideration of this lawsuit.

## Background

The lawsuit concerns Kurier, a Russian language weekly newspaper with a circulation in the New York area of about 20,000. It is published in New York City by defendant Kurier. Defendant Pogrebnoy is president and sole shareholder of Kurier and editor-in-chief of Kurier. The plaintiffs include corporations that publish, daily or weekly, major Russian language newspapers in Russia and Russian language magazines in Russia or Israel; Itar-Tass Russian News Agency ("Itar-Tass"), formerly known as the Telegraph Agency of the Soviet Union (TASS), a wire service and news gathering company centered in Moscow, functioning similarly to the Associated Press; and the Union of Journalists of Russia ("UJR"), the professional writers union of accredited print and broadcast journalists of the Russian Federation.

The Kurier defendants do not dispute that Kurier has copied about 500 articles that first appeared in the plaintiffs' publications or were distributed by Itar-Tass. The copied material, though extensive, was a small percentage of the total number of articles published in Kurier. The Kurier defendants also do not dispute how the copying occurred: articles from the plaintiffs' publications, sometimes containing headlines, pictures, bylines, and graphics, in addition to text, were cut out, pasted on layout sheets, and sent to Kurier's printer for photographic reproduction and printing in the pages of Kurier.

Most significantly, the Kurier defendants also do not dispute that, with one exception, they had not obtained permission from any of the plaintiffs to copy the articles that appeared in Kurier. Pogrebnoy claimed at trial to have received permission from the publisher of one newspaper, but his claim was rejected by the District Court at trial. Pogrebnoy also claimed that he had obtained permission from the authors of six of the copied articles. The District Court made no finding as to whether this testimony was credible, since authors' permission was not pertinent to the District Court's view of the legal issues.

### Preliminary injunction ruling.

After a hearing in May 1995, the District Court issued a preliminary injunction, prohibiting the Kurier defendants from copying the "works" of four plaintiff news organizations. Since the Court's analysis framed the key issue that would be considered at trial and is raised on appeal, the Court's opinion and the Russian statutory provisions relied on need to be explained.

Preliminarily, the Court ruled that the request for a preliminary injunction concerned articles published after March 13, 1995, the date that Russia acceded to the Berne Convention. The Court then ruled that the copied works were "Berne Convention works," 17 U.S.C. § 101, and that the plaintiffs' rights were to be determined according to Russian copyright law.

The Court noted that under Russian copyright law authors of newspaper articles retain the copyright in their articles unless there has been a contractual assignment to their employer or some specific provision of law provides that the author's rights vest in the employer. Since the defendants alleged no claim of a contractual assignment, the Court next considered the provision of the 1993 Russian Federation Law on Copyright and Neighboring Rights ("Russian Copyright Law") (World Intellectual Property Organization (WIPO) translation) concerning what the United States Copyrights Act calls "works made for hire," 17 U.S.C. § 201(b). See Russian Copyright Law, Art. 14(2). That provision gives employers the exclusive right to "exploit" the "service-related work" produced by employees in the scope of their employment, absent some contractual arrangement. However, the Court noted, Article 14(4) specifies that subsection 2 does not apply to various categories of works, including newspapers. Accepting the view of plaintiffs' expert, Professor Vratislav Pechota, Judge Koeltl therefore ruled that the Russian version of the work-for-hire doctrine in Article 14(2), though exempting newspapers, applies to press agencies, like Itar-Tass.

Turning to the rights of the newspapers, Judge Koeltl relied on Article 11, captioned "Copyright of Compiler of Collections and Other Works." This Article contains two sub-sections. Article 11(1) specifies the rights of compilers generally:

> The author of a collection or any other composite work (compiler) shall enjoy copyright in the selection or arrangement of subject matter that he has made insofar as that selection or arrangement is the result of a creative effort of compilation.
>
> The compiler shall enjoy copyright subject to respect for the rights of the authors of each work included in the composite work.
>
> Each of the authors of the works included in the composite work shall have the right to exploit his own work independently of the composite work unless the author's contract provides otherwise. . . . .

Article 11(2), the interpretation of which is critical to this appeal, specifies the rights of compilers of those works that are excluded from the work-for-hire provision of Article 14(2):

> The exclusive right to exploit encyclopedias, encyclopedic dictionaries, collections of scientific works – published in either one or several installments – newspapers, reviews and other periodical publications shall belong to the editor thereof. The editor shall have the right to mention his name or to demand such mention whenever the said publications are exploited.
>
> The authors of the works included in the said publications shall retain the exclusive rights to exploit their works independently of the publication of the whole work. Art. 11(2).

In another translation of the Russian Copyright Law, which was in evidence at the trial, the last phrase of Article 11(2) was rendered "independently from the publication as a whole." Russian Copyright Law, Art. 11(2) (Newton Davis translation). Because the parties' experts focused on the phrase "as a whole" in the Davis translation of Article 11(2), we will rely on the Davis translation for the rendering of this key phrase of Article 11(2), but all other references to the Russian Copyright Law will be to the WIPO translation.

The District Court acknowledged, as the plaintiffs' expert had stated, that considerable scholarly debate existed in Russia as to the nature of a publisher's right "in a work as a whole." Judge Koeltl accepted Professor Pechota's view that the newspaper could prevent infringing activity "sufficient to interfere with the publisher's interest in the integrity of the work." Without endeavoring to determine what extent of copying would "interfere with" the "integrity of the work," Judge Koeltl concluded that a preliminary injunction was warranted because what Kurier had copied was "the creative effort of the newspapers in the compilation of articles including numerous articles for the same issues, together with headlines and photographs." The Court's preliminary injunction opinion left it unclear whether at trial the plaintiffs could obtain damages only for copying the newspapers' creative efforts as a compiler, such as the selection and arrangement of articles, the creation of headlines, and the layout of text and graphics, or also for copying the text of individual articles.

*Expert testimony at trial.*

At trial, this unresolved issue was the focus of conflicting expert testimony. The plaintiffs' expert witness at trial was Michael Newcity, coordinator for the Center for Slavic, Eurasian and East European Studies at Duke University and an adjunct member of the faculty at the Duke University Law School. He opined that Article 11(2) gave the newspapers rights to redress copying not only of the publication "as a whole," but also of individual articles. He acknowledged that the reporters retained copyrights in the articles that they authored, but stated that Article 11(2) created a regime of parallel exclusive rights in both the newspaper publisher and the reporter. He rejected the contention that exclusive rights could not exist in two parties, pointing out that co-authors shared exclusive rights to their joint work.

Newcity offered two considerations in support of his position. First, he cited the predecessor of Article 11(2), Article 485 of the Russian Civil Code of 1964. That provision was similar to Article 11(2), with one change that became the subject of major disagreement among the expert witnesses. Article 485 had given compilers, including newspaper publishers, the right to exploit their works "as a whole." The 1993 revision deleted "as a whole" from the first paragraph of the predecessor of Article 11(2), where it had modified the scope of the compiler's right, and moved the phrase to the second paragraph of revised Article 11(2), where it modifies the reserved right of the authors of articles within a compilation to exploit their works "independently of the publication as a whole."

Though Newcity opined that even under Article 485, reprinting of "one or two or three, at most," articles from a newspaper would have constituted infringement of the copyright "as a whole," he rested his reading of Article 11(2) significantly on the fact that the 1993 revision dropped the phrase "as a whole" from the paragraph that specified the publisher's right. This deletion, he contended, eliminated whatever ambiguity might have existed in the first paragraph of Article 485.

Second, Newcity referred to an opinion of the Judicial Chamber for Informational Disputes of the President of the Russian Federation ("Informational Disputes Chamber"), issued on June 8, 1995. That opinion had been sought by the editor-in-chief of one of the plaintiffs in this litigation, Moskovskie Novosti (Moscow News), who specifically called the tribunal's attention to the pending litigation between Russian media organizations and the publisher of Kurier. The Informational Disputes Chamber stated, in response to one of the questions put to it, "In the event of a violation of its rights, including the improper printing of one or two articles, the publisher [of a newspaper] has the right to petition a court for defense of its rights."

Defendants' experts presented a very different view of the rights of newspapers. Professor Peter B. Maggs of the University of Illinois, Urbana-Champaign, College of Law, testifying by deposition, pointed out that Article 11(2) gives authors the exclusive rights to their articles and accords newspaper publishers only the "exclusive rights to the publication as a whole, because that's the only thing not reserved to the authors." He opined that a newspaper's right to use of the compiled work "as a whole" would be infringed by the copying of an entire issue of a newspaper and probably by copying a substantial part of one issue, but not by the copying of a few articles, since the copyright in the articles belongs to the reporters. He also disagreed with Newcity's contention that exclusive rights to individual articles belonged simultaneously to both the newspaper and the reporter. Exclusive rights, he maintained, cannot be held by two people, except in the case of co-authors, who have jointly held rights against the world.

The defendants' first expert witness at trial was Michael Solton, who has worked in Moscow and Washington as an associate of the Steptoe & Johnson law firm. Under Article 11, he testified, authors retain exclusive rights to their articles in compilations, the compiler acquires a copyright in the selection and creative arrangement of materials in the compilation, and a newspaper publisher typically acquires the limited rights of the compiler by assignment from the compiler. The publisher, he said, does not acquire any rights to the individual articles. Solton declined to attach any significance to the decision issued by the Informational Disputes Chamber because, he explained, the bylaws of that body accord it authority only over limited matters concerning the mass media and explicitly preclude it from adjudicating matters that Russian law refers to courts of the Russian Federation, such as copyright law.

The defendants' second expert trial witness was Svetlana Rozina, a partner of the Lex International law firm, who has consulted for the Russian government. She wrote the first draft of what became the 1993 revision of the Russian Copyright Law. She also testified that authors of works in compilations retain the exclusive right to their works, and that publishers of compilations do not have any rights to individual articles. Turning to the change in the placement of the phrase "as a whole" from Article 11(1) to Article 11(2), she explained that no substantive change was intended; the shift was made "for the purpose of Russian grammar." She also agreed with Solton that the Informational Disputes Chamber renders advice on matters concerning freedom of mass information and lacks the competence to adjudicate issues of copyright law.

*Trial ruling.*

The District Court resolved the dispute among the experts by accepting Newcity's interpretation of Russian copyright law. As he had previously ruled in granting the preliminary injunction, Judge Koeltl recognized that newspapers acquire no rights to individual articles by virtue of Article 14 since the Russian version of the work-for-hire doctrine is inapplicable to newspapers. Nevertheless, Judge Koeltl accepted Newcity's view of Article 11, relying on both the movement of the phrase "as a whole" from the first paragraph of Article 11(2) to the second paragraph of Article 11(2), and the opinion of the Informational Disputes Chamber. He also reasoned that publishers have "the real economic incentive to prevent wholesale unauthorized copying," and that, in the absence of assignments of rights to individual articles, widespread copying would occur if publishers could not prevent Kurier's infringements.

The District Court estimated Kurier's profits during the relevant years at $2 million and found that 25 percent of these profits were attributable to the copied articles. The Court therefore awarded the plaintiffs $500,000 in actual damages against Kurier and Pogrebnoy. The Court also ruled that the plaintiffs were entitled to statutory damages with respect to 28 articles for which the plaintiffs had obtained United States copyright registrations. The Court found that the registered articles had originally appeared in 15 different publications and concluded that the plaintiffs were entitled to 15 awards of statutory damages. The Court found the violations willful, see 17 U.S.C. §504(c)(1), and set each statutory award at $2,700. However, to avoid duplicative recovery, the Court ruled that the actual and statutory damages could not be aggregated and afforded the plaintiffs their choice of whether to receive statutory damages (offsetting the statutory award from the actual damages award) or actual damages. The Court awarded $3,934 in total damages against defendant Linco Printing, which prints Kurier; this sum comprised actual damages of $1,017, reduced to $934 to avoid partial duplication with statutory damages, plus $3,000 in statutory damages.

*Discussion*

I.  *Choice of Law*

The threshold issue concerns the choice of law for resolution of this dispute. That issue was not initially considered by the parties, all of whom turned directly to Russian law for resolution of the case. Believing that the conflicts issue merited consideration, we requested supplemental briefs from the parties and appointed Professor William F. Patry as Amicus Curiae. Prof. Patry has submitted an extremely helpful brief on the choice of law issue.

Choice of law issues in international copyright cases have been largely ignored in the reported decisions and dealt with rather cursorily by most commentators. Examples pertinent to the pending appeal are those decisions involving a work created by the employee of a foreign corporation. Several courts have applied the United States work-for-hire doctrine, see 17 U.S.C. § 201(b), without explicit consideration of the conflicts issue. See, e.g., *Aldon Accessories Ltd. v. Spiegel, Inc.*, 738 F.2d 548, 551-53 (2d Cir. 1984) (U.S. law applied to determine if statuettes crafted abroad were works for hire); *Dae Han Video Productions, Inc. v. Kuk Dong Oriental Food, Inc.*, 1990 U.S.Dist.LEXIS 18329, 19 U.S.P.Q.2D (BNA) 1294 (D. Md. 1990) (U.S. law applied to determine if scripts written abroad were works for hire); *P & D International v. Halsey Publishing Co.*, 672 F.Supp. 1429, 1435-36 (S.D.Fla. 1987) (U.S. work for hire law assumed to apply). Other courts have applied foreign law. See *Frink America, Inc. v. Champion Road Machinery Ltd.*, 961 F.Supp. 398 (N.D.N.Y. 1997) (Canadian copyright law applied on issue of ownership); *Greenwich Film Productions v. DRG Records Inc.*, 1992 U.S.Dist.LEXIS 14770, 1992 WL 279, at *357 (S.D.N.Y. 1992) (French law applied to determine ownership of right to musical work commissioned in France for French film); *Dae Han Video Production Inc. v. Dong San Chun*, 1990 U.S.Dist.LEXIS 18496, 17 U.S.P.Q.2D (BNA) 1306, 1310 n.6 (E.D. Va. 1990) (foreign law relied on to determine that alleged licensor lacks rights); see also *Autoskill, Inc. v. National Educational Support Systems, Inc.*, 994 F.2d 1476, 1489 n.16 (10th Cir. 1993) (U.S. work for hire law applied where claim that contrary Canadian law should apply was belatedly raised and for that reason not considered); *Pepe (U.K.) Ltd. v. Grupo Pepe Ltda.*, 1992 U.S.Dist.LEXIS 17144, 24 U.S.P.Q.2D (BNA) 1354, 1356 (S.D.Fla. 1992) (congruent foreign and U.S. law both applied). In none of these cases, however, was the issue of choice of law explicitly adjudicated. The conflicts issue was identified but ruled not necessary to be resolved in *Greenwich Film Productions S.A. v. D.R.G. Records, Inc.*, 1992 U.S.Dist.LEXIS 14770, 25 U.S.P.Q.2D (BNA) 1435, 1437-38 (S.D.N.Y. 1992).

The Nimmer treatise briefly (and perhaps optimistically) suggests that conflicts issues "have rarely proved troublesome in the law of copyright." See *Nimmer on Copyright* § 17.05 (1998) ("Nimmer") (footnote omitted). Relying on the "national treatment" principle of the Berne Convention and the Universal Copyright Convention ("U.C.C."), Nimmer asserts, correctly in our view, that "an author who is a national of one of the member states of either Berne or the U.C.C., or one who first publishes his work in any such member state, is entitled to the same copyright protection in each other member state as such other state accords to its own nationals." *Id.* (footnotes omitted). Nimmer then somewhat overstates the national treatment principle: "The applicable law is the copyright law of the state in which the infringement occurred, not that of the state of which the author is a national, or in which the work is first published." *Id.* (footnote omitted). The difficulty with this broad statement is that it subsumes under the phrase "applicable law" the law concerning two distinct issues: ownership and substantive rights, i.e., scope of protection. Another commentator has also broadly stated the principle of national treatment, but described its application in a way that does not necessarily cover issues of ownership. "The principle of national treatment also means that both the question of whether the right exists and the question of the scope of the right are to be answered in accordance with the law of the country where the protection is claimed." S.M. Stewart, *International Copyright and Neighboring Rights* § 3.17 (2d ed. 1989). We agree with the view of the Amicus that the Convention's principle of national treatment simply assures that if the law of the country of infringement applies to the scope of substantive copyright protection, that law will be applied uniformly to foreign and domestic authors. See *Murray v. British Broadcasting Corp.*, 906 F.Supp. 858 (S.D.N.Y. 1995), aff'd, 81 F.3d 287 (1996).

  *Source of conflicts rules.*

Our analysis of the conflicts issue begins with consideration of the source of law for selecting a conflicts rule. Though Nimmer turns directly to the Berne Convention and the U.C.C., we think that step moves too quickly past the Berne Convention Implementation Act of 1988, Pub L. 100-568, 102 Stat. 2853, 17 U.S.C.A. § 101 note. Section 4(a)(3) of the Act amends Title 17 to provide: "No right or interest in a work eligible for protection under this title may be claimed by virtue of . . . the provisions of the Berne Convention . . . . Any rights in a work eligible for protection under this title that derive from this title . . . shall not be expanded or reduced by virtue of . . . the provisions of the Berne Convention." 17 U.S.C. § 104(c).

We start our analysis with the Copyright Act itself, which contains no provision relevant to the pending case concerning conflicts issues.[10] [n10 The recently added provision concerning copyright in "restored works," those that are in the public domain because of noncompliance with formalities of United States copyright law, contains an explicit subsection vesting

123

ownership of a restored work "in the author or initial rightholder of the work as determined by the law of the *source country* of the work." 17 U.S.C. § 104A(b) (emphasis added); see *id.* § 104A(h)(8) (defining "source country"). This provision could be interpreted to be an example of the general conflicts approach we take in this opinion to copyright ownership issues, or an exception to some different approach. See Jane C. Ginsburg, *Ownership of Electronic Rights and the Private International Law of Copyright*, 22 Colum.-VLA J.L. & Arts 165, 171 (1998). We agree with Prof. Ginsburg and with the amicus, Prof. Patry, that section 104A(b) should not be understood to state an exception to any otherwise applicable conflicts rule.] We therefore fill the interstices of the Act by developing federal common law on the conflicts issue. In doing so, we are entitled to consider and apply principles of private international law, which are "'part of our law.'"

The choice of law applicable to the pending case is not necessarily the same for all issues. See *Restatement (Second) of Conflict of Laws* § 222 ("The courts have long recognized that they are not bound to decide all issues under the local law of a single state."). We consider first the law applicable to the issue of copyright ownership.

*Conflicts rule for issues of ownership.*

Copyright is a form of property, and the usual rule is that the interests of the parties in property are determined by the law of the state with "the most significant relationship" to the property and the parties. The *Restatement* recognizes the applicability of this principle to intangibles such as "a literary idea." Since the works at issue were created by Russian nationals and first published in Russia, Russian law is the appropriate source of law to determine issues of ownership of rights. That is the well-reasoned conclusion of the Amicus Curiae, Prof. Patry, and the parties in their supplemental briefs are in agreement on this point. In terms of the United States Copyrights Act and its reference to the Berne Convention, Russia is the "country of origin" of these works, see 17 U.S.C. §101 (definition of "country of origin" of Berne Convention work); Berne Convention, Art. 5(4), although "country of origin" might not always be the appropriate country for purposes of choice of law concerning ownership.[11] [n11 *In deciding that the law of the country of origin determines the ownership of copyright, we consider only initial ownership, and have no occasion to consider choice of law issues concerning assignments of rights.* [Emphasis added.]]

To whatever extent we look to the Berne Convention itself as guidance in the development of federal common law on the conflicts issue, we find nothing to alter our conclusion. The Convention does not purport to settle issues of ownership, with one exception not relevant to this case.[12] [n12 The Berne Convention expressly provides that "ownership of copyright in a cinematographic work shall be a matter for legislation in the country where protection is claimed." Berne Convention, Art. 14bis(2)(a). With respect to other works, this provision could be understood to have any of three meanings. First, it could carry a negative implication that for other works, ownership is not to be determined by legislation in the country where protection is claimed. Second, it could be thought of as an explicit assertion for films of a general principle already applicable to other works. Third, it could be a specific provision for films that was adopted without an intention to imply anything about other works. In the absence of any indication that either the first or second meanings were intended, we prefer the third understanding.]

See Jane C. Ginsburg, *Ownership of Electronic Rights and the Private International Law of Copyright*, 22 Colum.-VLA J.L. & Arts 165, 167-68 (1998) (The Berne Convention "provides that the law of the country where protection is claimed defines what rights are protected, the scope of the protection, and the available remedies; the treaty does not supply a choice of law rule for determining ownership.").

Selection of Russian law to determine copyright ownership is, however, subject to one procedural qualification. Under United States law, an owner (including one determined according to foreign law) may sue for infringement in a United States court only if it meets the standing test of 17 U.S.C. § 501(b), which accords standing only to the legal or beneficial owner of an "exclusive right."

*Conflicts rule for infringement issues.*

On infringement issues, the governing conflicts principle is usually *lex loci delicti*, the doctrine generally applicable to torts. We have implicitly adopted that approach to infringement claims, applying United States copyright law to a work that was unprotected in its country of origin. See *Hasbro Bradley, Inc. v. Sparkle Toys, Inc.*, 780 F.2d 189, 192-93 (2d Cir. 1985). In the pending case, the place of the tort is plainly the United States. To whatever extent *lex loci delicti* is to be considered only one part of a broader "interest" approach, United States law would still apply to infringement issues, since not only is this country the place of the tort, but also the defendant is a United States corporation.

The division of issues, for conflicts purposes, between ownership and infringement issues will not always be as easily made as the above discussion implies. If the issue is the relatively straightforward one of which of two contending parties owns a copyright, the issue is unquestionably an ownership issue, and the law of the country with the closest relationship to the work will apply to settle the ownership dispute. But in some cases, including the pending one, the issue is not simply who owns the copyright but also what is the nature of the ownership interest. Yet as a court considers the nature of an ownership interest, there is some risk that it will too readily shift the inquiry over to the issue of whether an alleged copy has infringed the asserted copyright. Whether a copy infringes depends in part on the scope of the interest of the copyright owner. Nevertheless, though the issues are related, the nature of a copyright interest is an issue distinct from the issue of whether the copyright has been infringed. The pending case is one that requires consideration not simply of who owns an interest, but, as to the newspapers, the nature of the interest that is owned.

*II. Determination of Ownership Rights Under Russian Law*

Since United States law permits suit only by owners of "an exclusive right under a copyright," 17 U.S.C. § 501(b), we must first determine whether any of the plaintiffs own an exclusive right. That issue of ownership, as we have indicated, is to be determined by Russian law. . . .

Under Article 14 of the Russian Copyright Law, Itar-Tass is the owner of the copyright interests in the articles written by its employees. However, Article 14(4) excludes newspapers from the Russian version of the work-for-hire doctrine. The newspaper plaintiffs, therefore, must locate their ownership rights, if any, in some other source of law. They rely on Article 11. The District Court upheld their position, apparently recognizing in the newspaper publishers "exclusive" rights to the articles, even though, by virtue of Article 11(2), the reporters also retained "exclusive" rights to these articles.

Having considered all of the views presented by the expert witnesses, we conclude that the defendants' experts are far more persuasive as to the meaning of Article 11. . . . As the defendants' experts testified, Article 11 lets authors of newspaper articles sue for infringement of their rights in the text of their articles, and lets newspaper publishers sue for wholesale copying of all of the newspaper or for copying any portions of the newspaper that embody their selection, arrangement, and presentation of articles (including headlines) copying that infringes their ownership interest in the compilation. . . .

Nor can the District Court's conclusion be supported by its observation that extensive copying of newspapers will ensue unless newspapers are permitted to secure redress for the copying of individual articles. In the first place, copying of articles may always be prevented at the behest of the authors of the articles or their assignees. Second, the newspapers may well be entitled to prevent copying of the protectable elements of their compilations. Lastly, even if authors lack sufficient economic incentive to bring individual suits, as the District Court apprehended, Russian copyright law authorizes the creation of organizations "for the collective administration of the economic rights of authors . . . in cases where the individual exercise thereof is hampered by difficulties of a practical nature." Russian Copyright Law, Art. 44(1). Indeed, UJR, the reporters' organization, may well be able in this litigation to protect the rights of the reporters whose articles were copied by Kurier.

*Relief.*

Our disagreement with the District Court's interpretation of Article 11 does not mean, however, that the defendants may continue copying with impunity. In the first place, Itar-Tass, as a press agency, is within the scope of Article 14, and, unlike the excluded newspapers, enjoys the benefit of the Russian version of the work-for-hire doctrine. Itar-Tass is therefore entitled to injunctive relief to prevent unauthorized copying of its articles and to damages for such copying, and the judgment is affirmed as to this plaintiff.

Furthermore, the newspaper plaintiffs, though not entitled to relief for the copying of the text of the articles they published, may well be entitled to injunctive relief and damages if they can show that Kurier infringed the publishers' ownership interests in the newspaper compilations. Because the District Court upheld the newspapers' right to relief for copying the text of the articles, it had no occasion to consider what relief the newspapers might be entitled to by reason of Kurier's copying of the newspapers' creative efforts in the selection, arrangement, or display of the articles. Since Kurier's photocopying reproduced not only the text of articles but also headlines and graphic materials as they originally appeared in the plaintiffs' publication, it is likely that on remand the newspaper plaintiffs will be able to obtain some form of injunctive relief and some damages. On these infringement issues, as we have indicated, United States law will apply.

Finally, there remains for consideration what relief, if any, might be awarded to UJR, acting on behalf of any of its members whose articles have been copied. In its opinion granting the newspapers a preliminary injunction, the District Court noted that the plaintiffs had not "established the union's organizational standing to sue to enforce the rights of its members," an issue the Court expected would be considered later in the lawsuit. In its ruling on the merits, the District Court ruled that the UJR had standing to sue on behalf of its members. However, the Court noted that UJR sought only injunctive relief and then ruled that since UJR declined to furnish a list of its members, the Court was unable to frame an injunction that would be narrowly tailored and sufficient to give the defendants notice of its scope.

In view of our conclusion that the newspaper plaintiffs may not secure relief for the copying of the text of any articles as such, it will now become appropriate for the District Court on remand to revisit the issue of whether relief might be fashioned in favor of UJR on behalf of the authors. Despite UJR's unwillingness to disclose its entire membership list, it might be possible to frame some form of injunctive relief that affords protection for those author-members that UJR is willing to identify. And UJR should now be given an opportunity to amend its prayer for relief to state whatever claim it might have to collect damages for the benefit of its member-authors whose rights have been infringed. Finally, the District Court should consider the appropriateness and feasibility of giving some form of notice (perhaps at the defendants' expense) that is calculated to alert the authors of the infringed articles to their right to intervene in this lawsuit. Such notice might, for example, be addressed generally to the group of reporters currently employed at each of the plaintiff newspapers.

In view of the reckless conduct of the defendants in the flagrant copying that infringed the rights of Itar-Tass, the rights of the authors, and very likely some aspects of the limited protectable rights of the newspapers, we will leave the injunction in force until such time as the District Court has had an opportunity, on remand, to modify the injunction consistent with this opinion and with such further rulings as the District Court may make in light of this opinion.

### Conclusion

Accordingly, we affirm the judgment to the extent that it granted relief to Itar-Tass, we reverse to the extent that the judgment granted relief to the other plaintiffs, and we remand for further proceedings. . . .

Based on the *Itar-Tass* decision, which country's law determines who owns the U.S. copyright to a work of foreign origin?

The following decision illustrates how French law approaches the question of *who* owns the copyright to a work of foreign origin. At first blush, it appears that French law answers the question differently than U.S. law (or at least differently than Judge Newman did in the *Itar-Tass* case). But as you read this next decision, consider whether the result might have been different, even in France, if the right asserted by the plaintiffs had been an economic right rather than a "moral right." That is, suppose that the next case did not involve the colorization of the American movie "Asphalt Jungle" (as it did), but instead involved the question of who was entitled *to be paid* for broadcast rights by a French television station that broadcast an original black and white version of the movie (so that no part of the case involved colorization or moral rights).

## Turner Entertainment Co. v. Huston
## Court of Appeal of Versailles France (1994)

1.  The cinematographic work entitled "Asphalt Jungle" was produced in 1950 in the United States by the Metro Goldwyn Mayer (MGM) company, a division of Loew's Inc. The film was shot in black and white by the late John Huston, a movie director of American nationality, at the time bound by a contract of employment to Loew's Inc., and co-author of the screenplay with Ben Maddow, bound to the same company by a contract as a salaried writer.

2.  On 2nd May 1950, Loew's Inc. obtained from the U.S. Copyright Office a certificate of registration of its rights to the film. This registration was duly renewed in 1977. On 26th September 1986 the benefit of this registration was transferred to the Turner Entertainment Co. by virtue of a merger with MGM, including transfer of the ownership of MGM's movie library and connected rights.

3.  The Turner company had the movie colorized, an operation which on 20th June 1988 resulted in registration of a copyright application, and it enabled the Fifth French Television Channel (La Cinq) to announce that it would broadcast this colorized version at 8:30 p.m. on 26th June 1988.

4.  The broadcast was objected to by John Huston's heirs, Angelica, Daniel and Walter Huston, who were subsequently joined by Mr Ben Maddow, the Societe des Auteurs et Compositeurs Dramatiques (SACD), the Societe des Realisateurs de Films (SRF), the Syndicat Frangais des Artistes Interpretes (SFA), the Federation Europeenne des Relisateurs de l'Audiovisuel (FERA), the Syndicat Francais des Realisateurs de Television CGT and the Syndicat National des Techniciens de la Production Cinematographique et de Television. They opposed the broadcast because they deemed it a violation of the author's moral right, aggravated in their opinion by the fact that John Huston had opposed colorization of his works during his life.

5.  The dispute thus arising with La Cinq and the Turner Entertainment Co. (TEC) resulted in France in the following decisions:

a)  An order in summary proceedings on 24th June 1988, confirmed by a judgment of the Court of Appeal of Paris on 25th June 1988, which suspended the broadcast of the colorized film as being likely to cause unacceptable and irreparable damage;

b)  On 23rd November 1988 the Court of First Instance of Paris judged as follows:

> "Declares the action of Messrs and Mrs Huston and Mr Ben Maddow and the voluntary intervention of TEC admissible insofar as they are limited to the television broadcasting of the colorized version of the film entitled 'Asphalt Jungle'; Declares the claims of the secondary voluntary intervenors admissible; Formally takes cognizance of the fact that Societe d'Exploitation de la Cinquieme Chaine has abandoned its plans for broadcasting the colorized version of the film entitled 'Asphalt Jungle'; As necessary forbids it from broadcasting this version on television; Dismisses all other claims; Dismisses the claim of the TEC company."

In admitting the claim, this judgment referred in substance to the Universal Copyright Convention signed in Geneva on 6th September 1952, ratified by the United States, to deduce that this convention provides citizens of member States in France with the benefit of the Law of 11th March 1957, notably Section 6, which provides that the moral right is attached to the person and is perpetual, inalienable and imprescribable. Thus it distinguished between this moral right and the economic rights held by the Turner company to the work, notably under contracts signed with John Huston and Ben Maddow.

Finally, it held that John Huston and Ben Maddow, by their art, had imbued their work with an original and personal character and that, because Huston's renown is based on the interplay of black and white, creating an atmosphere, the said atmosphere would be jeopardized by colorization.

c) The Court of Appeal of Paris, appealed to by the Turner company, judged as follows on 6th July 1989:

"States that the author of the film entitled 'Asphalt Jungle' is the Turner company and that the heirs of John Huston as well as Ben Maddow have no moral right to this work shot in black and white; Notes that the colorized version of the said film is an adaptation, under U.S. law, for which the Turner company obtained a registration certificate on 20th June 1988; States that the principle of colorization could not be criticized by the heirs of John Huston and by Ben Maddow, even if they could claim a moral right to the black and white film; Accordingly, reversing the judgment, Dismisses the claims of the heirs of John Huston and Ben Maddow and judges admissible but unfounded the interventions of the six legal entities supporting their claims; Authorizes the Fifth Channel to broadcast the colorized version of the film entitled 'Asphalt Jungle,' formally recognizing the cognizance petitioned for."

The judgment further provided for various warning notices intended for television viewers, with respect to the possibility of using the color control device and respect for the memory of John Huston.

In reversing the judgment against which the appeal was brought, the Court of Appeal of Paris settled the conflict of laws in favor of U.S. law, the law of the first publication of the work having, according to said court, granted the status of author solely to Loew's, which cannot be defeated by the Berne Convention, effective from 1st March 1989, which is an instrument to harmonize relations between the member countries and is not competent to affect acquired rights or the effect of contracts between producer and director. Moreover, it dismissed the exception according to which the French conception of international law was violated and held that the copyright granted to the "derivative work" transferred in 1988 to the Turner company made it impossible for Messrs and Mrs Huston and Mr Maddow to raise it if they had a moral right to claim.

6. Messrs and Mrs Huston and Mr Maddow and the intervenors appealed against this judgment of the Court of Appeal of Paris to the Cour de Cassation. In a ruling dated 28th May 1991, the Supreme Court reversed and cancelled every provision of the judgment of the Court of Appeal for violation of Section 1.2 of Law 64-689 of 8th July 1964 and Section 6 of the Law of 11th March 1957, stating:

"According to the first of these texts, the integrity of a literary or art work cannot be affected in France, regardless of the State in whose territory the said work was made public for the first time. The person who is its author, by its creation alone, enjoys the moral right stipulated in his favor by the second of the aforesaid texts; these are laws of mandatory application."

1.  The Turner Entertainment Co. duly referred the case to the Court of Appeal of Versailles, appointed as Court of Remand, and petitioned it to reverse the judgment of the Court of First Instance of Paris, to judge that the claims of Messrs and Mrs Huston are inadmissible or that they have in any case no grounds to claim the moral right to which they refer and therefore to dismiss their case and all other intervenors. It also claims as follows:

In support of its argument of inadmissibility, that Messrs and Mrs Huston cannot claim the status of foreign author, which is reserved for the Turner company under the laws applicable at the place of creation and the agreements governed by them; that they are therefore not entitled to claim French law, under the Geneva Convention, in order to protect themselves and exercise rights which they have not acquired;

That it is in any event the recognized holder of the patrimonial rights of the authors and that it was therefore entitled to introduce the colorized version by applying a technique which does not alter the essence of the work.

2.  Messrs and Mrs Huston and Mr Maddow petitioned the Court of Remand to confirm the judgment of the Court of First Instance of Paris, further petitioning the court to add that the broadcasting of the colorized version of the film entitled "Asphalt Jungle" has violated their moral right and thus to order the Turner company to pay them FRF 1,000,000 [$170,000] by way of damages and costs and a further FRF 100,000 [$17,000] under Section 700 of the New Code of Civil Procedure; thus:

They oppose [i.e., they replied to Turner's argument] that French law alone is competent to determine the status of author, as pointed out by the Cour de Cassation in a decision which stresses the importance of moral right and results in dismissal of the law applicable to the agreement between director and producer; and that their claim is therefore admissible;

That black and white is the form of expression in which the authors and especially John Huston have delivered their esthetic conception to the public; that colorization therefore alters the very essence of the work, of which it is no "adaptation" at all but a "transformation" or "modification"; that, moreover, John Huston was formally opposed to this during his life.

3.  Societe des Auteurs et Compositeurs Dramatiques (SACD) intervened voluntarily and joined itself to the submissions of Messrs and Mrs Huston, whose claims it supports in application of Section 3.1 of its bylaws and Section 65, paragraph 2 of the Law of 11th March 1957 and Section 38 of the Law of 3rd July 1985.

4.  Societe des Realisateurs de Films (SRF), Syndicat Francais des Artistes Interpretes (SFA), Federation Europeenne des Realisateurs de l'Audiovisuel (FERA), Syndicat Francais des Realisateurs de Television CGT and Syndicat National des Techniciens de la Production Cinematographique et de Television pleaded the same and claimed FRF 10,000 [$1,700] from the Turner company by virtue of Section 700 of the New Code of Civil Procedure. . . .

6.  Maitre Pierrel ex-officio petitioned the court to declare his appeal admissible and well-founded, to take formal cognizance of the fact that La Cinq, in accordance with the judgment of the Court of Appeal of Paris on 6th July 1989, broadcast the film accompanied by the ordered notices, to reverse the referred judgment of the Court of First Instance of Paris and, judging again, to judge that Messrs and Mrs Huston and Mr Maddow do not have

status as the film's authors and that they cannot claim in France the benefit of the moral right, to judge secondarily that colorization is in principle a legal adaptation and does not violate any moral right, to dismiss the claims of the opponents and to order Messrs and Mrs Huston and Mr Maddow to pay them FRF 30,000 [$5,100] by virtue of Section 700 of the New Code of Civil Procedure. He thus reiterated the arguments already produced by the Turner company, stressing that John Huston could not be unaware of the fact that he did not have the status of an author by virtue of the law governing the contracts signed with the producer.

7.  The Turner Entertainment Co. maintained its initial claims, notably on the inadmissibility of the opponents' claims in submissions in answer to which it maintains:

That it is the constant rule in private international law that the situation is governed by the law of the place where it occurs; that, therefore, the status of author of an art work is the status recognized in the country where the work has been created, i.e. in this case the United States of America; that this means Loew's Inc., to which the rights have been transferred;

That the Court of Remand is not bound by the judgment of the Cour de Cassation, criticized by an authorized doctrine;

That, in fact, the Law of 8th July 1964, incorporated as Section L 111-4 in the Code of Intellectual Property, does not apply in that it assumes that the foreign State does not provide French works with adequate and effective protection, which is not the case in the United States; that the second paragraph of Section 1 of this law, which alone is referred to in the judgment of the Cour de Cassation, is not severable;

That, lastly, the Geneva Convention does not govern the formation of rights and the pre-existing status of author, for which it only organizes protection;

That, secondarily, the Cour de Cassation has not pronounced itself on the violation of the moral right alleged to result from the colorization and that this violation has not been shown.

8.  SACD opposed in replication the submissions produced ex-officio by Me Pierrel and maintained its claims as an intervenor.

9.  In their turn, Messrs and Mrs Huston and Mr Maddow replicated as follows:

That the Cour de Cassation found for a solution which alone enables the authors to exercise their moral right in France; that this position complies with Section 14*bis* 2 of the Berne Convention, which provides for application of the law of the country of protection in designating the holder of the rights to a cinematographic work;

That U.S. law only protects economic rights, wherefore the Law of 8th July 1964 remains applicable for lack of reciprocal agreements on moral right;

That, contrary to the submissions of the Turner company, colorization violates the moral right retained.

They furthermore petitioned the court to take cognizance of the violation of the authors' moral right by La Cinq's broadcasting of the "colorized" film and to order Me Pierrel ex-officio to pay them one million francs in damages and costs on this ground.

10. In its rejoinder, the Turner Entertainment Co. petitioned the court again to judge that Messrs and Mrs Huston and Mr Maddow cannot claim the benefit of the Berne Convention and Law of 8th July 1985, which have no retroactive application, to dismiss application of the Law of 8th July 1964

because of the protection afforded by U.S. law for every attribute of copyright; to judge

That colorization is by its nature an adaptation in the meaning of the law and to grant it the benefit of its earlier submissions;

That ratification by the United States of the Berne Convention postdates the disputed situation by a considerable time;

That, contrary to the ground produced by Messrs and Mrs Huston and Mr Maddow, U.S. caselaw sanctions violation of the integrity or authorship of a work, which excludes application of the Law of 8th July 1964;

That the Law of 3rd July 1985 cannot be claimed whereas it is not disputed that the Turner company is the holder of the patrimonial rights, including the right to adapt the work and therefore to introduce a colorized version.

11. The closing order was pronounced on 17th February 1994.

III . . .

3.   The Turner company first opposes to Messrs and Mrs Huston and Mr Maddow and the intervenors that U.S. law should be applied to determine who has the status of the film's author; it designates the producer, i.e. Loew's Inc., which obtained the copyright on 2nd May 1950 and whose rights, renewed on 2nd May 1977, were transferred to the Turner company; the action of Messrs and Mrs Huston and Mr Maddow to protect rights which they have not acquired is therefore not admissible.

4.   But the judges in first instance correctly stressed the "very different conceptions" of U.S. and French laws, the first focusing exclusively on the protection of economic rights without referring to the creative act underlying the inalienable moral right recognized by French law, viz. Section 6 of the Law of 11th March 1957, at the time applicable, which provides that "the author enjoys the right to respect for his name, his status, his work  this right is attached to his person it is perpetual, inalienable and imprescribable  it is transmitted after death to the author's heirs."

John Huston and Ben Maddow, of whom it is not disputed that the first is the co-author of the screenplay and the director of the film entitled "Asphalt Jungle" and the second the co-author of the same film, as already referred to under (I-1), are in fact its authors, having created it, and whereas they are therefore, in the meaning of the aforesaid law, vested with the corresponding moral right, which is part of public law and therefore mandatorily protected.

5.   Section 1 of Law No 64-689 of 8th July 1964 on the application of the principle of reciprocity with respect to copyright provides as follows:

"Subject to the provisions of the international conventions to which France is a party, in the event that it is noted, after consultation of the Minister of Foreign Affairs, that a State does not provide adequate and effective protection for works disclosed for the first time in France, irrespective of the form thereof, works disclosed for the first time in the territory of the said State shall not benefit from the copyright protection recognized by French law. However, the integrity or authorship of such works may not be violated. In the case provided for in paragraph 1 heretofore, royalties shall be paid to organizations of general interest designated by decree."

The defect in protection thus likely to affect the foreign work on the conditions governing reciprocity, as laid out in paragraph 1, can only concern its economic aspects, i.e., the patrimonial rights attached thereto, in that it is limited by the general mandatory rule providing for respect of an author's moral right as proclaimed without reservation in paragraph 2.

6.    It follows that the moral rights attached to the person of the creators of the work entitled "Asphalt Jungle" could not be transferred and, therefore, the judges in first instance correctly ruled that Messrs and Mrs Huston and Ben Maddow were entitled to claim recognition and protection thereof in France.

7.    However, the Turner company, which it is not disputed is the holder of the author's economic rights, maintains that these rights include the right to adapt the work and therefore to colorize the film entitled "Asphalt Jungle," arguing that it cannot be maintained that this denatures the work; Me Pierrel, ex-officio, follows the same argument, submitting that the colorized version of the film is merely an adaptation of the original black-and-white version which is left intact and is therefore not affected.

8.    However, "colorization" is a technique based on the use of computer and laser and it makes it possible, after transferring the original black-and-white tape onto a videographic media, to give color to a film which did not originally have color; the application of this process is in no event to be considered an adaptation, defined as "an original work both in its expression and in its composition," even if it borrows formal elements from the pre-existing work; colorization, far from meeting these criteria, in fact merely consists in modifying the work by adding an element thus far not part of the creator's aesthetic conception.

9. The judges in first instance in the present case have precisely pointed out that the aesthetic conception which earned John Huston his great fame is based on the interplay of black and white, which enabled him to create an atmosphere according to which he directed the actor and selected the backdrops; moreover, he expressed himself clearly about his film entitled "The Maltese Falcon" when stating, "I wanted to shoot it in black and white like a sculptor chooses to work in clay, to pour his work in bronze, to sculpt in marble."

In 1950, while color film technique was already widespread and another option was available, the film entitled "Asphalt Jungle" was shot in black and white, following a deliberate aesthetic choice, according to a process which its authors considered best suited to the character of the work.

10. Therefore, the film's colorization without authorization and control by the authors or their heirs amounted to violation of the creative activity of its makers, even if it should satisfy the expectations of a certain public for commercially obvious reasons; the use of this process without the agreement of Messrs and Mrs Huston and Ben Maddow infringed the moral right of the authors as mandatorily protected under French law; Messrs and Mrs Huston and Ben Maddow have therefore good grounds to petition the court for reparation of their prejudice at the hands of the Turner company, and they will therefore be allotted FRF 400,000 [$68,000] by way of damages and costs for the damage done; moreover, the judges in first instance correctly recognized their right to demand that La Cinq SA be forbidden to broadcast the modified version of the film entitled "Asphalt Jungle."

11. It is constant that, contrary to the act required by the Court of First Instance, La Cinq SA broadcast the colorized version of the film entitled "Asphalt Jungle" further to a judgment by the Court of Appeal of Paris, quashed by the Cour de Cassation on the conditions reiterated under (I-5); this broadcasting is also a direct and definite violation of the moral right whose protection was demanded by Messrs and Mrs Huston and Ben Maddow, who are also well-founded to demand reparation on this head; the Court has the elements needed to allot them the sum of FRF 200,000

[$34,000] by reversing the referred judgment on the pronounced cognizance.
. . .

. . .[T]he . . . consideration of equity prompts the allotment, in application of the said Section 700 of the New Code of Civil Procedure, of FRF 60,000 [$10,200] to Messrs and Mrs Huston and Ben Maddow and FRF 2,000 [$340] each to SRF, SFA, FERA, Syndicat Francais des Realisateurs de Television CGT and Syndicat National des Techniciens de la Production Cinematographique et de Television.

On these grounds:

The Court, judging publicly, after hearing all parties and in last instance as Court of Remand; Pursuant to the closing order pronounced on 17th February 1994;

1. Declares that the Turner Entertainment Co. was entitled to petition the Court of Referral;

2. Declares admissible the interventions, before the same court, of Societe des Auteurs et Compositeurs Dramatiques (SACD), Societe des Realisateurs de Films (SRF), Syndicat Francais des Artistes Interpretes (SFA), Federation Europeenne des Realisateurs de l'Audiovisuel (FERA), Syndicat Frangcis des Realisateurs de Television CGT and Syndicat National des Techniciens de la Production Cinematographique et de Television; . . .

4. Confirms the judgment pronounced on 23rd November 1988 by the Court of First Instance of Paris, subject to the cognizance and the provisions dismissing application of Section 700 of the New Code of Civil Procedure in favor of Messrs and Mrs Huston and Ben Maddow and the secondary intervenors;

Judging again and adding:

5. States that the colorization of the film entitled "Asphalt Jungle" by the Turner Entertainment Co. and its broadcasting by La Cinq SA in this version, contrary to the will of the authors or their heirs, has violated their moral right;

6. Orders the Turner Entertainment Co. to pay Messrs and Mrs Huston and Ben Maddow Four Hundred Thousand French Francs (FRF 400,000) [$68,000] by way of damages and costs;

7. Orders Maitre Pierrel, ex-officio as court-appointed liquidator of Societe d'Exploitation de la Cinquieme Chaine (La Cinq SA) to pay them Two Hundred Thousand French Francs (FRF 200,000) [$34,000] in damages and costs; . . .

9. Orders it jointly and severally with the Turner Entertainment Co. to pay Messrs and Mrs Huston and Ben Maddow Sixty Thousand French Francs (FRF 60,000) [$10,200] under the same Section 700 of the New Code of Civil Procedure and to pay Two Thousand (FRF 2,000) [$340] to each of the intervenors referred to under (2), except SACD, which has lodged no claim in this respect;

10. Orders it further, jointly and severally with the Turner Entertainment Co., to bear the full cost of the appeal. . . .

This Judgment was pronounced and signed by: Mr Thavaud, President [and] Mrs Clem, District Registrar

Look back at the chart at the beginning of this chapter. Which combination (1 through 8) represents the result in *Turner Entertainment v. Huston*?

The 1991 decision of the French Supreme Court in the "Asphalt Jungle" colorization case (referred to in the opinion above) – which held that French rather than U.S. law determines who owns the authors' moral rights in France – was surprising to at least some observers in the United States. An American company, after all, produced the movie in the United States; and both John Huston and Ben Maddow were Americans. Indeed, in 1950, when "Asphalt Jungle" was produced, neither the movie nor any of those involved in its production had any connection with France, and none of them had any reason to suppose that French law would ever control ownership of any of the rights necessary to exploit the movie anywhere in the world.

The case was filed by Huston's heirs and by Maddow in 1988, *before* the United States joined the Berne Convention. From 1956 to 1989, copyright relations between the United States and France were governed by the UCC. In 1950, when "Asphalt Jungle" was produced, copyright relations between the two countries were governed by a bilateral treaty dating back to 1891. Neither the UCC nor the 1891 bilateral treaty contained provisions suggesting that the ownership of rights in an American work would be determined by applying French rather than American law.

However, the Berne Convention has governed copyright relations between the United States and France since the U.S. adhered to Berne in 1989. *If* the United States had become a member of the Berne Convention *before* "Asphalt Jungle" was produced, the ultimate result in the case would have been less surprising. This is so, because the Berne Convention contains a "Special Provision" concerning the ownership of the copyright in a "cinematographic work" (i.e., a movie).

### Berne Convention 14 *bis* (2)(a)

Ownership of copyright in a cinematographic work shall be a matter for legislation in the country where protection *is claimed*. [Emphasis added.]

Legislation in France provides that moral rights in all works, cinematographic works included, belong to the "author" as determined by French law; and French law also provides that moral rights may not be transferred (though economic rights may be). So if the U.S. had been a Berne adherent when "Asphalt Jungle" was produced, it would have been clear that moral rights to the film would have been governed by French – not American – law.

The Berne Convention is not the only law that contains "special provisions" concerning copyright ownership for specific types of works. As noted by Judge Newman in *Itar-Tass v. Russian Kurier*, the United States Copyright Act itself contains one such special provision.

### U.S. Copyright Act §104A(b)

Ownership of restored copyright. A restored work vests initially in the author or initial rightholder of the work as determined by the law of the *source country* of the work. [Emphasis added.]

This section means, for example, that if the copyright to a French movie or German photograph went into the public domain in the United States, and that copyright was restored in the U.S., the owner of the restored copyright would be the "author" of the movie or photo as determined by the law of

France or Germany, without regard to who the "author" of the work would have been under United States law.

Does this section also mean that the "author" of the restored copyright would be its owner, without regard to who the *owner* of the copyright would have been under U.S. law? Restoration of U.S. copyright, and the answer to this question, will be considered in detail in Chapter 6, when we consider what advice should be given to a hypothetical filmmaker concerning from *whom* she should obtain a license, if the U.S. restored the copyrights to once public domain photos she wishes to use in her documentary. In the hypothetical, a German photographer was the "author" of the photos under German law, but, before their copyrights were restored, the photographer granted an American company an exclusive license under U.S. law to use them, or to authorize others to use them, in the United States "in perpetuity," thus making the American company the "owner" of their U.S. copyrights.

### 3. Transfer of copyright issues

The previous section of this book dealt with who owns a copyright *initially*, from the time a work is created up *until* – but not after – its copyright is transferred to someone else. This section of the book deals with which country's law is applied to determine who owns a copyright *after* its copyright has been transferred. In other words, which country's law determines the validity and consequences of the transfer of a copyright?

This is an important question, because international copyright transfers – assignments and licenses – are very common. For every transfer, there are at least three countries whose law might be applicable and sound reasons to use each of the three:

- *The law of the country where protection is sought*. This is where the transfer will have actual consequences, though for works that are licensed for use in many countries of the world, applying the law of the country where protection is sought would mean that many different laws would be applicable, even to a single transfer, if the transfer is a worldwide license.
- *The law of the work's country-of-origin*. Applying the law of the work's country-of-origin would require the use of the law of just a single country; and even though it would not be the law of the country where the assignee or licensee is located, it would not be unreasonably burdensome to determine the law of the countries from which works are acquired.
- *The law of the country where the transfer actually took place*. Transfers frequently take place in countries that are neither the country-of-origin nor the country where protection will be sought. It happens every year at international licensing events like the Cannes Film Festival, MIP-TV television market and MIDEM music market (all in Cannes, France), and the Frankfurt Book Fair (in Germany). Applying the law of the country where the transfer took place would require the use of the law of just a single country, and since the major international markets take place year after year in the same

few places, the cost of learning the laws of those few countries could be amortized over many transactions, year after year.

The question of which of these three possibilities is "the law" is surprisingly difficult to answer. Indeed, conflicting answers appear to be found within pages of one otherwise excellent international copyright treatise, *International Copyright and Neighboring Rights* by S.M. Stewart. At page 30 (of the 2nd edition published in 1989), Stewart wrote:

> [I]f an English author makes a publishing contract to have his work published in France and the published work is then performed in a slightly altered form without permission in Germany, the issue whether that performance constitutes an infringement will probably be judged according to German law as the country where protection is claim, that is where the infringement is committed. . .but the validity of the transfer of the right to the French publisher will probably be judged according to French law if the contract is a French contract. . . .

This seems to mean that the law to be applied is the law of the country where the transfer took place. Just four pages later, however, at page 34, Stewart wrote:

> In the realm of the law of movable (physical) property the law applicable to decide ownership is generally the law of the country where the property is acquired. If one bought goods in country A and takes them to country B, the question of whether one has become the rightful owner of the goods is to be decided by the law of country A. The position is different in copyright. The law applying to the physical property . . . such as the book, the film, the record containing the work is governed by the above mentioned rules. The property in the work, however, is governed by the law of country B, if that is where the right is claimed. Thus "the centre of gravity" of the work is the country where protection is claimed.

This says that the law to be applied is the law of the country where protection is sought.

If a single treatise by highly-regarded author leaves you uncertain about which law should be applied, the separately-decided opinions by different judges are likely to do so as well.

No published case has applied the law of the work's country-of-origin. Indeed, in *Hermann Luchterhand v. Albert Langen-Georg Muller*, 7 IIC 134 (Germany S.Ct. 1975), the Supreme Court of Germany expressly rejected the argument that the effectiveness of a license to publish Soviet author Alexander Solzhenitsyn's novel *August Fourteen* in Germany should be determined under Soviet law, which would have made the license invalid. Instead, the German Supreme Court held that the license was valid, even though it had been obtained from a Swiss attorney who had a power of attorney from Solzhenitsyn rather than from the Soviet government agency that then had the exclusive authority, under Soviet law, to grant copyright licenses to non-Soviets. The basis for the court's ruling appears to have been that Soviet law was effective only within the USSR, and the effectiveness, within Germany, of the power of attorney, had to be determined under German rather than Soviet law.

While no case has relied on the work's country-of-origin, some cases have applied the law of the country where the transfer took place, and at least one case has applied the law of the country where protection was sought.

In the earliest published opinion to address the issue, *Khan v. Leo Feist*, 165 F.2d 188 (2d Cir. 1947), a U.S. court applied the law of Trinidad to determine the validity of an assignment of the copyright to "Rum and Coca-Cola," a (once famous) song written by Rupert Grant. Grant was "a native of Trinidad," but the court's reliance on the law of Trinidad appears to have been based on the fact that Grant's assignment to Mohamed Khan took place "in Trinidad." The validity of that assignment was challenged in a copyright infringement suit filed in the United States by Khan against the publisher and writer of another song, some of whose lyrics were "practically identical" to those of "Rum and Coca-Cola." In an opinion by Judge Augustus Hand, the court held that the assignment was valid under the law of Trinidad. The defendants did not argue that the validity of the assignment – an oral assignment later confirmed in a signed writing – should have been determined under the law of the United States rather than Trinidad. The defendants may not have made that argument because the law of Trinidad was so clearly applicable. On the other hand, they may not have made that argument simply because U.S. law was the same as the law of Trinidad, so the outcome did not turn on which country's law was applied. In either event, the "Rum and Coca-Cola" case merely *illustrates* the use of the law of the country where the transfer took place; it did not *hold* that the law of Trinidad, rather than U.S. law, should be applied.

The next two cases do address the choice-of-law question directly. One case, from the U.K., and the other, from the U.S., are a matched pair, because (by coincidence) both deal with the same quite specific question: Which country's law should be applied to decide whether music publishing contracts, that were negotiated and signed *outside* the United States, had the effect of transferring the *U.S.* renewal terms to songs written (before 1978) by songwriters who were *not* Americans to music publishers that were *not* Americans either? The British decision held that British law applied to a publishing contract entered into in the U.K. between a British songwriter and British publishing company; and that as interpreted under British law, the contract *did* transfer the U.S. renewal term to the British company. By contrast, the American decision held that U.S. law applied to a publishing contract entered into in Brazil between a Brazilian songwriter and Brazilian publishing company; and that as interpreted under U.S. law, the contract did *not* transfer the renewal term to the Brazilian company.

### Campbell Connelly & Co. v. Noble
### [1963] 1 All E.R. 237 (U.K.Chancery Div.)

Wilberforce, J.:

In or about the year 1934 the defendant, Mr. Ray Noble, a well-known [English] dance band leader, composed a lyric, consisting of words and music, which he called "The very thought of you". That composition has become successful and has demonstrated its survival value to such an extent that it still sells large numbers of copies. But in 1934 it was, of course, unknown, and in order to procure its exploitation the defendant entered into a publishing contract with the plaintiffs, Campbell Connelly & Co., Ltd., who are a well-known [British] company of music publishers. That agreement was dated Mar. 2, 1934; and I need read only one clause of it, which is cl. 1. That runs as follows:

> "In consideration of the sum of 1s. on account of the royalties hereinafter made payable paid to the composer by the publishers (the receipt of which sum of 1s. is hereby acknowledged) the composer hereby assigns to the publishers the full copyright for all countries in the musical composition entitled 'The very thought of you' including the title, words and music thereof in all countries for the period of copyright as far as it is assignable by law, together with all rights therein which he now has or may hereafter become entitled to whether now or hereafter known including the publishing rights, the performing rights, the synchronisation rights, the rights to use the same for mechanical reproduction and the right to make, publish, perform and reproduce any arrangement alteration or adaptation of the same."

There were the usual provisions for the payment of royalties and so on, but nothing turns on them.

That agreement was a purely English contract and must plainly be interpreted according to English law. But it did relate to the rights in all countries of the world, and in particular to the United States of America. In fact the work did obtain copyright protection in the United States of America on Apr. 16, 1934, which was the date on which it was first published in that county.

Now the law of the United States of America differs from the law of this country in that, whereas under English law there is a single term of copyright, in the United States there are two terms. Copyright is first granted for a term of twenty-eight years from the date of publication, but if the author is alive at the commencement of the twenty-eighth year of the first period he has the right to renew the copyright for a further period of twenty-eight years. That further period of twenty-eight years was in fact obtained by the defendant, Mr. Noble, who was living at the relevant time and is alive now. The plaintiffs now claim that they are entitled to the benefit of the copyright for that renewal period, as it is called; but Mr. Noble denies that, and he has in fact entered into another agreement, on Sept. 15, 1959, by which he assigned the renewal copyright in "The very thought of you" to other parties, namely, a concern called M. Witmark & Sons. The plaintiffs consequently bring this action seeking to establish that the renewal copyright (as the extended copyright is commonly called) falls within the terms of the agreement of Mar. 2, 1934, and, in particular, within the terms of c. 1, which I have read.

Now, in deciding whether this contract applies in the circumstances of the present case, it is necessary first to ascertain the precise nature of that to which it is claimed to apply. The disputed subject-matter is the creation of the law of the United States of America, and I must look at that law in order to ascertain whether it is assignable at all, and if so in what conditions it is assignable. . . .

The nature of the renewal copyright has been considered in a number of reported cases. From these it appears (as indeed one would assume from the terms of the statute) that this right is an item of property, or "estate", as it has been called, quite separate and distinct from the original copyright, and that if it is to pass to an assignee it must be separately assigned. I will refer only to one of the cases cited, which I do with the preliminary comment that both this case and the others referred to in the evidence were decided subsequently to the contract now in question, so that the parties cannot be said to have contracted with these decisions in mind. The case to which I shall refer is *Fred Fisher Music Co. v. M. Witmark & Sons*, which was decided in the Supreme Court of the United States. . . .

The opinion of the majority of the Supreme Court was delivered by Frankfurter, J., and . . . the court came to the conclusion that there was nothing in the law which prevented an author from agreeing to assign the renewal copyright after he had secured it. This case, then, clearly establishes not only that the renewal copyright is capable of assignment but that it may be made the subject of a contract to assign it, entered into at the same time as the original copyright is assigned, which will be effective when the renewal copyright has been secured.

There have been a number of decisions in American courts on the nature of the expressions which it is necessary to use in order effectively to assign the renewal copyright. I do not propose to refer to these except as establishing what seems to me to be indisputable – that the renewal copyright is separate and distinct from the original copyright. It seems to me that decisions as to the construction and effect of United States contracts are not helpful or indeed admissible guides to me in interpreting this English contract. Nearer to the point, and not without interest, are two English decisions given at a time when English law created two separate copyright periods. The first is Carnan v. Bowles, decided in 1786.

> "In 1771, [says the report] Captain Paterson, having prepared a book of roads, sold all his interest in the copyright of it to the plaintiff. . ."

Then . . . the report states that by s. 11 of the Act of 8 Anne . . . referred:

> "... it is provided, that, after the expiration of the term of fourteen years, the sole right of printing, or disposing of copies of books, shall return to the authors thereof, if they are then living, for a further term of fourteen years; but the question is, whether the conveyance of the author's property in the copy did not convey to the plaintiff his right to that contingent return. The words of the grant are, all his right, which must convey the contingent interest in the second term of fourteen years, as well as the absolute interest in the first fourteen."

That was the argument for the plaintiff. For the defendant the argument was expressed in the following sentence:

> "In selling the right, the author sells all that is in him, not the contingent right that may return to him."

Lord Thurlow, L.C., in dealing with this point, said this:

> "With respect to the first point, it strikes me that the contingent interest must pass by the word interest in the grant. He conveys all his interest in the copyright: the assignment must have been made upon the idea of a perpetuity; and it is probable not a syllable was said or thought of, respecting the contingent right. They merely followed the old precedents of such conveyances. It must, I think, be considered as conveying his whole right. If he had meant to convey his first term only, he should have said so."

The second case is Rundell v. Murray, decided in 1821. That was also a decision on the statute of Anne as amended by 41 Geo. 3 c. 107, s. 1. It was a case where an author had given his work to a publisher and sought to restrain him after the first fourteen years from continuing with the publication. I cite one passage from the argument which is expressed in the following way:

> "Where copyright is assigned by the author, his contingent right in the event of his surviving the first fourteen years does not in general pass; the statutes . . . having provided that it shall return to the author. If it be intended to pass, it is necessary to introduce special words, as in Carnan v. Bowles."

Lord Eldon, L.C., said this with reference to the relevant point:

> "I conceive that an author will not be taken to have assigned his contingent right in case of his surviving the fourteen years, unless the assignment is so expressed as to purport to pass it. . ."

Although these were decisions on a statute which can fairly be regarded as the parent or at least the ancestor of the present United States Title 17, it would be wrong to regard them as binding authorities as to the manner in which the modern United States renewal copyrights are to be assigned; but in the words of Lord Eldon, L.C., which I have just cited. I find considerable support for the approach which independently I should be inclined to make to this contract, which is to ask this question: given the separate proprietary character of the renewal copyright, is this clause so expressed as to pass it? To that question I now address myself.

Now if there is one characteristic of this contract which makes an immediate and clear impact on the reader, it is that it, and particularly cl. 1, is intended to have world-wide application. Clause 1 is expressed in the widest and most general terms and is evidently designed to bring within its grasp every right to exploit this composition, of whatever character, in whatever country. As applied to any particular country it includes not only the full copyright but all rights which the composer has or may hereafter become entitled to, whether now or hereafter known, so that, on the assumption that he had, in addition to a present copyright, some additional future or contingent right, it would seem on the first impression of the clause that it was intended to be caught. The defendant, however, says that on a more careful analysis of the words used, the intention necessary to assign the renewal right does not appear. He begins by dividing the clause into two phrases. The first consists of the words "the full copyright for the period of copyright so far as it is assignable by law", the second of the words following "together". The first limb, he contends, can only refer to the original copyright, and the "period" can only be the first twenty-eight years. This reference to "period" is the only reference in the clause to the duration of the rights assigned by it. Then he says that the second phrase commencing with "together" does not refer to any separate period from the period already mentioned and can only pass rights the duration of which is limited to that period, not rights extending, as is claimed, twenty-eight years beyond it, and the nature of the rights so passed is indicated by those specifically referred to. They are limited rights, rights to exploit in particular ways (including new ways which might be discovered) the musical composition. Further, the defendant contends that it cannot have been the intention to include renewal copyright in the right assigned: if it had been so intended, first some such words as "or any renewal thereof" would certainly have been added after "the period of copyright"; secondly, some machinery would have been provided in the contract for the vesting of the renewal copyright in the publishers, either a power of attorney or at least some covenant for further assurance; and thirdly (rather a far-fetched argument, if I may say so) the publishers would surely have taken steps to obtain the concurrence in the contract of the author's wife in case she should be the person who under s. 24 in fact obtained the renewal copyright.

Dealing first with the latter series of arguments, it appears to me that they might have great force if this was a contract dealing specifically with the United States copyright. In such a contract one might expect specific attention to be directed to the renewal copyright and to the mechanism for securing it. But they lose all validity, to my mind, once it is appreciated that this clause is a clause of world-wide application. If it is specifically directed towards the copyright law of any one country, that country is the United Kingdom, and indeed the words "the period of copyright so far as it is assignable by law" seem to be related to . . . s. 5 (2) of the Copyright Act, 1911. As regards other countries, one would expect nothing more than words of a general character and of sufficient width to bring in any right in the nature of copyright, however, different from English copyright that might be.

I recognise, of course, that it is reasonable to assume that the parties to this contract had, inter alia, United States copyright in mind. Not only is copyright in the United States of great and obvious value on account of the superficial similarity of the two languages, but we know that the plaintiffs at this time had a United States associate company which was actively concerned with their rights in America. But giving full weight to this, it is in my view quite natural that cl. 1 should still have been expressed in a general form and that this should have been thought preferable rather than to attempt to bring in the United States rights by specific language, which might cause embarrassment in other directions.

Turning to the more general argument on the two phrases in this clause, I am unable to read the second phrase in the limited sense urged on me by the defendant. I see no reason why the duration of the rights assigned by it should be limited to the period fixed by the first clause. The composer might well under the law of some country have acquired some particular right (for example the television rights) for a period extending beyond the original copyright period, and I would see no reason why it should not pass. The second phrase is quite general and unlimited as regards its duration. Further, one cannot but be struck by the great width of the rights conferred by the second phrase. It enumerates the main rights which the inclusive expression "the copyright" confers – to publish, to perform, to reproduce mechanically, to arrange, and to adapt. This seems to me to show that there is nothing ancillary or subsidiary about the second phrase. It is intended to bring in all rights normally included in the copyright, whatever their exact status or nomenclature in the particular country in question and whenever they arise. Indeed it may well be the case that it is this phrase rather than the first phrase which made available to the publishers the original copyright in the United States, because that right was, at the date of the contract, not an existing right but a future right to which the composer became entitled only on publication in the United States. In any event, and whether that be so or not, the second phrase is, in my view, fully wide enough to cover the renewal copyright as an independent future or contingent right. . . .

This being the case, cl. 1, being, as I hold, an assignment of a future or contingent right to copyright as and when acquired, confers on the assignees, the publishers, an equitable right as against the composer the moment his right accrues. For this proposition, which was not disputed, I need only refer to one authority specifically on copyright – *Performing Right Society v. London Theatre of Varieties*.

Accordingly, the plaintiffs make out their case, in my judgment, and they are entitled to a declaration, which should be in the form: that under and by virtue of the agreement the plaintiffs became entitled, subject to the royalties specified in the said agreement, to the benefit of the copyright in the musical composition entitled "The very thought of you" in the United States of America for the full renewal period of such copyright in the United States of America.

## Corcovado Music Corp. v. Hollis Music, Inc
### 981 F.2d 679 (2d Cir. 1993)

Feinberg, Circuit Judge:

Plaintiff Corcovado Music Corp. (Corcovado) appeals from a judgment of the United States District Court for the Southern District of New York, Kevin T. Duffy, J., dismissing an action for copyright infringement on the condition that defendants submit to the jurisdiction of the Brazilian courts. For the reasons stated below, we reverse the judgment of the district court and remand.

*I. Facts and Proceedings Below*

In 1958 and 1960, the composer Antonio Carlos Jobim entered into a series of contracts with a Brazilian publisher, Editora Musical Arapua (Arapua), pursuant to which Arapua and its designee obtained United States copyrights for five songs (the Five Songs)[1] composed by Jobim. [n1 The songs are "Desafinado," "Eu sei que vou te amar," "Modinha," "Janelas abertas" and "Mulher, sempre mulher."] Soon thereafter, Arapua assigned its copyrights in the Five Songs to Bendig Music Corp. (Bendig). Bendig in turn assigned the rights in one of the songs, the *bossa nova* classic "Desafinado," to Hollis Music, Inc. (Hollis). Songways Service, Inc. (Songways), an affiliate of Hollis, administers the rights in "Desafinado." Bendig, Hollis and Songways are all defendants in this action.

Jobim, apparently believing that he retained United States copyright renewal rights for the Five Songs, assigned those rights in 1987 and 1988 to plaintiff Corcovado. Corcovado's complaint alleges that after the expiration of the original term copyrights, defendants Bendig, Hollis, and Songways continued to receive payments in connection with the Five Songs notwithstanding Jobim's assignment of the renewal rights to Corcovado. Accordingly, the complaint alleges that defendants[2] are infringing the renewal copyrights and seeks relief under the Copyright Act, 17 U.S.C. § 101 et seq. [n2 In addition to Bendig, Hollis and Songways, Corcovado also named The Harry Fox Agency (Fox) and Broadcast Music, Inc. (BMI) as defendants. The latter are licensing and collection organizations in the music industry. They have collected money in connection with performances of the Five Songs and are thus stakeholders in this action. After the complaint was filed, all parties to the action entered into a dismissal stipulation, subsequently signed into an order by the district judge, which dismissed the action against Fox and BMI on condition that they hold money earned from the Five Songs in escrow to be paid out pursuant to order of the court.]

Defendants moved to dismiss the complaint on the ground that the 1958 and 1960 contracts in which Jobim had conveyed copyrights to Arapua – negotiated and executed in Brazil and written in Portuguese – required interpretation by a Brazilian court. Defendants claimed that these contracts, which unquestionably conveyed original term copyrights, also conveyed renewal rights. They argued further that Corcovado, as Jobim's contractual successor, was bound by the forum selection clause in the Jobim-Arapua contracts. This clause, defendants contend, required the parties, i.e., Jobim and Arapua, to resolve any disputes in the courts of Brazil. Corcovado responded that it was suing to vindicate its rights under the Copyright Act, not as Jobim's successor under the Jobim-Arapua contracts. Therefore, the Jobim-Arapua contracts and the forum selection clause contained therein were relevant to the cause of action, if at all, only as a defense.

The district court agreed with defendants and granted the motion to dismiss with the following handwritten memorandum endorsement:

> This case is by the initial agreement of the parties [i.e., Jobim and Arapua] to be resolved in the courts of Brazil. It involves citizens of Brazil and the interpretation of a Brazil contract and Brazil law. It is dismissed on condition that defendants submit to the jurisdiction of the Brazilian courts.

This appeal followed.

## II. Discussion

### A. Effect of forum selection clause

Corcovado argues to us that the district court erred, pointing out that Corcovado and defendants, the parties to this action, never had any agreement with each other, that none of the parties to this action is a citizen of Brazil (indeed, all – including Fox and BMI – are New York corporations doing business in New York) and that United States copyright law, not the law of Brazil, is involved. What is fundamentally at stake, Corcovado argues, is the vindication of rights under the Copyright Act, not the interpretation of a contract.

This is a copyright action. . . . The Jobim-Arapua contracts are relevant only as a defense. The complaint asserts no rights whatsoever arising out of those contracts, and they form no part of plaintiff Corcovado's case. Plaintiff's position is simply that the defendants infringed its renewal term copyrights....

It is true, as defendants argue, that plaintiff Corcovado could receive a renewal term copyright from Jobim only if Jobim had something left to give. It can with equal justification be said of anyone who acquires *anything* by contract that he or she acquired it only if the seller had something left to give. That, and the fact that the defendants have a separate contract with the seller (Jobim) containing a forum-selection clause, do not, without more, entitle defendants to haul plaintiff halfway across the world to enforce its rights.

As an illustration, consider the following. Buyer 1 buys a house and proceeds to move in. Buyer 2 is already there and says: "You can't move in. Seller sold *me* this house a month ago." Buyer 1 replies, "Really? We'd better go to court," to which Buyer 2 answers: "Yes, but in *Brazil,* because when *I* bought the house from Seller, we put in a forum-selection clause. See you in Brazil." In this example, the essence of Buyer 1's claim is: "My deed is valid; you're interfering with my right of ownership." Buyer 2 wants to rewrite Buyer 1's claim as if it were based on a contract between Buyer 2 and Seller. In reality, the Buyer 2-Seller contract, like the contracts between Jobim and Arapua, is at most a defense to Buyer 1's claim of ownership.

Accordingly, we believe that the district court erred in dismissing Corcovado's copyright action with instructions, in effect, to pursue it in Brazil.

We would ordinarily, at this point, simply remand the case to the district court for further proceedings, including a determination of the defense offered by defendants that they, rather than plaintiff Corcovado, are the owners of the renewal copyrights in the Five Songs. However, a careful examination of the record and principles of sound judicial administration persuade us that we should determine that issue at this time.

## B.  Owner of renewal rights

The ownership right at stake in this action is the author's right of renewal found in § 24 of the 1909 Copyright Act, reenacted in § 304 of the 1976 Act, 17 U.S.C. §  304(a). The purpose of the right of renewal is to "provide[] authors a second opportunity to obtain remuneration for their works." *Stewart v. Abend*, 495 U.S. 207, 110 S. Ct. 1750, 1758, 109 L. Ed. 2d 184 (1990). . .
.

Although *Stewart* tells us what a renewal right is and why it is important to federal copyright law, it does not tell us how an author may convey that right. In the present case, two factors are of primary importance: (1) The Jobim-Arapua contracts did not explicitly convey renewal rights; and (2) the Jobim-Arapua contracts contain no language that is ambiguous enough to permit the inference that they implicitly conveyed renewal rights. Together, these factors compel the conclusion that Jobim did not, as a matter of law, convey renewal rights to Arapua in 1958-60. The reasoning underlying that conclusion follows.

First, there is a strong presumption against the conveyance of renewal rights. . . . The seminal case is *Fred Fisher Music Co. v. M. Witmark & Sons*, in which the Supreme Court held that "an assignment by the author of his 'copyright' in general terms did not include conveyance of his renewal interest." In other words, a contract that conveyed original term copyrights without mentioning future rights did not as a matter of federal copyright law convey renewal rights. . . . The presumption against conveyance of renewal rights serves the congressional purpose of protecting authors' entitlement to receive new rights in the 28th year of the original term. In the present case, Jobim's 1958 and 1960 contracts with Arapua were silent as to renewal rights.[7]

[n7 In defendants' translation from the Portuguese, the assignment clause of the 1958 contract conveying the rights to "Desafinado" reads as follows:

> The Authors assign and transfer to the Publisher, the full property, for the exercise of the corresponding rights in all the countries of the world, of their ownership rights in the musical composition of which they are the authors with the corresponding lyrics, titled "Desafinado" soft slow samba, in the form, scope and application which they hold by virtue of the laws and treaties in force and those which become effective hereinafter.

Plaintiff's translation of the same clause is as follows:

> The AUTHORS assign and transfer to the PUBLISHER, in full ownership, for the exercise of the appropriate authority, in all countries of the world, their copyright to the musical composition authored by them, with the respective lyrics, which is entitled: Desafinado — samba song[,] in such manner, to such extent and with such application as provided for by current or future laws and treaties.]

145

Accordingly, under federal copyright law Jobim retained renewal rights to the Five Songs and could validly assign them to Corcovado.

Defendants cite *Siegel v. National Periodical Publications, Inc.*, 508 F.2d 909, 913-14 (2d Cir. 1974), for the proposition that "general words of assignment can include renewal rights if the parties had so intended. That intent is to be determined by the trier of the facts." In *Siegel*, however, "the agreement by the parties did not simply purport to convey a copyright . . . . Rather, [it] conveyed the 'exclusive right to the use [of the intellectual property] . . . *forever*'"; "moreover, the authors agreed not to [employ or sell said property] at any time *hereafter*." (emphasis in original). *Siegel* is consistent with *Fred Fisher* because the contract language in *Siegel*, by using the words "forever" and "hereafter," embraced a renewal term copyright. In this case, unlike *Siegel*, the contracts conveying original term rights contain no such language. Hence, as noted above, they did not convey renewal rights. . . .

Citing the English case of *Campbell Connelly & Co., Ltd. v. Noble*, 1 All E.R. 237 (1963), defendants argue that Brazilian law should apply to the interpretation of the Jobim-Arapua contracts. We disagree. We believe that Campbell Connelly is distinguishable on the facts,[8] and, in any event, conclude that its reasoning could not be applied here to preclude the use of United States law. [n8 *Campbell Connelly* was a suit by a publisher against a composer asserting right's under a contract in which the composer assigned copyrights to the publisher. It is as though Arapua or its assignees were suing on Arapua's contract with Jobim.] Factors arguing for the application of United States law include the following: United States renewal copyrights reflect a vital policy of United States copyright law; the forum in which the Jobim-Arapua contracts are to be construed is in the United States (for reasons set forth above); and the place of performance of the contracts is also the United States. Under these circumstances, we believe that United States law is applicable.

The judgment of the district court is reversed and the case is remanded to the district court for further proceedings consistent with this opinion.

These two opinions – *Campbell Connelly* and *Corcovado Music* – raise many important questions. Here are some:

1. Which of the two opinions strikes you as being the most realistic about the actual way in which contracts are negotiated and drafted?

2. Are you satisfied that *Corcovado* persuasively distinguished *Campbell Connelly*? That is,

   a. Couldn't Hollis Music (the successor to Jobim's original Brazilian publisher) have filed a lawsuit against Corcovado Music (Jobim's successor) that was identical, as a procedural matter, to the lawsuit filed by Campbell Connelly against Noble?

   b. In other words, wasn't the *Corcovado* court over-influenced by who sued whom, and under-influenced by the actual nature of the dispute, which was who owned the renewal term?

3. Why was the *Corcovado* court influenced at all by the fact that "the place of performance of the contracts is . . . the United States" – given that the court characterized the case as "a copyright action. . ." and the "Jobim-Arapua contracts are relevant only as a defense"?

4. Did the *Corcovado* court give adequate – indeed any – consideration to the facts that: Jobim and his original publisher both were Brazilian; their lawyers no doubt were Brazilian too; the contract was negotiated in Brazil and written in Portugese (Brazil's national language); the contract was sufficient to transfer the full term of the copyrights pursuant to the law of Brazil where all parties were located when the language of the contract was drafted?

5. Although the *Corcovado* court said that "United States renewal copyrights reflect a *vital policy* of the United States copyright law" (emphasis added), it acknowledged that if the Jobim-Arapua contracts contained just slightly different language – that is, if they had used the words "forever" and "hereafter" – those contracts could have *and would have* transferred U.S. renewal terms. What was the "vital policy," and how "vital" could it have been, if it could have been avoided by so slight a step as adding the words "forever" and (maybe even "or") "hereafter" to the contract?

6. So, did the *Corcovado* decision penalize Jobim's original publisher, and give Jobim and his new publisher a windfall, simply because the original publisher's Brazilian lawyers did not know that in order to accomplish their mission they had to insert the words "forever" and "hereafter" into the contracts?

*Corcovado* was decided by the same court that later held – in *Itar-Tass Russian News Agency v. Russian Kurier* – that copyright *ownership* is determined by the law of a work's country-of-origin rather than by the law of the country where protection is sought. In fact, the two opinions were decided by practically the same judges. *Corcovado* was decided by Judges Feinberg, Newman and Cardamone, while *Itar-Tass* was decided by Judges Feinberg, Newman and McLaughlin. In *Itar-Tass*, Judges Feinberg and Newman ruled that the law of a work's country-of-origin should be applied to determine who owns a copyright initially, and what the consequences are of that ownership. But those same judges ruled in *Corcovado* that the law where protection is sought should be applied to determine the effect of a contract transferring ownership.

Initial ownership is somewhat different from ownership by virtue of a transfer. But how different are they, really? In the United States, the copyright to a work created by an independent contractor is owned *initially* by the commissioning party if – but only if – there is a signed agreement that it is a work-made-for-hire. Even then, a work is a work-for-hire only if it is a specified type of work, and neither "software" nor "computer programs" are specified. U.S. Copyright Act §101 (definition of "work made for hire").

Consider the question that follows this provision of Brazilian law.

## Brazilian Law on the Protection of Intellectual Property of Software

2. The protection system for intellectual property of software is the same granted to literary works by the copyright laws and connected provisions in Brazil, under the terms of this Law. . . .

4. Unless covenanted otherwise, the employer, [or] service contracting party . . . shall have full title over the rights associated to the software program, developed and elaborated throughout the duration of an agreement or by-law obligation . . . or in which the employee's, service contractor's or server's activities are provided. . . .

The preceding paragraph is an English language translation of a Portugese language statute, so if its meaning is not perfectly clear, it may help to know that it has been explained as follows:

> Article 4 of the Software Act provides that, unless agreed otherwise, an employer or *commissioning party* . . . initially owns all economic rights arising from the development of a computer program on the job or *on commission*. (Emphasis added.)

Otto B. Licks, Dr. Antonio Chaves, Henrique Gandelman, *Brazil* §4[1][b][ii], in Paul Edward Geller, *International Copyright Law and Practice* (2000).

Nothing in the Brazilian Software Act requires a commissioning agreement to be in writing.

To see the significance of all this, answer the following hypothetical question:

A computer program (for the management of small businesses) was created in Brazil "on commission." There was *no* written agreement between the Brazilian company that commissioned the program and the Brazilian programmer who created it. The Brazilian company granted Office Depot (the American company) the exclusive right to make and sell copies of an English-language version of the program in the United States, while the Brazilian programmer granted Staples (the American company) the exclusive right to make and sell copies of an English-language version of the program in the United States. Office Depot and Staples both made and sold copies of the program in the U.S., and then sued one another in the U.S. for copyright infringement. Which country's law should be applied to determine whether Office Depot or Staples is the owner of the program's copyright in the U.S. – the law of Brazil, or the law of the United States?

Here is another provision of Brazilian law:

## Brazilian Copyright Law

49. Author's rights may be wholly or partly transferred to third parties by the author or by his successors, in a universal or individual transfer effected in person or through representatives with special powers, by licensing, concession, assignment or any other means recognized by law, subject to the limitations set forth below: . . .

    IV. unless otherwise specified, assignment shall be valid only in the country in which the contract has been signed;

    V. the assignment shall be valid only for the modes of exploitation existing on the date of the contract. . . .

The United States Copyright Act does not contain a provision that is equivalent to the Brazil's existing-modes-only provision. In fact, U.S. cases have held that an agreement does validly transfer exploitation rights in not-yet-existing and unknown modes, if the agreement transfers the right to use a work by "any means or methods now or hereafter known," or "by any present or future methods or means" or by "any . . . means now known or unknown." See, e.g., *Platinum Record Co. v. Lucasfilm, Ltd.*, 566 F.Supp. 226 (D.N.J. 1983), *Rooney v. Columbia Pictures*, 538 F.Supp. 211 (S.D.N.Y. 1982), aff'd, 714 F.2d 117 (2d Cir. 1982), cert. denied, 460 U.S. 1084 (1983).

Nor does the United States Copyright Act contain a provision that is equivalent to Brazil's valid-only-where-signed provision.

Answer this hypothetical question:

In 1984 – after the *Platinum Record* and *Rooney* cases were decided, but before the advent of the Internet or iTunes – Brazilian songwriter Luciana Veloso assigned her copyrights to a Brazilian music publishing company, in a transaction entered into in Brazil (in the Portuguese language). The assignment said nothing about its geographic scope. Ten years later, in 1994, Veloso's publisher licensed Digitone Records, an American record company, to make recordings of the songs Veloso had written. That license expressly authorized Digitone to distribute its recordings "as CDs and in any other format now or hereafter known." In 2006, Digitone licensed iTunes to sell recordings of Veloso's songs as digital downloads. Veloso has filed a copyright infringement lawsuit in the United States against Digitone and iTunes. Which country's law should be applied to determine whether Veloso or her Brazilian publisher is the owner of the songs' copyrights in the U.S. – the law of Brazil, or the law of the United States?

## Chapter 5

# International Trade Law and Its Relation to Copyright

International trade law is a field unto itself; and most of it is quite unrelated to copyright. Even when international trade law involves copyrighted goods and services, it doesn't concern itself with the *copyrighted* nature of those goods and services.

Instead, some trade law cases involve such esoterica as whether plastic digital date-and-time gadgets, decorated with copyrighted characters from the animated movie "A Bug's Life," were "toys" or "watches." It mattered, because they were manufactured abroad, and if they were "toys" they could be imported into the United States duty-free, but if they were "watches," the importer had to pay tariffs. (The Court of International Trade ruled they were watches. *Simon Marketing, Inc. v. United States*, 395 F.Supp.2d 1280 (CIT 2005)) In a similar case, the issue was whether "X-Men," "Spider-Man" and "Fantastic Four" action figures were "toys" or "dolls." At the time the case arose, importers of "dolls" had to pay a 12% tariff while importers of "toys" had to pay just 6.8%. (Both are duty-free today. When it mattered, though, the Court of International Trade ruled they were "toys." *Toy Biz, Inc. v. United States*, 248 F.Supp.2d 1234 (CIT 2003)). The important point (for present purposes) is that neither the toy/watch distinction nor the toy/doll distinction was based on the fact that these items were protected by copyright. These cases would have been litigated even if they involved public domain items, and their outcomes would have been the same.

Trade law also has been used by many countries (though not the United States) to create barriers to the exploitation of copyrighted works from other countries (usually from the United States). These trade law barriers include: "domestic content quotas" of various kinds, including laws that limit the number of foreign movies that may be exhibited by local theaters, and require radio and television stations to broadcast minimum percentages of local programming; and laws that discourage the importation and sale of magazines that contain advertising by local companies but articles and photos created abroad. Again, however, none of these barriers is triggered by the *copyrighted* nature of these works; these barriers would exist even if foreign movies, TV programs and magazines were not protected by copyright at all.

Although international trade law and copyright law are largely unrelated, they do intersect with one another in five important ways:

1. International trade laws have become an effective tool for requiring countries to upgrade their national copyright statutes in ways that are not required by international copyright treaties.

2. International trade laws have imposed limits on the extent to which copyright owners in many countries have been able to exercise the exclusive rights and privileges granted to them by the national copyright laws of those countries.

3.  International trade laws have required countries to "harmonize" – that is, to eliminate differences among – their national copyright laws, in ways not required by copyright treaties.
4.  International *trade* law has been used to provide remedies against nations that violate obligations imposed by *copyright* treaties – remedies that copyright treaties themselves simply do not provide.
5.  Trade *embargo* laws may prevent the United States from complying with some of its international copyright obligations.

## A. International trade law provisions requiring countries to upgrade national copyright statutes in ways not required by international copyright treaties

### 1. Infringement remedies

Copyright treaties are quite emphatic about what *works* they protect and what *rights* adhering countries must provide by national law. But – until the WIPO Copyright Treaty and WIPO Performances and Phonograms Treaty were adopted in 1996 – copyright treaties were not at all emphatic about what *remedies* adhering countries must provide for infringement of protected rights. Rights without remedies are worthless, so it is not surprising that eventually treaties were adopted or amended to cure both of these deficiencies. What is surprising is that (until the 1996 WIPO treaties) these treaties were not copyright treaties; they were instead international trade treaties. As you read the following materials, consider why copyright treaties were deficient when it comes to remedies, and consider why international trade treaties became the preferred (and largely successful) tool for improving copyright remedies.

The Berne Convention – also administered by WIPO – devotes several of its Articles to an enumeration of specific rights that authors "shall enjoy." But it contains only the following provision concerning the remedies that must be made available to authors whose rights are infringed:

### Berne Convention Article 16

(1) Infringing copies of a work shall be liable to seizure in any country of the Union where the work enjoys legal protection.
(2) The provisions of the preceding paragraph shall also apply to reproductions coming from a country where the work is not protected, or has ceased to be protected.
(3) The seizure shall take place in accordance with the legislation of each country.

Notice that this provision does not require adhering countries to provide damages, attorneys' fees or even injunctive relief. If a country decides to provide only the remedy required by Berne – "seizure" of infringing "copies" – how would authors be able to enforce any of the following rights, all of which Berne itself says authors "shall enjoy"?

## Berne Convention Article 11

(1) Authors of dramatic, dramatico-musical and musical works shall enjoy the exclusive right of authorizing:
  (i) the public performance of their works, including such public performance by any means or process;
  (ii) any communication to the public of the performance of their works.

## Berne Convention Article 11*bis*

(1) Authors of literary and artistic works shall enjoy the exclusive right of authorizing:
  (i) the broadcasting of their works or the communication thereof to the public by any other means of wireless diffusion of signs, sounds or images;
  (ii) any communication to the public by wire or by rebroadcasting of the broadcast of the work, when this communication is made by an organization other than the original one;
  (iii) the public communication by loudspeaker or any other analogous instrument transmitting, by signs, sounds or images, the broadcast of the work.

## Berne Convention Article 11*ter*

(1) Authors of literary works shall enjoy the exclusive right of authorizing:
  (i) the public recitation of their works, including such public recitation by any means or process;
  (ii) any communication to the public of the recitation of their works.

Note that Article 16 requires countries to make "liable to seizure" only "infringing copies" of works – not "allegedly" infringing copies or copies "claimed" to be infringing. As a result, Berne does not require countries to provide for pre-trial seizures (as the United States does in section 503(a) of its Copyright Act). So, if a country decides to provide only the remedy required by Berne – seizure of copies found, at trial, to be "infringing" – what is the probability that the infringer will still have in its possession, after trial, any infringing copies to be seized?

Other (pre-1996) international copyright treaties are even less adequate than Berne with respect to infringement remedies. The UCC, the Satellite Convention, and the Phonograms Convention contain no requirements at all for infringement remedies.

The absence of international infringement remedies was finally cured when the World Trade Organization – which (as its name indicates) is a "trade" rather than copyright organization – adopted its TRIPs Agreement in 1994. Here are the highlights of TRIPs' remedies provisions:

## World Trade Organization TRIPs Agreement

*Article 9: Relation to the Berne Convention*
  1. Members shall comply with . . . the Berne Convention. . . .

*Article 41*
1. Members shall ensure that enforcement procedures as specified in this Part are available under their law so as to permit effective action against any act of infringement of intellectual property rights covered by this Agreement, including expeditious remedies to prevent infringements and remedies which constitute a deterrent to further infringements. . . .

*Article 44: Injunctions*
1. The judicial authorities shall have the authority to order a party to desist from an infringement. . . .

*Article 45: Damages*
1. The judicial authorities shall have the authority to order the infringer to pay the right holder damages adequate to compensate for the injury the right holder has suffered because of an infringement of that person's intellectual property right by an infringer who knowingly, or with reasonable grounds to know, engaged in infringing activity.

2. The judicial authorities shall also have the authority to order the infringer to pay the right holder expenses, which may include appropriate attorney's fees. In appropriate cases, Members may authorize the judicial authorities to order recovery of profits and/or payment of pre-established damages even where the infringer did not knowingly, or with reasonable grounds to know, engage in infringing activity.

*Article 46: Other Remedies*
In order to create an effective deterrent to infringement, the judicial authorities shall have the authority to order that goods that they have found to be infringing be, without compensation of any sort, disposed of outside the channels of commerce in such a manner as to avoid any harm caused to the right holder, or, unless this would be contrary to existing constitutional requirements, destroyed. The judicial authorities shall also have the authority to order that materials and implements the predominant use of which has been in the creation of the infringing goods be, without compensation of any sort, disposed of outside the channels of commerce in such a manner as to minimize the risks of further infringements. . . .

*Article 47: Right of Information*
Members may provide that the judicial authorities shall have the authority, unless this would be out of proportion to the seriousness of the infringement, to order the infringer to inform the right holder of the identity of third persons involved in the production and distribution of the infringing goods or services and of their channels of distribution.

*Article 50*
1. The judicial authorities shall have the authority to order prompt and effective provisional measures: (a) to prevent an infringement of any intellectual property right from occurring . . . .

2. The judicial authorities shall have the authority to adopt provisional measures *inaudita altera parte* where appropriate, in particular where any delay is likely to cause irreparable harm to the right holder, or where there is a demonstrable risk of evidence being destroyed.

*Article 51: Suspension of Release by Customs Authorities*
Members shall . . . adopt procedures to enable a right holder, who has valid grounds for suspecting that the importation of . . . pirated copyright goods may take place, to lodge an application in writing with competent authorities . . . for the suspension by the customs authorities of the release into free circulation of such goods. . . .

*Article 59: Remedies*

Without prejudice to other rights of action open to the right holder and subject to the right of the defendant to seek review by a judicial authority, competent authorities shall have the authority to order the destruction or disposal of infringing goods in accordance with the principles set out in Article 46. . . .

*Article 61*

Members shall provide for criminal procedures and penalties to be applied at least in cases of . . . copyright piracy on a commercial scale. Remedies available shall include imprisonment and/or monetary fines sufficient to provide a deterrent, consistently with the level of penalties applied for crimes of a corresponding gravity. In appropriate cases, remedies available shall also include the seizure, forfeiture and destruction of the infringing goods and of any materials and implements the predominant use of which has been in the commission of the offence. . . .

On their face, these TRIPs provisions seem to do a thorough job of requiring WTO members to provide remedies for rights protected by the Berne Convention. Indeed, in order to join the WTO, China had to enact TRIPs-compliant copyright laws, including TRIPs-compliant infringement remedies; and it did so. This was a significant undertaking by China, because China had never developed its own version of intellectual property law "because of the character of Chinese political culture." (William Alford, *To Steal a Book is an Elegant Offense: Intellectual Property Law in Chinese Civilization* 2 (1997). More simply, the notion of copyright protection simply was not part of the fabric of Chinese culture.

Nevertheless, despite the seeming clarity of the TRIPs provisions, it didn't take long before a dispute arose over whether the infringement remedies enacted by China complied with TRIPs' requirements. The United States said they did not, and initiated a WTO dispute resolution proceeding against China – a proceeding in which Argentina, Australia, Brazil, Canada, the European Communities, India, Japan, Korea, Mexico, Chinese Taipei, Thailand and Turkey also participated. The United States lost, for reasons explained in the following excerpt from a 147-page decision (which the WTO calls a "Report").

As you read this excerpt, ask yourself whether it would have been possible to draft the TRIPs remedies provisions in a way that would have more clearly required China to do what the U.S. argued China should have done.

**Report of WTO Panel on**
**China – Measures Affecting the Protection and**
**Enforcement of Intellectual Property Rights**
**WTO Case WT/DS362/R (26 January 2009)**

. . .

The United States claims that China has not provided for criminal procedures and penalties to be applied in cases of wilful trademark counterfeiting or copyright piracy on a commercial scale that fail to meet certain thresholds. . . .

Article 217 of the [Chinese] Criminal Law may be translated as follows:
"Whoever, for the purpose of making profits, commits [described] acts of infringement of copyright shall, if the amount of illegal gains is relatively large, or if there are other serious circumstances, be sentenced to fixed-term imprisonment of not more than three years or criminal detention and shall also, or shall only, be fined; if the amount of illegal gains is huge or if there are other especially serious circumstances, the offender shall be sentenced to fixed-term imprisonment of not less than three years but not more than seven years and shall also be fined. . . . ."

. . . [T]he phrases "the amount of illegal gains is relatively large" and "there are other serious circumstances". . . . may be translated as follows:
"Whoever, for the purpose of making profits, commits any of the acts of infringement of copyright under Article 217 of the Criminal Law, with the amount of illegal gains of not less than 30,000 Yuan which shall be deemed as 'the amount of illegal gains is relatively large'; in any of the following circumstances which shall be deemed as 'there are other serious circumstances', shall be sentenced to fixed-term imprisonment of not more than three years or criminal detention for the crime of infringement of copyright, and shall also, or shall only, be fined:
- the illegal business operation volume of not less than 50,000 Yuan;
- reproducing, distributing, without permission of the copyright owner, a written work, musical work, cinematographic work, television or other video works, computer software and other works of not less than [500] in total;
- other serious circumstances."

. . . .

Article 218 of the Criminal Law may be translated as follows:
"Whoever, for the purpose of making profits, sells infringing reproductions, knowing that such infringing reproductions are those stipulated in Article 217 of this Law shall, if the amount of illegal gains is huge, be sentenced to fixed-term imprisonment of not more than three years or criminal detention and shall also, or shall only, be fined."

. . . . [T]he phrase "the amount of illegal gains is huge". . . . may be translated as follows:
"Whoever, for the purpose of making profits, commits any of the acts as stipulated in Article 218 of the Criminal Law, where the amount of illegal gains is not less than 100,000 Yuan, this shall be deemed as 'the amount of illegal gains is huge', and the offender shall be sentenced to fixed-term imprisonment of not more than three years or criminal detention for the crime of selling infringing reproductions, and shall also, or shall only, be fined."

. . . .

. . . .[T]he Panel concludes that, whilst the structure of the thresholds and the method of calculation of some of them can take account of various circumstances, acts of trademark and copyright infringement falling below *all* the applicable thresholds are not subject to criminal procedures and penalties. The Panel will now consider whether any of those acts of infringement constitute "wilful trademark counterfeiting or copyright piracy on a commercial scale" within the meaning of Article 61 of the TRIPS Agreement.

. . . .

The United States' claim relates to cases of wilful trademark counterfeiting and copyright piracy in respect of which China does not provide for criminal procedures and penalties to be applied but which the United States claims are "on a commercial scale".

. . . .

The terms of the obligation in the first sentence of Article 61 of the TRIPS Agreement are that Members shall "provide for criminal procedures and penalties to be applied". That obligation applies to "wilful trademark counterfeiting or copyright piracy on a commercial scale". Within that scope, there are no exceptions. The obligation applies to *all* acts of wilful trademark counterfeiting or copyright piracy on a commercial scale.

. . . . [I]n China, acts of trademark and copyright infringement falling below the applicable thresholds are not subject to criminal procedures and penalties. The issue that arises is whether any of those acts of infringement constitute "wilful trademark counterfeiting or copyright piracy on a commercial scale" within the meaning of the first sentence of Article 61. . . .

The . . . first sentence of Article 61 [contains] the word "wilful" that precedes the words "trademark counterfeiting or copyright piracy". This word functions as a qualifier indicating that trademark counterfeiting or copyright piracy is not subject to the obligation in the first sentence of Article 61 unless it is "wilful". This word, focusing on the infringer's intent, reflects the criminal nature of the enforcement procedures at issue. . . . The penalties for criminal acts, such as imprisonment, fines and forfeiture of property, are relatively grave, as reflected in the second sentence of Article 61. There is no obligation to make such penalties available with respect to acts of infringement committed without the requisite intent.

The . . . first sentence of Article 61 [also contains] . . . the phrase "on a commercial scale" that follows the words "trademark counterfeiting or copyright piracy". This phrase, like the word "wilful", appears to qualify both "trademark counterfeiting" and "copyright piracy". . . .

The principal interpretative point in dispute is the meaning of the phrase "on a commercial scale". This phrase functions in context as a qualifier, indicating that wilful trademark counterfeiting or copyright piracy is included in the scope of the obligation provided that it also satisfies the condition of being "on a commercial scale". Accordingly, certain acts of wilful trademark counterfeiting or copyright piracy are excluded from the scope of the first sentence of Article 61.

Despite the fact that trademark counterfeiting and copyright piracy infringe the rights of right holders, and despite the fact that they can be grave, the two qualifications of wilfulness and "on a commercial scale" indicate that Article 61 does not require Members to provide for criminal procedures and penalties to be applied to such counterfeiting and piracy *per se* unless they satisfy certain additional criteria. . . .

The parties adopt different approaches to the task of interpreting the phrase "on a commercial scale". . . .

[The Panel then undertook a very lengthy review and analysis of the parties' differing approaches to interpreting "on a commercial scale," and reached the following conclusion.]

The Panel . . . finds that a "commercial scale" is the magnitude or extent of typical or usual commercial activity. Therefore, counterfeiting or piracy "on a commercial scale" refers to counterfeiting or piracy carried on at the magnitude or extent of typical or usual commercial activity with respect to a given product in a given market. The magnitude or extent of typical or usual commercial activity with respect to a given product in a given market forms a benchmark by which to assess the obligation in the first sentence of Article 61. It follows that what constitutes a commercial scale for counterfeiting or piracy of a particular product in a particular market will depend on the magnitude or extent that is typical or usual with respect to such a product in such a market, which may be small or large. The magnitude or extent of typical or usual commercial activity relates, in the longer term, to profitability.

. . . The Panel will now apply that interpretation to the measures at issue.

. . .

The United States argues that the criminal thresholds exclude certain commercial activity. The United States relies, in particular, on the text of the measures establishing the criminal thresholds themselves.

The Panel has reviewed the measures and agrees that, on their face, they do exclude certain commercial activity from criminal procedures and penalties. For example, some of the criminal thresholds are set in terms that refer expressly to commercial activity, such as "illegal business operation volume", which is defined in terms of "manufacture, storage, transportation, or sales" of infringing products, and "illegal gains" which is defined in terms of profit. However, based solely on the measures on their face, the Panel cannot distinguish between acts that, in China's marketplace, are on a commercial *scale*, and those that are not.

Certain thresholds are set in monetary terms, ranging from ¥20,000 profit to ¥50,000 turnover or sales. The measures, on their face, do not indicate what these amounts represent as compared to a relevant commercial benchmark in China. Each of these amounts represents a range of volumes of goods, which vary according to price. Another factor to take into account is the period of time over which infringements can be cumulated to satisfy these thresholds. One threshold is set not in monetary terms but rather at 500 张 (份) ("copies" for the sake of simplicity). Whilst it is reasonably clear to the Panel how many goods that comprises with respect to certain traditional media, this is not, on its face, related to any relevant market benchmark in China either.

. . .

The Panel has reviewed the evidence [submitted by the U.S., but concludes that] . . . the information that was provided was too little and too random to demonstrate a level that constitutes a commercial scale for any product in China.

. . .

For the above reasons, the Panel finds that the United States has not made a prima facie case with respect to the first limb of its claim [based on numerical thresholds] under the first sentence of Article 61 of the TRIPS Agreement.

. . . [T]he United States also alleges that China's thresholds are tied to finished goods and therefore ignore other indicia of commercial scale operations, such as the impact that the piracy or counterfeiting has on the commercial marketplace and by extension, right holders. . . . The United States mentions the example of HDVDs (high-definition digital video discs) that can hold up to ten episodes of a TV series or several films.

The Panel notes that the United States has not attempted to substantiate its assertion regarding HDVDs. This example appears to be based on the view that the term 张 (份) in the thresholds ("copies" for the sake of simplicity) refers only to physical discs and cannot be applied in any other way in a novel situation. There is no evidence on the record indicating that the thresholds have ever been applied to HDVDs, so this example is merely speculation based on the indirect reference to flat objects in the word 张 and to copies in the word 份. This example can be compared to an assertion that a copyright law does not provide protection to computer programs simply on the basis that the legislation refers to the term "literary and artistic works" and computer programs are not obviously literary or artistic. Some evidence is required that the authorities could not or would not apply that measure in the appropriate manner to new technology. The Panel notes China's assertion that, at such time as this issue arises for consideration, its authorities can apply the threshold in terms of the number of films or episodes on each disc.

. . .

For all the above reasons, the Panel does not consider that the United States has made a prima facie case with respect to impact on the commercial marketplace.

. . .

. . . [T]he Panel concludes that the United States has not established that the criminal thresholds are inconsistent with China's obligations under the first sentence of Article 61 of the TRIPS Agreement.

. . .

TRIPs – an intellectual property annex to an international trade agreement – "broke the ice" by requiring countries to adopt effective copyright infringement remedies. TRIPs did not prompt revisions to the UCC, the Satellite Convention or the Phonograms Convention. But it did pave the way for remedies provisions in the two post-TRIPs copyright treaties adopted in 1996 – the WIPO Copyright Treaty and the WIPO Performances and Phonograms Treaty. These two treaties provide (in identically worded Articles):

### WIPO Copyright Treaty Article 14
### WIPO Performances and Phonograms Treaty Article 23

(1) Contracting Parties undertake to adopt, in accordance with their legal systems, the measures necessary to ensure the application of this Treaty.

(2) Contracting Parties shall ensure that enforcement procedures are available under their law so as to permit effective action against any act of infringement of rights covered by this Treaty, including expeditious remedies to prevent infringements and remedies which constitute a deterrent to further infringements.

## 2. Substantive protections

International trade treaties also have required countries to upgrade the substantive copyright protections their laws provide, *beyond* what is required by *copyright* treaties. For example, here is what the WIPO Copyright Treaty and WIPO Performances and Phonograms Treaty have to say about technological protection measures (in virtually identical language):

### WIPO Copyright Treaty Article 11

Contracting Parties shall provide adequate legal protection and effective legal remedies against the circumvention of effective technological measures that are used by authors in connection with the exercise of their rights under this Treaty or the Berne Convention and that restrict acts, in respect of their works, which are not authorized by the authors concerned or permitted by law.

### WIPO Performances and Phonograms Treaty Article 18

Contracting Parties shall provide adequate legal protection and effective legal remedies against the circumvention of effective technological measures that are used by performers or producers of phonograms in connection with the exercise of their rights under this Treaty and that restrict acts, in respect of their performances or phonograms, which are not authorized by the performers or the producers of phonograms concerned or permitted by law.

The United States implemented these treaty obligations by enacting the anti-circumvention provisions that are codified at 17 U.S.C. sections 1201 through 1205. Those provisions of U.S. law are far more detailed than the WIPO treaties. The anti-circumvention provisions of U.S. law have been extremely controversial. What's more, because they prohibit circumvention under certain circumstances where, arguably, prohibition is not required by the WIPO treaties, it is likely that at least some other countries – perhaps many – would not have followed the lead of the United States, if the matter were left entirely to them. The United States prefers its own anti-circumvention provisions to others that are less stringent, even if less-stringent versions would be WIPO-compliant. As a result, in a number of instances, the United States has persuaded other countries to adopt anti-circumvention provisions similar to its own, in the course of bilateral trade treaty negotiations. See, e.g., *U.S.-Australia Free Trade Agreement* Article 17.4 (effective January 1, 2005) available at http://www.ustr.gov/ Trade_Agreements/Bilateral/Australia_FTA/ Final_Text/Section_Index.html

How do you suppose the United States was able to persuade other countries, like Australia, to enact U.S.-style anti-circumvention provisions? Would it help to know that the U.S.-Australia Free Trade Agreement is 264 pages long, *not* including its "Annexes" and "Side Letters," and that most of those pages deal with topics *other than* copyright?

## B. Limits imposed by international trade law on rights and privileges granted by national copyright statutes

The relationship between copyright and international trade may not be obvious, but there is one. There is, because copyright owners have the exclusive right, within individual countries, to sell their works there (or to grant exclusive licenses to others to do so).

Here is a bit of copyright law background that will enable you to put the following materials in proper context. The United States Copyright Act:

- gives copyright owners the exclusive right to distribute their works, including the exclusive right to import their works into the U.S. from abroad, *but*
- the exclusive right to distribute works comes to an end, with respect to each particular copy of a work, when that particular copy is first sold by the copyright owner to someone else.

The copyright laws of most other countries also contain an exclusive right to distribute and import. And in most other countries, that right also comes to an end, with respect to a particular copy, when that copy is sold. In the U.S., the legal doctrine that brings the exclusive distribution right to an end is called the "First Sale Doctrine"; elsewhere, it is usually referred to as the "Doctrine of Exhaustion." By whatever name, the doctrine permits the buyer of a particular copy of a copyrighted work to re-distribute that particular copy to others, without the consent of the copyright owner.

Here is a bit of factual background you should keep in mind, as you read the following case. Copyrighted works located in other countries (prior to being imported into the U.S.)

- may have been manufactured *in the United States* to begin with, and then sold (the "First Sale") to a foreign buyer, from whom an importer purchased them for resale back in the U.S., in which case the copyrighted works have made a "round trip" out of and then back into the U.S., *or* they
- may have been manufactured *outside* the U.S. to begin with, and then purchased outside the U.S. by an importer who imports them into the U.S. for resale in the U.S., in which case the copyrighted works have made a "one-way" trip into the U.S.

---

*Questions:*

- What types of works were involved in the following case: those that were manufactured *in* the United States to begin with, or those that were manufactured *outside* the U.S. to begin with?
- Does the answer to this question matter to Justice Stevens, who wrote the "opinion of the Court"? To Justice Ginsburg, who wrote a concurring opinion?

---

## Quality King Distributors, Inc. v. L'Anza Research International, Inc.
### 523 U.S. 135 (1998)

*Justice Stevens delivered the opinion of the Court.*

Section 106(3) of the Copyright Act of 1976 (Act), 17 U.S.C. §106(3), gives the owner of a copyright the exclusive right to distribute copies of a copyrighted work. That exclusive right is expressly limited, however, by the provisions of §§107 through 120. Section 602(a) gives the copyright owner the right to prohibit the unauthorized importation of copies. The question presented by this case is whether the right granted by §602(a) is also limited by §§107 through 120. More narrowly, the question is whether the "first sale" doctrine endorsed in §109(a) is applicable to imported copies.

I

Respondent, L'Anza Research International, Inc. (L'Anza), is a California corporation engaged in the business of manufacturing and selling shampoos, conditioners, and other hair care products. L'Anza has copyrighted the labels that are affixed to those products. In the United States, L'Anza sells exclusively to domestic distributors who have agreed to resell within limited geographic areas and then only to authorized retailers such as barber shops, beauty salons, and professional hair care colleges. L'Anza has found that the American "public is generally unwilling to pay the price charged for high quality products, such as L'Anza's products, when they are sold along with the less expensive lower quality products that are generally carried by supermarkets and drug stores." . . . L'Anza promotes the domestic sales of its products with extensive advertising in various trade magazines and at point of sale, and by providing special training to authorized retailers.

L'Anza also sells its products in foreign markets. In those markets, however, it does not engage in comparable advertising or promotion; its prices to foreign distributors are 35% to 40% lower than the prices charged to domestic distributors. In 1992 and 1993, L'Anza's distributor in the United Kingdom arranged the sale of three shipments to a distributor in Malta; each shipment contained several tons of L'Anza products with copyrighted labels affixed. . . . [I]t is undisputed that the goods were manufactured by L'Anza and first sold by L'Anza to a foreign purchaser.

It is also undisputed that the goods found their way back to the United States without the permission of L'Anza and were sold in California by unauthorized retailers who had purchased them at discounted prices from Quality King Distributors, Inc. (petitioner). . . . [W]e assume that petitioner bought all three shipments from the Malta distributor, imported them, and then resold them to retailers who were not in L'Anza's authorized chain of distribution.

After determining the source of the unauthorized sales, L'Anza brought suit against petitioner and several other defendants. The complaint alleged that the importation and subsequent distribution of those products bearing copyrighted labels violated L'Anza's "exclusive rights under 17 U.S.C. §§106, 501 and 602 to reproduce and distribute the copyrighted material in the United States." The District Court rejected petitioner's defense based on the "first sale" doctrine recognized by §109 and entered summary judgment in favor of L'Anza. Based largely on its conclusion that §602 would be "meaningless" if §109 provided a defense in a case of this kind, the Court of Appeals affirmed. . . . Because its decision created a conflict with the Third Circuit, . . . we granted the petition for certiorari. . . .

161

## II

This is an unusual copyright case because L'Anza does not claim that anyone has made unauthorized copies of its copyrighted labels. Instead, L'Anza is primarily interested in protecting the integrity of its method of marketing the products to which the labels are affixed. Although the labels themselves have only a limited creative component, *our interpretation of the relevant statutory provisions would apply equally to a case involving more familiar copyrighted materials such as sound recordings or books.* [Emphasis added.] Indeed, we first endorsed the first sale doctrine in a case involving a claim by a publisher that the resale of its books at discounted prices infringed its copyright on the books. *Bobbs-Merrill Co.* v. *Straus,* 210 U.S. 339, 52 L. Ed. 1086, 28 S. Ct. 722 (1908). . . .

The statute in force when *Bobbs-Merrill* was decided provided that the copyright owner had the exclusive right to "vend" the copyrighted work. Congress subsequently codified our holding in *Bobbs-Merrill* that the exclusive right to "vend" was limited to first sales of the work. Under the 1976 Act, the comparable exclusive right granted in 17 U.S.C. §106(3) is the right "to distribute copies . . . by sale or other transfer of ownership." The comparable limitation on that right is provided not by judicial interpretation, but by an express statutory provision. Section 109(a) provides:

"Notwithstanding the provisions of section 106(3), the owner of a particular copy or phonorecord lawfully made under this title, or any person authorized by such owner, is entitled, without the authority of the copyright owner, to sell or otherwise dispose of the possession of that copy or phonorecord . . . ."

## III

The most relevant portion of §602(a) provides:

"Importation into the United States, without the authority of the owner of copyright under this title, of copies or phonorecords of a work that have been acquired outside the United States is an infringement of the exclusive right to distribute copies or phonorecords under section 106, actionable under section 501 . . . ."

It is significant that this provision does not categorically prohibit the unauthorized importation of copyrighted materials. Instead, it provides that such importation is an infringement of the exclusive right to distribute copies "under section 106." Like the exclusive right to "vend" that was construed in *Bobbs-Merrill,* the exclusive right to distribute is a limited right. The introductory language in §106 expressly states that all of the exclusive rights granted by that section – including, of course, the distribution right granted by subsection (3) – are limited by the provisions of §§107 through 120. One of those limitations, as we have noted, is provided by the terms of §109(a), which expressly permit the owner of a lawfully made copy to sell that copy "notwithstanding the provisions of section 106(3)."

After the first sale of a copyrighted item "lawfully made under this title," any subsequent purchaser, whether from a domestic or from a foreign reseller, is obviously an "owner" of that item. Read literally, §109(a) unambiguously states that such an owner "is entitled, without the authority of the copyright owner, to sell" that item. Moreover, since §602(a) merely provides that unauthorized importation is an infringement of an exclusive right "under section 106," and since that limited right does not encompass resales by lawful owners, the literal text of §602(a) is simply inapplicable to both domestic and foreign owners of L'Anza's products who decide to import them and resell them in the United States.[14] [n14 Despite L'Anza's contention to the contrary, the owner of goods lawfully made under the Act is entitled to the protection of the first sale doctrine in an action in a United States court even if the first sale occurred abroad. Such protection does not require the extraterritorial application of the Act any more than §602(a)'s "acquired abroad" language does.] . . .

The judgment of the Court of Appeals is reversed. It is so ordered.

*Justice Ginsburg, concurring.*

This case involves a "round trip" journey, travel of the copies in question from the United States to places abroad, then back again. I join the Court's opinion recognizing that we do not today resolve cases in which the allegedly infringing imports were manufactured abroad. See W. Patry, *Copyright Law and Practice* 166-170 (1997 Supp.) (commenting that provisions of Title 17 do not apply extraterritorially unless expressly so stated, hence the words "lawfully made under this title" in the "first sale" provision, 17 U.S.C. §109(a), must mean "lawfully made in the United States"); see generally P. Goldstein, *Copyright* §16.0, pp. 16:1-16:2 (2d ed. 1998) ("Copyright protection is territorial. The rights granted by the United States Copyright Act extend no farther than the nation's borders.").

---

The question of whether copyright may be used to block "one-way" imports from abroad was answered "yes," in *Omega v. Costco*, 541 F.3d 982 (9th Cir. 2008), *petition for cert. pending*, 2009 U.S. LEXIS 6827 (2009). The Ninth Circuit noted that the *Quality King* majority did not disagree with Justice Ginsburg's concurring opinion, in which she said that the case involved only a "round trip" import. Assume that the Supreme Court denies certiorari in the *Omega v. Costco* case, or that the Supreme Court affirms *Omega*. In other words, assume that one way or another, Justice Ginsburg's concurring opinion in *Quality King* is accepted as a correct statement of the law. With that assumption in mind, answer the following questions.

*Questions:*

- A U.S.-based Spanish language television program production company manufactures, in the United States, DVDs of old episodes of its programs. The episodes are protected by U.S. copyright law, and the company owns those copyrights. The company sells some of the DVDs to retail stores in the United States, at wholesale prices that are customary in the U.S. The company also sells some of the DVDs to retail stores in Mexico, at wholesale prices that are customary in Mexico. The customary wholesale price in Mexico is much less than it is in the United States. The owner of a retail store in San Diego, California, drives a rented U-Haul truck across the border to Tijuana, Mexico, where the store owner is able to buy the DVDs in bulk from a retail store at a price that is less than the San Diego store owner would have to pay in the United States. If the production company sues the owner of the San Diego retail store for copyright infringement in federal District Court in

San Diego, alleging the infringement of the company's exclusive right to import, what result is likely?

- A Mexican television program production company manufactures, in Mexico, DVDs of old episodes of its programs. The company sells some of the DVDs to retail stores in the United States, at wholesale prices that are customary in the U.S. The company also sells some of the DVDs to retail stores in Mexico, at wholesale prices that are customary in Mexico. The customary wholesale price in Mexico is much less than it is in the United States. The owner of a retail store in San Diego, California, drives a rented U-Haul truck across the border to Tijuana, Mexico, where the store owner is able to buy the DVDs in bulk from a retail store at a price that is less than the San Diego store owner would have to pay in the United States. The United States and Mexico are parties to a copyright treaty, so the Mexican company does own U.S. copyrights to all of its episodes. If the Mexican production company sues the owner of the San Diego retail store for copyright infringement in federal court in San Diego, alleging the infringement of the company's exclusive right to import, what result is likely?

---

The *Quality King* case involved imports into the United States from Malta. Malta is a member of the European Union, but the United States of course is not. Suppose that a similar case arose involving imports into one member of the European Union from another member of the European Union. In such a case, a treaty that played no role at all in the *Quality King* case would be very important. Here are the relevant provisions of that treaty.

### Treaty Establishing the European Community (aka "EEC Treaty" and "Treaty of Rome")

*Article 28 [Article 30 in original version of the Treaty cited in the opinions that follow]*
Quantitative restrictions on imports *and all measures having equivalent effect* shall be prohibited between Member States. [Emphasis added.]

*Article 30 [Article 36 in original version of the Treaty cited in the opinions that follow]*
The provisions of [Article] 28 . . . shall *not* preclude prohibitions or restrictions on imports . . . justified on grounds of . . . *the protection of industrial and commercial property.* Such prohibitions or restrictions shall not, however, constitute a means of arbitrary discrimination or a disguised restriction on trade between Member States. [Emphasis added.]

Before reading the materials that follow, are you able to see how Article 28 *could* be interpreted to prohibit the enforcement of exclusive territorial rights granted by national copyright statutes? Are you able to see how Article 30 *could* be interpreted to permit the enforcement of those rights? Assuming copyrights are "industrial property" (as that term is defined within the European Union), what impact do you think Articles 28 and 30 would have on the enforceability of exclusive territorial rights granted by national copyright statutes?

The Court of Justice of the European Communities is the court that interprets the Treaty of Rome – the treaty that created what is now known as the European Union – so in a sense, it can be thought of as the EU Supreme Court. (Despite their similar names, the EU's "Treaty of Rome" should not be confused with the "Rome Convention" which is a copyright treaty that protects phonograms. In some decisions, the Treaty of Rome is referred to as the "EEC Treaty.")

## 1. Limits on exclusive rights

Although the Treaty of Rome applies only to EU members, the following decisions are important to copyright owners from other countries too (including the United States), if those owners export their copyrighted goods to EU countries or license their copyrighted works for use in EU countries. As you read these cases, think about *why* and *how* they would affect copyright owners from non-EU countries. Why, in other words, would you – as a lawyer for American copyright owners who do business with those in the EU – need to know about the legal principles discussed in these cases?

### Deutsche Grammophon Gesellschaft GmbH
### v. Metro-SB-Grossmarkte GmbH & Co. Ltd
### [1971] ECR 487, [1971] CMLR 631, 2 IIC 429
### (Court of Justice of the European Communities 1971)

The facts of the case . . . may be summarized as follows.

Deutsche Grammophon . . . produces gramophone records (for which it has certain artists under exclusive contracts) and markets its products under a number of marks. In the German Federal Republic the records are supplied direct to retailers and to two book-wholesalers which exclusively supply retail bookshops. The retail prices of the records are mostly controlled; in any event, all the numbers that are sold under the "Polydor" mark are subject to a retail price-maintenance system. Retailers have to sign an appropriate form to this effect. The form in addition provides that the price-maintenance undertaking also applies to Deutsche Grammophon records acquired from third parties and that such products can only be imported from abroad with the authorisation of Deutsche Grammophon (and the consent is only given if the retailer also undertakes to observe the price-maintenance system in this respect). Deutsche Grammophon, on its part, is bound to supply solely to retailers who sign the undertaking. In addition, it has to ensure that the price-maintenance system is kept watertight and proceed against infringements. The records are marketed abroad through subsidiaries of Deutsche Grammophon or Philips. This is the case in particular in France where Polydor SA, Paris (99.55 per cent of the capital of which is held by Deutsche Grammophon), supplies the market from its factories in Paris and Strasbourg. Deutsche Grammophon has concluded a licensing agreement with it, whereby the licensee has inter alia the exclusive right in . . . France to exploit Deutsche Grammophon recordings . . . through retailers and to use the appropriate marks. For this purpose Deutsche Grammophon supplies matrixes for reproduction against payment of licence fees. In special cases records manufactured in the Federal Republic are also supplied to Polydor Paris.

Metro-SB-Grossmarkte . . . bought Polydor records from Deutsche Grammophon in the period from April to October 1969 but did not observe the retail price-maintenance system. Since Metro was not prepared to sign a retailer's undertaking, business relations were broken off at the end of October 1969. However, in January and February 1970 Metro succeeded in obtaining Polydor records manufactured by Deutsche Grammophon in Germany from a Hamburg wholesaler. Apparently these records had been supplied by Deutsche Grammophon to its Paris subsidiary. They had then reached the Hamburg wholesaler through the Strasbourg branch and a Swiss enterprise. Metro also sold these records to retail customers at a price below that fixed by Deutsche Grammophon for the Federal Republic.

When Deutsche Grammophon learned of this it obtained a provisional injunction from [a German court] on 20 March 1970 prohibiting Metro from selling or distributing in any other way Deutsche Grammophon records with certain serial numbers under the Polydor mark. The application and the court's decision were based on the [German copyright statute] which, in accordance with the [Rome] Convention . . . , created an original protection right, similar to copyright, for manufacturers of sound recordings. . . . The [German court] invoked sections 85 and 97 of the German [copyright] statute, which provide as follows:

> Section 85: "The manufacturer of a sound recording has the exclusive right to reproduce and to distribute the recording."

> Section 97: "Any person who unlawfully infringes the copyright or any other right protected by this statute may, at the suit of the person whose rights are infringed, be ordered to abate the infringement, or, if there is a danger of repetition, be restrained by injunction, and if he is found to have acted with intent or negligence he may be ordered to pay damages."

In addition, the court evidently found that the exclusive right attributed to Deutsche Grammophon to distribute its records in Germany had not been exhausted by the delivery to Polydor Paris. Thus it held that there was no exhaustion of the right as provided in the appropriately applicable section 17 of the [German] Copyright Statute in the following words:

> "If the original or reproductions of the work have been brought into circulation with the consent of the person entitled to distribute them in the territory to which this statute applies by means of alienation their further distribution is permitted."

In the view of the court, this provision would only have applied if a distribution had occurred in the German Federal Republic. Otherwise the marketing of re-imported records in Germany had to be regarded as impermissible.

The protest lodged by Metro against the provisional injunction was unsuccessful. In a judgment of 22 May 1970 all the arguments submitted against the order of the court were held to be of no avail. Metro then lodged an appeal against this judgment and the matter thus came before the Hanseatische Oberlandesgericht [a German appeals court]. In support of the appeal it was submitted inter alia that Deutsche Grammophon no longer had the distribution rights in the records in question as these rights had been extinguished by the delivery to the French subsidiary. . . .

In view of these arguments the Oberlandesgericht [the German appeals court], by an order of 8 October 1970, suspended the proceedings and in accordance with Article 177 of the EEC Treaty submitted the following questions for a preliminary ruling [by this court, i.e., the Court of Justice of the European Communities]:

> 1. Does an interpretation of Sections 97 and 85 of the [German] Statute concerning Copyright, whereby a German manufacturer of sound recordings, by virtue of its distribution rights, can prohibit the marketing in the German Federal Republic of recordings which it has itself supplied to its subsidiary France which is legally separate but economically completely dependent, conflict with Article 5(2) . . . of the EEC Treaty? . . .

According to Article 177 [of the EEC Treaty] the Court [of Justice of the European Communities] can only give preliminary rulings regarding the interpretation of the [EEC] Treaty and the measures taken by the organs of the Community or concerning the validity of these measures, and not with regard to the interpretation of a provision of national law. Nevertheless, it may extract from the wording of the question submitted by the national court, in the light of the facts found by that court, the questions that relate to the interpretation of the Treaty.

From the findings of the Hanseatische Oberlandesgericht, Hamburg, [the German appeals court,] it must be supposed that the question posed really seeks to ascertain whether [European] Community law is infringed if the exclusive right conferred on a manufacturer of recordings by national legislation to distribute the protected products can be used to prohibit the domestic marketing of products that have been brought into the market in the territory of another member-State by this manufacturer or with his consent. Thus the Court is asked to ascertain the content and scope of the applicable Community rules, particularly with regard to Article 5(2) . . . of the Treaty.

According to Article 5(2) of the Treaty the member-States must "abstain from any measures which could jeopardise the attainment of the objectives of [the] Treaty." This provision imposes a general obligation on the member-States the concrete content of which depends in a particular case on the provisions of the Treaty or the rules of law derived from the general system of the Treaty. . . .

Although the Treaty otherwise permits prohibitions or restrictions on the movement of goods between member-States laid down in Article 36, it nevertheless sets clear limits to these prohibitions or restrictions by providing that these exceptions may not amount "either to a means of arbitrary discrimination or to a disguised restriction on trade between the member-States."

. . . [I]t must therefore be considered to what extent the marketing of products imported from another member-State may be prohibited in exercise of a national protection right similar to copyright.

Article 36 mentions among the prohibitions or restrictions on the free movement of goods permitted by it those that are justified for the protection of industrial and commercial property. [It may] be assumed that a right analogous to copyright can be covered by these provisions[.] [Nevertheless] it follows . . . from this Article that although the Treaty does not affect the existence of the industrial property rights conferred by the national legislation of a member-State, the exercise of these rights may come within the prohibitions of the Treaty. Although Article 36 permits prohibitions or restrictions on the free movement of goods that are justified for the protection of industrial and commercial property, it only allows such restrictions on the freedom of trade to the extent that they are justified for the protection of the rights that form the specific object of this property.

If a protection right analogous to copyright is used in order to prohibit in one member-State the marketing of goods that have been brought onto the market by the holder of the right or with his consent in the territory of another member-State solely because this marketing has not occurred in the domestic market, such a prohibition maintaining the isolation of the national markets conflicts with the essential aim of the Treaty, the integration of the national markets into one uniform market. This aim could not be achieved if by virtue of the various legal systems of the member-States private persons were able to divide the market and cause arbitrary discriminations or disguised restrictions in trade between the member-States.

Accordingly, it would conflict with the provisions regarding the free movement of goods in the Common market if a manufacturer of recordings exercised the exclusive right granted to him by the legislation of a member-State to market the protected articles in order to prohibit the marketing in that member-State of products that had been sold by him himself or with his consent in another member-State solely because this marketing had not occurred in the territory of the first member-State. . . .

The Court, for these reasons, giving judgment on the questions submitted to it by the Hanseatische Oberlandesgericht Hamburg in its order of 8 October 1970,

Hereby Decides:

1. It conflicts with the provisions regarding the free movement of goods in the Common Market if a manufacturer of recordings so exercises the exclusive right granted to him by the legislation of a member-State to market the protected articles as to prohibit the marketing in that member-State of products that have been sold by himself or with his consent in another member-State solely because this marketing has not occurred in the territory of the first member-State. . . .

As a consequence of the *Deutsche Grammophon* decision, is it possible for an American book publishing company to grant a license to a British publisher, giving it the *exclusive* right to publish a book *in the U.K.*, and another license to a French publisher, giving it the *exclusive* right to publish the book *in France*? Is it possible for an American movie studio to grant a license to an Italian homevideo company, giving it the *exclusive* right to distribute DVDs of a movie *in Italy*, and another license to a German homevideo company, giving it the *exclusive* right to distribute DVDs of the movie *in Germany*? Exclusive license agreements purporting to do just that could be drafted and signed, of course. *Deutsche Grammophon* doesn't make such agreements illegal. The question is whether the exclusivity clause could be enforced by exclusive licensees, if others were to buy licensed books or DVDs in another country and then offer them for sale in the country where exclusive rights were granted.

What if the exclusive rights holder does not seek to prevent importation into or sales within its territory, but does attempt to collect royalties from the importer? That question is answered by the next opinion.

### Musik-Vertrieb Membran GmbH v. GEMA
### [1981] ECR 147, [1981] 2 CMLR 44, [1981] FSR 433, 12 IIC 526
### (Court of Justice of the European Communities 1981)

. . . Musik-Vertrieb Membran GmbH imported sound recordings (records and cassettes) from other countries, including Member States of the European Community, in which those products were in free circulation, into the Federal Republic of Germany. The sound recordings were of musical works protected by copyright. Licenses were granted in the country of manufacture for the reproduction and distribution of the protected musical works and the appropriate royalties were paid.

GEMA [the German society that collects mechanical royalties from record companies on behalf of music publishers and songwriters] obtained a judgment from the Landgericht Hamburg [a German Regional Court] ordering Musik-Vertrieb Membran to supply detailed information about the sound recordings imported by it into Germany from abroad since 1 April 1973. GEMA had based its application on Article 87 of the [German] Copyright Law (Urheberrechtsgesetz) on the ground that the defendant had infringed the distribution rights of the authors represented by GEMA and was therefore liable to pay damages equivalent to the difference between the license fee already paid abroad and the royalty in force in Germany. It was in order to be able to put a figure to that difference that GEMA initially confined itself to requiring information.

When ruling on the appeal by the defendant the Hanseatisches Oberlandesgericht [the German appeals court] upheld the judgment [of the Regional Court]. . . .

In 1974 . . . K-tel International imported records from the United Kingdom into the Federal Republic on which protected musical works were recorded. A license to reproduce and distribute the protected musical works had been granted in the United Kingdom by the management company "Mechanical Copyright Protection Society Ltd. (MCPS)," the copyright owner, to a sister company of K-tel, K-tel International Ltd. The English firm paid a royalty to MCPS. The amount of that royalty is the same as the rate demanded by MCPS for records intended to be marketed in the United Kingdom.

MCPS tried without success to obtain payment in the United Kingdom by K-tel International Ltd., in regard to the records exported to Germany, of the difference between the royalty fee paid in the United Kingdom and that charged in Germany.

GEMA obtained a judgment from the Landgericht Frankfurt [a German Regional Court] ordering K-tel to pay it in regard to the records imported into Germany the difference between the royalty fee paid in the United Kingdom to MCPS by K-tel International Ltd., and that charged in Germany. GEMA had sought that sum as damages payable under Article 97 of the [German] Copyright Law (Urheberrechtsgesetz) on the ground that K-tel had infringed the distribution rights of the authors represented by GEMA.

When ruling on the appeal by the defendant the Oberlandesgericht Frankfurt upheld the judgment . . . .

In both cases the courts held that the right to distribute records in the Federal Republic of Germany was not exhausted by their entry into circulation in the United Kingdom and that the provisions of the EEC Treaty on the free movement of goods did not prevent the difference between the royalty fees from being claimed....

Musik-Vertrieb Membran GmbH and K-tel International (hereinafter called "the appellants") appealed against those judgments on a point of law before the Bundesgerichtshof [the German Supreme Court].

By two orders of 19 December 1979 the Bundesgerichtshof stayed the proceedings and in both cases referred the following question to the Court [of Justice of the European Communities] for a preliminary ruling:

> Is it compatible with the provisions concerning the free movement of goods (Article 30 et seq. of the EEC Treaty) for a management company entrusted with the exploitation of copyrights to exercise the exclusive rights held by the composer in Member State A to the transcription of his musical works onto sound recordings, their reproduction and marketing in such a way as to require, in respect of the marketing in Member State A of sound recordings which have been produced and placed on the market in Member State B – the composer's authorization being however restricted to Member State B against payment of a license fee which is calculated on the quantity and final selling price relevant to that Member State – a payment which is equal to the customary license fee in respect of production and marketing in Member State A, but which takes into account the (lower) license fee which has already been paid in respect of production and marketing in Member State B?

[In both orders for reference, the German Supreme Court stated that in its opinion, the decisions of the lower German courts were correct, on the basis of German law alone.] . . .

That question has been raised in the context of two disputes between GEMA, a German copyright management society, and two [companies] which imported into the Federal Republic of Germany sound recordings of protected musical works. In [the Musik-Vertrieb case] the imports consisted of gramophone records and musical tape cassettes from various countries, including other Member States of the Community; and in [the K-tel case] the importation consisted of a consignment of 100,000 gramophone records from the United Kingdom. It is common ground that the sound recordings from other Member States had been manufactured and marketed in those Member States with the consent of the owner of the copyright in the musical works concerned, and that the requisite licenses had been granted by those owners and the appropriate royalties had been calculated only on the basis of distribution in the country of manufacture.

GEMA contends that the importation of those sound recordings into German territory constitutes an infringement of the copyrights which it is responsible for protecting in the name of the owners of those rights. As a result it considers that it is entitled to claim payment of the royalties payable on sound recordings put into circulation on German Territory less the amount of the lower royalties already paid in respect of distribution in the Member State of manufacture.

The Bundesgerichtshof [the German Supreme Court] has stated that under German law the fact that the composers involved consented to their musical works' being reproduced in another Member State of the Community and put into circulation on the territory of that Member State in return for a royalty calculated according to the number of copies sold and the retail selling price in that Member State does not prevent them from claiming, pursuant to the exclusive exploitation right which they hold on the German market when sound recordings are distributed on that market, the royalties ordinarily paid on that market, which are calculated according to the number of copies sold and the retail selling price prevailing on the domestic market, less the royalties already paid in respect of distribution in the Member State of manufacture.

However, the [German] national court questions whether such an exercise of copyright is compatible with the provisions of the Treaty relating to the free movement of goods. It has brought the matter before the Court [of Justice of the European Community] in order to clarify this point.

From the papers placed before the Court it seems that in the two disputes before the German courts, GEMA based its case on Article 97 of the German Law on Copyright (Urheberrechtsgesetz), a provision setting forth the various remedies which are available to an author should his copyright be infringed and which include actions requiring the person infringing the copyright to put an end to the infringement, to desist therefrom and to pay damages.

In those circumstances the question submitted by the national court is in effect whether Articles 30 and 36 of the Treaty must be interpreted as precluding the application of national legislation under which a copyright management society empowered to exercise the copyrights of composers of musical works reproduced on gramophone records or other sound recording in another Member State is permitted to invoke those rights where such sound recordings are distributed on the national market after having been put into circulation in the Member State of manufacturer by or with the consent of the owners of those copyrights in order to claim payment of a fee equal to the royalties ordinarily paid for marketing on the national market less the lower royalties paid in the Member State of manufacture for marketing in that Member State alone.

It should first be emphasized that sound recordings, even if incorporating protected musical works, are products to which the system of free movement of goods provided for by the Treaty applies. It follows that national legislation whose application results in obstructing trade in sound recordings between Member States must be regarded as a measure having an effect equivalent to a quantitative restriction within the meaning of Article 30 of the Treaty. That is the case where such legislation permits a copyright management society to object to the distribution of sound recordings originating in another Member State on the basis of the exclusive exploitation right which it exercises in the name of the copyright owner.

However, Article 36 of the Treaty provides that the provisions of Articles 30 to 34 shall not preclude prohibitions or restrictions on imports justified on grounds of the protection of industrial and commercial property. The latter expression includes the protection conferred by copyright, especially when exploited commercially in the form of licenses capable of affecting distribution in the various Member States of goods incorporating the protected literary or artistic work.

It is apparent from the well-established case-law of the Court . . . that the proprietor of an industrial or commercial property right protected by the law of a Member State cannot rely on that law to prevent the importation of a product which has been lawfully marketed in another Member State by the proprietor himself or with his consent.

In these proceedings before the Court, the French Government has argued that that case-law cannot be applied to copyright, which comprises inter alia the right of an author to claim authorship of the work and to object to any distortion, mutilation or other alteration thereof, or any other action in relation to the said work which would be prejudicial to his honour or reputation. It is contended that, in thus conferring extended protection, copyright is not comparable to other industrial and commercial property rights such as patents or trade-marks.

It is true that copyright comprises moral rights of the kind indicated by the French Government. However, it also comprises other rights, notably the right to exploit commercially the marketing of the protected work, particularly in the form of licenses granted in return for payment of royalties. It is this economic aspect of copyright which is the subject of the question submitted by the national court and, in this regard, in the application of Article 36 of the Treaty there is no reason to make a distinction between copyright and other industrial and commercial property rights.

While the commercial exploitation of copyright is a source of remuneration for the owner it also constitutes a form of control on marketing exercisable by the owner, the copyright management societies acting in his name and the grantees of licenses. From this point of view commercial exploitation of copyright raises the same issues as that of any other industrial or commercial property right.

The argument put to the Court by the Belgian and Italian Governments that in the absence of harmonization in this sector the principle of the territoriality of copyright laws always prevails over the principle of freedom of movement of goods within the Common Market cannot be accepted. Indeed, the essential purpose of the Treaty, which is to unite national markets into a single market, could not be attained if, under the various legal systems of the Member States, nationals of those Member States were able to partition the market and bring about arbitrary discrimination or disguised restrictions on trade between Member States.

It follows from the foregoing considerations that neither the copyright owner or his licensee, nor a copyright management society acting in the owner's or licensee's name, may rely on the exclusive exploitation right conferred by copyright to prevent or restrict the importation of sound recordings which have been lawfully marketed in another Member State by the owner himself or with his consent.

GEMA has argued that such an interpretation of Articles 30 and 36 of the Treaty is not sufficient to resolve the problem facing the national court since GEMA's application to the German courts is not for the prohibition or restriction of the marketing of the gramophone records and tape cassettes in question on German territory but for equality in the royalties paid for any distribution of those sound recordings on the German market. The owner of a copyright in a recorded musical work has a legitimate interest in receiving and retaining the benefit of his intellectual or artistic effort regardless of the degree to which his work is distributed and consequently it is maintained that he should not lose the right to claim royalties equal to those paid in the country in which the recorded work is marketed.

It should first be observed that the question put by the national court is concerned with the legal consequences of infringement of copyright. GEMA seeks damages for that infringement pursuant to the applicable national legislation and it is immaterial whether the quantum of damages which it seeks is calculated according to the difference between the rate of royalty payable on distribution in the national market and the rate of royalty paid in the country of manufacture or in any other manner. On any view its claims are in fact founded on the copyright owner's exclusive right of exploitation, which enables him to prohibit or restrict the free movement of the products incorporating the protected musical work.

It should be observed next that no provision of national legislation may permit an undertaking which is responsible for the management of copyrights and has a monopoly on the territory of a Member State by virtue of that management to charge a levy on products imported from another Member State where they were put into circulation by or with the consent of the copyright owner and thereby cause the Common Market to be partitioned. Such a practice would amount to allowing a private undertaking to impose a charge on the importation of sound recordings which are already in free circulation in the Common Market on account of their crossing a frontier; it would therefore have the effect of entrenching the isolation of national markets which the Treaty seeks to abolish.

It follows from those considerations that this argument must be rejected as being incompatible with the operation of the Common Market and with the aims of the Treaty.

GEMA and the Belgian Government have represented to the Court that, in any event, a system of free movement of sound recordings may not be permitted as regards sound recordings manufactured in the United Kingdom because the provisions of section 8 of the United Kingdom Copyright Act 1956 have the effect of instituting a statutory license in return for payment of a royalty at a reduced rate and the extension of such a statutory license to other countries is contrary to the provisions of the Berne Convention for the Protection of Literary and Artistic Works.

Section 8 of the Copyright Act provides in effect that the copyright of a composer of a musical work is not infringed by the manufacture of a sound recording of that work if the work has already been reproduced in the United Kingdom on a sound recording for the purpose of retail sale by the author himself or with his consent and if, in addition, the manufacturer notifies the copyright owner of his intention to make a recording of the work for the purpose of sale and pays him a royalty of 6.25% of the retail selling price of the sound recording.

It appears from the papers before the Court that the practical result of that system is that the royalty for any manufacture of a sound recording is established at 6.25% of the retail selling price since no prospective licensee is willing to agree to a higher rate. As the rate of 6.25% is thus the rate which is in fact agreed for contractual licenses, the United Kingdom legislation has the effect of putting a ceiling on the remuneration of the copyright holder.

Where, therefore, a copyright management society exercising an exclusive right of exploitation in the name of an owner claims the difference between the rate of 6.25% already paid and that charged on its domestic market, it is in fact seeking to neutralize the price differences arising from the conditions existing in the United Kingdom and thereby eliminate the economic advantage accruing to the importers of the sound recordings from the establishment of the Common Market.

As the Court has already stated in [earlier, non-copyright cases], the existence of a disparity between national laws which is capable of distorting competition between Member States cannot justify the maintenance or introduction by a Member State of measures which are incompatible with the rules concerning the free movement of goods. Such disparities must be abolished by the means provided for to that end by the Treaty, and in particular through the harmonization of national laws.

It should further be observed that in a common market distinguished by free movement of goods and freedom to provide services an author, acting directly or through his publisher, is free to choose the place, in any of the Member States, in which to put his work into circulation. He may make that choice according to his best interests, which involve not only the level of remuneration provided in the Member State in question but other factors such as, for example, the opportunities for distributing his work and the marketing facilities which are further enhanced by virtue of the free movement of goods within the Community. In those circumstances, a copyright management society may not be permitted to claim, on the importation of sound recordings into another Member State, payment of additional fees based on the difference in the rates of remuneration existing in the various Member States.

It follows from the foregoing considerations that the disparities which continue to exist in the absence of any harmonization of national rules on the commercial exploitation of copyrights may not be used to impede the free movement of goods in the Common Market.

The answer to the question put by the Bundesgerichtshof should therefore be that Articles 30 and 36 of the Treaty must be interpreted as precluding the application of national legislation under which a copyright management society empowered to exercise the copyrights of composers of musical works reproduced on gramophone records or other sound recordings in another Member State is permitted to invoke those rights where those sound recordings are distributed on the national market after having been put into circulation in that other Member State by or with the consent of the owners of those copyrights, in order to claim payment of a fee equal to the royalties ordinarily paid for marketing on the national market less the lower royalties paid in the Member State of manufacture. . . .

On those grounds, the Court, in answer to the question submitted to it by the Bundesgerichtshof by two orders of 19 December 1979, hereby rules:

> Articles 30 and 36 of the Treaty must be interpreted as precluding the application of national legislation under which a copyright management society empowered to exercise the copyrights of composers of musical works reproduced on gramophone records or other sound recordings in another Member State is permitted to invoke those rights where those sound recordings are distributed on the national market after having been put into circulation in that other Member State by or with the consent of the owners of those copyrights, in order to claim the payment of a fee equal to the royalties ordinarily paid for marketing on the national market less the lower royalties paid in the Member State of manufacture.

In the case you just read, both Musik-Vertrieb and K-tel imported recordings from other countries *in* the European Union (beginning in 1973 and 1974). Suppose that today they begin to import recordings from countries *outside* the European Union – say, from the United States.

Since 2006, the statutory mechanical royalty rate in the U.S. is 9.1 cents per song per album; so a 12-song album now generates mechanical royalties of about $1.09 (9.1 cents/song x 12 songs = $1.092). Record companies in the U.S. will pay those royalties, directly or through The Harry Fox Agency, to the music publishers that own the copyrights to the songs that are recorded on each album. Those publishers, in turn, will pay songwriters their share of these mechanical royalties, in accordance with terms of their music publishing contracts.

The mechanical royalty rate in Germany is 9.009% of the Published Price to Dealers (roughly, the wholesale price), regardless of the number of songs on the recording. [Source: GEMA press release dated 19 May 2005 available at http://www.gema.de/en/press/press-releases/press-release/archive/2005// browse/1/?tx_ttnews%5Btt_news%5D=73&tx_ttnews %5BbackPid%5D=73&cHash=14afa2e040]. If the wholesale price of CDs in Germany is €12 [12 Euros], an album manufactured in Germany will generate mechanical royalties of about €1.08 (9.009% x €12 = €1.081). Record companies in Germany will pay those royalties to GEMA which will distribute them to composers, lyricists and music publishers. The exchange rate from Euros to Dollars (as of January 2007) is about €1 = $1.31. This means that mechanical royalties paid on albums manufactured in Germany would be about $1.41 (€1.081 x 1.31 = $1.4148) – which is 32¢ per CD more than the mechanical royalties paid on the CDs imported from the United States.

What result would you expect if GEMA sues Musik-Vertrieb and K-tel in connection with albums they import from the United States, seeking damages of €0.24 (i.e., 32¢) per imported album? Before answering this question, reread *SDRM v. Givaudan* in Chapter 4. Note that *SDRM* was decided by the Paris District Court a year *before* the Court of Justice of the European Communities decided *Musik-Vertrieb*. Does the *SDRM* opinion still indicate, reliably, what the law is today?

The *Deutsche Grammophon* and *Musik-Vertrieb* opinions show how free trade treaties, that say nothing on their face about copyright, have limited – in some cases, eliminated – the ability of copyright owners to assert exclusive distribution rights clearly granted to them by the national copyright statutes of their countries. Not surprisingly, copyright owners were not pleased with these decisions, though importers, some retail stores, and many consumers presumably were pleased.

## 2. Limits on statutory copyright privileges

In addition to imposing limits on exclusive copyright *rights*, free trade agreements sometimes impose limits on statutory copyright *privileges*.

The following opinion dramatically illustrates how the WTO TRIPs Agreement has limited a statutory privilege found in United States Copyright

Act section 110(5). That section is commonly referred to as the "homestyle receiver" exemption – though (as you will read below), the section now exempts more than "homestyle" receivers, as a result a 1998 amendment called the "Fairness in Music Licensing Act." The opinion begins with a detailed description of the 1998 amendment, because an understanding of what the amendment did to U.S. law is necessary in order to follow *why* the opinion concludes that only *part* of the amendment violates TRIPs. As you read the opinion, watch for (and make note of) the answers to the following questions:

1. What two kinds of performances do section 110(5) exempt from the requirement that public performance fees be paid?
2. Which of the two exemptions violates TRIPs?
3. What was the legal standard the WTO Panel used to decide?
4. Why did the standard used by the WTO Panel invalidate one of the exemptions?
5. Why didn't that standard invalidate the other exemption?

With the answers to those questions in mind, see if you can answer these questions too:

6. Which of the two exemptions is more important to copyright owners and copyright users, as a *business* matter?
7. So, who *really* won the case, and who really lost?

The following opinion is important far beyond the question of whether the 1998 Fairness in Music Licensing Act violates TRIPs. It shows how TRIPs limits the ability of the United States (and all other WTO members) to enact copyright *privileges* (that is, statutory exemptions from exclusive rights). Thus, this opinion shows that TRIPs should be kept in mind by Congress whenever it considers proposed Copyright Act amendments that would diminish or weaken the rights of copyright owners.

## Report of WTO Panel on Section 110(5) of U.S. Copyright Act (WTO 2000)

*I.   Introduction*

On 26 January 1999, the European Communities and their member States (hereafter referred to as the European Communities) requested consultations with the United States under Article 4 of the Understanding on Rules and Procedures Governing the Settlement of Disputes ("DSU") and Article 64.1 of the Agreement on Trade-Related Aspects of Intellectual Property Rights ("TRIPS Agreement") regarding Section 110(5) of the United States Copyright Act as amended by the "Fairness in Music Licensing Act" enacted on 27 October 1998.

The European Communities and the United States held consultations . . . , but failed to reach a mutually satisfactory solution. . . .

*II.   Factual Aspects*

The dispute concerns Section 110(5) of the US Copyright Act of 1976, as amended by the Fairness in Music Licensing Act of 1998 ("the 1998 Amendment"), which entered into force on 26 January 1999. The provisions of Section 110(5) place limitations on the exclusive rights provided to owners of copyright in Section 106 of the Copyright Act in respect of certain performances and displays.

The relevant parts of the current text of Section 106 read as follows:

"§ 106. Exclusive rights in copyrighted works

Subject to sections 107 through 120, the owner of copyright under this title has the exclusive rights to do and to authorize any of the following: . . .

(4) in the case of literary, musical, dramatic, and choreographic works, pantomimes, and motion pictures and other audiovisual works, to perform the copyrighted work publicly. . . .

The relevant parts of the current text of Section 110(5) read as follows:

"§ 110. Limitations on exclusive rights: Exemption of certain performances and displays

Notwithstanding the provisions of section 106, the following are not infringements of copyright:...

(5)(A) except as provided in subparagraph (B), communication of a transmission embodying a performance or display of a work by the public reception of the transmission on a single receiving apparatus of a kind commonly used in private homes, unless

(i) a direct charge is made to see or hear the transmission; or

(ii) the transmission thus received is further transmitted to the public;

(B) communication by an establishment of a transmission or retransmission embodying a performance or display of a nondramatic musical work intended to be received by the general public, originated by a radio or television broadcast station licensed as such by the Federal Communications Commission, or, if an audiovisual transmission, by a cable system or satellite carrier, if—

(i) in the case of an establishment other than a food service or drinking establishment, either the establishment in which the communication occurs has less than 2,000 gross square feet of space (excluding space used for customer parking and for no other purpose), or the establishment in which the communication occurs has 2,000 or more gross square feet of space (excluding space used for customer parking and for no other purpose) and—

(I) if the performance is by audio means only, the performance is communicated by means of a total of not more than 6 loudspeakers, of which not more than 4 loudspeakers are located in any 1 room or adjoining outdoor space; or

(II) if the performance or display is by audiovisual means, any visual portion of the performance or display is communicated by means of a total of not more than 4 audiovisual devices, of which not more than 1 audiovisual device is located in any 1 room, and no such audiovisual device has a diagonal screen size greater than 55 inches, and any audio portion of the performance or display is communicated by means of a total of not more than 6 loudspeakers, of which not more than 4 loudspeakers are located in any 1 room or adjoining outdoor space;

(ii) in the case of a food service or drinking establishment, either the establishment in which the communication occurs has less than 3,750 gross square feet of space (excluding space used for customer parking and for no other purpose), or the establishment in which the communication occurs has 3,750 gross square feet of space or more (excluding space used for customer parking and for no other purpose) and—

(I) if the performance is by audio means only, the performance is communicated by means of a total of not more than 6 loudspeakers, of which not more than 4 loudspeakers are located in any 1 room or adjoining outdoor space; or

(II) if the performance or display is by audiovisual means, any visual portion of the performance or display is communicated by means of a total of not more than 4 audiovisual devices, of which not more than one audiovisual device is located in any 1 room, and no such audiovisual device has a diagonal screen size greater than 55 inches, and any audio portion of the performance or display is communicated by means of a total of not more than 6 loudspeakers, of which not more than 4 loudspeakers are located in any 1 room or adjoining outdoor space;

(iii) no direct charge is made to see or hear the transmission or retransmission;

(iv) the transmission or retransmission is not further transmitted beyond the establishment where it is received; and

(v) the transmission or retransmission is licensed by the copyright owner of the work so publicly performed or displayed. . . ."

Subparagraph (A) of Section 110(5) essentially reproduces the text of the original "homestyle" exemption contained in Section 110(5) of the Copyright Act of 1976. When Section 110(5) was amended in 1998, the homestyle exemption was moved to a new subparagraph (A) and the words "except as provided in subparagraph (B)" were added to the beginning of the text.

A House Report (1976) accompanying the Copyright Act of 1976 explained that in its original form Section 110(5) "applies to performances and displays of all types of works, and its purpose is to exempt from copyright liability anyone who merely turns on, in a public place, an ordinary radio or television receiving apparatus of a kind commonly sold to members of the public for private use." "The basic rationale of this clause is that the secondary use of the transmission by turning on an ordinary receiver in public is so remote and minimal that no further liability should be imposed." "[The clause] would impose liability where the proprietor has a commercial 'sound system' installed or converts a standard home receiving apparatus (by augmenting it with sophisticated or extensive amplification equipment) into the equivalent of a commercial sound system." A subsequent Conference Report (1976) elaborated on the rationale by noting that the intent was to exempt a small commercial establishment "which was not of sufficient size to justify, as a practical matter, a subscription to a commercial background music service."

The factors to consider in applying the exemption are largely based on the facts of a case decided by the United States Supreme Court immediately prior to the passage of the 1976 Copyright Act. In *Aiken*, the Court held that an owner of a small fast food restaurant was not liable for playing music by means of a radio with outlets to four speakers in the ceiling; the size of the shop was 1,055 square feet (98 m$^2$), of which 620 square feet (56 m$^2$) were open to the public. The House Report (1976) describes the factual situation in *Aiken* as representing the "outer limit of the exemption" contained in original Section 110(5). This exemption became known as the "homestyle" exemption.

As indicated in the first quotation in the preceding paragraph, the homestyle exemption was originally intended to apply to performances of all types of works. However, given that the present subparagraph (B) applies to "a performance or display of a nondramatic musical work," the parties agree . . . that the effect of the introductory phrase "except as provided in subparagraph (B)," that was added to the text in subparagraph (A), is that it narrows down the application of subparagraph (A) to works other than "nondramatic musical works."

The Panel notes that it is the common understanding of the parties that the expression "nondramatic musical works" in subparagraph (B) excludes from its application the communication of music that is part of an opera, operetta, musical or other similar dramatic work when performed in a dramatic context. All other musical works are covered by that expression, including individual songs taken from dramatic works when performed outside of any dramatic context. Subparagraph (B) would, therefore, apply for example to an individual song taken from a musical and played on the radio. Consequently, the operation of subparagraph (A) is limited to such musical works as are not covered by subparagraph (B), for example a communication of a broadcast of a dramatic rendition of the music written for an opera.

The 1998 Amendment has added a new subparagraph (B) to Section 110(5), to which we, for the sake of brevity, hereinafter refer to as a "business" exemption. It exempts, under certain conditions, communication by an establishment of a transmission or retransmission embodying a performance or display of a nondramatic musical work intended to be received by the general public, originated by a radio or television broadcast station licensed as such by the Federal Communications Commission, or, if an audiovisual transmission, by a cable system or satellite carrier.

The beneficiaries of the business exemption are divided into two categories: establishments other than food service or drinking establishments ("retail establishments"), and food service and drinking establishments. In each category, establishments under a certain size limit are exempted, regardless of the type of equipment they use. The size limits are 2,000 gross square feet (186 m$^2$) for retail establishments and 3,750 gross square feet (348 m$^2$) for restaurants.

In its study of November 1995 prepared for the Senate Judiciary Committee, the Congressional Research Service ("CRS") estimated that 16 per cent of eating establishments, 13.5 per cent of drinking establishments and 18 per cent of retail establishments were below the area of the restaurant ran by Mr. Aiken, i.e. 1,055 square feet. Furthermore, the CRS estimated that 65.2 per cent of eating establishments and 71.8 per cent of drinking establishments would have fallen at that time under a 3,500 square feet limit, and that 27 per cent of retail establishments would have fallen under a 1,500 square feet limit.

In 1999, Dun & Bradstreet, Inc. ("D&B") was requested on behalf of the American Society of Composers, Authors and Publishers (ASCAP) to update the CRS study based on 1998 data and the criteria in the 1998 Amendment. In this study, the D&B estimated that 70 per cent of eating establishments and 73 per cent of drinking establishments fell under the 3,750 square feet limit, and that 45 per cent of retail establishments fell under the 2,000 square feet limit.

The studies conducted by the National Restaurant Association (NRA) concerning its membership indicate that 36 per cent of table service restaurant members (those with sit-down waiter service) and 95 per cent of quick service restaurant members are less than 3,750 square feet. . . .

Section 110(5) does not apply to the use of recorded music, such as CDs or cassette tapes, or to live performances of music.

Holders of copyright in musical works (composers, lyricists and music publishers) normally entrust the licensing of nondramatic public performance of their works to collective management organizations ("CMOs" or performing rights organizations). The three main CMOs in the United States in this area are ASCAP, the Broadcast Music, Inc. (BMI) and SESAC, Inc. CMOs license the public performance of musical works to users of music, such as retail establishments and restaurants, on behalf of the individual right holders they represent, collect licence fees from such users, and distribute revenues as royalties to the respective right holders. They normally enter into reciprocal arrangements with the CMOs of other countries to license the works of the right holders represented by them. Revenues are distributed to individual right holders through the CMOs that represent the right holders in question. The above-mentioned three US CMOs license nondramatic public performances of musical works, including nondramatic renditions of "dramatic" musical works.

*III. Findings and Recommendations Requested by the Parties*

The European Communities alleges that the exemptions provided in subparagraphs (A) and (B) of Section 110(5) of the US Copyright Act are in violation of the United States' obligations under the TRIPS Agreement. In particular, it alleges that these US measures are incompatible with Article 9.1 of the TRIPS Agreement together with Articles 11(1)(ii) and 11*bis*(1)(iii) of the Berne Convention and that they cannot be justified under any express or implied exception or limitation permissible under the Berne Convention or the TRIPS Agreement. In the view of the EC, these measures cause prejudice to the legitimate rights of copyright owners, thus nullifying and impairing the rights of the European Communities.

The European Communities requests the Panel to find that the United States has violated its obligations under Article 9.1 of the TRIPS Agreement together with Articles 11*bis*(1)(iii) and 11(1)(ii) of the Berne Convention and to recommend that the United States bring its domestic legislation into conformity with its obligations under the TRIPS Agreement.

The United States contends that Section 110(5) of the US Copyright Act is fully consistent with its obligations under the TRIPS Agreement. The Agreement, incorporating the substantive provisions of the Berne Convention , allows Members to place minor limitations on the exclusive rights of copyright owners. Article 13 of the TRIPS Agreement provides the standard by which to judge the appropriateness of such limitations or exceptions. The exemptions embodied in Section 110(5) fall within the Article 13 standard.

The United States requests the Panel to find that both subparagraphs (A) and (B) of Section 110(5) of the US Copyright Act meet the standard of Article 13 of the TRIPS Agreement and the substantive obligations of the Berne Convention . Accordingly, the United States requests the Panel to dismiss the claims of the European Communities in this dispute. . . .

*VI. Findings . . .*
    *D. Substantive aspects of the dispute*
        *1. General considerations about the exclusive rights concerned and limitations thereto*
            *(a) Exclusive rights implicated by the EC claims*

Articles 9-13 of Section 1 of Part II of the TRIPS Agreement entitled "Copyright and Related Rights" deal with the substantive standards of copyright protection. Article 9.1 of the TRIPS Agreement obliges WTO Members to comply with Articles 1-21 of the Berne Convention (with the exception of Article 6*bis* on moral rights and the rights derived therefrom) and the Appendix thereto. The European Communities alleges that subparagraphs (A) and (B) of Section 110(5) are inconsistent primarily with Article 11*bis*(1)(iii) but also with Article 11(1)(ii) of the Berne Convention as incorporated into the TRIPS Agreement.

We note that through their incorporation, the substantive rules of the Berne Convention, including the provisions of its Articles 11*bis*(1)(iii) and 11(1)(ii), have become part of the TRIPS Agreement and as provisions of that Agreement have to be read as applying to WTO Members.

### (i) Article 11bis of the Berne Convention

The provision of particular relevance for this dispute is Article 11*bis*(1)(iii). Article 11*bis*(1) provides:
"Authors of literary and artistic works shall enjoy the exclusive right of authorizing: . . .

> (iii) the public communication by loudspeaker or any other analogous instrument transmitting, by signs, sounds or images, the broadcast of the work."

Subparagraph (iii) provides an exclusive right to authorize the public communication of the broadcast of the work by loudspeaker, on a television screen, or by other similar means. Such communication involves a new public performance of a work contained in a broadcast, which requires a licence from the right holder. For the purposes of this dispute, the claims raised by the European Communities under Article 11*bis*(1) are limited to subparagraph (iii).

### (ii) Article 11 of the Berne Convention

Of relevance to this dispute are also the exclusive rights conferred by Article 11(1)(ii) of the Berne Convention . Article 11(1) provides:
"Authors of dramatic, dramatico-musical and musical works shall enjoy the exclusive right of authorizing:

> (i) the public performance of their works, including such public performance by any means or process;
> (ii) any communication to the public of the performance of their works."

As in the case of Article 11*bis*(1) of the Berne Convention , which concerns broadcasting to the public and communication of a broadcast to the public, the exclusive rights conferred by Article 11 cover *public* performance; private performance does not require authorization. Public performance includes performance by any means or process, such as performance by means of recordings (e.g., CDs, cassettes and videos). It also includes communication to the public of a performance of the work. The claims raised by the European Communities under Article 11(1) of the Berne Convention are limited to its subparagraph (ii).

Regarding the relationship between Articles 11 and 11*bis*, we note that the rights conferred in Article 11(1)(ii) concern the communication to the public of performances of works in general. Article 11*bis*(1)(iii) is a specific rule conferring exclusive rights concerning the public communication by loudspeaker or any other analogous instrument transmitting, by signs, sounds or images, the broadcast of a work.

As noted above, the United States acknowledges that subparagraphs (A) and (B) of Section 110(5) implicate Articles 11*bis*(1)(iii) and 11(1)(ii) of the Berne Convention . Consequently, the core question before this Panel is which of the exceptions under the TRIPS Agreement invoked are relevant to this dispute and whether the conditions for their invocation are met so as to justify the exemptions under subparagraphs (A) and (B) of Section 110(5) of the US Copyright Act.

### (b) Limitations and exceptions

A major issue in this dispute is the interpretation and application to the facts of this case of Article 13 of the TRIPS Agreement. The US defense is firmly based upon it. . . .

Article 13 of the TRIPS Agreement, entitled "Limitations and Exceptions," is the general exception clause applicable to exclusive rights of the holders of copyright. It provides:

"Members shall confine limitations or exceptions to exclusive rights to certain special cases which do not conflict with a normal exploitation of the work and do not unreasonably prejudice the legitimate interests of the right holder." . . .

As we noted above, the US view is that Article 13 of the TRIPS Agreement clarifies and articulates the scope of the minor exceptions doctrine, which is applicable under the TRIPS Agreement. . . .

We note that, in addition to the explicit provisions on permissible limitations and exceptions to the exclusive rights embodied in the text of the Berne Convention , the reports of successive revision conferences of that Convention refer to "implied exceptions" allowing member countries to provide limitations and exceptions to certain rights. The so-called "minor reservations" or "minor exceptions" doctrine is being referred to in respect of the right of public performance and certain other exclusive rights. Under that doctrine, Berne Union members may provide minor exceptions to the rights provided, *inter alia*, under Articles 11*bis* and 11 of the Berne Convention . . .

. . . We note that the parties and third parties have brought to our attention several examples from various countries of limitations in national laws based on the minor exceptions doctrine. [Fn: For example, Australia exempts public performance by wireless apparatus at premises of, *inter alia*, hotels or guest houses. Belgium exempts a work's communication to the public in a place accessible to the public where the aim of the communication is not the work itself, and exempts the performance of a work during a public examination where the purpose is the assessment of the performer. Finland exempts public performance in connection with religious services and education. Finland and Denmark provide for exceptions where a work's performance is not the main feature of the event, provided that no fee is charged and the event is not for profit. New Zealand exempts public performance of musical works at educational establishments. The Philippines exempts public performances for charitable and educational purposes. A similar exception applies in India, where also performances at amateur clubs or societies are exempted. Canadian law provides for exceptions with respect to different exclusive rights for educational, religious or charitable purposes, and also at conventions and fairs. South Africa exempts public performances in the context of demonstrations of radio or television receivers and recording equipment by dealers of or clients for such equipment. Brazil allows free use of works in commercial establishments for the purpose of demonstration to customers in establishments that market equipment that makes such use possible.] . . . .

. . . [T]he incorporation of Articles 11 and 11*bis* of the Berne Convention into the [TRIPS] Agreement includes the entire *acquis* of these provisions, including the possibility of providing minor exceptions to the respective exclusive rights. . . .

In our view, Section 110(5) of the US Copyright Act contains exceptions that allow use of protected works without an authorization by the right holder and without charge. Whether these exceptions meet the United States' obligations under the TRIPS Agreement has to be examined by applying Article 13 of the TRIPS Agreement . . . .

We now proceed to applying the three conditions contained in Article 13 of the TRIPS Agreement to the exemptions contained in Section 110(5) of the US Copyright Act in relation to Articles 11*bis*(1)(iii) and 11(1)(ii) of the Berne Convention as incorporated into the TRIPS Agreement.

### 2. The three criteria test under Article 13 of the TRIPS Agreement

Article 13 of the TRIPS Agreement requires that limitations and exceptions to exclusive rights (1) be confined to certain special cases, (2) do not conflict with a normal exploitation of the work, and (3) do not unreasonably prejudice the legitimate interests of the right holder. . . .

### (b) "Certain special cases" . . .

In our view, the first condition of Article 13 requires that a limitation or exception in national legislation should be clearly defined and should be narrow in its scope and reach. . . .

In the case at hand, in order to determine whether subparagraphs (B) and (A) of Section 110(5) are confined to "certain special cases," we first examine whether the exceptions have been clearly defined. Second, we ascertain whether the exemptions are narrow in scope, *inter alia*, with respect to their reach. In that respect, we take into account what percentage of eating and drinking establishments and retail establishments may benefit from the business exemption under subparagraph (B), and in turn what percentage of establishments may take advantage of the homestyle exemption under subparagraph (A)....

### (ii) The business exemption of subparagraph (B)

The factual information presented to us indicates that a substantial majority of eating and drinking establishments and close to half of retail establishments are covered by the exemption contained in subparagraph (B) of Section 110(5) of the US Copyright Act. Therefore, we conclude that the exemption does not qualify as a "certain special case" in the meaning of the first condition of Article 13. . . .

### (iii) The homestyle exemption of subparagraph (A)

We believe that from a quantitative perspective the reach of subparagraph (A) in respect of potential users is limited to a comparably small percentage of all eating, drinking and retail establishments in the United States. . . .

. . . In our view, the term "homestyle equipment" expresses the degree of clarity in definition required under Article 13's first condition. . . .

We have noted the common view of the parties that the addition of the introductory phrase "except as provided in subparagraph (B)" to the homestyle exemption in the 1998 Amendment should be understood . . . as limiting the coverage of the exemption to works other than "nondramatic" musical works. As regards musical works, the currently applicable version of the homestyle exemption is thus understood to apply to the communication of music that is part of an opera, operetta, musical or other similar dramatic work when performed in a dramatic context. All other musical works are covered by the expression "nondramatic" musical works, including individual songs taken from dramatic works when performed outside any dramatic context. Subparagraph (B) would, therefore, apply for example to an individual song taken from a musical and played on the radio. Consequently, given the common view of the parties, the operation of subparagraph (A) is limited to such musical works as are not covered by subparagraph (B), for example a communication of a broadcast of a dramatic rendition of the music written for an opera, operetta, musical or other similar works. . . .

In practice, this means that most if not virtually all music played on the radio or television is covered by subparagraph (B). Subparagraph (A) covers, in accordance with the common understanding of the parties, dramatic renditions of operas, operettas, musicals and other similar dramatic works. We consider that limiting the application of subparagraph (A) to the public communication of transmissions embodying such works, gives its provisions a quite narrow scope of application in practice. . . .

Taking into account the specific limits imposed in subparagraph (A) and its legislative history, as well as in its considerably narrow application in the subsequent court practice on the beneficiaries of the exemption, permissible equipment and categories of works, we are of the view that the homestyle exemption in subparagraph (A) of Section 110(5) as amended in 1998 is well-defined and limited in its scope and reach. We, therefore, conclude that the exemption is confined to certain special cases within the meaning of the first condition of Article 13 of the TRIPS Agreement. . . .

(c) "Not conflict with a normal exploitation of the work" . . .
(ii) The business exemption of subparagraph (B) . . .

Right holders of musical works would expect to be in a position to authorize the use of broadcasts of radio and television music by many of the establishments covered by the exemption and, as appropriate, receive compensation for the use of their works. Consequently, we cannot but conclude that an exemption of such scope as subparagraph (B) conflicts with the "normal exploitation" of the work in relation to the exclusive rights conferred by Articles 11bis(1)(iii) and 11(1)(ii) of the Berne Convention .

In the light of these considerations, we conclude that the business exemption embodied in subparagraph (B) conflicts with a normal exploitation of the work within the meaning of the second condition of Article 13.

(iii) The homestyle exemption of subparagraph (A) . . .

We recall that it is the common understanding of the parties that the operation of subparagraph (A) is limited, as regards musical works, to the public communication of transmissions embodying dramatic renditions of "dramatic" musical works, such as operas, operettas, musicals and other similar dramatic works. Consequently, performances of, e.g., individual songs from a dramatic musical work outside a dramatic context would constitute a rendition of a nondramatic work and fall within the purview of subparagraph (B).

It is our understanding that the parties agree that the right holders do not normally license or attempt to license the public communication of transmissions embodying dramatic renditions of "dramatic" musical works in the sense of Article 11bis(1)(iii) and/or 11(1)(ii). We have not been provided with information about any existing licensing practices concerning the communication to the public of broadcasts of performances of dramatic works (e.g., operas, operettas, musicals) by eating, drinking or retail establishments in the United States or any other country. In this respect, we fail to see how the homestyle exemption, as limited to works other than nondramatic musical works in its revised form, could acquire economic or practical importance of any considerable dimension for the right holders of musical works.

Therefore, we conclude that the homestyle exemption contained in subparagraph (A) of Section 110(5) does not conflict with a normal exploitation of works within the meaning of the second condition of Article 13.

> (d) "Not unreasonably prejudice the legitimate interests of the right holder" . . .
> (ii) The business exemption of subparagraph (B) . . .

The United States estimates that the maximum annual loss to EC right holders of distributions from the largest US collecting society, ASCAP, as a result of the Section 110(5) exemption, is in the range of $294,113 to $586,332. Applying the same analysis, it estimates that the loss from the second largest society, BMI, is $122,000. . . .

The European Communities estimates that the annual loss to all right holders amounts to $53.65 million. . . .

. . . [T]he ultimate burden of proof concerning whether all of the conditions of Article 13 are met lies with the United States as the Member invoking the exception. In the light of our analysis of the prejudice caused by the exemption, including its actual and potential effects, we are of the view that the United States has not demonstrated that the business exemption does not unreasonably prejudice the legitimate interests of the right holder.

Accordingly, we conclude that the business exemption of subparagraph (B) of Section 110(5) does not meet the requirements of the third condition of Article 13 of the TRIPS Agreement.

> (iii) The homestyle exemption of subparagraph (A) . . .

. . . [A]s regards the exemption as amended in 1998 to exclude from its scope nondramatic musical works, the European Communities has not explicitly claimed that the exemption would currently cause any prejudice to right holders.

In the light of the considerations above, we conclude that the homestyle exemption contained in subparagraph (A) of Section 110(5) does not cause unreasonable prejudice to the legitimate interests of the right holders within the meaning of the third condition of Article 13.

VII. *Conclusions and Recommendations*

. . . [T]he Panel concludes that:

(a) Subparagraph (A) of Section 110(5) of the US Copyright Act meets the requirements of Article 13 of the TRIPS Agreement and is thus consistent with Articles 11*bis*(1)(iii) and 11(1)(ii) of the Berne Convention as incorporated into the TRIPS Agreement by Article 9.1 of that Agreement.

(b) Subparagraph (B) of Section 110(5) of the US Copyright Act does not meet the requirements of Article 13 of the TRIPS Agreement and is thus inconsistent with Articles 11*bis*(1)(iii) and 11(1)(ii) of the Berne Convention as incorporated into the TRIPS Agreement by Article 9.1 of that Agreement.

The Panel *recommends* that the Dispute Settlement Body request the United States to bring subparagraph (B) of Section 110(5) into conformity with its obligations under the TRIPS Agreement.

The WTO Panel Report you just read was the equivalent of a trial court decision. The United States could have appealed its decision to a WTO Appellate Body; but the U.S. chose not to. Instead, the United States informed the WTO that it would implement the Panel's recommendation that "the United States . . . bring subparagraph (B) of Section 110(5) into conformity with its obligations under the TRIPS Agreement." The only way to do that, of course, would be to repeal the Fairness in Music Licensing Act. That is something only Congress has the power to do; it cannot be done by the U.S. Trade Representative or by anyone else in the Executive Branch of the government. Though several years have passed since the Panel issued its Report, the Fairness in Music Licensing Act has not been repealed yet (as of January 2007). The United States' failure to do so raises the question of what remedies TRIPs provides against violators – an issue addressed below in the final section of this chapter.

For more about the extent to which TRIPs limits the ability of WTO members to grant copyright privileges, especially in the context of P2P file "sharing," see, Alexander Peukert, *A Bipolar Copyright System for the Digital Network Environment*, 28 Comm/Ent: Hastings Communications and Entertainment Law Journal 1 (2005).

## C. Harmonization of national copyright laws required by international trade law

International trade laws also have been used to harmonize the copyright laws of countries that are members of free trade areas. Free trade areas are groups of countries that have agreed to eliminate (or at least reduce) tariffs and other impediments to the exchange of goods and services. The European Union is a prime example, as is the North American Free Trade Area (whose members are Mexico, Canada and the United States, commonly referred to as "NAFTA").

Copyrighted works are embodied in goods, such as books, homevideos and CDs; and they are delivered as services, such as movie theater exhibitions, concerts and television broadcasts. As a result, differences in the national copyright laws of countries that belong to free trade areas may have the effect of interfering with, or distorting, the cross-border exchange of copyrighted goods and services. These differences arise because they involve issues which are not controlled by copyright treaties, so uniformity is not required.

Free trade areas – especially the EU – have used their trade law powers to require members to eliminate (or reduce) their copyright differences. On several occasions, the EU has done so by requiring EU countries to amend their national copyright statutes. At least once, the EU did so by judicial decree.

## 1. Harmonization by legislation

The EU has required its members to harmonize their copyright laws, by enacting legislation if necessary, in at least four areas: artist resale royalties; duration of copyright; rental rights; and cable retransmission of television broadcasts.

### Artists resale royalties

The laws of most members of the European Union contained artists resale royalty rights, long before 2006. Though most EU member nations had such a right, not all did. The UK, for example, did not. Moreover, the exact details of the right varied from country to country, even among those EU members that had it. They differed with respect to the types of works covered, those who were entitled to receive royalties, the royalty rate, the transactions that required the payment of royalties, and the basis on which the royalties were calculated.

As a result of these differences, many art works were moved from one EU country to another, simply for the purpose of selling them. Doing so made sense to sellers, because artworks could be shipped among countries in the EU without the payment of tariffs, and because shipping artworks from a country whose law *did* include a resale royalty right to another EU country that did *not* would save the seller the amount of the royalty that otherwise would have been payable. You read about one such case – *Joseph Beuys' Works*, 24 IIC 139 (Germany Ct.App. 1992) – in Chapter 4, where a painting was shipped for resale from Germany, which does have such a right, to the UK, which did not, simply so the seller could avoid paying the German royalty.

To bring an end to the impact that the resale royalty right was having on trade in artworks within the European Union, the EU adopted a "directive" with the descriptive (though cumbersome) title "Directive 2000 of the European Parliament and of the Council on the resale right for the benefit of the author of an original work of art." The directive required EU members to add a resale royalty right to their law or to amend their existing law (by January 1, 2006), so the right is uniform throughout the EU and thus no longer will have an effect on free trade in artworks.

### Duration of copyright

After the Court of Justice decided the *Deutsche Grammophon* and *Musik-Vertrieb* cases, a German import-export company imported records from Denmark into Germany, without licenses from the owners of the records' German copyrights. The import-export company was not licensed to import the recordings; but the two Court of Justice decisions lead the company to believe that it could sell the recordings in Germany without liability, even though doing so infringed the exclusive distribution right granted by German copyright law. Despite the apparent applicability of *Deutsche Grammophon* and *Musik-Vertrieb*, the German copyright owner sued the importer for infringement. The case made its way to the Court of Justice, which – contrary to the expectations of many – ruled against the importer and in favor of the copyright owner!

### EMI Electrola GmbH v. Patricia Im-und Export
### [1989] ECR 79, [1989] 2 CMLR 413, [1989] 1 FSR 544
### (Court of Justice of the European Communities 1989)

By order of 2 October 1987 . . . the Landgericht, Hamburg [a German Regional Court], requested a preliminary ruling . . . on the interpretation of Articles 30 and 36 of the Treaty to enable it to determine whether the application of certain national provisions concerning copyright in musical works would be compatible with those Articles.

The question has arisen in the context of an action brought by EMI Electrola GmbH, a German [company] to which a British company, EMI Records Ltd, assigned the rights of reproduction and distribution of musical works performed by a well-known British singer [Cliff Richard], and two other German [companies], Patricia Im-und Export and Lune-ton, which sold in the Federal Republic of Germany sound recordings from Denmark incorporating some of those works.

On the ground that its exclusive rights of distribution for recordings incorporating the works in question in German territory had been infringed, EMI Electrola brought an action before the Landgericht, Hamburg, for an injunction against Patricia and Lune-ton restraining the sale of sound recording imported from Denmark and claiming damages. However, the two defendants contended that the disputed recordings had been marketed lawfully in Denmark as the protection period granted by Danish copyright legislation for exclusive rights had already expired.

It appears from the file that the disputed recordings were manufactured in German territory by Patricia on an order from a Danish [company] and that they were then delivered to that [company] in Denmark before being re-exported to the Federal Republic of Germany. The Danish enterprise is not the one to which EMI Records Ltd assigned rights of reproduction and distribution for the musical works in question in Danish territory.

The [German] national court took the view that the application by EMI Electrola was justified according to German law, but that the question could arise of whether Articles 30 and 36 EEC precluded application of national legislation. In order to decide this problem it stayed judgment and referred the following question to the Court for a preliminary ruling:

> Is it compatible with the provisions on the free movement of goods (Articles 30 et seq. EEC) for a manufacturer of sound recordings in member-State A to exercise his exclusive rights in that State over the production and sale of certain musical works in such a manner as to prohibit the sale in the territory of member-State A of sound recordings of the same musical works manufactured and sold in member-State B, where the manufacturer of sound recordings previously enjoyed copyright protection for the musical works in member-State B but the copyright period has already expired?

. . . Pursuant to Article 36 of the Treaty, the provisions of Article 30 prohibiting all measures having an equivalent effect to quantitative restrictions on imports between member-States do not preclude prohibitions or restrictions on imports justified on grounds of the protection of industrial and commercial property. Such protection covers the protection of literary and artistic property including copyright, if it is exploited commercially. Therefore it also covers protection for exclusive rights of reproduction and distribution of sound recordings, if that is treated in the same way as copyright by the relevant national law.

Therefore the object of Articles 30 and 36 is to reconcile the requirements of the free movement of goods with upholding the lawful exercise of exclusive rights in literary and artistic property. In particular, that reconciliation means that protection must be refused to any improper exercise of those rights which would be likely to maintain or create artificial partitioning in the Common Market.

From this the Court's case law has inferred that a copyright owner cannot rely on the exclusive exploitation right conferred by his copyright to prevent or restrict the importation of sound recordings which have been lawfully marketed in another member-State by the owner himself or with his consent.

However, that situation differs from the situation envisaged by the [German] national court. The question before the Court shows that the fact that sound recordings were marketed lawfully in the market of another member-State is due, not to an act or consent of the copyright owner or his licensee, but to expiry of the protection period granted by the legislation of that member-State. Therefore the problem arises from the disparity between legislation of different countries regarding the protection period given by copyright and by similar rights. The disparity lies either in the duration of protection itself or the details or protection, such as the time when the protection period begins to run.

In this connection it should be observed that, in the present state of Community law, which is characterized by the absence of harmonization or approximation of legislation on the protection of literary and artistic property, it is for national legislatures to specify the conditions and rules for such protection.

To the extent that the disparity between national laws is likely to create restrictions on sound recordings in the Community, such restrictions are justified by Article 36 of the Treaty if they arise from the difference in arrangements relating to the duration of protection and if the protection period is inseparably linked with the existence of the exclusive rights themselves.

There would be no justification if the restrictions on trade imposed or allowed by the national legislation on which the owner of exclusive rights or his licensee rely were such as to constitute a means of arbitrary discrimination or a disguised measure for restricting trade. However, there is nothing in the file which would permit the presumption that this situation could arise in a case such as the present.

Consequently the reply to the question submitted should be the Articles 30 and 36 of the Treaty must be interpreted as not precluding the application of legislation of a member-State which allows a producer of sound recordings in that member-State to rely on the exclusive rights of reproduction and distribution of certain musical works of which he is the owner in order to prohibit the sale, in the territory of that member-State, of sound recordings of the same musical works when those recordings are imported from another member-State in which they had been lawfully marketed, without the consent of the aforesaid owner of his licensee, and in which the producer of those recordings had enjoyed protection which has in the meantime expired. . . .

On those grounds, the Court, in reply to the question submitted to it by the Landgericht, Hamburg [a German Regional Court], by order of 2 October 1987, hereby rules:

> Articles 30 and 36 of the EEC Treaty must be interpreted as not precluding the application of legislation of a member-State which allows a producer of sound recordings in that member-State to rely on the exclusive rights of reproduction and distribution of certain musical works of which he is the owner in order to prohibit the sale, in the territory of that member-State, of sound recordings of the same musical works when those recordings are imported from another member-State in which they had been lawfully marketed without the consent of the aforesaid owner or his licensee, and in which the producer of those recordings had enjoyed protection which has in the meantime expired.

Why was the outcome in *EMI Electrola v. Patricia* different from the outcome in *Deutsche Grammophon*? In *EMI Electrola v. Patricia*, "the disputed recordings were manufactured in German territory by Patricia on an order from a Danish [company] and . . . they were then delivered to that [company] in Denmark before being re-exported to the Federal Republic of Germany." Did it matter, though, to the outcome of the case that the "disputed recordings" were manufactured in Germany, or even that they were manufactured by the same company that then imported them back into Germany from Denmark? That is, doesn't it appear (from the Court's opinion) that the result would have been the same, even if the disputed recordings had been manufactured in Denmark by a Danish company and then imported into Germany by Patricia? In fact, given that the recordings were in the public domain in Denmark because their copyrights had expired there, wouldn't it have been more likely that the recordings would have been made in Denmark than in Germany where they were still protected by copyright? Couldn't the same ultimate result in the case have been achieved, without implicating the Treaty of Rome at all, by ignoring altogether the fact that they had been exported to Denmark and then imported back into Germany, and simply finding that Patricia was liable for manufacturing unauthorized copies of the recordings in Germany, where they were still protected by copyright?

Isn't the most important difference between *EMI Electrola* and *Deutsche Grammophon* the fact that:

- in *Deutsche Grammophon*, the records imported into Germany from France had been manufactured in France by a company licensed by the owner of their German copyrights, or were manufactured in Germany by the German copyright owner and then shipped to France, while
- in *EMI Electrola*, the "Danish enterprise [from which the records were purchased] is *not* the one to which EMI Records Ltd assigned rights of reproduction and distribution for the musical works in question in Danish territory." [Emphasis added.]

But why did that matter? In *Deutsche Grammophon*, it was legal for the French company to manufacture and sell the recordings, because it was licensed to do so in France. In *EMI Electrola*, it was legal for the Danish company to sell the recordings (and it would have been legal for it to manufacture them too), because they were in the public domain in Denmark. In other words, in both cases, what the French and Danish companies did was legal where they did it. What difference does it make *why* it was legal?

Of course, as a consequence of the *EMI Electrola* decision, recordings that were in the public domain in one EU country could not be imported into other EU countries where they were still protected by copyright (unless the copyright owner consented), despite the usual rule that goods should travel freely within the EU. In 1993 – four years after the *EMI Electrola* decision – the EU decided to do something about this. Rather than overrule the *EMI* decision (legislatively), it decided that the duration of copyright should be the same in all EU countries. The EU did so by adopting a Directive, the following excerpt from which appears to be in direct response to the *EMI* decision. As you read this excerpt, ask yourself whether it *authorizes* German record distributors to import recordings from Denmark, or whether instead it simply eliminates copyright-related reasons for manufacturing recordings in one EU country rather than another.

### Council Directive 93/98/EEC of 29 October 1993
### harmonizing the term of protection of copyright and certain related rights

The Council of the European Communities,

Having regard to the Treaty establishing the European Economic Community . . . ,

(2) Whereas there are . . . differences between the national laws governing the terms of protection of copyright and related rights, which are liable to impede the free movement of goods . . . , and to distort competition in the common market; whereas therefore with a view to the smooth operation of the internal market, the laws of the Member States should be harmonized so as to make terms of protection identical throughout the Community . . .

Has Adopted this Directive:

Article 3. . . .

2. The rights of producers of phonograms shall expire 50 years after the fixation is made. However, if the phonogram is lawfully published or lawfully communicated to the public during this period, the rights shall expire 50 years from the date of the first such publication or the first such communication to the public, whichever is the earlier.

*Rental rights*

The next case is another in which the Court of Justice recognized the primacy of national copyright rights over free trade (and again surprised many by doing so). The result was welcomed by copyright owners, of course; but it was followed by a Directive that required EU members to harmonize their copyright statutes in yet another way.

## Warner Bros. Inc. v. Christiansen
### [1988] ECR 2605, [1990] 3 CMLR 684, [1991] FSR 161
### (Court of Justice of the European Communities 1988)

The film "Never Say Never Again" was produced by . . . Warner Brothers Incorporated, which assigned the video-production rights [i.e., homevideo reproduction and distribution rights] for Denmark to . . . Metronome Video ApS.

In July 1984, while video-cassettes of the film could be purchased in England but were not available either for purchase or for hire in Denmark, the defendant in the main proceedings, Mr. Christiansen, who manages a video shop in Copenhagen, bought a copy of the film in London for the purpose of hiring it out [i.e., renting it to customers] in Denmark.

It is common ground between the parties that, as is stated in the order of the [Danish] national court,

- the video-cassette in question was lawfully manufactured, marketed and purchased in the United Kingdom;
- it was lawfully imported into Denmark by Mr. Christiansen;
- British copyright law does not confer any right of dissemination within the United Kingdom of the author or producer, so that the purchaser of a film recorded on video-cassette may hire it out in the United Kingdom without the consent of the owner of the exclusive rights;
- by virtue of . . . Danish Law . . . , the exclusive right to authorize the hiring-out of a musical or cinematographic work is not exhausted when the copyright owner sells a copy of the work but only when he authorizes the hiring-out of the work. Those articles [of Danish copyright law] therefore make it possible to prohibit the hiring-out to the public of a video-cassette without the copyright owner's consent, irrespective of how the video-cassette was purchased.

On the basis of that Danish legislation the two plaintiffs in the main proceedings obtained an injunction from the Copenhagen City Court restraining the defendant from hiring out the video-cassette in Denmark.

The plaintiffs then requested confirmation of the injunction from the Ostre Landsret [the Eastern Division of the Danish High Court] which, before giving judgment, made an order dated 11 June 1986 staying the proceedings and referring the following question to the Court of Justice [of the European Communities] for a preliminary ruling:

> Must the provisions . . . of the EEC Treaty, on the elimination of quantitative restrictions between Member States, namely Articles 30 and 36 . . . , be interpreted as meaning that the owner of exclusive rights (copyright) in a video cassette which is lawfully put into circulation by the owner of the exclusive right or with his consent in a Member State under whose domestic copyright law he may not prohibit the (resale and) hiring-out of the video cassette is prevented from restraining the hiring-out of that video cassette in another Member State into which it has been lawfully imported, where the copyright law of that State allows such prohibition without distinguishing between domestic and imported video-cassettes and without preventing the actual importation thereof?

. . . It should be noted that, unlike the national copyright legislation which gave rise to the judgment of 20 January 1981 in *Musik Vertrieb Membran v GEMA*, the legislation which gives rise to the present preliminary question does not enable the author to collect an additional fee on the actual importation of recordings of protected works which are marketed with his consent in another Member State, or to set up any further obstacle whatsoever to importation or resale. The rights and powers conferred on the author by the national legislation in question comes into operation only after importation has been carried out.

Nonetheless, it must be observed that the commercial distribution of video-cassettes takes the form not only of sales but also, and increasingly, that of hiring out to individuals who possess video-tape recorders. The right to prohibit such hiring-out in a Member State is therefore liable to influence trade in video-cassettes in that State and hence, indirectly, to affect intra-Community trade in those products. Legislation of the kind which gave rise to the main proceedings must therefore, in the light of established case-law, be regarded as a measure having an effect equivalent to a quantitative restriction on imports, which is prohibited by Article 30 of the Treaty.

Consideration should therefore be given to whether such legislation may be considered justified on grounds of the protection of industrial and commercial property within the meaning of Article 36 – a term which was held by the Court . . . to include literary and artistic property.

In that connection it should first be noted that the Danish legislation applies without distinction to video-cassettes produced in [Denmark] and video-cassettes imported from another Member State. The determining factor for the purposes of its application is the type of transaction in video-cassettes which is in question, not the origin of those video-cassettes. Such legislation does not therefore, in itself, operate any arbitrary discrimination in trade between Member States.

It should further be pointed out that literary and artistic works may be the subject of commercial exploitation, whether by way of public performance or of the reproduction and marketing of the recordings made of them, and this is true in particular of cinematographic works. The two essential rights of the author, namely the exclusive right of performance and the exclusive right of reproduction, are not called in question by the rules of the Treaty.

Lastly, consideration must be given to the emergence . . . of a specific market for the hiring-out of such recordings, as distinct from their sale. The existence of that market was made possible by various factors such as the improvement of manufacturing methods for video-cassettes which increased their strength and life in use, the growing awareness amongst viewers that they watch only occasionally the video-cassettes which they have bought and, lastly, their relatively high purchase price. The market for the hiring-out of video-cassettes reaches a wider public than the market for their sale and, at present, offers great potential as a source of revenue for makers of films.

However, it is apparent that, by authorizing the collection of royalties only on sales to private individuals and to persons hiring out video-cassettes, it is impossible to guarantee to makers of films a remuneration which reflects the number of occasions on which the video-cassettes are actually hired out and which secures for them a satisfactory share of the rental market. That explains why . . . certain national laws have recently provided specific protection of the right to hire out video-cassettes.

Laws of that kind are therefore clearly justified on grounds of the protection of industrial and commercial property pursuant to Article 36 of the Treaty.

However, the defendant in the main proceedings, relying on . . . *Musik Vertrieb Membran v GEMA*, contends that the author is at liberty to choose the Member State in which he will market his work. The defendant in the main proceedings emphasizes that the author makes his choice according to his own interests and must, in particular, take into consideration the fact that the legislation of certain Member States, unlike that of certain others, confers on him an exclusive right enabling him to restrain the hiring-out of the recording of the work even when that work has been offered for sale with his consent. That being so, a maker of a film who has offered the video-cassette of that film for sale in a Member State whose legislation confers on him no exclusive right of hiring it out (as in the main proceedings) must accept the consequences of his choice and the exhaustion of his right to restrain the hiring-out of that video-cassette in any other Member State.

That objection cannot be upheld. It follows from the foregoing considerations that, where national legislation confers on authors a specific right to hire out video-cassettes, that right would be rendered worthless if its owner were not in a position to authorize the operations for doing so. It cannot therefore be accepted that the marketing by a film-maker of a video-cassette containing one of his works, in a Member State which does not provide specific protection for the right to hire it out, should have repercussions on the right conferred on that same film-maker by the legislation of another Member State to restrain, in that State, the hiring-out of that video-cassette.

In those circumstances, the answer to be given to the question submitted by the national court is that Articles 30 and 36 of the Treaty do not prohibit the application of national legislation which gives an author the right to make the hiring-out of video-cassettes subject to his permission, when the video-cassettes in question have already been put into circulation with his consent in another Member State whose legislation enables the author to control the initial sale, without giving him the right to prohibit hiring-out. . . .

On those grounds, the Court, in answer to the question referred to it by the Ostre Landsret, Copenhagen [the Eastern Division of the Danish High Court], by order of 11 June 1986, hereby rules:

> Articles 30 and 36 of the EEC Treaty do not prohibit the application of national legislation which gives an author the right to make the hiring-out of video-cassettes subject to his permission, when the video-cassettes in question have already been put into circulation with his consent in another Member State whose legislation enables the author to control the initial sale, without giving him the right to prohibit hiring-out.

In its opinion in the *Warner Bros.* case, did the Court of Justice persuasively distinguish its own earlier opinion in the *Musik-Vertrieb* case? In *Warner Bros.*, the Court said that "where national legislation confers on authors a specific right to hire out video-cassettes, that right would be rendered worthless if its owner were not in a position to authorize the operations for doing so." Couldn't something quite similar have been said in *Musik-Vertrieb*? That is, couldn't the Court have said, in its *Musik-Vertrieb* opinion, that Germany's "national legislation confers on authors [of musical compositions, and on their publishers] a specific right" to be paid mechanical royalties at a rate set by law, which rate was higher than the rate set by law in the United

Kingdom, and "that right would be rendered worthless if its owner were not in a position to [collect the German royalty]?"

Or would it be *in*accurate to say that the right to collect mechanical royalties was made "worthless" by *Musik-Veritrieb*, because royalties at the rate of 6.25% of retail actually were collected in the U.K. (and were paid to songwriters and publishers in Germany, using a mechanism that will be considered in Chapter 8). Suppose the mechanical royalty rate in the U.K. were 0%? That would have "rendered worthless" the right of songwriters and publishers (under German law) to be paid royalties for recordings of their music – wouldn't it? Yet, did the holding of *Musik-Vertrieb* turn at all on the fact that a 6.25% royalty had already been collected in the U.K. – or did it focus, instead, on the fact that allowing GEMA to collect an additional royalty in Germany would have had the effect of discouraging the importation of recordings into Germany from other EU countries?

Yet, in *Warner Bros.*, the Court of Justice acknowledged, didn't it, that its ruling would have the effect of discouraging the importation of movie videos into Denmark from other EU countries? Because of that effect, the EU adopted the following Directive.

### Council Directive 92/100/EEC of 19 November 1992 on rental right and lending right and on certain rights related to copyright in the field of intellectual property

*The Council of the European Communities,*
Having regard to the Treaty establishing the European Economic Community. . .

Whereas differences exist in the legal protection provided by the laws and practices of the Member States for copyright works . . . as regards rental . . . ;

Whereas such differences are sources of barriers to trade and distortions of competition which impede the achievement and proper functioning of the internal market;

Whereas such differences in legal protection could well become greater as Member States adopt new and different legislation or as national case-law interpreting such legislation develops differently;

Whereas such differences should therefore be eliminated in accordance with the objective of introducing an area without internal frontiers . . . so as to institute . . . a system ensuring that competition in the common market is not distorted;

Whereas rental . . . of copyright works . . . is playing an increasingly important role in particular for authors, performers and producers of phonograms and films;

. . .

Whereas the adequate protection of copyright works . . . by rental . . . rights . . . can accordingly be considered as being of fundamental importance for the Community's economic and cultural development;

Whereas copyright . . . protection must adapt to new economic developments such as new forms of exploitation;

Whereas the creative and artistic work of authors . . . necessitates an adequate income as a basis for further creative and artistic work, and the investments required particularly for the production of phonograms and films are especially high and risky;

Whereas the possibility for securing that income and recouping that investment can only effectively be guaranteed through adequate legal protection of the rightholders concerned; . . .

Whereas the pursuit of such activities must be made easier by providing a harmonized legal protection within the Community; . . .

Whereas the legislation of the Member States should be approximated in such a way so as not to conflict with the international conventions on which many Member States' copyright . . . laws are based;...

Whereas the harmonized rental . . . rights . . . should not be exercised in a way which constitutes a disguised restriction on trade between Member States. . . .

*Has adopted this Directive:* . . .

Article 1 - Object of harmonization

1. . . . Member States shall provide . . . a right to authorize or prohibit the rental . . . of originals and copies of copyright works . . . as set out in Article 2(1).

2. For the purposes of this Directive, "rental" means making available for use, for a limited period of time and for direct or indirect economic or commercial advantage. . . .

4. The rights referred to in paragraph 1 shall not be exhausted by any sale or other act of distribution of originals and copies of copyright works . . . and other subject matter as set out in Article 2(1).

Article 2 - Rightholders and subject matter of rental . . . right

1. The exclusive right to authorize or prohibit rental . . . shall belong:
— to the author in respect of the original and copies of his work,
— to the performer in respect of fixations of his performance,
— to the phonogram producer in respect of his phonograms, and
— to the producer of the first fixation of a film in respect of the original and copies of his film. For the purposes of this Directive, the term "film" shall designate a cinematographic or audiovisual work or moving images, whether or not accompanied by sound. . . .

Article 15 - Final provisions

1. Member States shall bring into force the laws, regulations and administrative provisions necessary to comply with this Directive not later than 1 July 1994. . . .

[Available at http://europa.eu.int/eur-lex/lex/LexUriServ/site/en/consleg/1992/L/ 01992L0100 -20010622-en.pdf]

How, exactly, did the "rental right" Directive address the issue raised in *Warner Bros. Inc. v. Christiansen*? In other words, does the Directive mean that homevideos of "Never Say Never Again" and other movies now may be imported into Denmark from the U.K. and then rented to customers in Denmark without the consent of the movies' Danish copyright owners? Or does the Directive require the U.K. to adopt a "rental right" of its own, so that Danish importers have no basis for arguing that they may legally rent homevideos in Denmark even without the consent of Danish copyright owners?

By the way (and by way of review), how does it happen that Danish video stores are legally able to import homevideos from the U.K. (and elsewhere in the EU) in the first place, without the consent of the videos' Danish copyright owners? If Christiansen had *sold* – rather than rented – videos of "Never Say Never Again," without the consent of Metronome Video (Warner Bros.' exclusive Danish homevideo licensee), would Christiansen have violated any *enforceable* provision of Danish copyright law (assuming that Danish copyright law gives copyright owners and their licensees the exclusive right to distribute their works within Denmark)?

*Cable retransmissions of television broadcasts*

All of the Court of Justice decisions you've read to this point dealt with the cross-border shipment of *physical copies* of copyrighted works. Copyrighted works also are delivered to consumers as *intangible services*. And when those works are delivered as television broadcasts, they sometimes are delivered across national borders, especially in Europe where countries are relatively small in size, and major population centers are close together even if they are in different countries. What (you may wonder) has the EU done about the rights of copyright owners, or their licensees, under national copyright law, to show movies and TV programs *exclusively* within specific countries?

As you'll read immediately below, in 1980, the Court of Justice decided to treat cable retransmissions from abroad differently than record imports from abroad. It decided, in other words, to permit copyright owners to assert their exclusive territorial rights. But, as you'll also see, in 1993, the European Union decided that the EEC Treaty *does* require *some* limits on territorial exclusivity, after all.

### S.A. Compagnie Generale pour la Diffusion de la Television, Coditel
### v. S.A. Cine Vog Films
### [1980] ECR 881, [1981] 2 CMLR 362, 12 IIC 207
### (Court of Justice of the European Communities 1980)

Cine Vog Films (. . . "Cine Vog"), a cinematographic film distribution company, acquired under a contract made on 8 July 1969 with the producer, the company "Les Films la Boetie" (. . . "La Boetie"), the exclusive right to show the [French] film "Le Boucher" ["The Butcher"] publicly in Belgium in all its versions in the form of cinema performances and television broadcasts. Exclusivity was given for a period of seven years starting from the first cinematographic showing in Belgium, which took place on 15 May 1970. The right to broadcast the film on Belgian television could not, however, be exercised until forty months after the first performance in Belgium.

At a later unspecified date La Boetie assigned the right to broadcast the film on television in the Federal Republic of Germany to the German television broadcasting station. The Belgian cable television companies, Coditel, picked up directly on their aerial at their reception sites in Belgium the film "Le Boucher" broadcast on 5 January 1971 in the Federal Republic of Germany on the first German television channel and distributed the film by cable to their subscribers, the film being contained in the German programme which they diffuse on a regular basis.

Upon the application of Cine Vog and the Chambre Syndicale Belge de la Cinematographie, the Tribunal de Premiere Instance, Brussels [the Belgium Court of First Instance], decided in a judgment of 19 June 1975 that, by acting as they did without the authorization of Cine Vog, the . . . cable television companies were guilty of infringing the copyright held by Cine Vog.

The cable television companies appealed from that judgment. They relied, inter alia, upon the incompatibility of the exclusive right granted by La Boetie to Cine Vog and the exercise of that right with the provisions of the EEC Treaty on competition (Article 85), on the one hand, and on the freedom to provide services (Article 59), on the other. By a judgment of 30 March 1979, the Court d'Appel, Brussels [the Belgium court of appeals], ruled that, subject to the effect of Community law, under the copyright legislation the appellants required the authority of Cine Vog to show the film "Le Boucher" on their networks on 5 January 1971.

The Court d'Appel based its decision upon the Berne Convention . . . approved by the Belgian Law of 26 June 1951 and in particular upon the first paragraph of Article 11bis, which is worded as follows:

> Authors of literary and artistic works shall have the exclusive right of authorizing:
>
> (i) The radio-diffusion of their works or the communication thereof to the public by any other means of wireless diffusion of signs, sounds or images;
>
> (ii) Any communication to the public, whether over wires or not, of the radio-diffusion of the work, when this communication is made by a body other than the original one;
>
> (iii) The communication to the public by loudspeaker or any other similar instrument transmitting, by signs, sounds or images, the radiodiffusion of the work.

The Court d'Appel ruled that that provision was applicable in the case before it and declared that the cable television undertakings must be considered as a body "separate" from the broadcaster of the film, namely the German broadcasting station, and that the communication of the film to Belgian viewers was a communication "to the public" as understood in the said provision.

As regards Community law, the Cour d'Appel first of all held that a performing right is part of the specific subject-matter of copyright and that consequently Article 85 of the Treaty did not apply.

Having subsequently decided that the submission based upon Article 59 of the Treaty [on the freedom to provide services] raised the problem of the interpretation of that provision, it decided to stay the proceedings and to refer to the Court of Justice the following two questions for a preliminary ruling under Article 177 of the Treaty:

> 1. Are the restrictions prohibited by Article 59 of the Treaty establishing the European Economic Community only those which prejudice the provision of services between nationals established in different Member States, or do they also comprise restrictions on the provision of services between nationals established in the same Member State which however concern services the substance of which originates in another Member State?
>
> 2. If the first limb of the preceding question is answered in the affirmative, is it in accordance with the provisions of the Treaty on freedom to provide services for the assignee of the performing right in a cinematographic film in one Member State to rely upon his right in order to prevent the defendant from showing that film in that

State by means of cable television where the film thus shown is picked up by the defendant in the said Member State after having been broadcast by a third party in another Member State with the consent of the original owner of the right?"

... The Court of Justice will first of all examine the second question. If the answer to this question is in the negative because the practice it describes is not contrary to the provisions of the Treaty on freedom to provide services – on the assumption that those provisions are applicable – the national court will have all the information necessary for it to be able to resolve the legal problem before it in conformity with Community law.

The second question raises the problem of whether Articles 59 and 60 of the Treaty prohibit an assignment, limited to the territory of a Member State, of the copyright in a film, in view of the fact that a series of such assignments might result in the partitioning of the Common Market as regards the undertaking of economic activity in the film industry.

A cinematographic film belongs to the category of literary and artistic works made available to the public by performances which may be infinitely repeated. In this respect the problems involved in the observance of copyright in relation to the requirements of the Treaty are not the same as those which arise in connection with literary and artistic works the placing of which at the disposal of the public is inseparable from the circulation of the material form of the works, as in the case of books or records.

In these circumstances the owner of the copyright in a film and his assigns have a legitimate interest in calculating the fees due in respect of the authorization to exhibit the film on the basis of the actual or probable number of performances and in authorizing a television broadcast of the film only after it has been exhibited in cinemas for a certain period of time. It appears from the file on the present case that the contract made between Les Films la Boetie and Cine Vog stipulated that the exclusive right which was assigned included the right to exhibit the film "Le Boucheur" publicly in Belgium by way of projection in cinemas and on television but that the right to have the film diffused by Belgian television could not be exercised until 40 months after the first showing of the film in Belgium.

These facts are important in two regards. On the one hand, they highlight the fact that the right of a copyright owner and his assigns to require fees for any showing of a film is part of the essential function of copyright in this type of literary and artistic work. On the other hand, they demonstrate that the exploitation of copyright in films and the fees attaching thereto cannot be regulated without regard being had to the possibility of television broadcasts of those films. The question whether an assignment of copyright limited to the territory of a Member State is capable of constituting a restriction on freedom to provide services must be examined in this context.

While Article 59 of the Treaty prohibits restrictions upon freedom to provide services, it does not thereby encompass limits upon the exercise of certain economic activities which have their origin in the application of national legislation for the protection of intellectual property, save where such application constitutes a means of arbitrary discrimination or a disguised restriction on trade between Member States. Such would be the case if that application enabled parties to an assignment of copyright to create artificial barriers to trade between Member States.

The effect of this is that, while copyright entails the right to demand fees for any showing or performance, the rules of the Treaty cannot in principle constitute an obstacle to the geographical limits which the parties to a contract of assignment have agreed upon in order to protect the author and his assigns in this regard. The mere fact that those geographical limits may coincide with national frontiers does not point to a different solution in a situation where television is organized in the Member States largely on the basis of legal broadcasting monopolies, which indicates that a limitation other than the geographical field of application of an assignment is often impracticable.

The exclusive assignee of the performing right in a film for the whole of a Member State may therefore rely upon his right against cable television diffusion companies which have transmitted that film on their diffusion network having received it from a television broadcasting station established in another Member State, without thereby infringing Community law.

Consequently the answer to the second question referred to the Court by the Cour d'Appel, Brussels, should be that the provisions of the Treaty relating to the freedom to provide services do not preclude an assignee of the performing right in a cinematographic film in a Member State from relying upon his right to prohibit the exhibition of that film in that State, without his authority, by means of cable diffusion if the film so exhibited is picked up and transmitted after being broadcast in another Member State by a third party with the consent of the original owner of the right.

It is clear from the answer given to the second question that Community law, on the assumption that it applies to the activities of the cable diffusion companies which are the subject-matter of the dispute brought before the national court, has no effect upon the application by that court of the provisions of copyright legislation in a case such as this. Therefore there is no need to answer the first question. . . .

On those grounds, the Court, in answer to the questions referred to it by the Cour d'Appel, Brussels, by judgment of 30 March 1979, hereby rules:

> The provisions of the Treaty relating to the freedom to provide services do not preclude an assignee of the performing right in a cinematographic film in a Member State from relying upon his right to prohibit the exhibition of that film in that State, without his authority, by means of cable diffusion if the film so exhibited is picked up and transmitted after being broadcast in another Member State by a third party with the consent of the original owner of the right.

### Council Directive 93/83/EEC of 27 September 1993 on the coordination of certain rules concerning copyright and rights related to copyright applicable to satellite broadcasting and cable retransmission

*The Council of the European Communities,*

Having regard to the Treaty establishing the European Economic Community . . . ,

(1) Whereas the objectives of the Community as laid down in the Treaty include establishing an ever closer union among the peoples of Europe, fostering closer relations between the States belonging to the Community and ensuring the economic and social progress of the Community countries by common action to eliminate the barriers which divide Europe;

(2) Whereas, to that end, the Treaty provides for the establishment of a common market and an area without internal frontiers; whereas measures to achieve this include the abolition of obstacles to the free movement of services and the institution of a system ensuring that competition in the common market is not distorted; whereas, to that end, the Council may adopt directives for the coordination of the provisions laid down by law, regulation or administrative action in Member States concerning the taking up and pursuit of activities as self-employed persons;

(3) Whereas broadcasts transmitted across frontiers within the Community, in particular by . . . satellite and cable, are one of the most important ways of pursuing these Community objectives, which are at the same time political, economic, social, cultural and legal; . . .

(5) Whereas, however, the achievement of these objectives in respect of cross-border . . . cable retransmission of programmes from other Member States is currently still obstructed by a series of differences between national rules of copyright and some degree of legal uncertainty; whereas this means that holders of rights are exposed to the threat of seeing their works exploited without payment of remuneration or that the individual holders of exclusive rights in various Member States block the exploitation of their rights; whereas the legal uncertainty in particular constitutes a direct obstacle in the free circulation of programmes within the Community; . . .

(8) Whereas, furthermore, legal certainty, which is a prerequisite for the free movement of broadcasts within the Community, is missing where programmes transmitted across frontiers are fed into and retransmitted through cable networks;

(9) Whereas the development of the acquisition of rights on a contractual basis by authorization is already making a vigorous contribution to the creation of the desired European audiovisual area; whereas the continuation of such contractual agreements should be ensured and their smooth application in practice should be promoted wherever possible;

(10) Whereas at present cable operators in particular cannot be sure that they have actually acquired all the programme rights covered by such an agreement;

(11) Whereas, lastly, parties in different Member States are not all similarly bound by obligations which prevent them from refusing without valid reason to negotiate on the acquisition of the rights necessary for cable distribution or allowing such negotiations to fail; . . .

(27) Whereas the cable retransmission of programmes from other Member States is an act subject to copyright and, as the case may be, rights related to copyright; whereas the cable operator must, therefore, obtain the authorization from every holder of rights in each part of the programme retransmitted; whereas, pursuant to this Directive, the authorizations should be granted contractually . . . ;

(28) Whereas, in order to ensure that the smooth operation of contractual arrangements is not called into question by the intervention of outsiders holding rights in individual parts of the programme, provision should be made, through the obligation to have recourse to a collecting society, for the exclusive collective exercise of the authorization right to the extent that this is required by the special features of cable retransmission; whereas the authorization right as such remains intact and only the exercise of this right is regulated to some extent, so that the right to authorize a cable retransmission can still be assigned; whereas this Directive does not affect the exercise of moral rights; . . .

(30) Whereas contractual arrangements regarding the authorization of cable retransmission should be promoted by additional measures; whereas a party seeking the conclusion of a general contract should, for its part, be obliged to submit collective proposals for an agreement; whereas, furthermore, any party shall be entitled, at any moment, to call upon the assistance of impartial mediators whose task is to assist negotiations and who may submit proposals; whereas any such proposals and any opposition thereto should be served on the parties concerned in accordance with the applicable rules concerning the service of legal documents, in particular as set out in existing international conventions; whereas, finally, it is necessary to ensure that the negotiations are not blocked without valid justification or that individual holders are not prevented without valid justification from taking part in the negotiations; whereas none of these measures for the promotion of the acquisition of rights calls into question the contractual nature of the acquisition of cable retransmission rights; . . .

(33) Whereas minimum rules should be laid down in order to establish and guarantee free and uninterrupted . . . simultaneous, unaltered cable retransmission of programmes broadcast from other Member States, on an essentially contractual basis; . . .

*Has Adopted this Directive:*

*Article 1. . .*

3.   For the purposes of this Directive, "cable retransmission" means the simultaneous, unaltered and unabridged retransmission by a cable or microwave system for reception by the public of an initial transmission from another Member State, by wire or over the air, including that by satellite, of television or radio programmes intended for reception by the public.

4.   For the purposes of this Directive "collecting society" means any organization which manages or administers copyright or rights related to copyright as its sole purpose or as one of its main purposes.

5.   For the purposes of this Directive, the principal director of a cinematographic or audiovisual work shall be considered as its author or one of its authors. Member States may provide for others to be considered as its co-authors. . . .

*Article 8  Cable retransmission right*

1.   Member States shall ensure that when programmes from other Member States are retransmitted by cable in their territory the applicable copyright and related rights are observed and that such retransmission takes place on the basis of individual or collective contractual agreements between copyright owners, holders of related rights and cable operators. . . .

*Article 9  Exercise of the cable retransmission right*

1.   Member States shall ensure that the right of copyright owners and holders or related rights to grant or refuse authorization to a cable operator for a cable retransmission may be exercised only through a collecting society.

2.   Where a rightholder has not transferred the management of his rights to a collecting society, the collecting society which manages rights of the same category shall be deemed to be mandated to manage his rights. Where more than one collecting society manages rights of that category, the rightholder shall be free to choose which of those collecting societies is deemed to be mandated to manage his rights. A rightholder referred to in this paragraph shall have the same rights and obligations resulting from the agreement between the cable operator and the collecting society which is deemed to be mandated to manage his rights as the rightholders who have

mandated that collecting society and he shall be able to claim those rights within a period, to be fixed by the Member State concerned, which shall not be shorter than three years from the date of the cable retransmission which includes his work or other protected subject matter.

3.    A Member State may provide that, when a rightholder authorizes the initial transmission within its territory of a work or other protected subject matter, he shall be deemed to have agreed not to exercise his cable retransmission rights on an individual basis but to exercise them in accordance with the provisions of this Directive. . . .

*Article 11  Mediators*

1. Where no agreement is concluded regarding authorization of the cable retransmission of a broadcast, Member States shall ensure that either party may call upon the assistance of one or more mediators.

2.    The task of the mediators shall be to provide assistance with negotiation. They may also submit proposals to the parties.

3.    It shall be assumed that all the parties accept a proposal as referred to in paragraph 2 if none of them expresses its opposition within a period of three months. Notice of the proposal and of any opposition thereto shall be served on the parties concerned in accordance with the applicable rules concerning the service of legal documents.

4.    The mediators shall be so selected that their independence and impartiality are beyond reasonable doubt.

*Article 12  Prevention of the abuse of negotiating positions*

1.    Member States shall ensure by means of civil or administrative law, as appropriate, that the parties enter and conduct negotiations regarding authorization for cable retransmission in good faith and do not prevent or hinder negotiation without valid justification. . . .

*Article 14  Final provisions*

1.    Member States shall bring into force the laws, regulations and administrative provisions necessary to comply with this Directive before 1 January 1995. . . .

[Available at http://europa.eu.int/eur-lex/lex/LexUriServ/LexUriServ.do?uri=CELEX: 31993L0083:EN:HTML]

How did this Directive harmonize the national copyright laws of EU members?

## 2.  Harmonization by judicial decree

Free trade treaties also may have the effect of harmonizing the copyright laws of countries that adhere to them, *whether or not* those countries are required to amend their copyright statutes to do so. This point is well illustrated by the following case in which harmonization was accomplished by judicial decree.

# Collins v. Imtrat Handelsgesellschaft MbH
## [1993] 3 CMLR 773
### (Court of Justice of the European Communities 1993)

. . .

*Case C-92/92 [The Phil Collins case]*

The plaintiff in Case C-92/92 is Phil Collins, a singer and composer of British nationality. The defendant – Imtrat Handelsgesellschaft mbH ('Imtrat') – is a producer of phonograms. In 1983 Mr. Collins gave a concert in California which was recorded without his consent. Reproductions of the recording were sold in Germany by Imtrat on compact disc under the title 'Live and Alive.' Mr. Collins applied to the Landgericht Munchen I [a German trial court] for an injunction restraining Imtrat from marketing such recordings in Germany and requiring it to deliver copies in its possession to a court bailiff.

It appears that if Mr. Collins were a German national his application would undoubtedly have succeeded. Section 75 of the Gesetz uber Urheberrecht und verwandte Schutzrechte (Law on copyright and related rights, hereafter 'Urheberrechtsgesetz') provides that a performing artist's performance may not be recorded without his consent and recordings may not be reproduced without his consent. Section 125(1) of the Urheberrechtsgesetz provides that German nationals enjoy the protection of section 75, amongst other provisions, for all their performances regardless of the place of performance. However, foreign nationals have less extensive rights under the Urheberrechtsgesetz. Under section 125(2) they enjoy protection in respect of performances which take place in Germany, and under section 125(5) they enjoy protection in accordance with international treaties.

. . .

*Case C-326/92 [The Cliff Richard case]*

The plaintiff and respondent in Case C-326/92 – EMI Electrola GmbH ('EMI Electrola') – produces and distributes phonograms. It owns the exclusive right to exploit in Germany recordings of certain works performed by Cliff Richard, a singer of British nationality. The defendants and appellants are Patricia Im- und Export Verwaltungsgesellschaft mbH ('Patricia'), a company which distributes phonograms, and Mr. L. E. Kraul, its managing director. EMI Electrola applied for an injunction restraining Patricia and Mr. Kraul (together with other persons) from infringing its exclusive rights in recordings of certain performances by Cliff Richard. The recordings were first published in the United Kingdom in 1958 and 1959, apparently by a British phonogram producer to which Cliff Richard had assigned his performer's rights in the recordings. That company subsequently assigned the rights to EMI Electrola.

The Landgericht [German trial court] granted EMI Electrola's application and that decision was confirmed on appeal. Patricia and Mr. Kraul appealed on a point of law to the Bundesgerichtshof [German Federal Supreme Court], which considered that, under German law, EMI Electrola would be entitled to an injunction if Cliff Richard were of German nationality but is not so entitled because he is British. . . .

It is . . . common ground that a difference in treatment, depending on the nationality of the performer, exists in German law. . . .

*The issues raised by the two cases*

Both cases raise essentially the same issues: (a) whether it is compatible with Community law, in particular Article 7 EEC, for a member-State to grant more extensive protection in respect of performances by its own nationals than in respect of performances by nationals of other member-States and (b) if such a difference in treatment is not compatible with Community law, whether the relevant provisions of Community law produce direct effect, in the sense that a performer who has the nationality of another member-State is entitled to claim, in proceedings against a person who markets unauthorised recordings of his performances, the same rights as a national of the member-State in question.

I note in passing that, although both the national courts refer to copyright, the cases are in fact concerned not with copyright in the strict sense but with certain related rights known as performers' rights.

The prohibition of discrimination on grounds of nationality is the single most important principle of Community law. It is the leitmotiv of the EEC Treaty. It is laid down in general terms in Article 7 of the Treaty, the first paragraph of which provides:

> Within the scope of application of this Treaty, and without prejudice to any special provisions contained therein, any discrimination on grounds of nationality shall be prohibited.

. . . There cannot be any doubt that Article 7, either alone or in conjunction with other provisions of the Treaty, has the effect that nationals of a member-State are entitled to pursue any legitimate form of economic activity in another member- State on the same terms as the latter State's own nationals. . . .

Certainly there can be no doubt about the economic importance of the performing artist's exclusive right to authorise the reproduction and distribution of recordings embodying his performance. The exercise of that right is essential to the commercial exploitation of a performance. The sale of unauthorised recordings damages the performing artist in two ways: first, because he earns no royalties on such recordings, the sale of which must inevitably reduce the demand for his authorised recordings, since the spending power of even the most avid record collector is finite; secondly, because he loses the power to control the quality of the recordings, which may, if technically inferior, adversely affect his reputation. . . .

Performers' rights also play a role in the field of consumer protection: the consumer doubtless assumes that recordings made by well-known, living performers are not released without the performer's authorisation and that such persons would not jeopardise their reputation by authorising the distribution of low-quality recordings; that limited guarantee of quality is lost entirely if recordings may be distributed without the performer's consent. It may thus be seen that performers' rights operate in much the same way as trade marks. . . .

The defendants in both the present cases advance a number of arguments purporting to show that the contested German legislation is not contrary to the prohibition of discrimination on grounds of nationality. I shall briefly summarise the main arguments and state why, in my view, none of them is convincing.

Both defendants contend that the discrimination lies outside the scope of application of the Treaty. Imtrat reaches that conclusion on the grounds that the performance in question took place outside the territory of a member-State and that the existence of intellectual property rights is a matter for national law by virtue of Article 222 EEC. That cannot be correct. The place where the original performance took place is irrelevant; what matters is that Phil Collins and his licensees are denied protection, in an overtly discriminatory manner, when they attempt to exploit – or prevent others from exploiting – the performance in a member-State. . . .

It is contended on behalf of Patricia and Mr. Kraul that the absence of Community legislation harmonising the laws of member-States on copyright and related rights removes such matters from the scope of the Treaty entirely. That argument is of course doomed to failure. The application of the principle of non-discrimination is not dependent on the harmonisation of national law; on the contrary, it is precisely in areas where harmonisation has not been achieved that the principle of national treatment assumes special importance. . . .

### The direct effect of Article 7(1)

I turn now to the issue of direct effect. In my view, it is clear from the considerations set out above that the Treaty provisions which prohibit discrimination must be capable of being invoked by performers in the circumstances of the present cases. . . . [N]ational courts are under a duty to disapply national provisions that are contrary to Article 7. It is equally clear that that duty arises not only in proceedings against the State but also in litigation between individuals.

### A factual difference between Case C-92/92 and Case C-326/92

A final issue that remains to be explored is whether any significance attaches to an obvious factual difference between Case C-92/92 and Case C-326/92: in the former case the performer, Phil Collins, has remained the proprietor of the performer's rights and has granted an exclusive licence to a producer of phonograms to exploit those rights in Germany; in the latter case the performer, Cliff Richard, has assigned his rights to a British company, which has reassigned them to a German company. I am satisfied that that difference is not relevant to the issue of discrimination. Although in Case C-326/92 the direct victim of the discriminatory German legislation is a German company, the indirect victim will, on the assumption that royalties are paid to the performer by EMI Electrola, be Cliff Richard himself. Even in the case of an outright assignment without any provision for the payment of royalties, it would be wrong in principle to discriminate on the basis of the nationality of the performer and original right-holder. If such discrimination were permitted, it would mean that the exclusive right granted to a German performer would be an assignable asset, potentially of considerable value, while a British performer's exclusive right would have virtually no assignable value, since it would be extinguished on assignment. Thus the indirect victim of the discrimination would always be the performer himself. It would in any case be illogical, in the circumstances of the present cases, to distinguish between a performer's right which has been the subject of an exclusive licence and a performer's right which has been the subject of an assignment. . . .

### Order

On those grounds, the Court, in answer to the questions referred to it by the Regional Court, Munich I, by order of 4 March 1992, and by the Federal Supreme Court by order of 30 April 1992, Hereby rules:

1.  Copyright and related rights are within the scope of application of the Treaty within the meaning of Article 7(1); the general principle of non-discrimination laid down by that Article is consequently applicable to those rights.
2.  Article 7(1) EEC must be interpreted as meaning that it prevents the law of a member-State from refusing authors and performing artists of other member-States and their successors in title the right, which is granted by the same law to nationals, to prohibit the marketing in national territory of a phonogram made without their consent, if the performance in question was given outside national territory.
3.  Article 7(1) EEC must be interpreted as meaning that the principle of non-discrimination which it lays down can be relied upon directly before the national court by an author or artist of a member-State or his successor in title in order to seek the protection given to national authors and artists.

If Phil Collins and Cliff Richard had been Americans, rather than British nationals, would the Court of Justice have ruled in their favor, just the same? The EEC Treaty prohibits EU countries from discriminating in copyright (and other) matters against nationals of other EU countries, but does it permit EU countries to discriminate against Americans (and nationals of other non-EU countries)? Why, in other words, didn't the German court that decided the following opinion say anything about the EEC Treaty, or at least refer the case to the Court of Justice of the European Communities?

### Re Copyright in an Unauthorized U.S. Recording
### [1993] ECC 428
### (German Regional Court of Appeal, Cologne 1991)

Spatgens, Schneider and Fox, Judges

The plaintiff cannot require the defendant to desist from marketing the records [in issue] containing recordings of one of his concerts, given in New Orleans, USA, in 1981.

The plaintiff, who [is not identified by name in this opinion] is a U.S. citizen and is claiming performing rights protection as a performing artist, has no rights under German copyright law which go beyond the minimum protection for foreign nationals under section 125(6) of the Copyright Act. [Section 125(6) protects foreign performers against: the unauthorized "public communication" of their performances "by screen, loudspeaker or similar technical device in a place other than that in which it takes place"; the unauthorized audio or video recording of their performances; and against the "distortion" of their performances.]

Section 125(2) of the Copyright Act cannot provide a basis for the plaintiff's injunction application, since the performance for which protection is sought took place in the USA, in New Orleans. [Section 125(2) protects foreign performers against unauthorized uses of any of their performances that took place in Germany.]

Section 125(5) of the Copyright Act, under which foreign nationals are to be given protection in accordance with any treaties in force, also does not apply in the present case. [Section 125(5) provides protection for foreign performers "as provided by international treaty."] It has already been pointed out correctly by the Landgericht [the German trial court] . . . that the Rome Convention of 26 October 1961 does not apply in the plaintiff's favour, and he no longer seeks to challenge this matter. As the plaintiff also no longer disputes, the agreement between Germany and the USA on the mutual protection of copyright of 15 January 1892 likewise provides no support for the injunction application. . . .   Accordingly, it is only section 125(6) of the Copyright Act [described above] which might provide a basis for the plaintiff's claims under copyright law. But this provision too, with the rights for foreign artists which it specifies, does not lead to the prohibition of the marketing of the compact disc in issue.

    . . . German copyright law already grants foreign artists a considerable degree of protection for their artists in Germany by acceding to international conventions or by concluding reciprocal agreements (which at the same time grant German artists an increased level of protection abroad). If other countries (like the USA in the present case) do not make use of that opportunity, the gap cannot be filled by an extension of the sphere of application of section 125(6). Otherwise there would be no point in the incentive, deliberately created by the scheme of sections 121 and 125 [which set forth the conditions under which "Foreign Nationals" are entitled to copyright protection in Germany] in the interests of protecting German claimants abroad, for other states to act in accordance with the opportunity provided for in section 125(5) of the Act [i.e., by entering into a treaty with Germany]. . . .

    Accordingly, if the injunction application is not justified on any legal basis, the further application for the confiscation of the discs must also fail for that reason. . . .

### D. Remedies provided by international trade law for copyright treaty violations

Copyright treaties are surprisingly silent about what remedies are available if an adhering country violates its treaty obligations – by, for example, failing to protect works or rights for which the treaty requires protection. The United States itself provides three perfect examples of ways in which the question of remedies for treaty violations could arise – and indeed have.

*Example 1:*

You will recall (from Chapter 3) that the Berne Convention requires newly-adhering countries to provide retroactive copyright protection to works from other Berne countries, so long as those works haven't fallen into the public domain in their country-of-origin. You also will recall that when the United States adhered to Berne in 1989, it expressly (by statute) refused to provide retroactive protection, and that its reason for refusing to do so was thought by some to be a stretch or even tortured. Russia and Thailand reportedly rejected the U.S. position out of hand. But the validity of the United States' denial of retroactive protection to works from other Berne countries was never tested in any legal forum. You may have wondered, why not? The answer is buried in Berne itself. Here is everything Berne has to say about what Russia and Thailand could have done, if they had wanted to challenge the United States' failure to restore copyrights to Russian and Thai works, when the U.S. adhered to Berne:

## Berne Convention Article 33(1)

Any dispute between two or more countries of the Union concerning the interpretation or application of this Convention, not settled by negotiation, may, by any one of the countries concerned, be brought before the International Court of Justice by application in conformity with the Statute of the Court, unless the countries concerned agree on some other method of settlement. The country bringing the dispute before the Court shall inform the International Bureau; the International Bureau shall bring the matter to the attention of the other countries of the Union.

Berne does not say what remedy the International Court of Justice could award, or what penalty it could impose, if – in a proceeding authorized by Article 33(1) – it finds that a country has violated a Berne provision.

The World Trade Organization filled this void. It adopted a detailed *Understanding on Rules and Procedures Governing the Settlement of Disputes* under TRIPs (as well as other WTO agreements). The *Understanding* creates an elaborate set of procedures, including appeals, following which actual remedies are authorized.

## WTO Understanding on Rules and Procedures Governing the Settlement of Disputes - Article 22(2)

. . . [A]ny party having invoked the dispute settlement procedures may request authorization from the DSB [Dispute Settlement Body] to suspend the application to the Member concerned of concessions or other obligations under the covered agreements.

"Suspend . . . obligations" is a polite way of saying "fight a trade war." Trade wars are fought by imposing tariffs – something WTO members are generally prohibited from doing. So the remedy provided by the *Understanding* is one which would *authorize* the complaining WTO member to impose tariffs on goods it imports from the offending WTO member. Tariffs, of course, increase the cost of imported goods and thus decrease demand for them. For countries that depend on exports for the economic well-being of their workers, the possibility that tariffs will be imposed on their goods is a powerful incentive to comply with TRIPs, which in turn means comply with the Berne Convention.

Do you suppose that the *Understanding* is what finally persuaded the United States to grant retroactive copyright protection (that is, to restore copyrights) to WTO members when the U.S. joined the WTO in 1995, as it should have done six years earlier in 1989 when it joined Berne?

*Example 2:*

The possibility of having tariffs imposed on its goods was sufficient to cause the United States to be certain that TRIPs would not require compliance with one provision of Berne – the moral rights provision. Moral rights will be considered later in this book, but for now, it is necessary to know that Berne contains this provision:

## Berne Convention Article 6 *bis* (1)

Independently of the author's economic rights, and even after the transfer of the said rights, the author shall have the right to claim authorship of the work and to object to any distortion, mutilation or other modification of, or other derogatory action in relation to, the said work, which would be prejudicial to his honor or reputation.

In the United States, these rights are granted to some visual artists by section 106A of the U.S. Copyright Act. They are not however granted to other kinds of "authors" by the Copyright Act. The "right to claim authorship" was given to other kinds of authors by judicial interpretations of section 43(a) of the Lanham Act; but those decisions were overturned by the United States Supreme Court in *Dastar Corp. v. Twentieth Century Fox Film Corp.*, 123 S.Ct. 2041 (2003), which held that the Lanham Act does not provide authors with a right to claim authorship of their works.

As a result, it can be argued (and has been) that the United States does not comply with its obligation to provide authors with the moral rights required by Berne Convention Article 6*bis*. Between the time the U.S. adhered to Berne in 1989 and the time it joined the WTO in 1995, no one challenged the United States' failure to satisfy its moral rights obligations – quite probably for the same reason no one challenged the United States' failure to restore copyrights to works from other Berne countries when the U.S. adhered to Berne in 1989.

However, membership in the WTO automatically makes TRIPs applicable, including the TRIPs provision that requires countries to "comply" with the Berne Convention. WTO membership also makes applicable its *Understanding on . . . the Settlement of Disputes*, including the provision that authorizes countries to impose tariffs on goods imported from countries that violate TRIPs by violating Berne. In short, as the United States contemplated its then-forthcoming membership in the WTO, and it considered the likelihood that its laws do not satisfy the moral rights obligations imposed by Article 6 *bis* of Berne, the U.S. negotiated for, and got, a sentence, shown below in italics, inserted into Article 9.1 of the TRIPs Agreement:

## World Trade Organization TRIPs Agreement

*Article 9: Relation to the Berne Convention*
1.  Members shall comply with Articles 1 through 21 of the Berne Convention (1971) and the Appendix thereto. *However, Members shall not have rights or obligations under this Agreement in respect of the rights conferred under Article 6bis of that Convention or of the rights derived therefrom.* [Emphasis added.]

In other words, international trade law – in the form of TRIPs – is so effective in providing remedies for the violation of the Berne Convention that the United States had to be certain it doesn't violate TRIPs. To do so, the United States persuaded the WTO to make TRIPs easier for the U.S. to comply with.

*Example 3:*

The Panel Report in the "Fairness in Music Licensing Act" case (which you read earlier in this chapter) was issued in June 2000, just months before the end of the then-current session of Congress, and just months before the 2000 Presidential election. As a result, repealing the Fairness in Music Licensing Act was not a high priority for anyone in Congress (and for some, it wasn't a priority at all). As a result, – although the United States advised the WTO that it would comply with the Panel's "recommendation" – the U.S. also told the WTO that it needed a "reasonable period of time" within which to do so. Because the United States and the European Communities were not able to agree on how long a time would be "reasonable," that issue was referred to arbitration (as permitted by WTO procedural rules).

The European Communities argued that the Panel's recommendation should be implemented by May 27, 2001, which was 10 months from the date of adoption of the Panel Report. Ten months was sufficient, the EU said, because doing so merely "requires a 'repeal' of Section 110(5)(B) of the Copyright Act, as well as a 'modest adaptation' to Section 110(5)(A) of that Act."

The United States, on the other hand, argued that it needed "at least 15 months" from the adoption of the Panel Report, but added that it would be "even more prudent" to give it until the adjournment of the next session of Congress which might have occurred as late as December 31, 2001. The U.S. justified its request by explaining the multi-step legislative process that is required to enact legislation, and by noting that because the United States had recently elected a new President, Congress would be spending its first few months getting organized and confirming President George Bush's appointments. As a result, the U.S. explained that the process of repealing the Fairness in Music Licensing Act was unlikely to begin until March or April 2001.

The WTO Dispute Settlement Understanding provides that although "particular circumstances" may require shorter or longer times, 15 months from the adoption of a Panel Report is a "guideline" for arbitrators to consider when deciding how much time is "reasonable" for the implementation of recommendations.

Arbitrator Julio Lacarte-Muro agreed with the European Communities that "that the period of time proposed by the United States . . . is not justified by the 'particular circumstances' of this case." On the other hand, the Arbitrator agreed with the United States that "Given that the Congressional schedule for 2001 begins, at the earliest, in January, a 'reasonable period of time' of 10 months, ending on 27 May 2001, does not seem sufficient in the particular circumstances of this case."

The Arbitrator therefore concluded that "that the 'reasonable period of time' for the United States to implement the recommendations and rulings of the [Panel] in this case is 12 months from the date of adoption of the Panel Report by the DSB on 27 July 2000. The 'reasonable period of time' will thus expire on 27 July 2001." *United States – Section 110(5) of the US Copyright Act, Arbitration under Article 21.3(c) of the Understanding on*

*Rules and Procedures Governing the Settlement of Disputes*, WT/DS160/12 (15 January 2001)

Just a few days before the July 27, 2001, deadline, the EU agreed to extend the deadline until December 31, 2001 (the date the U.S. had originally requested in arbitration).

In the meantime, however, the case proceeded to the next stage. That stage required a determination of "the nature and level of the benefits [that otherwise would have been received by EU publishers and songwriters] which are being nullified or impaired" by the Fairness in Music Licensing Act. The EU and the U.S. could not agree on an amount. The EU contended that its music publishers and songwriters are losing almost $25.5 million a year in royalties, while the U.S. contended they are losing only $773,000 a year or less.

Since the U.S. and the EU could not agree, that issue too was submitted to arbitration. A panel of three arbitrators decided that the Fairness in Music Licensing Act is costing European songwriters and music publishers $1.1 million a year in lost royalties. While that amount was more than the U.S. estimate, it was less than one-twentieth of the EU estimate. In this respect, then, it can be said that the United States "won" that round of the case.

There were several reasons the U.S. and the EU were so far apart on how much damage the Fairness in Music Licensing Act is doing to EU publishers and songwriters.

- The EU and U.S. had different views about whether the damage should be measured by the amount of royalties that *all* U.S. restaurants, bars and retail stores should have been paying (the EU's position), or only by those royalties that would have been paid by restaurants, bars and stores that ASCAP and BMI *would have licensed* (the U.S.'s position) if the Fairness in Music Licensing Act had not been passed.

- They also disagreed about whether the damage should be measured by the royalties that would have been *collected* by ASCAP and BMI on behalf of EU publishers and songwriters (the EU's position), or only the amount that would have been *distributed* by ASCAP and BMI to EU publishers (or their U.S. subpublishers) and songwriters (the U.S.'s position).

- They could not agree on whether the amount should be calculated by taking, as a starting point, the number of restaurants, bars and stores that are improperly exempted from paying public performance royalties by the Fairness in Music Licensing Act (the EU's position), or whether the starting point should be the amount of royalties that were actually paid by ASCAP and BMI to EU publishers and songwriters before the Fairness in Music Licensing Act became law (the U.S.'s position).

- Finally, because the arbitrators could not obtain all of the exact data necessary for making their calculations, estimates had to be made in some areas; and the U.S. and EU were unable to agree on the proper figures for some of those estimates.

The arbitrators – Mr. Ian F. Sheppard, Mrs. Margaret Lian, and Mr. David Vivas-Eugui – agreed with the United States on most of these issues.

While the arbitrators agreed with the EU that *all* U.S. users of music *should* be licensed and *should* pay licensing fees, the arbitrators noted that in actual practice, EU publishers and songwriters rely on ASCAP and BMI to collect their public performance royalties; and ASCAP and BMI do not in fact attempt to license all restaurants, bars and stores, because the cost of licensing some would exceed the fees that could be collected from them. The arbitrators therefore decided that damages should be measured by reference to licenses that ASCAP and BMI actually would have issued if the Fairness in Music Licensing Act had not been passed.

The arbitrators determined that the EU's damages should be determined by reference to the amount of *distributions* that ASCAP and BMI would have made to EU publishers and songwriters, rather than the license fees ASCAP and BMI would have collected from restaurants, bars and stores. This was so, the arbitrators explained, because the amounts actually lost by EU publishers and songwriters are those they would have received, after ASCAP and BMI deducted their own collection and administrative costs.

The arbitrators determined that they should start with the amounts paid to EU publishers and songwriters by ASCAP and BMI before the Fairness in Music Licensing Act became law, rather than with the number of restaurants, bars and stores that are improperly exempted by the Act. They reached this conclusion, because even before the Act was passed in 1998, some restaurants, bars and stores were exempt under the old "home style receiver" exemption; and the arbitrators decided that amounts lost by EU publishers and songwriters under that exemption were not at issue in this case.

To calculate the amount lost by EU publishers and songwriters as a result of the Fairness in Music Licensing Act, the arbitrators:

- took the amount ASCAP and BMI distributed to EU publishers and songwriters annually, before the Act was passed (an amount the decision does not reveal, because it was considered to be confidential);
- determined how much of that amount was attributable to license fees paid by restaurants, bars and stores, by multiplying the total amount paid by 18.45% which is the percentage of total domestic receipts attributable to the "general licensing" category (by ASCAP), and then multiplying that by 50% which is the estimated percentage of "general licensing" fees attributable to restaurants, bars and stores; and
- determined how much of that amount was attributable to radio and television play (rather than, say, live performances or the use of CD players), by multiplying that amount by an undisclosed percentage (because the percentage was considered confidential).

These calculations led the arbitrators to conclude that before the Fairness in Music Licensing Act was passed, EU publishers and songwriters received $1.55 million a year on account of radio and television play of their compositions by restaurants, bars and stores in the U.S. The arbitrators then:

- determined that 58.5% of this $1.55 million – or $0.91 million – was paid by restaurants, bars and stores that became exempt because of the Act; and the arbitrators
- adjusted this $0.91 million to take into account "the evolution of the market" from 1998 until the arbitration began in July 2001; they did so

- by increasing the $0.91 million by the percentage of growth in the U.S. gross domestic product for 1998, 1999, 2000 and the first six months of 2001 (i.e., 5.6%, 5.5%, 6.5% and 1.7%).

These calculations yielded the $1.1 million figure the arbitrators decided was the amount per year EU publishers and songwriters have lost, as a result of the public performance fee exemptions that the Fairness in Music Licensing Act has improperly given to restaurants, bars and stores. *United States – Section 110(5) of the US Copyright Act – Recourse to Arbitration under Article 25 of the DSU*, WT/DS160/ARB25/1 (Nov. 9, 2001).

The December 31, 2001 deadline came and went, and Congress did nothing to repeal the Fairness in Music Licensing Act. However, the arbitrators' decision that EU publishers and songwriters have suffered damage of $1.1 million a year since 1998 did *not* lead to a "judgment" that the EU could collect from the U.S. Instead, under WTO rules, the EU became eligible to suspend "obligations" it owes the U.S. under the WTO agreement.

As previously mentioned, "suspension of obligations" is a polite way of describing the initiation of a trade war. The WTO Dispute Settlement Understanding provides that "the general principle is that the complaining party" – in this case, the EU – "should first seek to suspend . . . obligations in the same sector(s) as that in which the panel . . . found a violation. . . ." This "general" principle would authorize the EU to impose tariffs on, say, American-made copyrighted goods imported by Europe.

The WTO Dispute Settlement Understanding contains an "alternate" principle as well. The alternate principle would have authorized the EU "to suspend . . . obligations in other sectors." It would, for example, permit the EU to impose tariffs on other types of goods (having nothing to do with copyright) manufactured in the United States and exported to Europe.

For a while, there was reason to suppose that the EU might take advantage of the "alternate" principle – to impose tariffs on non-copyrighted goods – for reasons buried in the U.S. legislative and political process.

When originally enacted, the Fairness in Music Licensing Act was approved by a majority of the members of both the House and the Senate, and it was signed (rather than vetoed) by President Bill Clinton – even though all were told in advance that the Act probably would be found to violate TRIPs, just as it actually was.

While this means that blame for the Act can fairly be spread around, a bigger share should go to Representative James Sensenbrenner Jr. The Act's original enactment was spearheaded by Representative Sensenbrenner, and in January 2001, he became Chairman of the House Judiciary Committee – the very committee that would have jurisdiction over legislation to repeal the Fairness in Music Licensing Act. In the wake of the WTO's original ruling that the Act violates TRIPs, an unidentified Sensenbrenner "spokeswoman" told the *Hollywood Reporter* that the Fairness in Music Licensing Act "is U.S. law, and allowing an international body to say, 'You will change the law,' is not a good precedent to set." (*Hollywood Reporter*, Nov. 10-12, 2001, pg. 8) Sensenbrenner also reportedly wrote to the United States Trade Representative, protesting the government's decision not to appeal the WTO ruling, arguing that despite the WTO ruling, the Act is consistent with U.S. obligations as a WTO member, in his opinion.

It therefore seems likely that Representative Sensenbrenner is the person most responsible for Congress' failure even to consider repealing the Fairness in Music Licensing Act.

Representative Sensenbrenner, a Republican, represents a district in Wisconsin. The state of Wisconsin is home to a huge number of manufacturers, including, for example, Harley-Davidson, Inc., the manufacturer of Harley-Davidson motorcycles. In the year 2000, Harley-Davidson shipped 19,870 motorcycles to Europe (just over 10% of all its shipments that year). How perfectly ironic it would have been if the EU chose to impose tariffs on Harley-Davidson motorcycles and other Wisconsin-made goods. If the EU chose to do that, Representative Sensenbrenner might have understood why compliance with international law – as determined by an international body that the U.S. has used to good advantage in other disputes – is in fact a good precedent to set.

Alas, that was not to be, though for a while, it looked as though the EU would not impose tariffs on American made goods of any type.

On December 19, 2001 – less than two weeks before the extended deadline for U.S. compliance with the WTO Panel's recommendations – the EU announced that it and the United States had agreed on a "temporary solution" of their dispute over the Fairness in Music Licensing Act. According to an EU press release, "the agreement came during a meeting between EU Trade Commissioner Pascal Lamy and . . . US Trade Representative Robert Zoellick." The release reported that "We have agreed on a process that will result in a US financial contribution to support projects and activities for the benefit of European music creators," though the release reported that the United States remains obliged to bring its copyright legislation into line with its WTO obligations.

The release said that the U.S. Trade Representative would propose that the Bush Administration seek authorization and funding from Congress to enable it to contribute to the financing of projects and activities for the benefit of European music creators. "Once the authorization is granted," the release said, "the EU and the US will be in a position to finalise an arrangement, which will be in place for three years." *EU and US agree on temporary solution in music copyright dispute*, Press Release (dated Dec. 19, 2001).

But December 31, 2001 came and went without any Congressional activity to repeal the Act or to fund the settlement. On January 7, 2002, the EU notified the WTO that the U.S. had failed to meet its deadline, and – despite its December 19, 2001 press release announcing a settlement – the EU informed the WTO that "no mutually acceptable arrangement has yet been made."

At the same time, the EU indicated what remedies it had chosen to pursue. It requested authorization "to suspend its obligations under the TRIPS Agreement in order to permit the levying of a special fee from US nationals in connection with border measures concerning *copyright[ed]* goods." [Emphasis added.] The EU noted that a WTO arbitration panel had found that the Fairness in Music Licensing Act had cost EU songwriters and music publishers $1.1 million per year in lost public performance royalties. Therefore, the EU promised to "fix the amount of the special fee . . . so as to ensure that the level of affected US benefits will not exceed the level of EC benefits nullified or impaired as a result of the WTO-inconsistent provisions of the US Copyright Act." That was just a polite way of telling the U.S. that if the EU does impose "special fees" – that is, "tariffs" – on copyrighted goods from the United States, those "special fees" will amount to as much as $1.1 million per year. *United States – Section 110(5) of the US Copyright Act: Recourse by the European Communities to Article 22.2 of the DSU*, WT/DS160/19 (WTO 7 January 2002)

The United States replied almost immediately. On January 17, 2002, it sent a missive of its own to the WTO, objecting "to the level of suspension of obligations proposed by the European Communities" on January 7th. What's more, the United States claimed that certain necessary "principles and procedures" had "not been followed." The U.S. therefore demanded that "the matter . . . be referred to arbitration." *Request by the United States for Arbitration under Article 22.6 of the DSU*, WT/DS160/20 (WTO 18 January 2002)

Just four days after the United States' demand for arbitration, a further development occurred, suggesting that the settlement was not dead after all, and that the public record during 2002 merely reflects the diplomacy that is necessary to keep it alive. This is what happened. On January 22, 2002, the U.S. sent the WTO a "status report" in which it assured the WTO that "the European Communities and the United States have been engaged in productive discussions with a view to resolving the dispute," and "Those discussions are continuing." *Status Report by the United States*, WT/DS160/18 (WTO 22 January 2002)

The WTO nevertheless appointed three arbitrators, in response to the United States' request. *Recourse by the United States to Article 22.6 of the DSU*, WT/DS160/21 (WTO 19 February 2002). Just one week later, the EC and the U.S. sent the arbitrators a joint communication saying, "The EC and the US would like to inform you that they are engaged in constructive discussions with a view to finding a solution to this dispute. Therefore, the EC and the US would respectfully request the Arbitrator to suspend the arbitration proceeding." The arbitrator therefore suspended the arbitration. *Recourse by the United States to Article 22.6 of the DSU*, WT/DS160/22 (WTO 1 March 2002).

That is where the case still stands (as of November 2009). To satisfy the United States' obligations under the settlement, Congress has appropriated, for payment to the EU, what is now $3.3 million ($1.1 million a year for three years). Eventually, it must repeal the Fairness in Music Licensing Act too. Representative Sensenbrenner is not a member of the House Appropriations Committee (let alone its Chair), so appropriating the needed $3.3 million in settlement funds was possible. On the other hand, since repeal of the Act had to be blessed by the Judiciary Committee, that didn't happen while Sensenbrenner was Chair of the House Judiciary Committee. However, as a consequence of the results of the November 2006 election, Democrats retook control of the House as of January 2007, so that John Conyers, Jr., a Democrat from Michigan – rather than Sensenbrenner – now Chairs the House Judiciary Committee. That may lead, finally, to the repeal of the Fairness in Music Licensing Act.

The WTO's dispute resolution procedure is, of course, a two-way street. And though the United States lost its Section 110(5) case to the EU, and lost its China IP remedies case to China, the United States has won at least its fair share (some say more than is fair share) of WTO cases. One of the cases that the United States won was part of the China IP case you read earlier in this chapter. In addition to complaining (unsuccessfully) about China's criminal IP enforcement laws, the United States also complained (successfully) that China provided no copyright protection at all to some types of works for which Berne, and therefore TRIPs, requires protection.

### Report of WTO Panel on
### China – Measures Affecting the Protection and
### Enforcement of Intellectual Property Rights
### WTO Case WT/DS362/R (26 January 2009)

. . .

The United States claims that China is acting inconsistently with its obligations under the TRIPS Agreement by denying the protection of its Copyright Law to creative works of authorship (and, to the extent Article 4 of the Copyright Law applies to them, sound recordings and performances) that have not been authorized for, or are otherwise prohibited from, publication or distribution within China. . . .

. . . China's Copyright Law . . . adopted by . . . National People's Congress and promulgated in 1990 then amended by a Decision . . . of the National People's Congress in 2001. The claims concerning the Copyright Law address, in particular, the first sentence of Article 4. The parties agreed to translate that sentence as follows:

"Works the publication and/or dissemination of which are prohibited by law shall not be protected by this Law."

This Report refers to the first sentence of Article 4 as "Article 4(1)" for ease of reference, although the original version does not use paragraph numbers within that Article.

. . .

The United States claims that Article 4(1) of China's Copyright Law denies the protection of the Copyright Law to certain categories of works. . . of which the publication or distribution was prohibited by such laws and regulations as the Criminal Law, the Regulation on the Administration of Publishing Industry, the Regulation on the Administration of Broadcasting, the Regulation on the Administration of Audiovisual Products, the Regulation on the Administration of Films and the Regulations on the Administration of Telecommunication. . . . The United States claims that Article 4(1) of China's Copyright Law denies to the authors of works "the publication or distribution of which is prohibited by law" the broad set of rights enumerated in Article 10 of the Copyright Law, which largely encompasses the rights contemplated by the provisions of the Berne Convention (1971). Nor do authors of works denied protection of the Copyright Law benefit from the remedies specified in Articles 46 and 47 of the Copyright Law. Consequently, the authors of such works do not enjoy the minimum rights that are "specially granted" by the Berne Convention, inconsistently with Article 5(1) of that Convention. . . .

217

China responds that copyright vests upon creation and is independent of publication. Article 2 of the Copyright Law grants full copyright protection by expressly incorporating into Chinese law the rights conferred under international agreements, including the Berne Convention and the TRIPS Agreement. In contrast, Article 4(1) of the Copyright Law is extremely limited in scope. China, like many other countries in the world, bans from publication and dissemination such works as those that consist entirely of unconstitutional or immoral content. Article 4(1) simply provides that such a work shall not be protected by the Copyright Law. . . .

. . .

The Panel [finds] that Article 4(1) of the Copyright Law denies the protection of Article 10 to certain works, including those of WTO Member nationals, as the United States claims. The Panel observes that no party alleges that the denial of protection under Article 4(1) of the Copyright Law is permitted by any of the exceptions available with respect to certain specific rights under Articles 9(2), 10 or 10*bis* of the Berne Convention (1971). Nor does any party allege that the denial of protection under Article 4(1) of the Copyright Law is permitted by the exceptions provision in Article 13 of the TRIPS Agreement.

. . .

The Panel [finds] that the class of works denied protection under Article 4(1) of the Copyright Law includes works that have failed content review and, to the extent that they constitute copyright works, the deleted portions of works edited to satisfy content review. . . . No party has disputed that the "works" to which the Copyright Law, in particular Article 4(1), applies include at least some, if not all, the categories of works falling within the definition of "literary and artistic works" in Article 2(1) of the Berne Convention (1971). It is not disputed that the "works" to which Article 4(1) of China's Copyright Law applies are more extensive than those for which protection may be refused or limited under other provisions of Article 2, and under Article 2*bis*, of the Berne Convention (1971).

For the above reasons, the Panel finds that the Copyright Law is sufficiently clear on its face for the United States to have established that the Copyright Law, specifically Article 4(1), is inconsistent with Article 5(1) of the Berne Convention (1971), as incorporated by Article 9.1 of the TRIPS Agreement. This finding is subject to the Panel's consideration of Article 17 of the Berne Convention (1971), set out below.

The Panel [finds] that this conclusion does not apply to works never submitted for content review in China, works awaiting the results of content review in China and the unedited versions of works for which an edited version has been approved for distribution in China. However, the Panel recognizes that the potential denial of copyright protection, in the absence of a determination by the content review authorities, implies uncertainty with respect to works that do not satisfy the content criteria prior to a determination under Article 4(1) of the Copyright Law, with the consequent impact on enjoyment of rights described above. Therefore, the Panel reiterates for the record the firm position of China taken in these proceedings that:

> "Copyright vests at the time that a work is created, and is not contingent on publication. Unpublished works are protected, foreign works not yet released in the Chinese market are protected, and works never released in the Chinese market are protected."; and

"Works that are unreviewed are decidedly not 'prohibited by law'."

China has an international obligation to protect copyright in such works in accordance with Article 5(1) of the Berne Convention (1971), as incorporated by Article 9.1 of the TRIPS Agreement.

China raises a defence under Article 17 of the Berne Convention (1971), as incorporated by Article 9.1 of the TRIPS Agreement. China submits that all rights granted to authors under the Berne Convention (1971) are limited by Article 17 of that Convention, that Article 17 is not an exhaustive codification of the sovereign right to censor and that Article 17 is drafted using very expansive language "that effectively denies WTO jurisdiction in this area".

The United States responds that Article 17 of the Berne Convention (1971) does not authorize a content review system that denies all enforceable copyright protection to all works that have not been approved for publication or distribution.

. . . Article 17 of the Berne Convention (1971) provides as follows:

"The provisions of this Convention cannot in any way affect the right of the Government of each country of the Union to permit, to control, or to prohibit, by legislation or regulation, the circulation, presentation, or exhibition of any work or production in regard to which the competent authority may find it necessary to exercise that right."

. . .

The parties agree that Article 17 confirms that governments have certain rights to control the exploitation of works. They do not agree as to whether those rights include a denial of all copyright protection with respect to particular works.

The Panel observes that the terms of Article 17 include certain broad phrases, notably "cannot in any way affect" and "any work or production". The use of the words "any work" (although it is slightly different in the French text) confirms that the subject-matter dealt with by Article 17 is the same as that addressed by the other substantive provisions of the Convention. However, these phrases are not used in isolation but refer to the right of a government to "permit, to control, or to prohibit ... the circulation, presentation, or exhibition" of any work or production.

The right of a government "to control, or to prohibit" the "circulation, presentation, or exhibition" of any work or production clearly includes censorship for reasons of public order. . . .

China draws the Panel's attention to the WIPO Guide to the Berne Convention, which states as follows regarding Article 17 of the Berne Convention (1971):

"It covers the right of governments to take the necessary steps to maintain public order. On this point, the sovereignty of member countries is not affected by the rights given by the Convention. Authors may exercise their rights only if that exercise does not conflict with public order. The former must give way to the latter. The Article therefore gives Union countries certain powers to control."

The Panel agrees with this interpretation. A government's right to permit, to control, or to prohibit the circulation, presentation, or exhibition of a work may interfere with the exercise of certain rights with respect to a protected work by the copyright owner or a third party authorized by the copyright owner.

However, there is no reason to suppose that censorship will eliminate those rights entirely with respect to a particular work.

With respect to those rights that are granted by the Berne Convention (1971), China is unable to explain why Article 4(1) of its Copyright Law provides for the complete denial of their protection with respect to particular works. . . .

. . .

The Panel notes that copyright and government censorship address different rights and interests. Copyright protects private rights, . . . whilst government censorship addresses public interests.

In response to a question from the Panel, China indicated that it "will always enforce copyrights against infringing edited versions, even when there is no edited version authorized by the author". It did not explain how this was possible under its law. In response to another question from the Panel, China indicated that if an unprotected, prohibited work later becomes legal, it will protect copyright in the work going forward. This might require a new court . . . determination but, in China's view, such a requirement does not constitute a formality under Article 5(2) of the Berne Convention (1971). In any event, the Panel recalls that Article 4(1) of the Copyright Law produces commercial uncertainty prior to a determination that a work is prohibited.

China maintains that public censorship renders private enforcement unnecessary, that it enforces prohibitions on content seriously, and that this removes banned content from the public domain more securely than would be possible through copyright enforcement. The Panel notes that these assertions, even if they were relevant, are not substantiated.

The Panel also recalls that if a measure infringes China's obligations under a covered agreement, . . . this is considered prima facie to constitute a case of nullification or impairment. Even if the measure at issue has had no actual impact on foreign works to date, it has a *potential* impact on works of WTO Member nationals.

For the above reasons, the Panel . . . concludes that, notwithstanding China's rights recognized in Article 17 of the Berne Convention (1971), the Copyright Law, specifically Article 4(1), is inconsistent with Article 5(1) of the Berne Convention (1971), as incorporated by Article 9.1 of the TRIPS Agreement.

*Question:*

Nothing in the United States Copyright Act purports to deny copyright protection to books or movies that are legally "obscene," even though the First Amendment permits governments (federal and state) to criminalize the distribution of "obscene" materials, and governments have in fact done so.

Nevertheless, there have been cases in which defendants were alleged to have infringed the copyrights to obscene works, and those defendants have argued that obscene works are not, or should not be, protected by copyright. Courts have rejected that argument and have held that obscene works, like their non-obscene relatives, *are* protected by copyright. *Mitchell Brothers Film Group v. Cinema Adult Theater*, 604 F.2d 852 (5th Cir. 1979), *cert. denied*, 445 U.S. 917 (1980) (under the 1909 Copyright Act); *Jartech, Inc. v. Clancy*, 666 F.2d 403 (9th Cir.), *cert. denied*, 459 U.S. 826 (1982) (under the 1978 Copyright Act).

The *Mitchell Brothers* and *Jartech* decisions are considered to be "the law" today. But suppose that Congress were to decide that "obscene" works should not be protected by copyright. Congress might conclude that the *Mitchell Brothers* and *Jartech* cases compel federal judges to use the power of the federal government to provide protection to works that cannot be distributed legally in the first place, by anyone – copyright owners or infringers – and thus infringement suits involving obscene works are an offensive waste of federal judicial time and money. Suppose, for that reason, Congress were to amend the Copyright Act to explicitly *deny* copyright protection for "obscene" works. Suppose further that Swedish producers of "obscene" movies were to discover that their movies are being duplicated and distributed in the U.S. without licenses, and those Swedish producers were to file copyright infringement lawsuits against the infringers in U.S. federal courts.

- What would the likely outcome of those lawsuits be?
- Is it likely that federal judges would take Berne, TRIPs, or the *WTO China Report* into account in reaching their decisions?
- If federal judges ruled against the Swedish movie producers, on the grounds that obscene works are no longer protected by copyright in the U.S., what recourse (if any) would the Swedish producers then have?

## E. Trade embargo laws vs. copyright treaty obligations

The United States generally favors free trade, as a matter of national policy. However, two federal statutes – and bevy of implementing regulations – authorize the President to impose the most restrictive of all restraints on trade: absolute embargoes. Presidents from both political parties have exercised this authority, sometimes with a vengeance.

The most newsworthy of the United States' current embargoes is the one against Cuba. But there are many others as well, including trade embargoes against Iran, Myanmar (formerly known as Burma), Sudan and Zimbabwe. The United States has copyright treaties with four of these countries (all except Iran; see, International Copyright Relations of the United States, U.S. Copyright Office Circular 38a, available at http://www.copyright.gov/circs/circ38a.pdf). So the question now to be considered is whether these embargoes affect the ability of the United States to comply with its copyright treaty obligations.

The first legislation that empowered the President to impose embargoes was the Trading with the Enemy Act (50 U.S.C. §§1-40). It was passed in 1917, shortly after the United States entered World War I. Originally, the Trading with the Enemy Act gave the President the power to impose embargoes only in times of war. But in 1933, it was amended to include peacetime national emergencies as well, thus making the Act a permanent weapon in the President's arsenal against disfavored nations.

In 1977, the Trading with the Enemy Act was amended again. At first blush, the 1977 amendment seems to cut back on the President's powers, because it once again limited the Act's effectiveness to times of actual war. In fact, though, the 1977 legislation didn't curtail the President's power at all, because the same bill that limited the Trading with the Enemy Act to wartime included a then-new law that gives the President powers in times of "peacetime crises." The 1977 law is the International Emergency Economic Powers Act (50 U.S.C. §§1701-06); and it gives the President the same authority to impose trade embargoes as had the Trading with the Enemies Act.

Here is the heart of the regulation that implements the embargo that President Kennedy first imposed on Cuba in 1963.

### Cuban Assets Control Regulations
### Title 31 Code of Federal Regulations

§ 515.201 Transactions involving designated foreign countries or their nationals . . .

(a) All of the following transactions are prohibited, except as specifically authorized by the Secretary of the Treasury . . . , if . . . such transactions are by, or on behalf of, . . . a foreign country designated under this part, or any national thereof, or such transactions involve property in which a foreign country designated under this part, or any national thereof, has . . . had any interest of any nature whatsoever, direct or indirect:

    (1) All . . . payments . . . through . . . any banking institution . . . with respect to any property . . . by any person . . . subject to the jurisdiction of the United States;

    (2) All transactions in foreign exchange by any person within the United States; and

    (3) The exportation . . . from the United States of . . . currency . . . by any person within the United States. . . .

(b) All of the following transactions are prohibited, except as specifically authorized by the Secretary of the Treasury . . . , if such transactions involve property in which any foreign country designated under this part, or any national thereof, has . . . had any interest of any nature whatsoever, direct or indirect:

    (1) All dealings in, including . . . transfers . . . or exportations of any property . . . by any person subject to the jurisdiction of the United States; and

    (2) All transfers outside the United States with regard to any property . . . subject to the jurisdiction of the United States. . . .

(d) For the purposes of this part, the term "foreign country designated under this part" and the term "designated foreign country" mean Cuba. . . .

In plain English, this regulation prohibits payments to Cuba, exports to Cuba, and imports from Cuba. The language of the ban on imports from Cuba is not as clear as it could be; but apparently the import-ban is the consequence of the regulation's ban on "transactions," "dealings" and "transfers" of any property in which any Cuban national has an interest. Moreover, imports almost always must be paid for, and that would run afoul of the ban on payments to Cuba.

In any event, the regulation was clear enough – in the opinion of the government – to authorize the seizure of books and magazines shipped to the United States from embargoed nations; and the United States did so. These seizures prompted Congress to amend the International Emergency Economic Powers Act in 1988 (in what is known as the "Berman Amendment") and again in 1994 (in the "Free Trade in Ideas Amendment") in order to prevent restrictions on the international flow of materials protected by the First Amendment. These amendments were then incorporated into the Cuban embargo regulations.

**Cuban Assets Control Regulations**
**Title 31 Code of Federal Regulations**

§ 515.206 Exempt transactions.
  (a) Information and informational materials.
    (1) The importation from any country and the exportation to any country of information or informational materials as defined in § 515.332, whether commercial or otherwise, regardless of format or medium of transmission, are exempt from the prohibitions and regulations of this part. . . .

§ 515.332 Information and informational materials.
  (a) For purposes of this part, the term information and informational materials means:
    (1) Publications, films, posters, phonograph records, photographs, microfilms, microfiche, tapes, compact disks, CD ROMs, artworks, news wire feeds, and other information and informational articles. . . .

Of course, the right to *import* films and music recordings – to take just two examples – does not, by itself, give Americans the ability to legally comply with copyright obligations. For example, films and music recordings that have been legally imported from Cuba may not be broadcast in the United States without copyright licenses, because broadcasts are public performances, and copyright treaties between Cuba and the United States require the U.S. to protect the public performance rights of the owners of copyrights to Cuban films and compositions.

So, consider whether the trade embargo on Cuba permits Americans to obtain public performance licenses from Cuban copyright owners – something that almost universally requires the *payment* of royalties. In other words, if the foregoing excerpts were all there was to the Cuban embargo, would it be legal for Americans to pay royalties – or copyright infringement damages – to Cuban copyright owners? If American infringers were barred by United States law from paying copyright royalties or infringement damages, wouldn't the United States be in violation of its copyright treaty obligations to Cuba?

As it happens, the foregoing excerpts are not all there is to the Cuban embargo. The following provisions are part of it too.

223

§ 515.527  Certain transactions with respect to United States intellectual property.

 (a)(1) Transactions related to the registration and renewal in the . . . United States Copyright Office of . . . copyrights in which the Government of Cuba or a Cuban national has an interest are authorized.

§ 515.545  Transactions related to information and informational materials.

 (a) . . . all financial and other transactions directly incident to the importation or exportation of information or informational materials are authorized.

 (b) Transactions relating to the dissemination of informational materials are authorized, including remittance of royalties paid for informational materials. . . .

By permitting Americans to register licenses and assignments they obtain from Cuban copyright owners, and permitting them to pay royalties to Cuban copyright owners in return for those licenses and assignments, these provisions certainly appear to satisfy the United States' copyright treaty obligations. And in fact, they may. But it's not perfectly clear that they do, as you will now see.

The following case concerns the efficacy of the copyright registration provision in the Iranian embargo regulations – a provision that is substantively similar to the Cuban copyright registration provision. The United States and Iran do not have a copyright treaty with one another, so you may wonder how and why the copyright to an Iranian work ever became the subject of litigation in the United States, or even why the Iranian embargo regulations permit the registration of copyrights to Iranian works. One explanation was offered back in Chapter 3, in the discussion of the copyright to Saddam Hussein's last novel. A second explanation is offered, quite summarily (in footnote 1), in the following decision.

## Kalantari v. NITV, INC.
### 352 F.3d 1202 (9th Cir. 2003)

Susan P. Graber, Circuit Judge:

In this copyright infringement case, we are called on to decide whether the Iranian trade embargo prohibits the commercial importation of movies from Iran, the copyright of such movies, or the assignment to a "United States person" of the exclusive rights to copyright, distribute, and exhibit the movies in North America. We answer "no" to each of those questions and, accordingly, we reverse.

*Factual and Procedural History*

Plaintiff Masood Kalantari is a producer of television programs and a promoter of Iranian cultural events in the United States. He is a "United States person," 31 C.F.R. § 560.314, who is subject to the Iranian trade embargo, *see, e.g., id.* § § 560.201-560.209.

Under a series of agreements, Plaintiff acquired the rights to three Farsi language films – "Snow Man," "Two Women," and "Corrupted Hands" – from their Iranian owners. For each film, Plaintiff's contract consists of an "Assignment," in English, and a "Contract," in Farsi. In relevant part, the agreements provide that, for a specified term: (1) Plaintiff is assigned, exclusively, all rights to the films, including the exclusive rights to copyright, distribute, and exhibit the films within the United States and Canada; (2) Plaintiff agrees to copyright the films in the United States and to use his "utmost efforts" to show and advertise the films; (3) the films' owners agree to send Plaintiff copies of the films and advertising materials; and (4) Plaintiff agrees to pay (a) for "Snow Man" and "Two Women," an initial deposit of $10,000, followed by quarterly payments of 50 percent of the net profit from showing the films, and (b) for "Corrupted Hands," three installment payments amounting to roughly $13,000.

As agreed, Plaintiff has made the contractual payments and displayed the three films in the United States. Plaintiff has also obtained copyright registrations for all three films.[1] [n1 The Berne Convention allows copyright registration in member countries (including the United States) of works from nonmember countries (including Iran) if publication in the member country is simultaneous with first publication in the nonmember country of origin. . . . "Publication," in the case of a motion picture, includes offering to distribute copies for the purpose of public showing in theaters. Plaintiff acquired United States copyrights for the films under this theory of simultaneous first publication.] Each copyright certificate lists the Iranian owner as the author of the work and indicates that Plaintiff became the owner of the copyright by way of an assignment of rights.

After Defendants NITV, Inc., d/b/a National Iranian TV, Zia Atabay, and Parvin Atabay allegedly broadcast the three movies on television in the United States without authorization, Plaintiff brought this action against them for copyright infringement. Defendants moved for summary judgment on the sole ground that the Iranian trade embargo prohibited Plaintiff from purchasing the rights that he purports to possess and that, without a valid assignment, he cannot have a valid copyright that could be infringed. The district court granted Defendants' motion. Plaintiff brought this timely appeal.
. . .

*Discussion . . .*

### B. The Iranian Trade Embargo

Pursuant to his authority under IEEPA, President Clinton issued Executive Order Nos. 12959 and 13059, in 1995 and 1997 (respectively), to prohibit most trade with Iran. The Iranian trade embargo was intended "to deal with the unusual and extraordinary threat to the national security, foreign policy, and economy of the United States" presented by "the actions and policies of the Government of Iran." As the Fourth Circuit has stated:

> The obvious purpose of [Executive Order No. 12959] is to isolate Iran from trade with the United States. . . . [Executive Order No. 12959] reflected the President's appraisal of the nation's interest in sanctioning Iran's sponsorship of international terrorism, its frustration of the Middle East peace process, and its pursuit of weapons of mass destruction.

The President's Executive Orders have largely been codified in the Iranian Transactions Regulations, 31 C.F.R. Part 560, which prohibit, with few exceptions, "the importation into the United States of any goods or services of Iranian origin" and any "transaction or dealing in" such goods or services.

Notwithstanding their broad scope, however, the regulations permit trade in certain items through general and specific licenses, and they reflect the IEEPA exemption for informational materials:

> The importation from any country . . . of information and informational materials as defined in § 560.315, whether commercial or otherwise, regardless of format or medium of transmission, [is] exempt from the prohibitions and regulations of this part. *Id.* § 560.210(c)(1).

*1. Importation*

The first question that we must answer is whether Plaintiff's importation of the three movies ran afoul of the Iranian embargo. It is clear from the text of the statute and regulation that the bare importation of a movie is permitted. 50 U.S.C. § 1702(b)(3); 31 C.F.R. § 560.210(c)(1). But, because Plaintiff paid Iranians for the movies that he imported, to answer our first question, we also must consider whether a commercial transaction that results in importation is likewise permitted.

The regulation provides, as relevant: "The importation from any country . . . of information and informational materials . . . , whether commercial or otherwise . . . , [is] exempt from the prohibitions and regulations of this part."
. . .

In summary, the exemption plainly allows a United States person to pay Iranians in exchange for the importation of a movie.

*2. Copyright*

The applicable regulations grant an express general license for certain transactions related to intellectual property protection in the United States or Iran:

> All of the following transactions in connection with patent, trademark, copyright or other intellectual property protection in the United States or Iran are authorized:
>
> (1) The filing and prosecution of any application to obtain a patent, trademark, copyright or other form of intellectual property protection, including importation of or dealing in Iranian-origin services, payment for such services, and payment to persons in Iran directly connected to such intellectual property protection;
>
> (2) The receipt of a patent, trademark, copyright or other form of intellectual property protection;
>
> (3) The renewal or maintenance of a patent, trademark, copyright or other form of intellectual property protection; and
>
> (4) The filing and prosecution of opposition or infringement proceedings with respect to a patent, trademark, copyright or other form of intellectual property protection, or the entrance of a defense to any such proceedings.

31 C.F.R. § 560.509(a).

Without question, then, an Iranian movie may be copyrighted in the United States. The narrow question here is whether an assignee may copyright a lawfully imported Iranian movie in view of the absence of "assignment" from the foregoing list of authorized copyright transactions.

### 3. Assignment

In addition to exempting informational materials, the Iranian Transactions Regulations permit trade in some items by way of general licenses.[8] [n8 For example, the importation of Iranian carpets is allowed, not as an *exemption*, but as one of several general *licenses* granted in Subpart E, 31 C.F.R. Part 560. 31 C.F.R. § 560.534.] When the regulations license a transaction, they also authorize "any transaction ordinarily incident to [that] licensed transaction and necessary to give effect thereto." 31 C.F.R. § 560.405.

As discussed above, an Iranian author may copyright a film in the United States, pursuant to a general license. Thus, any transaction "ordinarily incident to [the copyright] and necessary to give effect thereto" is permitted, unless specifically prohibited by another regulation. For the following reasons, we hold that a copyright assignment is an incidental transaction authorized by 31 C.F.R. § 560.405 and not prohibited by any other regulation.

Upon obtaining a copyright, an author automatically acquires certain rights that are inherent in the very nature of a copyright. Specifically, the copyright owner obtains the six exclusive rights of copyright, 17 U.S.C. § 106, as well as the right to transfer any or all of those rights: "The ownership of a copyright may be transferred in whole or in part by any means of conveyance or by operation of law . . . ." *Id.* § 201(d)(1). Without question, an assignment qualifies as a transfer by "any means of conveyance."

The basic rights inherent in a copyright do not change simply because a movie's original owner is an Iranian who is expressly authorized to obtain the copyright. With the general license to obtain a copyright, Iranians as well as Americans obtain the right to transfer the copyright freely, by assignment or otherwise. Thus, because the right to assign a copyright is part of the bundle of rights inherent in holding a copyright, an assignment is a transaction "ordinarily incident" to ownership of a copyright and "necessary to give effect" to that ownership. . . .

### Conclusion

The Iranian embargo does not prohibit the commercial importation of an Iranian movie, the copyrighting of the movie, or the assignment to a United States person of rights to obtain and enforce such a copyright. Therefore, the district court erred in holding that Plaintiff lacked a valid assignment or lacked authority to obtain a valid copyright.

This decision is consistent with the United States' international copyright obligations. "But wait" – as infomercial announcers often say – "There's more!"

The "more" in question are two additional provisions of the Cuban embargo regulations.

§ 515.206 Exempt transactions.

    (a)(2) This section does not authorize transactions related to information or informational materials not fully created and in existence at the date of the transaction, or to the substantive or artistic alteration or enhancement of information or informational materials, or to the provision of marketing and business consulting services by a person subject to the jurisdiction of the United States. Such prohibited transactions include, without limitation, payment of advances for information or informational materials not yet created and completed, provision of services to market, produce or co-produce, create or assist in the creation of information or informational materials, and payment of royalties to a designated national with respect to income received for enhancements or alterations made by persons subject to the jurisdiction of the United States to information or informational materials imported from a designated national.

§ 515.545 Transactions related to information and informational materials.

    (b) . . .This section does not authorize the remittance of royalties or other payments relating to works not yet in being, or for marketing and business consulting services, or artistic or other substantive alteration or enhancements to informational materials. . . .

These two provisions make it appear that:

- although Americans are *permitted* to pay Cubans for
  - imported copies of already created works, and
  - the right to reproduce and distribute *preexisting* Cuban works
- Americans may *not pay* Cubans for
  - the right to use works that will be created in the future, or
  - the right to enhance, alter or market existing works.

These conclusions are confirmed by examples included right in the text of the Cuban embargo regulations.

§ 515.206 Exempt transactions. . . .

    Example #2:

        A Cuban party exports a single master copy of a Cuban motion picture to a U.S. party and licenses the U.S. party to duplicate, distribute, show and exploit in the United States the Cuban film in any medium, including home video distribution, for five years, with the Cuban party receiving 40% of the net income. All transactions relating to the activities described in this example are authorized under this section or § 515.545.

    Example #3:

        A U.S. recording company proposes to contract with a Cuban musician to create certain musical compositions, and to advance royalties of $10,000 to the musician. The music written in Cuba is to be recorded in a studio that the recording company owns in the

Bahamas. These are all prohibited transactions. The U.S. party is prohibited under §515.201 from contracting for the Cuban musician's services, from transferring $10,000 to Cuba to pay for those services, and from providing the Cuban with production services through the use of its studio in the Bahamas. No information or informational materials are in being at the time of these proposed transactions. However, the U.S. recording company may contract to purchase and import preexisting recordings by the Cuban musician, or to copy the recordings in the United States and pay negotiated royalties to Cuba under this section or § 515.545.

Example #4:

A Cuban party enters into a subpublication agreement licensing a U.S. party to print and publish copies of a musical composition and to sub-license rights of public performance, adaptation, and arrangement of the musical composition, with payment to be a percentage of income received. All transactions related to the activities described in this example are authorized under this section and § 515.545, except for adaptation, and arrangement, which constitute artistic enhancement of the Cuban composition. Payment to the Cuban party may not reflect income received as a result of these enhancements.

The ban on paying advances for works not yet in existence doesn't raise any obvious copyright issues. While advances for works to be created in the future are customary in all copyright-based businesses, copyright doesn't attach to a work until it's actually created – "fixed in any tangible medium" is the way the U.S. Copyright Act puts it (17 U.S.C. § 102(a)). Once a work is created, the embargo regulations permit it to be paid for.

On the other hand, the ban on paying for the right to make "enhancements or alterations" does raise copyright issues. Enhanced and altered versions are derivative works (17 U.S.C. §101). And the right to make derivative works is one of the exclusive rights granted to copyright owners (17 U.S.C. § 106(2)). Suppose that Example 4 above (which involved a voluntary agreement) is altered just a bit, so it reads:

A Cuban party enters into a subpublication agreement licensing a U.S. party to print and publish copies of a musical composition and to sub-license rights of public performance – but *not* the right to adapt or arrange the musical composition (thereby complying with the embargo regulations) – with payment to be a percentage of income received. The U.S. party then creates and uses an arrangement of the composition, even though it doesn't have a license to do so. By creating and using an arrangement of the composition without a license, the U.S. party has infringed the Cuban's copyright. The Cuban copyright owner sues the U.S. party for infringement of the Cuban's derivative work right.

Does the ban on paying for "enhancements or alterations" prohibit

- the U.S. party from paying the Cuban copyright owner to settle the infringement case?

- the U.S. party from paying the Cuban copyright owner to satisfy the infringement judgment the Cuban would obtain if the case were not settled?

If you answered "yes" to these questions, does that mean the

- Cuban embargo prevents the United States from complying with its international copyright treaty obligations to Cubans?

There is no direct authority answering these questions. But there is one additional bit of law that may be relevant (or at least insightful).

First, some background:

The penalties for violating embargo regulations are severe: as many as 10 years in federal prison, and fines of as much as $250,000 (for individuals) to $1 million (for corporations). These penalties are not just paper threats. The government office that enforces embargoes – the Office of Foreign Assets Control – is aggressive. It imposed penalties of almost $30 million in more than 8,000 matters, between 1993 and 2004. (That averages almost three matters a day, Monday through Friday, every week of the year, for 11 years.) Targets of these enforcement efforts weren't just American tourists who flew from Cancun to Havana and back with Cuban cigars in their luggage. Targets included musician Ry Cooter who was actually fined $25,000 for collaborating with Cuban musicians on what became the Grammy Award winning album "The Buena Vista Social Club." (And this occurred during the administration of Bill Clinton – a President whose attitudes about the Cuban embargo were more moderate than any President before or since – especially since.)

Those who deal regularly with authors in Cuba, Iran and other embargoed nations – as many American book and periodical publishers and editors do – take the embargo penalties very seriously. They take them so seriously, in fact, that sometimes they request written "guidance" from the Office of Foreign Assets Control, before they do anything that might violate the regulations.

In 2003, in response to written requests for guidance from publishers and editors, the Office of Foreign Assets Control issued (after delays of as much as a year and half) several astonishing letters asserting that Americans could not:

- edit or create illustrations for manuscripts written by Iranian authors – not even to correct syntax or grammar – because doing so "would result in a substantively altered or enhanced product" or
- publish books by Iranian authors, because "Inherent in the publication of a book are marketing, distribution, artistic, advertising and other services not exempt" from the regulations.

These letters provoked book publishers and editors to file a lawsuit in 2004 challenging the enforceability of certain of the embargo regulations. The case was captioned "Association of American University Presses v. Office of Foreign Assets Control." (Information concerning the case, including pleadings and legal memoranda, are available online at http://www.aaupnet.org/ofac/.) In a nutshell, the lawsuit alleged that the bans on

- paying advances for rights to works not yet in existence,
- paying royalties on the use of works that result from alterations and enhancements, and
- providing marketing and consulting services

violated the "Berman" and "Free Trade in Ideas" amendments as well as the First Amendment free speech rights of writers and publishers.

The lawsuit did *not* raise *copyright* issues, so even if it had produced a written opinion, the opinion would not have answered whether the Cuban embargo prevents the U.S. from complying with its copyright treaty obligations to Cubans. Nevertheless, the case and its outcome are relevant to that question, for this reason.

Just ten weeks after the lawsuit was filed, the government capitulated. It revised the embargo regulations to give the plaintiffs virtually everything their lawsuit sought. The case lingered a bit, while the plaintiffs negotiated for a few more concessions. The government finally agreed to those in August 2007, and the lawsuit was dismissed (without prejudice) in October.

Here is the language that was added to the Cuban embargo regulations, as a result of the lawsuit. (The lawsuit also challenged similar embargo regulations pertaining to Iran, Sudan and Myanmar/Burma, and the government revised those regulations as well, in a similar fashion.)

### Cuban Assets Control Regulations
### Title 31 Code of Federal Regulations

Sec. 515.577 Authorized transactions necessary and ordinarily incident to publishing.

    (a) . . . persons subject to the jurisdiction of the United States are authorized to engage in all transactions necessary and ordinarily incident to the publishing and marketing of manuscripts, books, journals, and newspapers in paper or electronic format (collectively, "written publications"). . . . Pursuant to this section, the following activities are authorized . . . :

    (1) Commissioning and making advance payments for identifiable written publications not yet in existence, to the extent consistent with industry practice;

    (2) Collaborating on the creation and enhancement of written publications;

    (3) (i) Augmenting written publications through the addition of items such as photographs, artwork, translation, explanatory text, and, for a written publication in electronic format, the addition of embedded software necessary for reading, browsing, navigating, or searching the written publication;

        (ii) Exporting embedded software necessary for reading, browsing, navigating, or searching a written publication in electronic format . . . ;

    (4) Substantive editing of written publications;

    (5) Payment of royalties for written publications;

    (6) Creating or undertaking a marketing campaign to promote a written publication; and

    (7) Other transactions necessary and ordinarily incident to the publishing and marketing of written publications as described in this paragraph (a).

(b) This section does not authorize transactions involving the provision of goods or services not necessary and ordinarily incident to the publishing and marketing of written publications as described in paragraph (a) of this section. For example, this section does not authorize persons subject to the jurisdiction of the United States:

(1) To provide or receive individualized or customized services (including, but not limited to, accounting, legal, design, or consulting services), other than those necessary and ordinarily incident to the publishing and marketing of written publications . . . . ;

(2) To create or undertake for any person a marketing campaign with respect to any service or product other than a written publication . . . .

Insofar as "written publications" are concerned, this 2007 addition to the embargo regulations seems to permit Americans to comply with the United States' obligation to protect the derivative work rights of Cuban and Iranian copyright owners (and those from Sudan and Myanmar as well). But notice how this provision emphasizes that it applies *only* to "written publications." What would the answer be, today, to the musical composition questions asked a couple of pages above? Indeed, even with respect to written publications, how would you analyze this hypothetical:

A Cuban author writes a novel, in Spanish, that is published in Cuba. An American book publishing company then acquires the right to translate the book into English and publish it in the United States, in hard and soft cover, and does so. The Cuban author retains all other rights in the novel. An American movie producer buys and reads the English-language version of the book and decides that it would make a terrific movie. The producer would like to acquire the movie rights to the book from the Cuban author, including the right to distribute, market and promote the movie, in the customary American fashion.

- As a matter of international copyright law, is the producer required to acquire movie rights from the Cuban author?
- May the producer do so, legally, under the Cuban embargo regulations?
- If the Cuban embargo regulations prohibit the producer from acquiring these rights from the Cuban author, and the producer produces, distributes, markets and promotes the movie anyway – without entering into any transaction at all with the author, and without paying the author anything – would the producer be exposed to any liability
  - to the Cuban author?
  - to the United States government?

Your answers to these questions indicate whether the Cuban embargo prevents the United States from complying with its international copyright treaty obligations to Cubans. If you conclude that the embargo does prevent the United States from complying with its treaty obligations, is there anything Cuba can do about it?

# Chapter 6

# Duration of Copyright

The Berne Convention requires countries to provide copyright protection for *at least* a specified period of time. (That's one of the reasons it took the United States so long to join Berne; until 1978, the duration of copyright in the United States – 28 years from first publication, plus 28 additional years if the copyright was renewed – was just too short.) But Berne *permits* countries to provide copyright protection for longer periods, if they wish to do so.

TRIPS too requires WTO members to provide copyright protection for at least a specified period of time, but also permits countries to provide longer protection, if they wish to do so. Some countries – the United States among them – have elected to provide longer-than-required copyright protection; and that's why copyright durations are *not* the same all around the world.

What's more, the Berne Convention *permits* countries to adopt a shorter-than-usual term of protection for certain kinds of works; and, as you will read below, some countries, including Germany, have done so, although the United States has not. This is another reason that copyright durations are not the same all around the world.

In the early years of international copyright protection (back in the 19th century), the disparity among copyright durations of different nations was a matter of significant concern for some countries. The concerned countries were those that protected copyrights for longer periods than other countries. To deal with their concerns, some countries with long durations included in their domestic copyright statutes something called "The Rule of the Shorter Term"; but other countries did not.

As a result of shorter-than-elsewhere copyright durations, many works went into the public domain in some countries before they did in others. Eventually, an international consensus developed that they shouldn't have. That led to treaty provisions that required copyright protection to be restored by countries where those works had gone into the public domain; and countries did so.

These two topics – the Rule of the Shorter Term, and copyright restoration – are what this chapter is about.

## A.  The Rule of the Shorter Term

The duration of copyright for works of *foreign* origin is treated in a unique way, in some countries. All countries apply their own law (as you would expect from the usual rule of national treatment), *if* their own duration is *shorter* than the duration in the work's country-of-origin. However, *some* countries apply the law of the work's country-of-origin, rather than their own, *if* the duration in the work's country-of-origin is *shorter* than their own. Countries that do this apply what is known as the "Rule of the Shorter Term."

The "Rule of the Shorter Term" provides that the duration of copyright is the term in the country where protection is sought, *or* the term in the work's country-of-origin, *whichever is shorter*. Countries that choose to apply this Rule – despite the usual rule that national treatment must be provided to foreign works – are permitted to do so by both Berne and the UCC.

### Berne Convention Article 7(8)

In any case, the term shall be governed by the legislation of the country where protection is claimed; however, *unless the legislation of that country otherwise provides, the term shall not exceed the term fixed in the country of origin of the work.* [Emphasis added.]

### Universal Copyright Convention Article IV(4)(a)

No Contracting State shall be *obliged to grant protection to a work for a period longer than that fixed . . . by the law of the Contracting State* of which the author is a national [for unpublished works] . . . [or] in which the work has been first published [for published works]. [Emphasis added.]

Australia, Japan, and European Union countries all apply the Rule of the Shorter Term; and others do as well. But the question of whether the United States applies the Rule is a bit complicated. The following provisions of the Berne Convention and U.S. copyright law illustrate how the question could arise and just how complicated it is. By themselves, these provisions may not make much sense, but the semi-hypothetical that follows these provisions should help you see how they work.

### Berne Convention Article 7(4)

It shall be a matter for legislation in the countries of the Union to determine the term of protection of photographic works and that of works of applied art in so far as they are protected as artistic works; however, this term shall last at least until the end of a period of twenty-five years from the making of such a work.

### U.S. Copyright Act of 1976, §302(a)

Copyright in a work created on or after January 1, 1978, subsists from its creation and . . . endures for a term consisting of the life of the author and 70 years after the author's death.

### U.S. Copyright Act of 1976, §304(a)(1)(A) & (C) and (2)(B)

Any copyright, in the first term . . . on January 1, 1978, shall endure for 28 years from the date it was originally secured. . . . [T]he author of such work, if the author is still living [or others, if the author is not living], . . . shall be entitled to a renewal and extension of the copyright in such work for a further term of 67 years . . . *if [for pre-1964 works]* an application to register a claim to such further term has been made to the Copyright Office within 1 year before the expiration of the original term of copyright. . . . [Emphasis added.]

## U.S. Copyright Act of 1909, § 24

The copyright secured by this title shall endure for twenty-eight years from the date of first publication. . . provided . . . That the author of such work . . . shall be entitled to a renewal and extension of the copyright in such work for a further term of twenty-eight years when application for such renewal and extension shall have been made to the copyright office and duly registered therein within one year prior to the expiration of the original term of copyright: And provided further, That in default of the registration of such application for renewal and extension, the copyright in any work shall determine [i.e., expire] at the expiration of twenty-eight years from first publication.

## U.S. Copyright Act of 1976 [as amended in 1994], §104A(h)(6)(B)

The term "restored work" means an original work of authorship that . . . is not in the public domain in its source country through expiration of term of protection. . . .

## U.S. Copyright Act of 1976 [as amended in 1994], §104A(a)(1)(B)

Any work in which copyright is restored under this section shall subsist for the remainder of the term of copyright that the work would have otherwise been granted in the United States if the work never entered the public domain in the United States.

To see how these provisions work, consider this semi-hypothetical, and answer the questions that follow it.

---

### Real facts

Elvis Presley was drafted into the United States Army in 1957, by which time he already was a worldwide celebrity. In 1958, after he completed basic training, the Army shipped him to Germany where he was stationed at Ray Barracks in Friedberg (near Frankfurt). The Barracks included housing for enlisted men, but Elvis was allowed to live off-base in a rented apartment in the city of Bad Nauheim, about 15 minutes from the Barracks. Because he lived off base and in town, Germans frequently saw Elvis, in and out of uniform, and they took many photographs of him.

### A bit of German law

Under then-existing German law, the duration of copyright for the kinds of photos taken of Elvis by Germans (i.e., snapshots rather than artistic works) was 25 years (from publication if they were published, or from the date they were taken, if they weren't published). The duration of German copyright for foreign snapshot photos was 25 years too.

### A bit of U.S. law

Any photographs taken of Elvis in Germany that were published anywhere in the world could have been registered for copyright in the United States, even if they weren't published in the U.S.

On the first day of 1996, the United States restored the copyrights to certain public domain works of foreign origin, including pre-1978 works whose U.S. copyrights had expired because they had not been renewed.

## Hypothetical "facts"

German photographer Heidi Heinrich shot hundreds of photographs of Elvis soon after he arrived in Germany; and many of those photos were published in a German magazine in 1958. Copyright notices, of the kind then required by U.S. law, were affixed to all of Heinrich's published photos of Elvis, even though they were not published in the U.S. until 1985.

In 1985 – to commemorate what would have been Elvis' 50th birthday (he died in 1977) – Picture Press, an American company, published *Elvis Remembered: Pictures of a Life*, a coffee-table size book containing hundreds of photos of Elvis, including two dozen taken by Heinrich in 1958. Until it published that book, Picture Press had been strictly a poster printing company, specializing in posters ordered by record companies, concert promoters and movie distributors. *Elvis Remembered* was the company's first book, and the first item of any kind it had printed for itself rather than for customers. For that reason, Picture Press did not have a copyright lawyer; and though it asked its corporate lawyer whether Heinrich's 1958 photos of Elvis were protected by copyright in the United States – because the U.S. was the only place Poster Press intended to sell the book – the lawyer simply did not know. Rather than authorize the lawyer to research the question and write an opinion letter (the lawyer said it might cost a few thousand dollars) Picture Press paid Heinrich a fee for a license to use her photos. In a written and signed license agreement, Heinrich gave Picture Press the "exclusive right to use and to authorize others to use [Heinrich's photographs of Elvis] in any and every way, in the United States, in perpetuity."

Because Picture Press was not an experienced book publisher and did not have a copyright lawyer, when *Elvis Remembered* was published, neither the book nor any of the photographs in it had copyright notices, and the book was never registered for copyright with the U.S. Copyright Office.

The copyright status of Heinrich's photos has become important once again, because Memphis filmmaker Felice Farrow is producing a documentary about his life for broadcast on U.S. television. Farrow intends to feature close-ups of Heinrich's photos in the documentary, and therefore needs to know whether they are protected by copyright in the U.S. now.

---

1.  In the Copyright Act of 1976, the United States changed the duration of its copyright from 28-years-from-publication (plus renewal) to life-of-the-author-plus-50-years (and later extended it further to life-plus-70 years). The U.S. did this for photographs (including snapshots), as well as other kinds of works. Germany has adhered to Berne for more than a hundred years. How was Germany able to limit copyright protection for (snapshot) photographs to a mere 25 years?

2.  When did the copyrights to Heinrich's photos of Elvis expire in Germany?

3.  Since Germany has adhered to Berne for more than a century, and Berne prohibits formalities like mandatory copyright notices, why would a German magazine publish photographs – in 1958 – with copyright notices of the kind then required by United States law? (Think: When would the copyrights to Heinrich's photos have expired in the United States, if they had been published in Germany in 1958 without copyright notices of the kind then required by United States law?)

4.  Since Heinrich's photos were published with copyright notices, when did their copyrights expire in the United States?

5.  Did the law you relied on to answer the previous question apply the Rule of the Shorter Term? Should it have?

6.  *If* the copyrights to Heinrich's photos had been registered and renewed in the United States, when would their U.S. copyrights have expired, or when will they expire?

7.  Did the law you relied on to answer the previous question apply the Rule of the Shorter Term? Should it have?

8.  *If* Heinrich's photos went into the public domain in the United States, were their copyrights restored?

9.  Did the law you relied on to answer the previous question apply the Rule of the Shorter Term? Should it have?

10. *If* the U.S. copyrights to Heinrich's photos were restored, when will those copyrights expire?

11. Did the law you relied on to answer the previous question apply the Rule of the Shorter Term? Should it have?

(*If* Heinrich's photos *are* protected by copyright in the U.S. now, Farrow also will want to know *from whom* she must obtain a license in order to be able to use the photos in her documentary. The answer to that question has nothing to do with the Rule of the Shorter Term. Instead, it has to do with restoration of copyright in the United States and in the European Union, so it will be considered later.)

Germany has a Rule of the Shorter term; and for a very long time, the duration of copyright in Germany was much longer than it was in the U.S. This might lead you to make an off-the-cuff guess that Germany would apply its Rule of the Shorter Term to find that American works are no longer protected in Germany (even though German works of comparable age still are). In fact, however, Germany's treatment of old American works has been surprisingly unpredictable. This has been so, because:

(1) since 1892, the U.S. and Germany have been parties to a bilateral copyright treaty which says nothing at all about copyright duration;

(2) in 1955, the U.S. and Germany became parties to the UCC which allows countries to adopt a Rule of the Shorter Term;

(3) Germany didn't have a Rule of the Shorter Term until 1965, when it first adopted one; and

(4) in 1966, Germany significantly extended its copyright duration.

Two cases – decided by the Supreme Court of Germany on the same day – show how that court has applied these four factors to decide that some American works were still protected in Germany while another was not. Here are descriptions of those decisions.

*Atlas Film v. Janus Film*, 10 IIC 358 (Germany Sup.Ct. 1978)

The issue in this case (between competing German film distributors) was whether

(a) Germany's Rule of the Shorter Term applied to Buster Keaton movies, so their copyrights had expired in Germany because they had expired in the U.S. (28 years after their release, because their copyrights were not renewed), or

(b) Germany's then-existing life-plus-50 year term applied, so the movies were still protected there (because Keaton didn't die until 1966).

By the time the case was filed, the German copyright act did contain a Rule of the Shorter Term, as authorized by the UCC. But the German Supreme Court held that the Rule did *not* apply, because the Keaton movies were first published before the UCC became effective in Germany. As a result, the movies were protected in Germany pursuant to the 1892 bilateral treaty between Germany and the U.S., which provided that U.S. citizens "shall enjoy, in the German Empire, the protection of copyright . . . on the same basis on which such protection is granted to subjects of the Empire."

In other words, the bilateral treaty did not permit Germany to apply a Rule of the Shorter Term to American works, because such a Rule would not be applied to Germans. Although the UCC did permit Germany to adopt a Rule of Shorter Term, the Court held that the Keaton movies were not affected by the UCC, because the UCC itself (in Article XIX) provides that "Rights in works acquired in any Contracting State under existing conventions or arrangements before the date on which this Convention comes into force in such State shall not be affected." According to the German Supreme Court, the owner of the copyrights to the Keaton movies acquired rights under the existing bilateral treaty before the UCC came into force; and those rights were the right to be protected by copyright "on the same basis" – which meant for the same length of time – as Germans.

Note, however, that *if* the Keaton movies had been released in, say, 1956, *after* the UCC became effective in Germany, and the movies' U.S.

copyrights had not been renewed 28 years later in 1984, Germany's Rule of the Shorter Term would have put the Keaton movies into the public domain in Germany at the same time they went into the public domain in the U.S. (at the beginning of 1985).

*Tele-Cine Film v. Constantine Film*, 10 IIC 363 (Germany Sup.Ct. 1978)

The issue in this case was whether Jack London's novel *White Fang* was still protected by copyright in Germany in 1972, even though its copyright had expired by then in the U.S.

The German Supreme Court confirmed (its same-day ruling in the *Atlas Films* case) that Germany's Rule of the Shorter Term did not apply to the novel, because it was protected in Germany under the 1892 bilateral treaty with the U.S., which did not allow the Rule to be applied to U.S. works. The Court also confirmed that nothing changed when Germany adhered to the UCC in 1955, or when Germany adopted its Rule of the Shorter Term in 1965, because the duration of the German copyright to the novel was established when the book was first published in 1905.

Because Jack London died in 1916, Germany's life-plus-50 copyright term – the term in effect when the novel was first published – meant that the novel's German copyright lasted until the *end* of 1966, even though its U.S. copyright had expired by then.

The defendant in this case made an unlicensed movie of *White Fang* in 1973 – seven years after the novel's copyright appeared to have expired. The plaintiff also made a movie based on *White Fang*, at about the same time the defendant did; but the plaintiff had acquired an exclusive license to do so.

The plaintiff argued that a license was necessary – and that its exclusive rights were infringed by the defendant – because when Germany extended the duration of German copyright from life-plus-50-years to life-plus-70-years at the *beginning* of 1966, *White Fang*'s German copyright was extended until the end of 1986. The Court, however, disagreed with the plaintiff.

The Court held that the 20-year *extension* applied only to works still protected in Germany under the UCC, and that meant they had to be protected still in their countries-of-origin. Because the novel was no longer protected in the U.S. in 1966, its German copyright was not extended.

In short, the Court held that Germany's Rule of the Shorter Term did *not* apply to the novel's original life-plus-50-years term but *did* apply to the 20-year extension of the term of German copyright!

## C. Copyright restoration

Copyrights expire for several reasons. First and foremost, of course, they expire when they get to be older than the duration given to them by law.

Copyrights may expire for other reasons too. For example, they may expire:

- if the work's country-of-origin does not have a copyright treaty with the country in which protection is sought;

- if the country in which protection is sought required compliance with certain formalities, such as publication with copyright notice, as the United States once did, and the work did not satisfy those formalities; or
- if some formal renewal process was required in order for a work to enjoy the full duration of copyright, as the United States once did, and the process was not satisfied.

Eventually, an international consensus developed that many of these copyrights should not have expired, and that copyright protection should be restored by the countries in which they did expire. Restoring copyright protection to specific works is easier said than done. That is, once the concept of doing so is accepted, questions about the details of doing so immediately begin to present themselves; and the answers aren't simple. Indeed, as you will see below, the answers are exceedingly complex.

### 1.  Restoration by the United States

Writer-director George Romero is an important figure to aficionados of horror films. Between 1968 and 1985, he made a trio of movies known as the "Living Dead" series. Entitled "Night of the Living Dead," "Dawn of the Dead" and "Day of the Dead," all three movies dramatized a single terrifying theme: dead people return from their graves, seeking the flesh of their still-living friends and neighbors.

Romero was a Pittsburgh advertising executive when he made the first movie, and according to at least one report, he was "quite naive" in the ways of the movie business. As a result, he apparently failed to affix a copyright notice to the movie – as was then required by U.S. law – and thereby put it in the public domain, where it has spawned a host unauthorized copies, imitations and parodies. (A 1990 remake of "Night of the Living Dead" was made by Romero himself.)

Though no one could have known so in 1968, it turned out to be prophetic that a movie about the "Living Dead" went into the public domain. A quarter-century later, the Congress of the United States followed in Romero's footsteps by creating its own "living dead" creatures in the context of copyright law. It did so by restoring the copyrights to countless public domain movies and other works. These "restored works" do not threaten the flesh of those still living. But "restored works" are as terrifying to some people as Romero's zombies ever were. The reason they are terrifying is that they do threaten the investments that many people and companies made because of their now-mistaken belief that works in the public domain are legally dead for all time and thus could be used without liability.

Unfortunately for George Romero, the 1968 version of "Night of the Living Dead" is not one of the movies whose copyrights were restored. His movie is of American origin, and Congress limited the benefits of its copyright restoration bill to works from foreign sources.

*Restoration of copyrights to foreign works*

In a nutshell, what Congress did was simple. It created a new section of the Copyright Act – section 104A – that restored the U.S. copyrights of certain foreign works, if those works went into the public domain in the U.S. for certain reasons. Once restored, those copyrights give their owners virtually all of the same rights their owners would have enjoyed, had those works not gone into the public domain at all. This simple statement of what Congress has done masks many complexities and ambiguities that are of practical importance in applying the section. But even this simple statement makes it apparent just how significant and dramatic the section is, within the larger fabric of American copyright law.

The copyright restoration provision raises (at least) five questions:

1. Why did Congress restore copyright protection to works in the public domain at all, and once it decided to do so, why did it restore the copyrights of foreign works only and not those of American works as well?
2. Which foreign works had their copyrights restored?
3. What term of protection is given to restored copyrights?
4. Who owns restored copyrights?
5. What effects does copyright restoration have on the continued use of restored works?

### Why U.S. restored copyrights

In two words, Congress restored copyrights because of "international trade." That is, in connection with international trade negotiations, other countries insisted that the U.S. copyrights to certain of their works be restored; and in order for the U.S. to get concessions that were desired from those countries, the U.S. agreed to their copyright restoration demands.

### NAFTA restoration

Congress restored copyrights for the first time in 1993 as part of the North American Free Trade Agreement (NAFTA) with Mexico and Canada. A small part of the NAFTA Implementation Act added a then-new section 104A to the Copyright Act, and that section provided for the restoration of the copyrights to certain Mexican and Canadian movies.

While conceptually significant, this first version of section 104A was of relatively little practical significance to the American entertainment industry, because it only restored the copyrights to Mexican and Canadian movies (not other types of works), if those movies had gone into the public domain in the U.S. because they were published without notice between 1978 and March 1, 1989, and only if the owners of the copyrights to those movies filed written statements with the Copyright Office during a specified one-year period. The NAFTA version of section 104A resulted in the restoration of the copyrights to only 345 movies, all or virtually all of which were from Mexico. (A list of the titles of those movies was published by the Copyright Office in *Copyright Restoration of Certain Motion Pictures*, 60 Fed.Regis. 8252 (1995).)

Though NAFTA-restoration was of little practical consequence, it showed Congress what it could do and gave it taste for doing it (much like the carnivorous plant in Roger Corman's "Little Shop of Horrors" which started by drinking a single drop of blood and soon was demanding entire carcasses with the menacing wail "Feed me, Seymour!").

*GATT restoration*

The NAFTA version of section 104A was replaced in just a year with what can be called the "GATT" version of section 104A, or more accurately the "Uruguay Round Agreements Act" version. The Uruguay Round negotiations resulted in an annex to GATT known as "TRIPs" which is short for "Agreement on Trade-Related Aspects of Intellectual Property Rights." TRIPs was added to GATT largely at the behest of the United States, Europe and Japan; and – as you know from Chapter 5 – it made adequate and effective protection for copyright (as well as other intellectual property) an obligation of membership in the World Trade Organization.

You'll recall that TRIPs requires all World Trade Organization members (of which the U.S. is one) to comply with most articles of the Berne Convention, including Article 18 which requires all Berne Union members to provide copyright protection for works from all other Berne countries. This Article 18 obligation is imposed on new Berne members as soon as they adhere to Berne, and thus it requires new members to provide retroactive protection to foreign works (so long as they have not yet fallen into the public domain in their country of origin when the new member joined). Old members are required to provide retroactive protection for works from newly-adhering countries too, so this retroactive-protection obligation is reciprocal.

Thus, TRIPs is the reason that the U.S. amended the Copyright Act to provide retroactive protection for certain works. (Recall from Chapter 2 that the Constitutionality of copyright restoration was challenged, and upheld, in *Luck's Music Library v. Gonzales*, 407 F.3d 1262 (D.C.Cir. 2005).)

*Why foreign works only*

Congress decided to make retroactive protection available only for foreign works and not for American works, because Berne and therefore TRIPs only require countries to provide retroactive protection for foreign works.

*Eligible works*

The preceding paragraphs described works whose copyrights have been restored as "foreign" works, for convenience. In fact, not all foreign works had their copyrights restored. The test for determining which ones did is a multi-step test involving inquiry into at least three things: the identity of the work's "source country"; whether the work was still protected by copyright in its source country; and the reason the work went into the public domain in the United States in the first place.

The Copyright Act creates this multi-step test in subsections that *define* what kinds of works were eligible to have their copyrights restored. This chart should help you make sense of the statutory definitions that follow it.

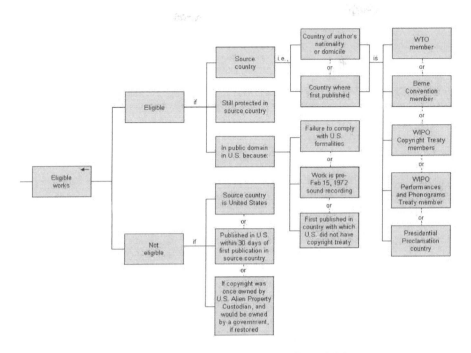

## United States Copyright Act §104A(h)

(3) The term "eligible country" means a nation, other than the United States, that —

    (A) becomes a WTO member country after the date of the enactment of the Uruguay Round Agreements Act;

    (B) on such date of enactment is, or after such date of enactment becomes, a nation adhering to the Berne Convention;

    (C) adheres to the WIPO Copyright Treaty;

    (D) adheres to the WIPO Performances and Phonograms Treaty; or

    (E) after such date of enactment becomes subject to a proclamation under subsection (g).

(6) The term "restored work" means an original work of authorship that —

. . .

    (B) is not in the public domain in its source country through expiration of term of protection;

    (C) is in the public domain in the United States due to —

        (i) noncompliance with formalities imposed at any time by United States copyright law, including failure of renewal, lack of proper notice, or failure to comply with any manufacturing requirements;

        (ii) lack of subject matter protection in the case of sound recordings fixed before February 15, 1972; or

        (iii) lack of national eligibility;

    (D) has at least one author or rightholder who was, at the time the work was created, a national or domiciliary of an eligible country, and if published, was first published in an eligible country and not published in the United States during the 30-day period following publication in such eligible country; and

(E) if the source country for the work is an eligible country solely by virtue of its adherence to the WIPO Performances and Phonograms Treaty, is a sound recording.

(8) The "source country" of a restored work is —
    (A) a nation other than the United States;
    (B) in the case of an unpublished work —
        (i) the eligible country in which the author or rightholder is a national or domiciliary, or, if a restored work has more than 1 author or rightholder, of which the majority of foreign authors or rightholders are nationals or domiciliaries; or
        (ii) if the majority of authors or rightholders are not foreign, the nation other than the United States which has the most significant contacts with the work; and
    (C) in the case of a published work —
        (i) the eligible country in which the work is first published, or
        (ii) if the restored work is published on the same day in 2 or more eligible countries, the eligible country which has the most significant contacts with the work.

These provisions seem understandable enough. Notice, though, that section 104A(h)(6)(B) requires American judges to determine whether a foreign work (for which copyright restoration is sought) is still protected by copyright in its "source country." This provision is significant for two reasons. First, it introduces into U.S. copyright law a "rule of the shorter term," because it means that even if a foreign work *would be* protected under U.S. law, its U.S. copyright will *not* be restored – and thus it will not be protected under U.S. law – if the work is no longer protected under the law of its source country. Second, this provision requires American judges to learn something – perhaps quite a bit – about the copyright law of the work's source country, as the following case illustrates.

**Alameda Films v. Authors Rights Restoration Corp.**
**331 F.3d 472 (5th Cir. 2003), cert. denied, 124 S.Ct. 814 (2003)**

Wiener, Circuit Judge:

Plaintiffs-Appellees-Cross-Appellants Alameda Films, S.A., et al. (collectively, "the Plaintiffs") are 24 Mexican film production companies that sued Defendants-Appellants-Cross-Appellees Authors Rights Restoration Corp., Inc., Media Resources International, Television International Syndicators, Inc., and H. Jackson Shirley, III (collectively, "the Defendants"), claiming copyright violations in 88 Mexican films that the Defendants distributed in the United States ("U.S."). Following a lengthy and vociferously disputed discovery process and the filing of numerous pre-trial motions, . . . the district court eliminated from consideration seven of the 88 films in question and conducted a jury trial on the Plaintiffs' claims concerning the remaining 81 Mexican films. The jury returned a verdict for the Plaintiffs on all claims.

. . .On appeal, the Defendants [made certain arguments discussed later in this chapter]. The Plaintiffs cross-appeal the district court's grant of partial summary judgment to the Defendants on the copyright status of seven of the 88 disputed films. We affirm the district court. . . .

*I.  Facts and Proceedings*

In the mid-1980s, the Defendants began distributing a variety of Mexican films in the U.S. This activity included 88 films that had been produced and released by the Plaintiffs in Mexico during that country's "golden age" of cinema, between the late-1930s and the mid-1950s. The Plaintiffs acknowledge that, at the time the Defendants began distributing these 88 films in the U.S., 69 of them had lost their copyrights here for failure of the authors to comply with U.S. copyright formalities, such as registering and renewing copyrights. According to the Plaintiffs, however, the legal status of these films changed in 1994 when the U.S. adopted the Uruguay Round Agreement Act ("URAA"), thereby amending the 1976 Copyright Act. The URAA eliminated many of the formalities previously required for copyrighting foreign works in the U.S., including registration and notice. The URAA also provided, effective January 1, 1996, for the automatic restoration of copyrights in various foreign works that had fallen into the public domain in the U.S. as a result of their foreign authors' failure to follow U.S. copyright formalities.

Following Congress's 1994 adoption of the URAA, the Defendants began to obtain assignments of "rights" to the films from some individual "contributors," such as screenwriters and music composers. The Defendants did not, however, contact any of the Plaintiffs to obtain assignments or licenses to these films. The Defendants continued to distribute Mexican films in the U.S. after January 1, 1996, the date on which the U.S. copyrights were automatically restored in those films that were eligible for copyright restoration under the URAA.

In June 1998, the Plaintiffs filed suit in the U.S. District Court for the District of Columbia, alleging that the Defendants violated the Plaintiffs' (restored) U.S. copyrights in the 88 films here at issue. . . .

Following discovery, Defendants filed [a motion] for partial summary judgment, claiming that . . . seven of the 88 films produced by Plaintiffs were ineligible for copyright restoration under the URAA because these seven had fallen into the public domain in Mexico. . . .

The district court . . . grant[ed] the Defendants' . . . motion for partial summary judgment concerning the copyright status of the seven particular films that had fallen into the public domain in Mexico. . . .

*II.  ANALYSIS . . .*

> *B.  Are the seven films excluded by the district court eligible for restoration of their U.S. copyrights under the URAA?*

The Defendants' . . . motion for partial summary judgment requested that the district court eliminate consideration of seven of the Plaintiffs' original 88 claims for copyright infringement, contending that the films had fallen into the public domain under Mexican copyright law, thereby precluding restoration of their U.S. copyrights under the URAA. The district court granted that motion, ruling that the seven films had fallen into the public domain in Mexico and thus were ineligible for copyright restoration in the U.S. . . .

> *2. Registration requirements of Mexican copyright law.*

. . . [T]he URAA predicates restoration of the work's U.S. copyright on its meeting three requirements: The work (1) is not in the public domain in the source country, (2) is in the public domain in the U.S. because of noncompliance with copyright formalities, lack of subject matter protection, or lack of national eligibility, and (3) was first published in the source country and was not published in the U.S. within 30 days after its initial foreign publication. The district court determined that the seven films in question were not eligible for copyright restoration under the URAA because they had fallen into the public domain in the source country – Mexico.

These seven films were produced and released between 1938 and 1946, and thus were governed by the copyright provisions of the 1928 Mexican Civil Code. . . . [T]hat Code states:

> The author who publishes a work cannot acquire the rights granted to him by this title if he does not register the work within a period of three years. At the conclusion of this term, the work enters the public domain [if not registered].

It is undisputed that the Plaintiffs never registered their copyrights in the seven films here at issue. In 1947, though, Mexico amended its copyright laws to eliminate the registration requirement. Article 2 of the 1947 Ley Federal de Derecho de Autor states that:

> [copyright] protection provided under this law to authors is conferred upon the simple creation of the work, without the necessity of deposit or registry previously [required] for its protection. . . .

Thus, for any works originally published in Mexico after the effective date of the abolition of that country's registration requirement (January 14, 1948), authors received automatic copyright protection.

The 1947 amendment of the Mexican copyright law also contained a safe harbor for any previously published works that had fallen into the public domain under the 1928 Code prior to the new law's effective date of January 14, 1948. Authors who had failed to register their works within three years following their publication, as required under . . . Mexico's 1928 Code, thereby allowing such works to fall into the public domain, were given a six-month period of repose following the aforesaid effective date of the 1947 revision during which to register their works and thereby restore their copyrights.

### 3. Is the restoration provision of the 1947 amendment applicable to the seven films at issue?

It is undisputed that four of the seven films that the district court ruled to have fallen into the public domain were released by the Plaintiffs less than three years before January 14, 1948, when the 1947 copyright provisions went into effect. On appeal, the Plaintiffs urge us to reverse the summary judgment concerning these four films, contending that the 1947 law, not the 1928 Code, is applicable. They direct us to that language of the 1947 copyright law stating that authors of works that (1) had been previously published under the 1928 Code, and (2) had fallen into the public domain prior to January 14, 1948, were accorded a six-month safe harbor during which to register these works and restore their copyrights. The Plaintiffs also note that any work created after the 1947 law went into effect received automatic copyright protection, with no registration requirement. Thus, urge the Plaintiffs, a temporal hiatus results from the effective dates of these two provisions of Mexico's 1947 copyright law for works that were published after 1945, but never registered: Works in this category had not yet lost their copyrights under the 1928 Code when the 1947 law went into effect; yet, the 1947 law did not provide for either an automatic copyright in, or a period of repose for registration of, works published during this short period.

Based on this analysis of the 1947 copyright law, the Plaintiffs first contend that the four films that they produced during this three-year gap between 1945 and 1948 should be granted copyright protection under the terms of the 1947 copyright law. In so claiming, however, the Plaintiffs are in essence asking us to rewrite Article 2 of Mexico's 1947 copyright law to apply retroactively its automatic copyright date three years earlier than is specified in the statute. This we decline to do. As the district court recognized in its summary judgment order, the automatic copyright provision expressly applies only to those works first published on or after January 14, 1948. Each of the Plaintiffs' four films were produced and released either in 1945 or 1946, and thus, by the plain words of the statute, do not qualify for the automatic copyright provision of the 1947 law.

The Plaintiffs alternatively maintain that canons of Mexican constitutional law support their interpretation of the automatic copyright provision as having retroactive effect, despite the statute's express terms to the contrary. They say that canons of Mexican constitutional law preclude retroactive application of statutes only when doing so would work to the detriment of a person's legal rights; retroactive application is actually sanctioned when it works in favor of both personal and property rights. The Plaintiffs thus conclude that retroactive application of the automatic copyright provision to works created after 1945 would advance Mexico's strong policy interest in favoring the moral rights of an author over the public interest.

We are not convinced by the Plaintiffs' alternative request that we judicially rewrite the 1947 statute to provide for automatic copyright protection as early as 1945, rather than the statute's express effective date of January 14, 1948. In fact, there is no reason for us to consider the canons of Mexican constitutional law in retroactive application of statutes because there is a completely reasonable explanation for the purported "gap" in the 1947 copyright law: There was simply no need to provide a safe harbor for works that remained within the three-year grace period for registration by or later than January 14, 1948, because authors of those works still had time remaining in which to register these works. The safe harbor was needed for works that had already fallen into the public domain: It was only the authors of these works who were given an explicit second bite at the apple. Works produced between January 1945 and January 1948 remained within the three-year grace period specified under the 1928 Code during which their authors could register them. Thus, Mexico's 1947 copyright law implicitly recognized that authors of works created within this three-year period still had time to register their works, as required under the terms of the 1928 Code, and thus were not in need of a grace period or safe harbor.

Simply put, the Plaintiffs should have realized in 1947 that they needed to register their copyrights in these four films before the 1928 Code's three-year grace period expired. It should have been obvious to them that, when the 1947 copyright provisions went into effect the following January, the new automatic copyright provisions would not apply to these four films. The Plaintiffs do not dispute the fact that they never registered the four films in question; neither is there evidence in the record indicating that they did so. By the plain terms of the applicable 1928 Code, these films fell into the public domain in Mexico. Thus, they are ineligible for U.S. copyright restoration under the URAA.

> 4. *Are the registration requirements of the 1928 Code applicable to all seven films?*

The Plaintiffs propose yet another theory for holding that all seven disputed films retained their copyright protection and thus did not fall into the public domain after the 1928 Code's three-year grace period expired. They note that the 1928 Code's registration requirement applied only to works that were "published." The Plaintiffs quibble semantically that films are never "published"; rather, they are "released." Thus, argue the Plaintiffs, the literal terms of the 1928 Code's registration provision do not apply to films at all.

The Plaintiffs identify no Mexican canon of constitutional law or statutory interpretation that should guide our construction of the 1928 Code's registration requirement. Neither do they identify any Mexican court opinion or other authoritative Mexican interpretation of the 1928 Code's registration requirement of films vis-à-vis books or other "published" works. When there are gaps in foreign law, though, a U.S. court may use forum law to fill them.[24]
[[24] See *Cantieri Navali Rieunitu v. M/V Skyptron*, 802 F.2d 160, 163 n.5 (5th Cir. 1986).]

In this regard, U.S. courts have broadly interpreted the U.S. copyright statutes to cover new types of works that clearly fall within the ambit of their protection, even though these new kinds of works are not covered literally by the terminology employed in the statutes at the time of their enactment. Furthermore, it would be anomalous for us to exempt films from the duties imposed on authors by the 1928 Code while affording these same films the benefits provided to authors by the very same code. Accordingly, we are satisfied that the term "publishes," as broadly used in the 1928 Code, was intended to encompass all appropriate forms of distributing copyrighted works to the public. As, in the mid-1940s, films could be distributed to the public only by being "released" to theaters, it would be nonsensical to construe the 1928 Code's registration requirement as not applicable to the very films that benefit from the copyright protections afforded by the other provisions of that Code. We hold that the 1928 Code's registration requirements are applicable to films, necessarily including the seven disputed here. . . .

## Restored term of protection

To determine the term of restored copyrights, it is necessary to identify the date that restoration did (or will) take effect and the duration of restored copyrights once restoration took effect. Here is the language of the Copyright Act, followed by a chart that visually depicts the following provisions.

### United States Copyright Act §104A(a)

(a) Automatic Protection and Term. —
   (1) Term. —
      (A) Copyright subsists, in accordance with this section, in restored works, and vests automatically on the date of restoration.
      (B) Any work in which copyright is restored under this section shall subsist for the remainder of the term of copyright that the work would have otherwise been granted in the United States if the work never entered the public domain in the United States.

### United States Copyright Act §104A(h)

(2) The "date of restoration" of a restored copyright is —
      (A) January 1, 1996, if the source country of the restored work is a nation adhering to the Berne Convention or a WTO member country on such date, or
      (B) the date of adherence or proclamation, in the case of any other source country of the restored work.

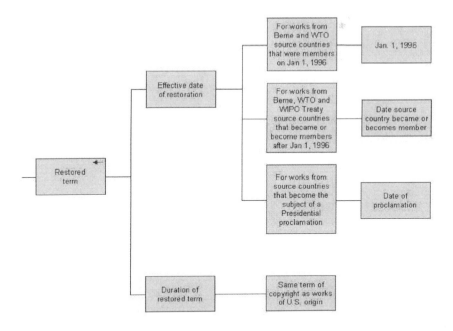

*Ownership of restored copyrights*

Ownership of restored copyrights is determined somewhat differently than the ownership of copyrights that never lapsed into the public domain. Determining the identity of the owner of a restored copyright requires a multi-step analysis: first, there are those steps that lead to a conclusion about ownership in cases where no transfers ever took place; and then, there are those steps that must be taken in those cases where transfers have taken place.

The following chart shows what the differences *look* like. The law's "details" follow the chart.

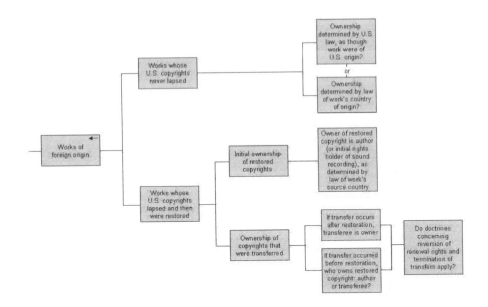

## United States Copyright Act §104A(b)
## Ownership of Restored Copyright

A restored work vests initially in the author or initial rightholder of the work as determined by the law of the source country of the work.

## United States Copyright Act §104A(h)

(7) The term "rightholder" means the person —
   (A) who, with respect to a sound recording, first fixes a sound recording with authorization, or
   (B) who has acquired rights from the person described in subparagraph (A) by means of any conveyance or by operation of law.

These subsections of the Copyright Act are *everything* the Act has to say about the ownership of restored copyrights.

Note that section 104A(b) says that the identity of the author or rightholder is to be determined by the law of the "source country," not by United States copyright law. In many cases, the identity of the author (or rightholder) will be the same, regardless of which country's law is applied. But not always. For example, under U.S. law, the "author" of a work for hire is the employer (or commissioning party). But some countries do not have a work for hire doctrine, or any equivalent; and in those countries, the author of a work is its human creator, even if the work is created by an employee within the course and scope of his or her employment. This difference could be – indeed has been – critical in cases where:

- Company A obtains an exclusive license from an employer to use a work whose U.S. copyright was restored, and
- Company B obtains an exclusive license to use that same work from its human creator.

In that kind of case, which company has the valid license, and which company is the infringer? This question matters, even if you are not a litigator. Suppose, for example, that you represent a company that wants an exclusive license to use a work whose U.S. copyright has been restored. From whom do you seek it?

### Alameda Films S A v. Authors Rights Restoration Corp.
### 331 F.3d 472 (5th Cir. 2003), cert. denied, 124 S.Ct. 814 (2003)

. . . On appeal, the Defendants [argued that the District Court erred in] determining that production companies, such as the Plaintiffs, can hold copyrights under Mexican law. . . .

*I. Facts and Proceedings*

. . . Defendants [claimed that] under Mexican law, only natural persons, such as the individual contributors, and not artificial or juridical persons, such as film production companies, could be "authors"....

The district court . . . acknowledged that interpretation of Mexican copyright law under 17 U.S.C. § 104A is a question of law for determination by the court.[5] [[5] See 17 U.S.C. § 104A(b) (noting that a "restored work vests initially in the author or initial rightholder of the work as determined by the law of the source country of the work"). See also Fed.R.Civ.P. 44.1 (noting that a "court's determination [of foreign law] shall be treated as a ruling on a question of law").] On this question, the district court ruled that film production companies can hold copyrights – a *derecho de autor* ("author's right") – under the Mexican Civil Code. The district court reserved for trial, though, the disputed issue whether the Plaintiffs had in fact obtained Mexican copyrights in the 81 remaining films. . . .

In the ensuing jury trial, the district court permitted both sides to adduce testimony about the requirements of Mexican copyright law; and the district court instructed the jury that a film production company can be an "author" under Mexican copyright law for purposes of the URAA. The jury returned a verdict for the Plaintiffs, finding that (1) the Plaintiffs own the U.S. copyrights in the 81 films remaining in dispute, [and] (2) the Defendants violated the copyrights in all 81 films. . . .

*II. ANALYSIS*

A. *Can film production companies hold copyrights under Mexican law?.*
. .

2. *The "author's right" under Mexican law.*

The URAA provides that a "copyright subsists . . . in restored works, and vests automatically on the date of restoration." The copyright in a restored work "vests initially in the author or initial rightholder of the work as determined by the law of the source country of the work." The URAA thus establishes two categories for foreign copyright owners whose U.S. copyrights can be restored: (1) authors, and (2) initial rightholders. The class of "initial rightholders" includes only owners of a copyright in a "sound recording," e.g., music composers; whereas, the class of "authors" includes all other creators of works originally copyrighted in foreign jurisdictions. Accordingly, the Plaintiffs can claim restored copyrights in their films under the URAA only if the Plaintiffs are considered "authors" under Mexican copyright law – the law of the source country of the work.

The Defendants' principal contention on appeal is that the Plaintiffs, as film production companies, cannot be "authors" under the Mexican Civil

251

Code. The Defendants maintain that the Mexican Civil Code permits only individuals, i.e., natural persons, to be "authors"; that the law does not permit corporations or other legal entities to be "authors" for purposes of claiming copyright entitlements. In contending that only natural persons can hold copyrights under Mexican law, the Defendants argue that we should never reach the restoration analysis under the URAA, because the Plaintiffs fail this threshold determination of qualification to hold copyrights under the "law of the source country of the work."

In response, the Plaintiffs – and the Government of Mexico, as *amicus curiae* – urge that the Defendants' failure even to mention the Collaboration Doctrine of the Mexican Civil Code is telling. They note that in Mexican law, the Collaboration Doctrine covers various provisions regarding copyrights claimed by corporations, which necessarily create copyrighted works only through the collaboration of individuals, viz., their agents and employees. Thus, . . . the 1928 Mexican Civil Code provides:

> The person or corporation that imprints or publishes a work made by various individuals with the consent of such individuals will have the property in the entire work, except each individual will retain the right to publish anew their own composition, independently, or in a collection.

Subsequent amendments and re-enactments of Mexico's copyright laws in 1947 and 1956 specify that "whoever" creates a work with the "collaboration" of one or more other authors is entitled to the "author's right" (*derecho de autor*) in the entire work, as long as the contributors are mentioned in the work and are paid for their respective contributions. Finally, the 1963 amendment of the Mexican copyright laws provides explicitly that "physical persons and legal entities who produce a work with the special and remunerated collaboration of one or more persons shall enjoy with respect to that work the author's right therein . . . ."

The Defendants devote a substantial portion of their briefs to discussing the role of Collective Bargaining Agreements ("CBA") in Mexico. The Defendants appear to believe that the Plaintiffs maintained before the district court (and continue to maintain on appeal) that they have copyrights in the films by virtue of having obtained assignments of the copyrights via the CBAs of the "natural persons" who worked for the production companies. If the Defendants harbor such a belief, they are mistaken. The CBAs that the Plaintiffs submitted into evidence were meant to prove only that the Plaintiffs' employees had been paid, thereby satisfying one of the requirements under the Collaboration Doctrine for the Plaintiffs, as production companies, to claim copyrights in the films that they produced.

The Defendants' insistence that an "author's right" under Mexican law vests only in a "natural person" is simply wrong. As *amicus*, the Government of Mexico explains that "throughout every iteration of its intellectual property laws, [Mexico] has recognized the producer as the rightful owner of the copyright of any film in its entirety." Provisions of the Mexican Civil Code identified by the Plaintiffs clearly support this position. Thus, the district court correctly determined that the Plaintiffs can be and are "authors" under Mexican law, and thus can hold Mexican copyrights (*derecho de autor*) in the films that they have produced. . . .

If the defendants' understanding of Mexican copyright law had been correct, who would have owned the restored U.S. copyrights in the Mexican films they were distributing and exhibiting in the United States?

Note also that section 104A(b) provides that ownership of a restored copyright vests "initially" in the author or initial rightholder. This certainly means that *after* a work's copyright has been restored, the initial owner may transfer the copyright to someone else, and that person or company will then be the owner. But what does section 104A(b) mean with respect to a restored copyright, ownership of which was transferred by the work's author (or initial rightholder) *before* ownership of the restored copyright vested? Does the author (or initial rightholder) become the owner of the restored copyright, despite the transfer? Or does section 104A(b) give automatic effect to the prior transfer, so that although ownership of the restored copyright vests "initially" in the author or initial rightholder, the prior transferee automatically becomes its owner immediately after vesting by operation of law?

These last few questions might have mattered in the *Alameda Films* case, even if the defendants' understanding of Mexican law had been correct. Did you notice that the defendants obtained many (perhaps all) of their licenses *before* the U.S. copyrights in those films actually were restored on January 1, 1996. (The court's opinion reports that "Following Congress's 1994 adoption of the URAA, the Defendants began to obtain assignments of 'rights' to the films from some individual 'contributors,' such as screenwriters and music composers.") So, if the defendants did obtain their licenses *before* the U.S. copyrights were restored, were the *defendants* the owners of the restored copyrights, or were the screenwriters and composers the owners, despite the assignments they had given to the defendants? If the screenwriters and composers were the owners, how would that have helped the defendants defeat the plaintiffs' claims?

### Peliculas Y Videos Internacionales v. Harriscope of Los Angeles, Inc. 302 F.Supp.2d 1131 (C.D.Cal. 2004)

William J. Rea, United States District Judge. . . .

*Factual Background*

On April 30, 2002, Peliculas Y Videos Internacionales, ("PVI") filed this lawsuit alleging copyright infringement . . . against Harriscope of Los Angeles, Inc. ("Harriscope"), Media Resources International, LLP ("MRI"), and Television International Syndicators, Inc. ("TIS"), (collectively "Defendants").

PVI alleges it owns exclusive copyrights to twenty-nine motion pictures, published in Mexico prior to March 1, 1989, through an assignment of those rights by the films' producers. For purposes of this motion, PVI and Defendants agree that these works fell into the public domain in the United States and were eligible for restoration under the Copyright Act and the Uruguay Round Agreements Act ("URAA"). 17 U.S.C. § 104A. PVI alleges that MRI and TIS licensed broadcast rights to Harriscope in violation of PVI's exclusive copyrights and that Harriscope broadcast those films in violation of PVI's exclusive broadcast rights.

Currently before the Court are the parties' cross motions for partial summary judgment. PVI moves for partial summary judgment, seeking to establish that a producer's assignee may qualify as an "author" under the URAA. Conversely, Defendants move for partial summary judgment, seeking to establish that PVI may not qualify as an author because of its assignee status. The Court will analyze these parallel motions together. . . .

*Discussion*

II. *Analysis*

A. *Cross Motions for Partial Summary Judgment on PVI's Status as an Author Under Mexican Law.*

In this lawsuit, PVI seeks to establish that it is the rightful owner of the copyright to twenty-nine films and that Defendants infringed this copyright by copying, licensing, and broadcasting these films without authorization. The films were produced in Mexico between 1930 and 1960 and fell into the public domain in the United States for failure to comply with copyright formalities. However, the Uruguay Round Agreements Act ("URAA") automatically restored the films' copyrights as of January 1, 1996. The copyright to these works "vests initially in the author or initial rightholder of the work as determined by the law of the source country of the work." 17 U.S.C. § 104A(b). The contentious issue to be decided in this motion is whether PVI qualifies as the author of the films under Mexican law.

The Fifth Circuit recently held that an author may be the producer of a film under the Mexican Collaboration Doctrine. *Alameda Films S.A. de C.V. v. Authors Rights Restoration Corp., Inc.*, 331 F.3d 472 (5th Cir. 2003). . . . This Court agrees with the Fifth Circuit.

However, PVI does not claim to be the original producer of the films at issue. Instead, PVI claims to be the assignee of the producer of each of the twenty-nine films. Thus, to establish its status as the "author" of the films under Mexican law, and its ownership of the copyrights, PVI must prove: (1) each film's producer remunerated the collaborators on the film, (2) an assignee of a producer may qualify as an author under Mexican law, and (3) the valid assignment to PVI of each producer's rights in each film. In this motion, PVI seeks only to establish the second point, that a producer's assignee may qualify as an author under Mexican law. To the Court's knowledge, no court has yet addressed this precise question. Thus, the Court will undertake to determine the content of Mexican copyright law on this point.

Applicable Mexican copyright law grants two distinct types of rights to an author: (1) moral rights, and (2) exploitation, or patrimonial, rights. Exploitation rights include the right to sell the use of the work for profit and may be sold or assigned in much the same manner as copyrights in the United States. . . . Moral rights, however, protect the author's dignity or personal artistic expression. Because these rights are personal to the author, Mexican law expressly prohibits the sale or assignment of moral rights. . . . Instead, ownership of moral rights may only pass by succession upon the death of the author. Mexican law clearly splits ownership of authors rights and, thus, anticipates the possibility that two separate groups might hold the two distinct types of rights.

Defendants argue that because PVI claims to be the assignee of the producers of the films, it cannot possess the moral rights to the films. Thus, Defendants argue, PVI cannot be deemed an "author" under Mexican law for purposes of the URAA.[5] [5 Defendants also argue that the URAA does not

254

recognize assignments, but instead restores the copyright in the original author, regardless of the author's disposition of its rights. However, the text of the URAA fails to support this reading. The URAA clearly mandates that the Court identify the author using Mexican law. 17 U.S.C. § 104A. Thus, the Court finds Mexican law on assignment of copyrights controlling.]

However, PVI contends that Defendants infringed its exploitation rights by unlawfully copying, licensing, and broadcasting, the films. Because Mexican law anticipates the possibility that two separate entities may hold the two types of rights, it must follow that each entity may enforce the right it holds. Thus, PVI may seek to enforce the exploitation rights it claims to hold, but may not seek to enforce the moral rights, which must belong to the original producers' successors. Accordingly, the Court grants PVI's motion for partial summary judgment and holds that an assignee may qualify as an author under the URAA for purposes of enforcing exploitation rights only.

The outcome of the *Peliculas Y Videos* case seems to have turned on Judge Rea's conclusion in footnote 5 that because section 104A "clearly mandates that the Court identify the *author* using Mexican law . . . the Court finds Mexican law on *assignment* of copyrights controlling." (Emphasis added.) Are "authorship" and ownership as a result of "assignment" the same thing? Are you satisfied with Judge Rea's conclusion that "an assignee may qualify as an author. . . ."?

*Effects of restoration*

The most important provisions of section 104A – as well as the lengthiest and most complex – are those that deal with the *consequences* of copyright restoration on the continued exploitation of those works that once were in the public domain in the U.S. but now are protected again.

These consequences are felt by two separate classes of people and companies:

- by those who did *not* exploit restored works while they were in the public domain, but who did exploit them (or would like to) after their copyrights were restored; and
- by those who *did* exploit restored works while they were in the public domain and continued to do so (or would like to) after their copyrights were restored.

Restoration also may have an effect on two types of legal commitments that were made before anyone knew or even dreamed that Congress might someday bring public domain works back to life. These two types of commitments are:

- warranties of non-infringement, and
- promises to perform.

The charts below show what the effects of restoration *look* like. Following each chart is the Copyright Act section the chart reflects.

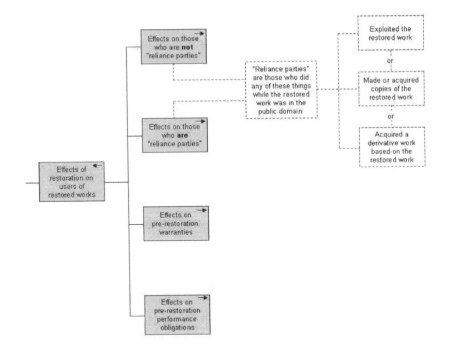

**United States Copyright Act §104A(h)**

(4) The term "reliance party" means any person who —
  (A) with respect to a particular work, engages in acts, before the source country of that work becomes an eligible country, which would have violated section 106 if the restored work had been subject to copyright protection, and who, after the source country becomes an eligible country, continues to engage in such acts;
  (B) before the source country of a particular work becomes an eligible country, makes or acquires 1 or more copies or phonorecords of that work; or
  (C) as the result of the sale or other disposition of a derivative work covered under subsection (d)(3), or significant assets of a person described in subparagraph (A) or (B), is a successor, assignee, or licensee of that person.

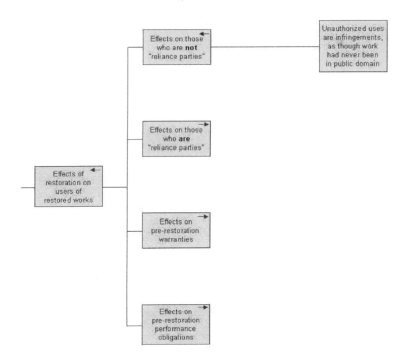

## United States Copyright Act §104A(d)
## Remedies for Infringement of Restored Copyrights

(1) Enforcement of copyright in restored works in the absence of a reliance party. — As against any party who is not a reliance party, the remedies provided in chapter 5 of this title shall be available on or after the date of restoration of a restored copyright with respect to an act of infringement of the restored copyright that is commenced on or after the date of restoration.

### Peliculas Y Videos Internacionales v. Harriscope of Los Angeles, Inc.
### 302 F.Supp.2d 1131 (C.D.Cal. 2004)

William J. Rea, United States District Judge. . . .

    *B.  Defendants' Motion for Partial Summary Judgment*

Defendants move for partial summary judgment, arguing they are not liable to PVI for statutory damages or attorneys fee's, because . . . Defendants qualify as reliance parties under 17 U.S.C. § 104A(h)(4). . . .

    *1.  Defendants' Status as Reliance Parties*

    . . . In general terms, a reliance party is someone who used a work prior to copyright restoration and who continues to use it after restoration. 17 U.S.C. § 104A(h)(4). A defendant qualifies as a reliance party if:

        (A) with respect to a particular work, [the defendant] engages in acts, before the source country of that work becomes an eligible country, which would have violated [17 U.S.C. § 106] if the restored work had been subject to copyright protection, and who, after the source country becomes an eligible country, continues to engage in such acts; . . . or

(c) as the result of the sale or other disposition of a derivative work covered under subsection (d)(3), or significant assets of a person described in subparagraph (A) or (B), [the defendant] is a successor, assignee, or licensee of that person.

17 U.S.C. § 104A(h)(4)

A reliance party may continue, in limited circumstances, to use the copyrighted material after the date of restoration and is not liable for statutory damages or attorney's fees. 17 U.S.C. § 104A(d) (absolving a reliance party of liability for statutory damages or attorney's fees under 17 U.S.C. § 412 if "acts which would have constituted infringement had the restored work been subject to copyright were commenced before the date of restoration"). The URAA, thus, balances the interests of foreign owners in copyright restoration against the interests of parties using the copyrighted material at the time of restoration. . . . The copyrights to the twenty-nine films at issue were restored as of January 1, 1996 because Mexico adheres to the Berne Convention. . . .

The uncontroverted evidence establishes that Defendants qualify as reliance parties as to twenty-two of the twenty-nine films because they engaged in infringing acts prior to January 1, 1996. Defendants and PVI both submitted broadcast logs showing actual broadcast dates for the twenty-nine films. . . .

Deposition testimony confirms this evidence. PVI's President, Mr. Ortega, testified at deposition that he learned as early as 1994 or as late as 1996 that Harriscope had broadcast the films at issue. Further, Mr. Ortega admits that Harriscope obtained the films from Jackson Shirley's companies, MRI and TIS. Finally, it is undisputed that MRI and TIS created "pan and scan" copies of the films prior to licensing them to Harriscope, which constitutes infringement under 17 U.S.C. § 106(1)-(3).

Thus, the evidence clearly establishes that infringing acts, that is, the creation of the pan and scan copies and the broadcast of the films, occurred prior to January 1, 1996. Because the broadcast logs additionally establish the continued broadcast of the films after January 1, 1996, the Court holds that Defendants qualify as reliance parties as to the twenty-two films listed above. The Court grants Defendants' motion for partial summary judgment as to these twenty-two films.

2. *Availability of Attorney's Fees and Statutory Damages Under 17 U.S.C. § 412.*

Defendants next argue that they are not liable for attorney's fees and statutory damages under 17 U.S.C. § 412. To prevail, Defendants must show: (1) that the works were published; (2) the date of copyright registration; and (3) that Defendants' infringement commenced prior to the registration.[11] [[11] Section 412 provides, in pertinent part: "no award of statutory damages or of attorney's fees . . . shall be made for . . . (2) any infringement of copyright commenced after first publication of the work and before the effective date of its registration, unless such registration is made within three months after the first publication of the work."] Because this case arises under the URAA, § 412 potentially applies to a narrow category of films: those that were first broadcast after January 1, 1996, the date of automatic copyright restoration, and before the date of PVI's copyright registration.

The uncontroverted evidence from the broadcast logs discussed above establishes that . . . four films meet those criteria. . . . [T]hese four films were published, by their broadcast, after the date of copyright restoration, January 1, 1996, and before the date of copyright registration. Accordingly, the Court holds that the requirements of § 412 are met and PVI is not entitled to statutory damages or attorney's fees as to these four films. The Court grants Defendants' motion for partial summary judgment as to these four films.

However, the Court denies Defendants' motion for partial summary judgment as to the three remaining films. . . . The evidence provided fails to establish that these three films were broadcast prior to their copyright registration dates. . . .

So, what remedies were available to the plaintiffs in the *Peliculas Y Videos* case with respect to:

- the four films that *were* broadcast *before* their restored U.S. copyrights were registered?
- the three films that were *not* broadcast *before* their restored U.S. copyrights were registered?

Equally important (indeed, perhaps more important): was there anything the plaintiffs in *Peliculas Y Videos* had to do in order to be eligible for *any* remedies at all for the infringement of their restored copyrights? Judge Rea didn't mention what else the plaintiffs may have had to do, so this question is answered by the next chart, the Copyright Act section that follows the chart, and the case that follows that.

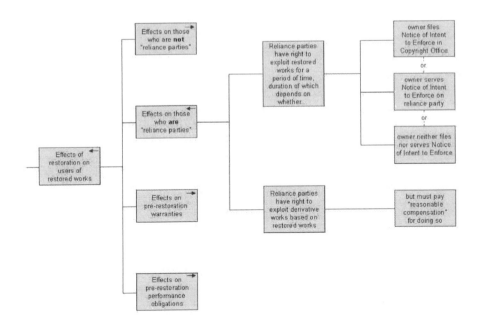

# United States Copyright Act §104A(d)
## Remedies for Infringement of Restored Copyrights

(2) Enforcement of copyright in restored works as against reliance parties. — As against a reliance party, except to the extent provided in paragraphs (3) and (4), the remedies provided in chapter 5 of this title shall be available, with respect to an act of infringement of a restored copyright, on or after the date of restoration of the restored copyright if the requirements of either of the following subparagraphs are met:

  (A) (i) The owner of the restored copyright (or such owner's agent) or the owner of an exclusive right therein (or such owner's agent) files with the Copyright Office, during the 24-month period beginning on the date of restoration, a notice of intent to enforce the restored copyright; and

    (ii) (I) the act of infringement commenced after the end of the 12-month period beginning on the date of publication of the notice in the Federal Register;

    (II) the act of infringement commenced before the end of the 12-month period described in subclause (I) and continued after the end of that 12-month period, in which case remedies shall be available only for infringement occurring after the end of that 12-month period; or

    (III) copies or phonorecords of a work in which copyright has been restored under this section are made after publication of the notice of intent in the Federal Register.

  (B) (i) The owner of the restored copyright (or such owner's agent) or the owner of an exclusive right therein (or such owner's agent) serves upon a reliance party a notice of intent to enforce a restored copyright; and

    (ii) (I) the act of infringement commenced after the end of the 12-month period beginning on the date the notice of intent is received;

    (II) the act of infringement commenced before the end of the 12-month period described in subclause (I) and continued after the end of that 12-month period, in which case remedies shall be available only for the infringement occurring after the end of that 12-month period; or

    (III) copies or phonorecords of a work in which copyright has been restored under this section are made after receipt of the notice of intent.

In the event that notice is provided under both subparagraphs (A) and (B), the 12-month period referred to in such subparagraphs shall run from the earlier of publication or service of notice.

(3) Existing derivative works. —

  (A) In the case of a derivative work that is based upon a restored work and is created —

    (i) before the date of the enactment of the Uruguay Round Agreements Act, if the source country of the restored work is an eligible country on such date, or

    (ii) before the date on which the source country of the restored work becomes an eligible country, if that country is not an eligible country on such date of enactment,

  a reliance party may continue to exploit that derivative work for the duration of the restored copyright if the reliance party pays to the owner of the restored copyright reasonable compensation for conduct which would be subject to a remedy for infringement but for the provisions of this paragraph.

(B) In the absence of an agreement between the parties, the amount of such compensation shall be determined by an action in United States district court, and shall reflect any harm to the actual or potential market for or value of the restored work from the reliance party's continued exploitation of the work, as well as compensation for the relative contributions of expression of the author of the restored work and the reliance party to the derivative work.

## Hoepker v. Kruger
### 200 F.Supp.2d 340 (S.D.N.Y. 2002)

Alvin K. Hellerstein, United States District Judge

*Factual Background*

Plaintiff Thomas Hoepker is a well-known German photographer. In 1960, during the early days of his career, Hoepker created a photographic image of plaintiff Charlotte Dabney. The image, "Charlotte As Seen By Thomas," pictures Dabney from the waist up, holding a large magnifying glass over her right eye. Dabney's eye fills the lens of the magnifying glass, and the lens covers a large portion of Dabney's face. The image was published once in the German photography magazine *Foto Prisma* in 1960.

Defendant Barbara Kruger also is a well-known artist, specializing in collage works combining photographs and text. In 1990, Kruger created an untitled work incorporating Hoepker's "Charlotte As Seen By Thomas." To create her work (the "Kruger Composite"), Kruger cropped and enlarged Hoepker's photographic image, transferred it to silkscreen and, in her characteristic style, superimposed three large red blocks containing words that can be read together as, "It's a small world but not if you have to clean it."

In April of 1990, Kruger sold the Kruger Composite to defendant Museum of Contemporary Art L.A. ("MOCA"). MOCA thus acquired the right to display the Kruger Composite . . . and, by separate license, acquired a non-exclusive right to reproduce the work. From October 17, 1999 to February 13, 2000, MOCA displayed the Kruger Composite as one of sixty-four works of art in an exhibit dedicated to Kruger (the "Kruger Exhibit"). In conjunction with the exhibition, MOCA sold gift items in its museum shop featuring the Kruger Composite in the form of postcards, note cubes, magnets and t-shirts. MOCA also sold a book respecting Kruger's works and ideas entitled "Barbara Kruger" (the "Kruger Catalog") that was published jointly with defendant M.I.T. Press. The Kruger Catalog contains three depictions of the Kruger Composite among the hundreds of pictures in the 200-plus page book. . . .

After closing in Los Angeles, the Kruger Exhibit traveled to New York and was presented at defendant Whitney Museum of American Art (the "Whitney") from July 13 through October 22, 2000. The Whitney advertised the Kruger Exhibit in various ways, including newsletters and brochures that incorporated the Kruger Composite. The Whitney also purchased from MOCA an inventory of the Kruger Catalog and various gift items to sell at its museum shop in conjunction with the exhibition. . . .

Around the time the Whitney presented the Kruger Exhibit, reproductions of the Kruger Composite appeared as five-story-high "billboard art" at one or more locations in Manhattan. The Amended Complaint alleges that these billboard installments were commissioned by the Whitney to advertise the Kruger exhibition. The Whitney denies that it paid for the billboards or that the billboards were used to advertise its exhibit. . . . Presumably, by denying that the billboards were advertisements, the Whitney contends they were instead art.

Defendant Education Broadcasting Systems ("EBS") maintained a now-retired website entitled "American Visions" at <www.thirteen.org/americanvisions>. From approximately June 1997 through mid-December 2000, the American Visions virtual "gallery" included a reproduction of the Kruger Composite in its digital collection of contemporary American art. The credit line below the digital reproduction stated that the image was "courtesy of Mary Boone Gallery, New York," and submissions by EBS confirm that the use was licensed by the gallery. . . .

*Discussion*

  *I.   Infringement of Hoepker's Copyright*

     *A.   Status of Hoepker's Copyright*

Hoepker, a German photographer, first published "Charlotte As Seen By Thomas" in Germany in 1960. Pursuant to the Universal Copyright Convention ("U.C.C."), to which both the United States and Germany are signatories,

> Published works of nationals of any Contracting State and works first published in that State shall enjoy in each other Contracting State the same protection as that other State accords to works of its nationals first published in its own territory. U.C.C. Article II(1).

Accordingly, . . . "Hoepker's work published in Germany was given 'in [the United States] the same protection as [the United States] accords to works of its nationals first published in its own territory.' Thus, in 1960, when Hoepker gained a German copyright, he simultaneously gained a copyright in the United States."

Under the terms of the U.C.C., Hoepker's copyright protection in the United States is governed by United States copyright laws. The laws in effect in 1960 afforded an initial copyright term of 28 years, subject to renewal at the end of the 28-year period for another 28 years. In Hoepker's case, his initial copyright term lasted from 1960 to 1988. Because Hoepker failed to renew protection as required by then-applicable United States law, his copyright terminated after this initial term. Thus, in 1988, "Charlotte As Seen by Thomas" fell into the public domain in the United States, and Kruger thereafter was free to incorporate the photographic image into her own work, as she did in 1990.

In 1994, six years after Hoepker's United States copyright expired and four years after Kruger created the Kruger Composite, Congress amended the Copyright Act to restore copyright protection to works of foreign origin that had entered the public domain in the United States for failure to comply with certain formal requirements of United States copyright law. Section 104A of the Copyright Act effectuates the restoration.

Section 104(h)(6) defines a "restored work" as "an original work of authorship that . . . is not in the public domain in its source country . . . [but] is in the public domain in the United States." 17 U.S.C. § 104A(h)(6). "Charlotte As Seen By Thomas" qualifies as a restored work. When Hoepker's photographic image was first published in Germany in 1960, German law provided a copyright term of 25 years. The German law subsequently was revised to afford protection enduring for the life of the author plus seventy years. Since Hoepker's copyright is still extant in Germany, but had fallen into the public domain in the United States, his United States copyright was restored by virtue of Section 104A as of January 1, 1996. . . . Hoepker's term of restored United States copyright endures through 2055, a period of 95 years as provided under the relevant statutes. . . .

### B.  Actions for Restored Copyrights

Recognizing that restoring copyright to works thought to be in the public domain could be problematic to those who had relied on the public domain status, Congress was careful to limit the restoration statute's potential for unanticipated infringement claims. First, the section provides a remedy only for infringing acts that occur after a copyright has been restored. See 17 U.S.C. § 104A(d)(1)-(2). More importantly, Section 104A provides safeguards to "reliance parties." A reliance party is a person or entity who

> engaged in acts before the source country of that work became an eligible country[5] which would have violated [the rights of an author of a restored work] if the restored work had been subject to copyright protection, and who, after the source country becomes an eligible country, continues to engage in such acts . . .; or . . . as the result of the sale or other disposition of [an existing] derivative work . . . is a successor, assignee or licensee of that person. [[5] December 8, 1994 is the relevant date for this case. Germany became an "eligible country" on the date the Uruguay Round Agreements Act was enacted in the United States (December 8, 1994) because Germany was a Berne Convention adherent nation as of that date.] *17 U.S.C. § 104A(h)(4).*

Infringement actions against reliance parties can be commenced (1) only after the restored copyright owner has provided notice of intent to enforce the restored copyright (either by filing a notice with the Copyright Office for publication in the Federal Register or by serving such a notice on the reliance party) and (2) only for those acts of infringement that either commence or continue 12 months or more after such notice is given.[7] See 17 U.S.C. § 104A(d)(2)(A)-(B). [[7] Where the act of infringement consists merely of reproducing the restored work, the 12-month grace period does not apply. See 17 U.S.C. §§ 104A(d)(2)(A)(ii)(III) and 104A(d)(2)(B)(ii)(III).]

Once notice is given and the grace period expires, Section 104A(d)(2) gives restored copyright holders full access to copyright remedies – except when the act of infringement is based on an "existing derivative work." The only remedy for the "exploitation" of an existing derivative work is the payment of "reasonable compensation for [the would-be infringing] conduct." 17 U.S.C. § 104A(d)(3). In other words, a person who created a new work of art by borrowing from a work then in the public domain but now protected by virtue of Section 104A restoration cannot be prohibited from exploiting that independent creation, but can be required to pay a licensing-type fee.

### C.  Application

. . . Hoepker has no cause of action for any infringement of "Charlotte, As Seen By Thomas" occurring between 1988 and 1994. At that time, his photographic image was in the public domain in the United States, and Section 104A restores copyright only for prospective acts of infringement.

As for alleged acts of infringement occurring after the restoration of Hoepker's copyright, Kruger clearly is a reliance party. By creating the Kruger Composite in 1990, Kruger engaged in an act which would have violated Hoepker's copyright – specifically, his exclusive right to create derivative works[10] – if Hoepker's photographic image had been subject to copyright protection at that time. [[10] Hoepker argues that the Kruger Composite is not a derivative work because it lacks sufficient additional creative elements. This argument is without merit, and cannot be the basis for allowing plaintiff to dispense with notice, as if the Kruger Composite were nothing more than a mere "reproduction."] According to the allegations of the complaint, she continued to engage in infringing acts post-restoration. Hence, she satisfies the requirements of a reliance party as set forth in 17 U.S.C. § 104(h)(4)(A). MOCA, too, is clearly a reliance party; having purchased the Kruger Composite, MOCA is, for some purposes, a successor to and, for other purposes, a licensee of Kruger.

As reliance parties, Kruger and MOCA may engage in acts that infringe Hoepker's restored work until, and for twelve months after, Hoepker gives them formal notice, as required by subsections (d)(2)(A) and (d)(2)(B) and as specified in subsections (e)(1) and (e)(2). Hoepker never gave the requisite notice, neither filing a notice of intent with the Copyright Office nor serving such a notice on Kruger or MOCA. Therefore, at this time, Hoepker may not seek redress for any alleged acts of infringement by these parties.

The "exploitation" language of subsection (d)(3) equally precludes Hoepker's current cause of action against the Whitney, M.I.T. Press and EBS. Although not defined anywhere in the Copyright Act, "exploitation" of a work of art at the very least must include the right to license that work to others for display (in the case of the Whitney and EBS) and reproduction (in the case of M.I.T. Press). Arguably, "exploitation" might also include the right to create new derivative works from the existing derivative work (such as MOCA's creation of the museum gift merchandise) – but, because Hoepker's claims against MOCA are precluded by his failure to give notice, Hoepker is unable to complain about these uses at this time.

Accordingly, I . . . dismiss[] Hoepker's copyright claims.

What was the significance of Hoepker's argument that the Kruger Composite was *not* a derivative work – an argument rejected by Judge Hellerstein in footnote 10? If the Kruger Composite were *not* a derivative work, would that have relieved Hoepker of the need to file or service a Notice of Intent to Enforce Copyright, as Hoepker apparently argued? If so, why?

The question of whether a defendant's work *is* a derivative work is an important question, because if it is, the defendant is permitted to continue to exploit its work, subject only to the requirement that it pay "reasonable compensation" to the owner of the restored copyright. You saw this in the chart and in section 104A(d)(3) above. In most cases, it should be apparent whether or not the defendant's work is a "derivative" work. If the defendant's work is a CD or MP3 of a pre-1972 recording, or even a paperback edition of a hardcover book, it isn't. If the defendant's work is a motion picture based on a book or play, it is. Suppose, however, the defendant's work is similar enough to be an infringement of the restored copyright to a once-public domain work, but is different enough that the differences are noticeable. Does that make it a "derivative" work that the defendant may continue to exploit, or despite the noticeable differences, is the defendant's work a "pure" infringement that may be enjoined?

## Dam Things from Denmark v. Russ Berrie & Co.
### 290 F.3d 548 (3rd Cir. 2002)

Rendell, Circuit Judge.

. . . The parties to this appeal, Dam Things from Denmark, a/k/a Troll Company ApS (together "Dam Things"), and Russ Berrie and Company, Inc. ("Russ"), are purveyors of trolls – short, pudgy, plastic dolls with big grins and wild hair. Dam Things, a Danish company, asserts that its copyright in its original troll design, the "Basic Good Luck Troll," has been restored pursuant to 17 U.S.C. § 104A. Section 104A is a highly unusual provision which has restored copyright protection in a vast number of foreign works previously in the public domain. Dam Things brought this action against Russ alleging infringement of its restored copyright. If restoration is proper under the statute, the key remaining issues are whether there is infringement, and if so, whether the infringing works will be totally prohibited or will be entitled to mandatory licenses under § 104A's safe harbor for derivative works.

Upon application by Dam Things, the District Court granted a preliminary injunction forbidding Russ from selling any trolls. . . . In its opinion and order, the District Court explained that the preliminary injunction was warranted because in all likelihood Dam Things could establish that the copyright in the "Good Luck Troll designs" was restored under § 104A and that Dam Things could also prove that Russ infringed its restored copyright.

Russ attacks the District Court's grant of the preliminary injunction. . . . Russ argues that . . . the injunction was improvidently granted because the Russ trolls at least qualify for the safe harbor protection § 104A provides for derivative works. . . .

*I.*

In the 1950s, Thomas Dam, a Danish woodcarver, created a troll figure for his daughter out of rubber. He called it the "Good Luck Troll," claiming that it had the ability to bring good luck to whomever possessed it. Apparently, his creation garnered much attention from the community and Dam decided to sell trolls to the public. He first manufactured them in his home, and soon established a factory outside of his home for this purpose. An article from the Danish weekly magazine *Se & HQr* dated September 4, 1959, features a photograph of Thomas Dam's daughter holding the trolls and tells of the troll's rising popularity – amounting to sales of 10,000 trolls each month in Denmark alone. In 1961, the trolls began to be produced in PVC instead of rubber, increasing their durability. As the troll's success continued, Dam began selling his trolls in other countries. According to Dam Things, the Dam trolls were first sold in the United States in 1961.

In 1960, Thomas Dam applied for a United States design patent for a troll doll, and the patent was issued in 1961. This troll doll was later described by Thomas Dam as "girl-like" as opposed to the original "boy-like" troll, and certain photographs of the troll submitted with the application reflect that the troll has hair pulled back in a ponytail. Dam Things filed applications for U.S. copyright registration of both the boy-like and girl-like trolls in 1964 and then again in 1965 after its initial applications were rejected for improperly designating the copyright holder as Denmark. Dam Things has held and continues to hold a valid Danish copyright in the trolls. In 1965, the

District Court for the District of Columbia held that the Dam Things' trolls submitted for patent and copyright protection were in the public domain, because they were published in the United States with improper notice – they were marked with "Denmark" and the date or with just the date, instead of with the company's name and date – or with no notice at all. *Scandia House Enters., Inc. v. Dam Things Establishment*, 243 F.Supp. 450, 453-54 (D.D.C. 1965) [hereinafter *Scandia*].

In the early 1950s, Russell Berrie was a manufacturer's representative for two companies who sold Dam Things trolls. Berrie started his own company, Russ Berrie and Company, Inc. in 1963 and began to sell trolls manufactured by Dam Things' U.S. licensee, Royalty Design, using the Dam Things molds, in 1967. When Royalty Design went bankrupt, Russ then used the Dam Things molds to manufacture trolls. Berrie claims that in 1987 his company began to modify the trolls. In 1988, Russ sent a Dam Things troll "pencil topper" to be used to make a mold and to manufacture trolls in China. In 1988 Russ also sent to China a photo of a Dam Things troll from the Russ catalog for the purpose of making a mold and manufacturing trolls. In the 1990s, Russ obtained fifteen copyright registrations for trolls – registered as derivative works of the photographs of the Dam Things trolls in the Russ catalogs.

Dam Things now claims copyright infringement of its public domain troll. This unusual claim is made possible by an act of Congress and is grounded on Dam Things' assertion that its copyright in its original troll has been restored pursuant to 17 U.S.C. § 104A. In this legislation, Congress declared that a wide range of foreign works previously in the public domain in this country, perhaps for many years, are once again afforded copyright protection. The United States took this action in an effort to comply with agreements it had entered into with foreign governments regarding intellectual property rights.

Although Russ points out the "extraordinary windfall" Dam Things will receive, and the "extraordinary burden" it will bear, if Dam Things' copyright is restored, the legislature's purpose in providing these protections for foreign copyright holders was to ensure greater protection for American copyright holders abroad.

This protection results from the United States' promise, in the context of the TRIPs annex to the Agreement Establishing the World Trade Organization ("WTO"), to adhere to the Berne Convention, which the United States had entered in 1989. In order to comply with the Berne Convention's "Rule of Retroactivity" contained in Article 18, Congress . . . provided for broad restoration of foreign works. . . .

Dam Things claims that its copyright in its original troll qualifies for automatic restoration in accordance with § 104A. If it does, then the copyright "shall subsist for the remainder of the term of copyright that the work would have otherwise been granted in the United States if the work never entered the public domain in the United States." 17 U.S.C. § 104A(a)(1)(B).

Section 104A also provides some relief for "reliance parties" – American authors who copied the restored works while they were in the public domain in the United States. Section 104A defines "reliance party" in relevant part as "any person who (A) with respect to a particular work, engages in acts, before the source country of that work becomes an eligible country, which would have violated section 106 if the restored work had been subject to copyright protection, and who, after the source country becomes an eligible country, continues to engage in such acts . . . ." Parties who were in fact copying the restored work are given one year to sell the now infringing works after being given a "notice of intent to enforce" ("NIE") by the author of the restored work. But, the statute also provides a safe harbor in the form of a mandatory license for authors of "derivative works"; they are allowed to continue manufacturing and selling their work, but must pay the author of the restored work reasonable compensation.

Dam Things filed this copyright infringement suit. . . . The District Court concluded that Dam Things had "demonstrated a likelihood of success on its copyright infringement claim" and on December 20, 2001 it . . . grant[ed] Dam Things a preliminary injunction . . . [that] . . . prohibited [Russ] from selling its troll dolls as of February 13, 2002 – one year after the date of the NIE. . . . The case comes before us on an expedited appeal.

*II.*

. . . . [W]e will examine the merits of Dam Things' claim under the statute and the District Court's treatment of it. This requires a three-step inquiry: first, does Dam Things hold a restored copyright, second, did Russ infringe Dam Things' copyright, and, third, is Russ protected by the 104A safe harbor for creators of derivative works?

*A. Eligibility for Restoration . . .*

The District Court concluded "that [Dam Things] can prove all of the requisite elements of § 104A and is therefore likely to succeed on the merits of its restoration claim." We agree with this aspect of the District Court's ruling, as it appears that Dam Things will be able to establish that [one of its trolls] satisfies all four requirements for restoration, including first publication in an eligible country.

*B. Copyright Infringement . . .*

We believe that the District Court's analysis was too conclusory, . . . in light of the unique challenges presented by § 104A. We are specifically concerned with the District Court's incomplete consideration of Russ's contention that its trolls would qualify as derivative works. As the United States Courts of Appeals have yet to provide any guidance as to the application of § 104A, . . . we will set forth the proper standards and analysis that needs to be conducted by a district court faced with an issue of whether a § 104A reliance party's work infringes and should be barred, or is a derivative work entitled to licensing.

*1. Infringement*

In cases where copyright infringement is at issue, the Court should first consider whether there has been infringement by comparing each of the allegedly infringing works against the restored work. . . .

*2. Derivative Works*

In light of the special provisions in § 104A, once a court has found infringement, it must consider whether the safe harbor provision is implicated, namely, whether the infringing works are derivatives of the restored work.[22] [[22] If, on the other hand, there was no infringement, Russ would succeed in this case and our analysis would be over. As Nimmer explains: "a work will be considered a derivative work only if it would be considered an infringing work if the material that it has derived from a pre-existing work had been taken without the consent of a copyright proprietor of such pre-existing work." 1 *Nimmer § 3.01.*] Just as with all other works, "originality is a constitutionally mandated prerequisite for copyright protection" for derivative works. However, all aspects of a work need not be original with the author. An author's work can utilize expression from an already existing work created by another author, or even that same author. A new work that utilizes expression from a previously existing work is considered to be derivative of that work. The Copyright Act defines a derivative work as "based upon one or more preexisting works, such as a translation, musical arrangement, dramatization, fictionalization, motion picture version, sound recording, art reproduction, abridgment, condensation, or any other form in which a work may be recast, transformed, or adapted." An author's right to protection of the derivative work only extends to the elements that he has added to the work; he cannot receive protection for the underlying work. Furthermore, if the underlying work is itself protected by copyright, then he will receive no protection at all; on the contrary, he is a copyright infringer, because in order to create his work he has copied the underlying work. However, section 104A obviously creates an exception to this rule and even though the foreign author has a restored copyright, the creator of the derivative work is given special dispensation and is not considered an infringer, and is instead treated as a licensee.

### 3. District Court's Analysis

These descriptions of the tests for copyright infringement and for derivative works illustrate the complex task that a court faces in addressing these issues. In this case, the District Court did assess the similarity between the trolls, and Russ does not challenge the Court's determination that the Russ trolls infringe Dam Things' restored copyright in [one of its trolls]. We therefore focus our discussion on the derivative works analysis. Unfortunately, it is not clear whether the Court actually addressed the derivative works issue which requires a determination as to originality, but, if so, it did not apply the proper standards for originality; instead, it conflated them with the requirements for infringement, which involve findings regarding similarity. Furthermore, the District Court did not properly compare the relevant trolls. . . .

### III.

As the District Court conducted an incomplete legal analysis of the likelihood of Dam Things' success on the merits in this case, we will vacate the District Court's preliminary injunction order and remand this case for further consideration consistent with this opinion. . . .

So, to be certain you're clear about what this opinion means, answer these questions:

- If Russ Berrie's troll *is* a derivative work based on Dam Things' troll, what remedies should the District Court award to Dam Things?
- If Russ Berrie's troll is *not* a derivative work based on Dam Things' troll, what remedies should the District Court award to Dam Things?

Here now are charts and the Copyright Act language they illustrate, dealing with the topics of pre-restoration warranties and performance obligations.

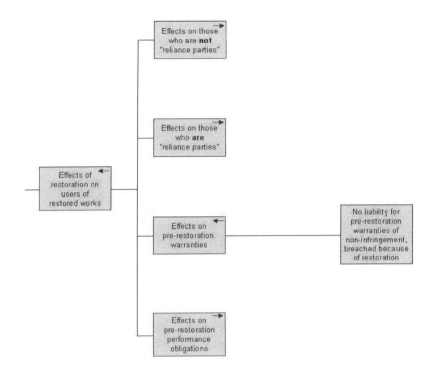

### United States Copyright Act §104A(f)
### Immunity from Warranty and Related Liability

(1) In general. — Any person who warrants, promises, or guarantees that a work does not violate an exclusive right granted in section 106 shall not be liable for legal, equitable, arbitral, or administrative relief if the warranty, promise, or guarantee is breached by virtue of the restoration of copyright under this section, if such warranty, promise, or guarantee is made before January 1, 1995.

This section is significant, because boilerplate provisions of entertainment industry contracts quite commonly require one party to warrant to the other that the work that is the subject of the contract does not infringe copyright. Before this paragraph was enacted, the use of works then in the public domain would not have infringed copyright. And thus warranties of non-infringement concerning such works could be truthfully given without concern for liability. As a result of restoration, however, many such warranties have turned out to be false – through no fault of those who gave them. Congress dealt with this issue, at least in part, by protecting those who gave such warranties. That is why Congress included this provision. Note, however, that Congress did not indicate what should happen if the person who gave such a warranty received an advance against money to be earned by the other party's exploitation of the work after its copyright was restored – by which time the other party may not be able to exploit the work precisely because its copyright has been restored.

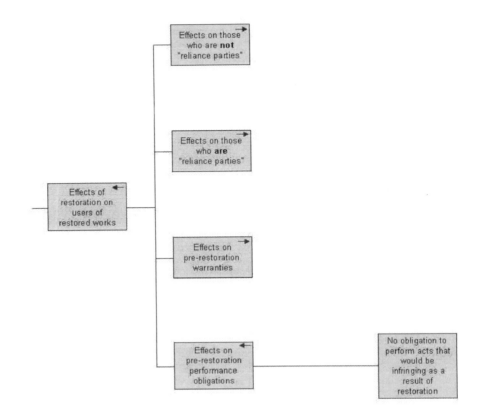

**United States Copyright Act §104A(f)**
**Immunity from Warranty and Related Liability**

(2) Performances. — No person shall be required to perform any act if such performance is made infringing by virtue of the restoration of copyright under the provisions of this section, if the obligation to perform was undertaken before January 1, 1995.

Entertainment industry contracts may also obligate one party to perform in the future in some fashion with respect to a particular work – to distribute, exhibit or publish it for example. Such contracts may have been entered into with respect to foreign works that were then in the public domain whose copyrights have been restored. As a result of the restoration, performance as agreed may constitute infringement that would lead to liability. Congress thought of this, at least in part; that's why this paragraph provides that no one shall be required to perform any act that would be infringing as a result of restoration. Again, however, Congress did not indicate what should happen if the person or company who was to have performed was paid in advance for the performance that is now infringing because of copyright restoration.

## 2. Restoration by the European Union

As you just read, the United States restored the copyrights to certain works of foreign origin when the U.S. joined the WTO, because it was obligated to do so by TRIPs.

European Union members joined the WTO at the same time the United States did, and they too were obligated by TRIPs to restore the copyrights to certain works of foreign – that is, non-EU – origin. But within the EU, membership in the WTO was not the same law-altering event that it was in the United States. Indeed, it doesn't appear that the EU or its members did anything at all to restore foreign copyrights in response to TRIPs. In all likelihood, they didn't, because there wasn't anything they had to do, in order to be in compliance with TRIPs.

Recall that insofar as restoration of copyright is concerned, TRIPs simply gave "teeth" to the already-existing obligation to restore copyrights that was imposed by Berne on its members. In 1996, when TRIPs took effect, all EU members already were Berne members. And EU members seem to have taken their Berne Convention obligations seriously. So if EU members had to do anything about copyright restoration, they already had done it, long before they joined the WTO.

What's more, there may have been little or nothing EU members ever had to do about Berne-required restoration. Recall that the U.S. had to restore the copyrights to works of foreign origin, because those works:

- were published without a copyright notice of the kind then required by the U.S. Copyright Act, or
- were not renewed in the U.S. Copyright Office when their initial 28-year terms of copyright expired, or
- were authored by nationals of countries with which the U.S. did not have a copyright treaty, and were first published in a country with which the U.S. did not have a copyright treaty.

By contrast, the copyright laws of EU members,

- never had copyright notice requirements that injected non-complying works into the public domain,
- never required works to be registered or renewed to be protected, and
- had been members of Berne for a very long time, so that few if any works were authored by nationals of *non*-treaty countries or first published in *non*-treaty countries.

This doesn't mean that EU members have *never* had to restore foreign copyrights. They did, but not because of Berne or TRIPs. They did because of the EC Directive in 1993 that harmonized the term of copyright protection throughout the European Union. You read a brief excerpt from that Directive in Chapter 5, where it illustrated the EU's response to the fact that Denmark had a much shorter duration than did Germany for sound recording copyrights. The rest of that Directive is reproduced below. As you read it, observe that its primary purpose was to lengthen the duration of copyright in most EU member countries – from life of the author plus 50 years, to life of the author plus 70 years – in order to bring them in line with the life-plus-70 copyright duration that already existed in Germany for most types of works.

As you read the Directive, note too that it does say something about copyright restoration. The reason it does is this. The Directive became effective in 1995, and when it became effective, it required EU members with life-plus-50 durations to add 20 years to the durations of any copyrights that had not yet expired. What, though, about works whose life-plus-50 copyrights had expired between 1976 and 1994? Did those works get another 20 years too? The answer matters, even today, because if it is "yes," then works whose copyrights expired before the Directive became effective are protected again, today.

### COUNCIL DIRECTIVE 93/98/EEC of 29 October 1993
### harmonizing the term of protection of
### copyright and certain related rights

*The Council of the European Communities,*

Having regard to the Treaty establishing the European Economic Community . . .

(1) Whereas the Berne Convention for the protection of literary and artistic works and the International Convention for the protection of performers, producers of phonograms and broadcasting organizations (Rome Convention) lay down only minimum terms of protection of the rights they refer to, leaving the Contracting States free to grant longer terms; whereas certain Member States have exercised this entitlement; . . .

(2) Whereas there are consequently differences between the national laws governing the terms of protection of copyright and related rights, which are liable to impede the free movement of goods and freedom to provide services, and to distort competition in the common market; whereas therefore with a view to the smooth operation of the internal market, the laws of the Member States should be harmonized so as to make terms of protection identical throughout the Community; . . .

(5) Whereas the minimum term of protection laid down by the Berne Convention, namely the life of the author and 50 years after his death, was intended to provide protection for the author and the first two generations of his descendants; whereas the average lifespan in the Community has grown longer, to the point where this term is no longer sufficient to cover two generations;

(6) Whereas certain Member States have granted a term longer than 50 years after the death of the author in order to offset the effects of the world wars on the exploitation of authors' works; . . .

(8) Whereas under the Community position adopted for the Uruguay Round negotiations under the General Agreement on Tariffs and Trade (GATT) the term of protection for producers of phonograms should be 50 years after first publication; . . .

(11) Whereas in order to establish a high level of protection which at the same time meets the requirements of the internal market and the need to establish a legal environment conducive to the harmonious development of literary and artistic creation in the Community, the term of protection for copyright should be harmonized at 70 years after the death of the author or

70 years after the work is lawfully made available to the public, and for related rights at 50 years after the event which sets the term running; . . .

(17) Whereas the protection of photographs in the Member States is the subject of varying regimes; whereas in order to achieve a sufficient harmonization of the term of protection of photographic works, in particular of those which, due to their artistic or professional character, are of importance within the internal market, it is necessary to define the level of originality required in this Directive; whereas a photographic work within the meaning of the Berne Convention is to be considered original if it is the author's own intellectual creation reflecting his personality, no other criteria such as merit or purpose being taken into account; whereas the protection of other photographs should be left to national law; . . .

(22) Whereas, for works whose country of origin within the meaning of the Berne Convention is a third country and whose author is not a Community national, comparison of terms of protection should be applied, provided that the term accorded in the Community does not exceed the term laid down in this Directive; . . .

(25) Whereas, for the smooth functioning of the internal market this Directive should be applied as from 1 July 1995; . . .

(27) Whereas respect of acquired rights and legitimate expectations is part of the Community legal order; whereas Member States may provide in particular that in certain circumstances the copyright and related rights which are revived pursuant to this Directive may not give rise to payments by persons who undertook in good faith the exploitation of the works at the time when such works lay within the public domain,

*Has Adopted this Directive:*

*Article 1     Duration of authors' rights*

1.   The rights of an author of a literary or artistic work within the meaning of Article 2 of the Berne Convention shall run for the life of the author and for 70 years after his death, irrespective of the date when the work is lawfully made available to the public. . . .

*Article 2     Cinematographic or audiovisual works*

1.   The principal director of a cinematographic or audiovisual work shall be considered as its author or one of its authors. Member States shall be free to designate other co-authors.

2.   The term of protection of cinematographic or audiovisual works shall expire 70 years after the death of the last of the following persons to survive, whether or not these persons are designated as co-authors: the principal director, the author of the screenplay, the author of the dialogue and the composer of music specifically created for use in the cinematographic or audiovisual work.

*Article 3     Duration of related rights*

1.   The rights of performers shall expire 50 years after the date of the performance. However, if a fixation of the performance is lawfully published or lawfully communicated to the public within this period, the rights shall expire 50 years from the date of the first such publication or the first such communication to the public, whichever is the earlier.

2.   The rights of producers of phonograms shall expire 50 years after the fixation is made. However, if the phonogram is lawfully published or lawfully communicated to the public during this period, the rights shall expire 50 years from the date of the first such publication or the first such communication to the public, whichever is the earlier.

3.   The rights of producers of the first fixation of a film shall expire 50 years after the fixation is made. However, if the film is lawfully published or lawfully communicated to the public during this period, the rights shall expire 50 years from the date of the first such publication or the first such communication to the public, whichever is the earlier. The term 'film' shall designate a cinematographic or audiovisual work or moving images, whether or not accompanied by sound.

4.   The rights of broadcasting organizations shall expire 50 years after the first transmission of a broadcast, whether this broadcast is transmitted by wire or over the air, including by cable or satellite. . . .

*Article 6     Protection of photographs*

Photographs which are original in the sense that they are the author's own intellectual creation shall be protected in accordance with Article 1. No other criteria shall be applied to determine their eligibility for protection. Member States may provide for the protection of other photographs.

*Article 7     Protection vis-à-vis third countries*

1.   Where the country of origin of a work, within the meaning of the Berne Convention, is a third country, and the author of the work is not a Community national, the term of protection granted by the Member States shall expire on the date of expiry of the protection granted in the country of origin of the work, but may not exceed the term laid down in Article 1.

2.   The terms of protection laid down in Article 3 shall also apply in the case of rightholders who are not Community nationals, provided Member States grant them protection. However, without prejudice to the international obligations of the Member States, the term of protection granted by Member States shall expire no later than the date of expiry of the protection granted in the country of which the rightholder is a national and may not exceed the term laid down in Article 3. . . .

*Article 10     Application in time . . .*

2.   The terms of protection provided for in this Directive shall apply to all works and subject matter which are protected in at least one Member State, on . . . [July 1, 1995]. . . .

3.   This Directive shall be without prejudice to any acts of exploitation performed before [July 1, 1995]. . . . Member States shall adopt the necessary provisions to protect in particular acquired rights of third parties. . .

.

As you see, the Directive did not give EU member countries much guidance about what to do about restoration. It required them to restore the copyrights of "all works . . . which are protected in at least one Member State [of which Germany, with its life-plus-70 term, was one], on . . . [July 1, 1995]. . . ." And the Directive required ("shall adopt") EU members to "protect" the "acquired rights" of third parties – that is, parties who had been using works that were in the public domain before their copyrights were restored. But the Directive didn't tell them how to do that. Here is how Germany and the United Kingdom complied with the Directive.

## German Law on Copyright and Neighboring Rights
### [In German: Gesetz über Urheberrecht und verwandte Schutzrechte or "Urheberrechtsgesetz"]

*Duration of Copyright*

64. Copyright shall expire 70 years after the author's death.

*Photographic Works*

137a. (1) The provisions of this Law as regards the term of copyright shall also apply to those photographic works whose term of protection under prior law has not yet expired on July 1, 1985.

(2) Where a right of exploitation in a photographic work has been assigned or transferred to another person, such assignment or transfer shall not extend, in case of doubt, to the period of time by which the term of copyright in photographic works has been extended.

*Transitional Provision for the Implementation of Directive 93/98/EEC*

137f. (1) . . . [T]he provisions of this Law concerning the term of protection are also of application . . . to works and neighboring rights whose protection has not yet expired on July 1, 1995.

(2) The provisions of this Law . . . shall also be of application to works whose protection under this Law has expired prior to July 1, 1995, but which still subsists at such date under the law of another Member State of the European Union or of a Contracting State to the Agreement on the European Economic Area. . . .

(3) Where the protection for a work within the territory to which this Law applies resumes in accordance with subsection (2), the resumed rights shall belong to the author. Any act of exploitation begun prior to July 1, 1995, may be continued, however, in the agreed form. Equitable remuneration shall be paid for exploitation after July 1, 1995. . . .

## UK Statutory Instrument 1995 No. 3297
### The Duration of Copyright and Rights in Performances Regulations 1995
### [amending the UK Copyright, Designs and Patents Act 1988]

*Duration of copyright in literary, dramatic, musical or artistic works . . .*

12 (1) The following provisions have effect with respect to the duration of copyright in a literary, dramatic, musical or artistic work.

(2) Copyright expires at the end of the period of 70 years [increased from 50 years] from the end of the calendar year in which the author dies. . . .

(6) Where the country of origin of the work is not an EEA state [i.e., the European Economic Area, consisting of EU countries plus Norway, Iceland and Liechtenstein] and the author of the work is not a national of an EEA state, the duration of copyright is that to which the work is entitled in the country of origin, provided that does not exceed the period which would apply under subsection[ ] (2). . . .

*Duration of copyright in sound recordings and films . . .*

13A(1) The following provisions have effect with respect to the duration of copyright in a sound recording.

(2) Copyright expires—

    (a) at the end of the period of 50 years from the end of the calendar year in which it is made, or

    (b) if during that period it is released, 50 years from the end of the calendar year in which it is released; . . .

(4) Where the author of a sound recording is not a national of an EEA state, the duration of copyright is that to which the sound recording is entitled in the country of which the author is a national, provided that does not exceed the period which would apply under subsection[ ] (2). . . .

13B(1) The following provisions have effect with respect to the duration of copyright in a film.
(2) Copyright expires at the end of the period of 70 years from the end of the calendar year in which the death occurs of the last to die of the following persons—
(a) the principal director,
(b) the author of the screenplay,
(c) the author of the dialogue, or
(d) the composer of music specially created for and used in the film;
. . .
(7) Where the country of origin is not an EEA state and the author of the film is not a national of an EEA state, the duration of copyright is that to which the work is entitled in the country of origin, provided that does not exceed the period which would apply under subsection[ ] (2) . . . .

*Duration of copyright: application of new provisions*

16 The new provisions relating to duration of copyright apply—
(a) to copyright works made after commencement [i.e., the "commencement" date of this law, January 1, 1996];
(b) to existing works which first qualify for copyright protection after commencement . . . ; and
(d) to existing works in which copyright expired before 31st December 1995 but which were on 1st July 1995 protected in another EEA state under legislation relating to copyright or related rights.

*Extended and revived copyright*

17 In the following provisions . . .
- "extended copyright" means any copyright which subsists by virtue of the new provisions after the date on which it would have expired under the 1988 provisions; and
- "revived copyright" means any copyright which subsists by virtue of the new provisions after having expired under the 1988 provisions or any earlier enactment relating to copyright.

*Ownership of extended copyright*

18 (1) The person who is the owner of the copyright in a work immediately before commencement is as from commencement the owner of any extended copyright in the work. . . .

*Ownership of revived copyright*

19 (1) The person who was the owner of the copyright in a work immediately before it expired (the "former copyright owner") is as from commencement the owner of any revived copyright in the work.
. . .

*Prospective ownership of extended or revived copyright*

20 (1) Where by an agreement made before commencement in relation to extended or revived copyright, and signed by or on behalf of the prospective owner of the copyright, the prospective owner purports

to assign the extended or revived copyright (wholly or partially) to another person, then if, on commencement the assignee or another person claiming under him would be entitled as against all other persons to require the copyright to be vested in him, the copyright shall vest in the assignee or his successor in title by virtue of this paragraph.

(2) A licence granted by a prospective owner of extended or revived copyright is binding on every successor in title to his interest (or prospective interest) in the right, except a purchaser in good faith for valuable consideration and without notice (actual or constructive) of the licence or a person deriving title from such a purchaser; . . .

(3) In paragraph (2) "prospective owner" includes a person who is prospectively entitled to extended or revived copyright by virtue of such an agreement as is mentioned in paragraph (1).

*Extended copyright: existing licences, agreement, &c.*

21 (1) Any copyright licence, any term or condition of an agreement relating to the exploitation of a copyright work, or any waiver or assertion of moral rights, which—

(a) subsists immediately before commencement in relation to an existing copyright work, and

(b) is not to expire before the end of the copyright period under the 1988 provisions, shall continue to have effect during the period of any extended copyright, subject to any agreement to the contrary. . . .

*Revived copyright: saving for acts of exploitation when work in public domain, &c*

23 (1) No act done before commencement shall be regarded as infringing revived copyright in a work.

(2) It is not an infringement of revived copyright in a work—

(a) to do anything after commencement in pursuance of arrangements made before 1st January 1995 at a time when copyright did not subsist in the work, or

(b) to issue to the public after commencement copies of the work made before 1st July 1995 at a time when copyright did not subsist in the work.

(3) It is not an infringement of revived copyright in a work to do anything after commencement in relation to a literary, dramatic, musical or artistic work or a film made before commencement, or made in pursuance of arrangements made before commencement, which contains a copy of that work or is an adaptation of that work if—

(a) the copy or adaptation was made before 1st July 1995 at a time when copyright did not subsist in the work in which revived copyright subsists, or

(b) the copy or adaptation was made in pursuance of arrangements made before 1st July 1995 at a time when copyright did not subsist in the work in which revived copyright subsists.

(4) It is not an infringement of revived copyright in a work to do after commencement anything which is a restricted act in relation to the work if the act is done at a time when, or is done in pursuance of arrangements made at a time when, the name and address of a person entitled to authorise the act cannot by reasonable inquiry be ascertained.

(5) In this Regulation "arrangements" means arrangements for the exploitation of the work in question.

(6) It is not an infringement of any moral right to do anything which by virtue of this Regulation is not an infringement of copyright.

*Revived copyright: use as of right subject to reasonable royalty*

24 (1) In the case of a work in which revived copyright subsists any acts restricted by the copyright shall be treated as licensed by the copyright owner, subject only to the payment of such reasonable royalty or other remuneration as may be agreed or determined in default of agreement by the Copyright Tribunal.

(2) A person intending to avail himself of the right conferred by this Regulation must give reasonable notice of his intention to the copyright owner, stating when he intends to begin to do the acts.

(3) If he does not give such notice, his acts shall not be treated as licensed.

(4) If he does give such notice, his acts shall be treated as licensed and a reasonable royalty or other remuneration shall be payable in respect of them despite the fact that its amount is not agreed or determined until later. . . .

Suppose that the copyright to a pre-1966 *American* recording was *not* restored by German law, but *was* restored by British law. Would that *American* recording be entitled to copyright protection *in Germany*, under the EU Directive, precisely because it was protected in the U.K. on January 1, 1966? This exact question arose in Germany, and was answered in the following Court of Justice decision.

### Sony Music Entertainment (Germany) GmbH
### v. Falcon Neue Medien Vertrieb GmbH
### Case C-240/07, Court of Justice of the European Communities
### (2009)

. . .

*Legal context*

*Community legislation*

Article 12 of Council Directive 92/100/EEC . . . on rental right and lending right and on certain rights related to copyright in the field of intellectual property, provided:

'. . . the rights referred to in this Directive of performers, phonogram producers and broadcasting organisations shall not expire before the end of the respective terms provided by the ... [International] Convention [for the Protection of Performers, Producers of Phonograms and Broadcasting Organisations. . .]. The rights referred to in this Directive for producers of the first fixations of films shall not expire before the end of a period of 20 years computed from the end of the year in which the fixation was made.'

The term of protection referred to in Article 12 of Directive 92/100 was extended to 50 years by Article 3 of Council Directive 93/98/EEC . . . harmonising the term of protection of copyright and certain related rights.

Directive 2006/116 codified Directive 93/98. Article 3(2) of Directive 2006/116 provides that:

'The rights of producers of phonograms shall expire 50 years after the fixation is made. . .

However, this paragraph shall not have the effect of protecting anew the rights of producers of phonograms where, through the expiry of the term of protection granted them pursuant to Article 3(2) of Directive 93/98/EEC in its version before amendment by Directive 2001/ 29/EEC . . . they were no longer protected on 22 December 2002.'

Article 7(1) and (2) of Directive 2006/116 provides that:

'1.  Where the country of origin of a work . . . is a third country, and the author of the work is not a Community national, the term of protection granted by the Member States shall expire on the date of expiry of the protection granted in the country of origin of the work, but may not exceed the term laid down in Article 1.

2.  The terms of protection laid down in Article 3 shall also apply in the case of rightholders who are not Community nationals, provided Member States grant them protection. However, without prejudice to the international obligations of the Member States, the term of protection granted by Member States shall expire no later than the date of expiry of the protection granted in the country of which the rightholder is a national and may not exceed the term laid down in Article 3.'

Article 10(1) to (3) of Directive 2006/116, headed 'Application in time', is worded as follows:

'1.  Where a term of protection which is longer than the corresponding term provided for by this Directive was already running in a Member State on 1 July 1995, this Directive shall not have the effect of shortening that term of protection in that Member State.

2.  The terms of protection provided for in this Directive shall apply to all works and subject-matter which were protected in at least one Member State on the date referred to in paragraph 1, pursuant to national provisions on copyright or related rights, or which meet the criteria for protection under . . . Directive 92/100. . . .

3.  This Directive shall be without prejudice to any acts of exploitation performed before the date referred to in paragraph 1. Member States shall adopt the necessary provisions to protect in particular acquired rights of third parties.'

*National legislation*

Paragraph 137f of the [German] Law on copyright . . . constitutes the transitional rule in respect of . . . Directive 93/98. . . .

Paragraph 137f(2) and (3) of the [German law] . . . is [ quoted above, in this chapter]. . . .

*The dispute in the main proceedings and the questions referred for a preliminary ruling*

.  .  .  Falcon distributes two phonograms containing recordings of performances by the artist Bob Dylan. The first CD is entitled 'Bob Dylan – Blowin in the Wind', the second 'Bob Dylan – Gates of Eden'.

Those phonograms include songs which feature on the albums 'Bob Dylan – Bringing It All Back Home', 'The Times They Are A-Changin'' and

'Highway 61 Revisited'. Those albums were released in the USA before 1 January 1966. . . .

Sony applied to [a German trial court] for an injunction prohibiting Falcon from copying and distributing the phonograms 'Bob Dylan – Blowin in the Wind' and 'Bob Dylan – Gates of Eden', or from having others copy and distribute them on its behalf. Further, Sony asked the court . . . to determine Falcon's liability for damages.

Falcon submitted that no phonogram producer owns the rights in Germany to Bob Dylan albums recorded prior to 1 January 1966.

The [German trial court] dismissed Sony's application. Upon appeal by Sony, the appellate court . . . dismissed Sony's appeal, considering that, under the Convention for the Protection of Producers of Phonograms against Unauthorised Duplication of their Phonograms . . . , in force both in Germany and the United States, such producers of phonograms are entitled to copyright protection pursuant to Paragraph 85 of the . . . German Copyright Law . . . only in relation to activities which took place after 1 January 1966. Moreover, the appellate court considered that music recordings produced prior to that date were also not entitled to protection under Paragraph 137f of the [German copyright law]. . . [because] Paragraph 137f(2) . . . did not apply to phonograms produced prior to 1 January 1966, as these had at no time been protected in Germany.

It was in those circumstances that, Sony applied for 'Revision' of the judgment of the appellate court to the [Supreme Court of Germany] which, taking the view that the outcome of the proceedings before it depended on the interpretation of Article 10(2) of Directive 2006/116, decided to stay proceedings and to refer the following questions to the Court [of Justice of the European Community]. . . .

*The questions referred. . .*

It is . . . clear . . . that, pursuant to [German copyright law], companies based in the United States are entitled in Germany to . . . protection [for sound recordings] . . . only in respect of activities from 1 January 1966, which is not the case of the phonograms at issue in the main proceedings. Nor does the application of Paragraph 137f(2) of the [German copyright law] grant protection to those phonograms on German territory, since that provision presupposes that the work at issue was protected on that territory before 1 July 1995, which was never the case of the phonograms at issue.

It should also be stated that . . . United Kingdom legislation affords protection to phonograms fixated before 1 January 1966 and this was extended to phonograms of American producers which were released in the United States.

*Question 1*

By its first question, the national court [i.e., the German Supreme Court] asks whether the term of protection provided for under Article 10(2) of Directive 2006/116 should be applied to subject-matter that has never been protected in the Member State in which that protection is sought.

According to Article 10(2) of Directive 2006/116, the terms of protection of phonogram producers, provided for in Article 3(2) of that directive are to apply to the subject-matter at issue if, on 1 July 1995, it was protected in the territory of at least one Member State, pursuant to national provisions on copyright or related rights, or if it met the criteria for protection provided for in Directive 92/100.

Thus, according to the wording of Article 10(2), the first alternative requirement under that provision concerns the prior existence of protection for the subject-matter at issue in at least one Member State. That provision does not require that Member State to be the State in which the protection for which Directive 2006/116 provides is sought.

Moreover, it should be pointed out that recital 3 in the preamble to Directive 2006/116 states that differences between national laws are liable to impede the free movement of goods and freedom to provide services and to distort competition in the common market. With a view to the smooth operation of the internal market, that directive is intended to harmonise the laws of the Member States so as to make terms of protection identical throughout the Community.

In those circumstances, to interpret Article 10(2) of Directive 2006/116 as meaning that application of the first alternative requirement of that provision is conditional on the prior existence of protection under the national legislation of the Member State in which the protection for which the directive provides is sought, even though such prior protection has been granted in another Member State, would comply neither with the terms of the provision at issue nor with the purpose of that directive.

Accordingly, the answer to the first question is that the term of protection laid down in Directive 2006/116 is also applicable, pursuant to Article 10(2) of that directive, where the subject-matter at issue has at no time been protected in the Member State in which the protection is sought.

*Question 2. . .*

By this question, the national court asks whether national provisions governing the protection of holders of copyright-related rights who are not Community nationals constitute national provisions within the meaning of Article 10(2) of Directive 2006/116.

It must be borne in mind that . . . the provisions of Article 10(2) of Directive 2006/116 pursue the objective of protection and apply to all works and subject-matter which on 1 July 1995 were protected under the provisions of at least one Member State on copyright or related rights.

In that regard, it is not apparent from its wording that Article 10(2) concerns only national provisions on copyright or related rights for the protection of holders of such rights who are Community nationals. Under the terms of that provision, Member States must grant the terms of protection for which Directive 2006/116 provides for all works and subject-matter which on 1 July 1995 were protected as such in at least one Member State.

In the context of the application of Article 10(2) of Directive 2006/116, it is thus necessary to examine whether it is possible to regard a work or subject-matter as being protected on 1 July 1995 in at least one Member State without consideration of the nationality of the holder of the copyright-related rights in that work or subject-matter.

. . . [The German Supreme Court] is uncertain whether an interpretation of Article 10(2) of Directive 2006/116 which recognised holders of copyright-related rights who are not Community nationals as entitled to the benefit of that provision would be compatible with Article 7(2) of that directive.

In that regard, it should be pointed out that the objective of Article 10(2) of Directive 2006/116 is to specify the conditions in which the terms of protection of copyright-related rights laid down by that directive are to apply . . . to existing situations. That provision provides for the application of those terms in respect of works and subject-matter which benefited on 1 July 1995

281

from the protection granted by national provisions on copyright or related rights in at least one Member State.

The intention of Article 10(2) is not to rule out the solution laid down by Article 7(2) of Directive 2006/116 in all cases where the terms of protection provided for by the directive are sought by holders of copyright-related rights who are not Community nationals in relation to a work or subject-matter which does not satisfy either of the two alternative conditions of the transitional provision of Article 10(2) of that directive.

The objective of Article 7(2) is to regulate the protection of copyright-related rights with regard to holders of such rights who are not Community nationals and the Article provides, to that end, for the terms of protection indicated in Article 3 of the directive to apply in respect of such rightholders, provided that Member States grant them protection.

In view of the foregoing, the question whether, in the context of Article 10(2) of Directive 2006/116, a holder of copyright-related rights in a work or subject-matter who is a national of a non-Member State was protected on 1 July 1995 in at least one Member State must be assessed in the light of the national provisions of that Member State and not in the light of the national provisions of the Member State in which the protection for which that directive provides is sought. . . .

It follows that, in respect of a work or subject-matter protected on 1 July 1995 in at least one Member State according to the national provisions of that Member State, the fact that the rightholder thus protected is a national of a non-Member State and is not entitled, in the Member State in which the term of protection provided for by Directive 2006/116 is sought, to protection under the national law of that Member State, is not decisive for the application of Article 10(2) of the directive. What matters is whether the work or the subject-matter at issue was covered by protection on 1 July 1995, under the national provisions of at least one Member State.

. . . [I]n the United Kingdom the protection provided for by national law applies to phonograms fixated before 1 January 1966 and the phonograms at issue in the main proceedings already benefited from protection in that Member State on 1 July 1995. . . .

Consequently, the answer to Question 2(a) is that Article 10(2) of Directive 2006/116 is to be interpreted as meaning that the terms of protection provided for by that directive apply in a situation where the work or subject-matter at issue was, on 1 July 1995, protected as such in at least one Member State under that Member State's national legislation on copyright and related rights and where the holder of such rights in respect of that work or subject-matter, who is a national of a non-Member State, benefited, at that date, from the protection provided for by those national provisions. . . .

So, what was the answer? Was Sony entitled to protection in *Germany* for the Bob Dylan recordings?

---

Italy took a different approach (from Germany and the U.K.) to protecting the acquired rights of third parties. Its approach did not satisfy at least one of those third parties; and the resulting dispute eventually made its way to the Court of Justice of the European Communities. As you read the following opinion, think about

- whether Germany and the UK gave third parties more or less protection – i.e., permission to continue to use works that used to be in the public domain – than Italy did, and
- whether it is likely that Germany's and the UK's approaches would be approved by the Court of Justice.

## Butterfly Music Srl v. Carosello Edizioni Musicali e Discografiche Srl (CEMED)
### Case C-60/98, [2000] ECR I-3939
### (Court of Justice of the European Communities 2000)

1. . . . [T]he Tribunale Civile e Penale . . . , Milan, referred to the Court for a preliminary ruling . . . a question on the interpretation of Article 10 of Council Directive 93/98/EEC of 29 October 1993 harmonising the term of protection of copyright and certain related rights ( . . . "the Directive").

2. That question has been raised in proceedings between Butterfly Music Srl ("Butterfly") and Carosello Edizioni Musicali e Discografiche Srl ("CEMED") [a record company], supported by the Federazione Industria Musicale Italiana ("FIMI") [a trade association representing Italian record producers], concerning the right to reproduce and exploit recordings which, after entering the public domain under the legislation previously in force, have again become protected as a result of the provisions transposing the Directive into national law.

3. The Directive is designed to put an end to the differences between national laws governing the terms of protection of copyright and related rights and to harmonise those laws by laying down identical terms of protection throughout the Community. Thus, under Article 3, the term of protection for rights of performers and of producers of phonograms was set at 50 years.

4. In accordance with Article 10(2) of the Directive, that term is to apply to all works and subject-matter protected in at least one Member State on the date laid down for implementation of the Directive, namely 1 July 1995 at the latest. However, Article 10(3) states that the "Directive shall be without prejudice to any acts of exploitation performed" before that date and that the "Member States shall adopt the necessary provisions to protect in particular acquired rights of third parties".

5. In Italy, the term of protection for phonograph records and analogous media and for performers was set at 30 years by Law No 633 of 22 April 1941 on Copyright. . . . That Law was amended by . . . Law No 52 of 6 February 1996 ( . . . "Law No 52/96"). . . .

6. Under Article 17(1) of Law No 52/96, the term of protection for the rights of the abovementioned persons was extended from 30 to 50 years. Article 17(2) of Law No 52/96 . . . specifies that that term of protection also applies to works and rights no longer protected under the periods of protection previously in force provided that, under the new periods, they are protected afresh as at 29 June 1995. However, under Article 17(4) of Law No 52/96 . . . those provisions are to apply without prejudice to instruments and contracts predating 29 June 1995 and to rights lawfully acquired and exercised by third parties thereunder. In particular, the following are not affected: . . .

"(b) the distribution, for three months following the date of entry into force of this Law, of phonograph records and analogous media in respect of which rights of use have expired under the previous legislation, by the persons who have reproduced and marketed the said media before the date of entry into force of this Law".

7. Butterfly, which is engaged in the production and distribution of music media, produced in November 1992, with the agreement of CEMED, a phonogram producer which held the rights over the original recordings, and with authorisation from the Società Italiana Autori e Editori (Italian Society of Authors and Publishers; "SIAE") [Italy's mechanical and performing rights society], a compact disc entitled "Briciole di Baci" ("the CD") containing 16 songs interpreted by the singer Mina, which had been recorded in the period from 1958 to 1962.

8. Those recordings entered the public domain at the end of 1992, but subsequently, in accordance with the Directive . . . and Law No 52/96 increased the term of protection for rights of producers of phonograms and of performers from 30 to 50 years.

9. At the end of 1995 and the beginning of 1996, CEMED, relying on the "revival" of its rights which resulted from the term of protection laid down by the Directive, sent Butterfly a letter of formal notice calling on it to cease the reproduction and distribution of the CD. Butterfly then brought an action, on 10 May 1996, before the Tribunale Civile e Penale, Milan, for a declaration that it was entitled to reproduce the recordings on the CD.

10. Before the national court, Butterfly contended in particular that the Directive implicitly precluded the renewal of rights which had expired and that, even if the "revival" of those rights were recognised, Law No 52/96 . . . did not comply with the obligation to protect acquired rights of third parties expressly laid down in Article 10(3) of the Directive. CEMED, supported by FIMI . . . counterclaimed for an order prohibiting Butterfly from making any further use of the works covered by the new period of protection.

11. The Tribunale Civile e Penale considered that it was clear from Article 10(2) of the Directive that the protection of rights could be revived following the extension of the periods which was required in certain Member States by harmonisation of the terms of protection. However, having regard to the obligation to protect acquired rights of third parties, it questioned the lawfulness of Article 17(4) of Law No 52/96 . . . which provides only a limited possibility for sound-recording media in respect of which rights of exploitation entered the public domain before the date on which the Law entered into force to be distributed by third parties who, before that date, had acquired the right to reproduce and market them. It therefore decided to refer the following question to the Court for a preliminary ruling:

> "Is the interpretation of Article 10 of Directive 93/98/EEC of 29 October 1993, particularly where it provides for the adoption of 'the necessary provisions to protect in particular acquired rights of third parties', compatible with Article 17(4) of Law No [52/96] . . . ?"

. . .

*The question submitted*

15. By its question, the national court asks the Court whether Article 10(3) of the Directive precludes a provision of national law such as the provision which, in Law No 52/96 . . . lays down a limited period in which sound-recording media may be distributed by persons who, by reason of the expiry of the rights relating to those media under the previous legislation, had been able to reproduce and market them before that Law entered into force.

16. Butterfly suggests that the Court should rule that Law No 52/96 . . . is inconsistent with Article 10 of the Directive in that it does not confer suitable protection for record producers who have undertaken in good faith the

exploitation of works whose protection is revived following the extension of the term of protection of copyright and related rights. It maintains, in particular, that the three-month limit, laid down in Article 17(4)(b) . . . of Law No 52/96, on the right to distribute records granted to persons who reproduced and marketed them before Law No 52/96 entered into force, is unreasonable and conflicts with the absence, under Article 17(4)(a) . . . of that Law, of a limit for the distribution of literary works which entered the public domain.

17. CEMED, FIMI, the Italian Government and the Commission, on the other hand, suggest that the Court should rule that Article 10 of the Directive does not preclude national legislation such as Law No 52/96. . . . They contend, in particular, that rules which restrict copyright and related rights must be interpreted restrictively. FIMI and the Italian Government maintain, furthermore, that the more favourable treatment accorded by Law No 52/96 . . . to publishers of literary works which have entered the public domain is justified by the high investment costs which they must bear. Finally, while the Commission does not share that last view, it considers that the period laid down for the distribution of stocks of phonographic media, which in fact lasted nearly a year taking account of the Decree-Laws promulgated in 1994 and 1995, is sufficient to comply with the obligation under the Directive to protect acquired rights of third parties.

18. As the national court has observed, it is clear from Article 10(2) of the Directive that application of the terms of protection laid down by the Directive may have the effect, in the Member States which had a shorter term of protection under their legislation, of protecting afresh works or subject-matter which had entered the public domain.

19. This consequence results from the express will of the Community legislature. While the Commission's original proposal for the Directive provided that its provisions would apply "to rights which have not expired on or before 31 December 1994", the European Parliament amended that proposal by introducing new wording which was, in essence, taken up in the final version of the Directive.

20. That solution was adopted in order to achieve as rapidly as possible the objective, formulated, in particular, in the second recital in the preamble to the Directive, of harmonising the national laws governing the terms of protection of copyright and related rights and to avoid the situation where rights have expired in some Member States but are protected in others.

21. However, Article 10(3) makes it clear that the Directive is without prejudice to any acts of exploitation performed before the date laid down for its implementation, that is to say 1 July 1995 at the latest, and that the Member States are to lay down the necessary provisions to protect in particular acquired rights of third parties.

22. Guidance on that provision is provided by the final two recitals in the preamble to the Directive. The 26th recital states that "Member States should remain free to adopt provisions on the interpretation, adaptation and further execution of contracts on the exploitation of protected works and other subject-matter which were concluded before the extension of the term of protection resulting from this Directive". According to the 27th recital, "respect of acquired rights and legitimate expectations is part of the Community legal order . . . Member States may provide in particular that in certain circumstances the copyright and related rights which are revived pursuant to this Directive may not give rise to payments by persons who

undertook in good faith the exploitation of the works at the time when such works lay within the public domain".

23. Reading these various provisions together, it is apparent that the Directive did provide for the possibility that copyright and related rights which had expired under the applicable legislation before the date of its implementation could be revived, without prejudice to acts of exploitation performed before that date, while leaving it to the Member States to adopt measures to protect acquired rights of third parties. In view of the wording of those provisions, such measures must be regarded as measures which the Member States are obliged to adopt, but whose detail is left to the discretion of the Member States, provided, however, that they do not have the overall effect of preventing the application of the new terms of protection on the date laid down by the Directive.

24. . . . [T]hat solution is, moreover, consistent with the principle that amending legislation applies, unless otherwise provided, to the future consequences of situations which arose under the previous legislation. . . . Since the revival of copyright and related rights has no effect on acts of exploitation definitively performed by a third party before the date on which revival occurred, it cannot be considered to have retroactive effect. Its application to the future consequences of situations which are not definitively settled means, on the other hand, that it has an effect on a third party's rights to continue the exploitation of a sound recording where the copies already manufactured have not yet been marketed and sold on that date.

25. Furthermore, while the principle of the protection of legitimate expectations is one of the fundamental principles of the Community, it is settled case-law that this principle cannot be extended to the point of generally preventing new rules from applying to the future consequences of situations which arose under the earlier rules. . . .

26. In view of those considerations, national legislation, such as Law No 52/96 . . . which permits persons, who were reproducing and marketing sound-recording media in respect of which the rights of use had expired under the previous legislation, to distribute those media for a limited period from its entry into force, meets the requirements of the Directive.

27. First, such legislation satisfies the obligation imposed on the Member States to adopt measures to protect acquired rights of third parties. . . .

28. Second, such legislation, by limiting in that way the protection of acquired rights of third parties with regard to the distribution of sound-recording media, meets the need to circumscribe a provision of that kind, which must necessarily be transitional in order not to prevent the application of the new terms of protection of copyright and related rights on the date laid down by the Directive, that being the Directive's principal objective. . . .

30. The answer to be given to the question referred for a preliminary ruling must therefore be that Article 10(3) of the Directive does not preclude a provision of national law such as the provision which, in Law No 52/96 . . . lays down a limited period in which sound-recording media may be distributed by persons who, by reason of the expiry of the rights relating to those media under the previous legislation, had been able to reproduce and market them before that Law entered into force. . . .

On those grounds, the Court, in answer to the question referred to it by the Tribunale Civile e Penale, Milan . . . hereby rules:

Article 10(3) of Council Directive 93/98/EEC of 29 October 1993 harmonising the term of protection of copyright and certain related rights does not preclude a provision of national law such as the provision which, in Italian Law No [52/96] . . . lays down a limited period in which sound-recording media may be distributed by persons who, by reason of the expiry of the rights relating to those media under the previous legislation, had been able to reproduce and market them before that Law entered into force.

Which countries' approach to copyright restoration strikes you as being "best": Germany's, the UK's, Italy's or the United States'? What characteristics make that country's approach seem better to you than the others'?

### 3. Why restoration by the U.S. may depend on restoration by the EU

Restoration of European copyrights is of course important to copyright owners and users within the European Union. But European restoration also could be important to copyright owners and users in the United States. This is so, because many European works lost their U.S. copyrights for reasons that made them eligible for restoration. Think, for example, of the Italian film "The Bicycle Thief," about which you read in Chapter 4. Think too about all of the snapshots of Elvis that were taken while he was in the Army in Germany and that were published in Germany *without* copyright notices.

The copyrights to those works actually were restored if, but only if, they were still protected in their countries of origin on January 1, 1996. And that in turn may depend on whether their country-of-origin copyrights were restored pursuant to the EC Directive!

# Chapter 7

# Litigation

Billions of dollars of copyright royalties flow across national borders every year, to their rightful recipients, without litigation or even the threat of it. How, exactly, that happens is the subject of the following chapter on Licensing. Nevertheless, on occasion, litigation (or the threat of it) is necessary to enforce the legal rights of copyright owners internationally, or to fend off the overly-aggressive assertion of rights that do not exist – just as litigation is sometimes necessary in purely domestic copyright disputes involving parties and uses within a single country.

Indeed, as the number of works used internationally has increased, and as American lawyers have become more familiar with international copyright law and its importance, the number of international copyright cases has increased dramatically. Lawyers and their clients no longer ignore what happens in other countries, simply because national borders separate them from those who are doing it.

International copyright cases begin and end with significant issues that in purely domestic cases might be classified as "procedural." They involve: the jurisdiction of courts; the availability of remedies; and the enforceability – in countries where infringers have assets – of judgments obtained in other countries. Though "procedural," they can't be ignored – not even by lawyers who don't litigate themselves. These issues also are critical to lawyers who merely give advice to clients about what they can do about suspected infringements occurring in other countries.

## A. Jurisdiction

It's likely that you spent a good deal of time studying general principles of "jurisdiction" in your first year Civil Procedure course. Now, we're going to look at "jurisdiction" in the context of cross-border copyright cases. The laws of most countries (perhaps all) contain doctrines that determine the circumstances under which their courts may hear cases. In the materials that follow, we'll begin by looking at the circumstances under which United States courts have jurisdiction to hear copyright cases. Then we'll look at some British cases to see how jurisdiction is handled in the UK. (You'll see some remarkable similarities.)

### 1. In U.S. courts

As you'll recall from your Civil Procedure course, in the United States two quite separate jurisdictional issues must be considered when determining whether a court may hear a particular case. One issue is whether the court has been given the legal authority to hear a case *of that particular type*. The other is whether the court has the power to hear a case against a *particular defendant*. These two types of issues are called "subject matter jurisdiction" (involving authority to hear a case of a particular type), and "personal jurisdiction" (involving power to hear a case against a particular defendant).

### a. Subject matter jurisdiction

Naturally, lawyers and their clients much prefer to litigate in the courts of their own country, rather than in the courts of their adversaries' countries. They do, because it is more convenient and less expensive, and because they want what in sports is referred to as the "home court advantage." As a result, copyright infringement lawsuits sometimes are filed in the United States, even though the allegedly infringing activity being complained of actually took place in another country. When that happens, the first issue to be decided in the case is whether the United States court has subject matter jurisdiction – that is, the legal authority – to hear and decide the case at all.

Here is what the law says about which courts in the United States have legal authority to hear copyright infringement cases, and what types of copyright cases they have the authority to hear.

### United States Judicial Code
### 28 U.S.C. §1338(a)

The district courts shall have original jurisdiction of any civil action arising under any Act of *Congress* relating to . . . copyrights . . . . Such jurisdiction shall be *exclusive* of the *courts of the states* in . . . copyright cases. [Emphasis added.]

Be certain you understand what section 1338(a) means. For example:

1. In a purely *domestic* copyright infringement case – one in which an American alleges that its copyright was infringed by another American as a result of an unauthorized use of the plaintiff's work inside the United States – could the plaintiff's lawyer elect to file suit in, say, the Superior Court of the State of California, because (for example) the lawyer has a lot of experience in Superior Court (and with Superior Court juries) but none in federal court?
2. In an *international* case – one in which an American alleges that its copyright was infringed by say, a Canadian national, as a result of the unauthorized use of the plaintiff's work in Canada – could the plaintiff's lawyer elect to file suit in a United States District Court rather than in Canada?

In order to answer question 2, it is necessary to determine whether the U.S. Copyright Act ever reaches activity that takes place in other countries, and if it does, under what circumstances it does reach that activity. The following cases answer those questions. Note that they are organized according to how much activity took place within the United States, rather than chronologically, because, as you'll see, the answers depend on how much activity did take place in the U.S.

### i. No activity in U.S.

**Ahbez v. Edwin H. Morris Co.**
**548 F.Supp. 664 (S.D.N.Y. 1982)**

District Judge Edelstein:
    This is an action for copyright infringement. . . .
    Plaintiff Eden Ahbez ("Ahbez") is an author of musical compositions, and alleges that he wrote the words and music to a composition entitled "Nature Boy." . . .
    Ahbez contends that in May, 1948, all of the defendants conspired "to defraud him and deprive him of revenue and sales of his copyrighted work throughout Europe by infringing his copyright by licensing, publishing, recording and commercially exploiting 'Nature Boy' throughout Europe.". . .
    . . . Ahbez seeks to recover damages sustained as a result of defendants' alleged infringement throughout Europe of his copyright in "Nature Boy." Ahbez also seeks a permanent injunction prohibiting defendants from infringing his copyright. . . .
    Defendants contend that this court lacks subject matter jurisdiction of this action insofar as Ahbez's claim of infringement arises from alleged acts undertaken by the defendants and others in Europe, and as such is not cognizable under the United States Copyright Act. Accordingly, defendants argue, the court lacks jurisdiction under 28 U.S.C. §1338(a). . . .
    As a general rule, acts of copyright infringement which occur outside the United States are not cognizable under the Copyright Act. In *Robert Stigwood* [a case you'll read below], the court . . . rejected plaintiffs' argument that where the acts in the United States constitute "an integral part" of the extraterritorial infringing act the defendants should be held liable for their foreign actions. The court held that at a minimum, an act of infringement within the United States is required to hold the defendant accountable for related infringing acts occurring outside this country.
    Ahbez has failed to allege any infringing acts occurring in the United States. Absent such a showing, Ahbez can not avoid application of the general rule that the copyright laws do not have extraterritorial operation. Accordingly, defendants' motion is granted as Ahbez has failed to establish subject matter jurisdiction. . . . The complaint herein is dismissed. . . .

    In the *Ahbez* case, it appears that literally nothing happened in the United States. Suppose, though, that some things happened in the U.S. – but not things that amounted to copyright infringement. Indeed, suppose that some of the things that happened in the U.S. were done while the defendant was in the U.S., though again, not things that amounted to infringement. Would that be enough to give subject matter jurisdiction to a U.S. District Court?

**De Bardossy v. Puski**
**763 F.Supp. 1239 (S.D.N.Y. 1991)**

United States District Judge John S. Martin, Jr.:
    Plaintiff Claire Kenneth De Bardossy, a Hungarian born writer of romance novels, commenced this copyright action against Sandor Puski and Corvin Hungarian Books to recover damages for and to enjoin the defendants' allegedly unauthorized publication of plaintiff's novels in Hungary. . . .

. . . . For the reasons discussed below, the Court finds that it lacks subject matter jurisdiction over plaintiff's claims. . . .

*Background*

According to the complaint, plaintiff was born and raised in Hungary and lived there until 1956 with her husband, Paul De Bardossy, and their son. Paul De Bardossy's uncle, Laszlo Bardossy, was the Prime Minister of Hungary in 1941 and 1942. During that time, Laszlo Bardossy declared war on the Soviet Union, was arrested in 1945 and was executed in 1946.

Given the Communist takeover of Hungary and the familial connections between plaintiff and Laszlo Bardossy, plaintiff was forced to adopt a *nom de plume* – Claire Kenneth – in order to have her books published in Communist Hungary.

In 1946 and 1947, plaintiff wrote two highly successful romance novels entitled "Night in Cairo" and "Rendezvous in Rome" (respectively the "Cairo book" and the "Rome book"). Sometime thereafter, plaintiff's true identity was discovered. Accused of being a "class enemy," plaintiff's works were banned and she was deported to an undeveloped area and drafted to do forced labor.

During the turmoil created by the Hungarian Revolution of 1956, plaintiff, her son and her husband, who himself had been imprisoned for three years for attempting to enter Austria, escaped from Hungary and settled in the United States.

Plaintiff resumed her writing after arriving in New York. Ultimately, plaintiff met defendant Sandor Puski sometime in the 1970's. Puski, also Hungarian born, states that he was a book publisher in Hungary from 1938 until 1950 when the Hungarian government nationalized his business and forced the defendant to seek other employment.

In 1970, Puski and his wife left Hungary and joined their sons who had previously settled in the United States. Puski eventually purchased the Corvin Book Store, a Hungarian language book store located on Second Avenue in New York City. Puski was also publishing books in the Hungarian language through May Publishing Company.

Plaintiff claims that in the 1970's, Puski approached plaintiff and requested that he be permitted to publish her books. . . . [An agreement was entered into covering some of Plaintiff's books.]

With respect to the Cairo and Rome books, defendants concede that there is no written agreement between Puski or his corporate entities and plaintiff. Defendants, however, claim that Puski acquired the rights to publish these two books in 1983 when he purchased the stock and existing publishing rights of Pilvax Publishing Corp . . . [a company which had previously acquired the Hungarian language rights to Plaintiff's books].

The story now shifts to the East Europe. In 1989, Janos Kadar, the head of the Communist Hungarian government since the Soviet Union crushed the 1956 uprising, was forced to retire and the country joined the rest of Eastern Europe in attempting to democratize the economy and political process. Defendants, apparently sensing a liberalization of society, one free of censorship, proceeded to contract with a state-owned publisher in Budapest to have plaintiff's books published in Hungary. . . .

Sometime in 1988 or 1989, Puski moved back to Hungary and started Puski Kiado (Publishers), a book publishing company. . . .

Although at that time, Puski had not yet published plaintiff's remaining books, he acknowledged at his deposition that he intended to do so. Hearing this, plaintiff, in the fall of 1990, contracted to have these last five novels published by Magyar Vilag in Hungary. Plaintiff claims that Puski, upon returning to Hungary after being deposed in the United States, learned of Magyar Vilag's intentions and, as result, proceeded to have Puski Kiado publish these same books.

As a result of defendants' actions as described above, plaintiff seeks an order enjoining defendants from infringing plaintiff's copyrights, damages flowing from the publication in Hungary of plaintiff's books and an accounting of all profits defendants have derived from the publication of plaintiff's books in Hungary. . . .

*Discussion*

### 1. Jurisdiction under the Copyright Act

At the outset, the Court must consider defendants' claim that the Court lacks subject matter jurisdiction under 28 U.S.C. §1338(a) since subject matter jurisdiction is a constitutional prerequisite to a federal court's power to act.

Defendants argue that jurisdiction is lacking in the present case because the United States Copyright laws generally do not have extraterritorial application and because the exceptions to this principle are inapplicable herein.

In *Update Art*, the Second Circuit succinctly set forth, as follows, both the general principle and the exception to extraterritorial jurisdictions:

> It is generally well established that copyright laws do not have extraterritorial application. There is an exception – when the type of infringement permits further reproduction abroad – such as the unauthorized manufacture of copyrighted material in the United States.

. . .

Thus, it appears that jurisdiction would be proper in the United States in the present case if plaintiff can show that an infringing act occurred in the United States and that this act has led to further infringement abroad. . . . .

[In this case], there was no unauthorized activity in the United States in the present action. Specifically, plaintiff does not allege that defendants' publication of Hungarian language editions of her books in the United States violated the Copyright Act since this is exactly what was called for under the . . . agreements.[10] [Fn.10 Plaintiff appears at times to argue that she never authorized the defendants to publish the Cairo and Rome books in the United States. If this was so, the improper publication of these works in the United States would certainly be an infringing act that could lead to continued infringement abroad. However, the Court finds that . . . she, indeed, did grant a Hungarian language license in these books and that defendants subsequently acquired the license. . . .]

Moreover, plaintiff does not – and, indeed, cannot – claim that the mere act of taking books legally produced in the United States to Hungary violated the Copyright Act . . ., and most significantly, the contracts authorizing the alleged improper use of plaintiff's copyright in Hungary were negotiated in Hungary and not in the United States. . . .

Having failed to produce any predicate act of infringement in the United States . . . , the Court finds that it lacks subject matter jurisdiction under the Copyright Act to entertain plaintiff's claims.

### 2. Jurisdiction under the Universal Copyright Convention

Although not pled in the complaint, plaintiff now alternatively argues that the Court has jurisdiction over this matter under the Universal Copyright Convention (the "Convention"). The Convention . . . provides that:

Published works of nationals of any Contracting State and works first published in that State shall enjoy in each other Contracting State the same protection as that other State accords works of its nationals first published in its own territory, as well as the protections granted by this Convention.

Plaintiff argues that, under the Convention, if the infringements took place in and entitled plaintiff to sue in Hungary, jurisdiction would also be conferred on an American court. This is not so.

The Convention does not expand a member state's copyright laws extraterritorially. Instead, the Convention simply provides that a contracting state must accord the same copyright protection to a work produced or created abroad but infringed in the contracting state that it would to a domestic work. For this reason, the Court holds that there is no subject matter jurisdiction over plaintiff's claims under the Convention.

*Conclusion*

For the reasons discussed above, the Court finds that it lacks subject matter jurisdiction over plaintiff's complaint. Accordingly, . . . the complaint [is] dismissed. So Ordered.

## ii. Slight activity in U.S.

Suppose now that some activity takes place in the United States, and suppose that activity *does* amount to copyright infringement under the U.S. Copyright Act. *But* suppose that the activity in the U.S. is slight in relation to the infringing activity alleged to have occurred in another country. Does a United States District Court have subject matter jurisdiction to hear and decide the infringement claims arising out of activities in the *other* country, as well as those arising out of the activities that took place in the U.S.?

## National Enquirer, Inc. v. News Group News, Ltd.
### 670 F.Supp. 962 (S.D.Fla. 1987)

United States District Judge Sidney M. Aronovitz:

In a six count complaint, the plaintiff, National Enquirer, Inc. ("Enquirer") has brought this action against News Group Newspapers, Ltd. ("News Group"), the defendant, essentially alleging the wrongful appropriation and use of photographic pictures of the wedding of actress Joan Collins and Peter Holm. Specifically, the Enquirer charges News Group with copyright infringement. . . .

Collins and Holm were married November 6, 1985 in a private ceremony in Las Vegas, Nevada. News Group published four black and white photos of the wedding in the November 10, 1985 edition of its British publication, *News of the World*. The Enquirer claims that this publication of the pictures was unauthorized and in contravention to its exclusive rights in the pictures. . . .

News Group has moved to dismiss . . . for lack of subject matter jurisdiction over the copyright claim, and lack of personal jurisdiction over News Group. . . .

*Jurisdictional Facts*

The parties do not dispute the preliminary facts relevant to this litigation. Collins and Holm employed Edward Sanderson, a professional photographer, to photograph their November 6, 1985 wedding in Las Vegas, Nevada.

Immediately after the wedding, Sanderson began to negotiate with various publications, including News Group and the Enquirer, in order to sell the publication and syndication rights to the photographs. Although Sanderson, on behalf of Collins and Holm, had reached a tentative deal with News Group for sale of the pictures, Holm intervened to reject News Group's offer. Instead, Holm accepted the Enquirer's offer in the early afternoon of November 7, 1985. On November 8, 1985 the Enquirer entered into a written contract with Collins, Holm and Sanderson. Under this contract, the Enquirer paid $160,000 for the exclusive right to publish and syndicate the wedding photographs. . . .

News Group has produced documentation of twelve Florida subscribers. News Group admits to a total of 85 subscribers to its newspaper in the United States. Furthermore, News Group sold a total of 5,021,630 copies of the November 10, 1985 issue of the News of the World. As computed by News Group, these U.S. sales comprise only .0017% of its total sales. News Group does not solicit U.S. subscribers, and it has no Florida offices, employees, telephone numbers, mailing addresses or bank accounts.

*Discussion*

. . .

The defendant . . . challenges the court's subject matter jurisdiction over the Enquirer's copyright claim. News Group first argues that all 5,021,630 copies of the November 10, 1985 edition of News of the World constitute only one alleged infringement. As an apparent alternative theory, News Group submits that the Enquirer's complaint limits its copyright claim to British infringement. In either event, the alleged infringement took place in the United Kingdom, where the United States copyright laws do not extend.

The defendant is undoubtedly correct that "[i]n general, United States copyright laws do not have extraterritorial effect." Consequently, infringing actions that take place entirely outside of the United States are not actionable in our courts. But News Group does admit to having distributed 85 copies of the November 10, 1985 edition of its newspaper in the United States.

News Group argues that as the 85 editions distributed in the United States constitute only .0017% of its total sales on that date, the rule of de minimis non curat lex applies. But in citing the case of *Knickerbocker Toy Co. v. Azrak-Hamway Intern.* (2d Cir. 1982), News Group has significantly overstated its argument. In *Knickerbocker*, the court held that a single undistributed sample display card could not constitute an infringing copy as it "was only an office copy which was never used." This completely trivial infringement hardly compares to the 85 copies News Group admits to having publicly distributed in the United States.

As either an off-shoot of its de minimis argument, or as an alternative, News Group suggests that all copies of the November 10, 1985 edition constitute just one alleged infringement which took place in the United Kingdom. The defendant fails to cite any decision rejecting subject matter jurisdiction on this theory. Instead, News Group cites *MCA, Inc. v. Wilson* (2d Cir. 1981), as treating multiple performances as a single infringement. But *MCA* only treated multiple performances as one for the issue of computing statutory damages. In any event, a critical issue in determining whether multiple acts constitute a single infringement is the relationship between them in time and place. In *Robert Stigwood*, for instance, the court held that the different "locales" of performance necessitated treating the performances severally for purposes of computing damages. Likewise, the 85 issues on News of the World distributed in the United States are sufficiently distinct from the United Kingdom sales to constitute a separate infringement (or infringements).

The Court has carefully reviewed and considered the extensive memoranda submitted by the parties, including supplemental memoranda filed upon the Court's request, the affidavits and deposition evidence submitted by both parties, and the oral argument heard on this matter, and News Group's motions to dismiss are denied. . . .

If publishing 85 infringing copies in the United States, as compared to more than 5 million copies abroad, is sufficient to give a U.S. District Court subject matter jurisdiction, is *any* infringement in the U.S. too slight to do so? What about making just a single infringing copy, which is then used to commit further infringements abroad?

## P & D International v. Halsey Publishing Co.
### 672 F.Supp. 1429 (S.D.Fla. 1987)

United States District Judge Edward Davis: . . .

*I. Factual Summary*

[Plaintiff] P & D is a Cayman Islands corporation with its principal place of business in George Town, Grand Cayman, Cayman Islands. P & D publishes magazines, films and videotapes, and sells advertising principally for use on cruise ships in the Caribbean Sea.

Defendant Cunard is a United Kingdom corporation with its principal place of business in New York. Cunard's cruise ships sail in and of the Port of Miami and Cunard otherwise conducts business in Florida....

On November 25, 1986, P & D filed a Complaint alleging that . . . Cunard . . . committed acts of copyright infringement. . . . The Complaint alleges that prior to August 1980, P & D created, wrote, and filmed an original audio-visual work (hereinafter referred to as the "St. Thomas Film") about the Island of St. Thomas, B.V.I. The St. Thomas Film was allegedly shown on Cunard cruise ships approximately 80 times a year during 1981, 1982, and 1983, pursuant to an agreement between P & D and . . . Cunard's advertising agency. . . .

P & D President Savill contends that after the relationship between Cunard and P & D ended in or about 1983, P & D requested that Cunard return all copies of the St. Thomas Film. Savill further states that Cunard complied, but at the time of the filing of this suit, was still showing the St. Thomas Film or parts of it on its cruises, and that consequently Cunard must have covertly kept one copy. P & D's Complaint alleges that Cunard has been performing and displaying on its cruise ships, without P & D's consent, the work produced by Halsey.

On June 11, 1986, P & D secured exclusive rights and privileges in and to the St. Thomas Film in compliance with United States copyright law.

*II. Discussion*

In . . . this proceeding, Defendants seek to have the copyright infringement count dismissed [for] . . . lack of subject matter jurisdiction . . . .

*A. Subject Matter Jurisdiction*

P & D's Complaint alleges that this action raises under the United States Copyright Act, United States Code, Title 17, Sections 101, 102 and 104(a), and the Universal Copyright Convention, Paris Act of 1974, as ratified by the United Kingdom on July 10, 1974. Cunard argues that this Court lacks subject

matter jurisdiction because: . . . U.S. copyright law has no extraterritorial effect.
. . .

### 2. Extraterritorial Reach of U.S. Copyright Law

As a general rule, U.S. copyright law has no extraterritorial effect and cannot be invoked to secure relief for acts of infringement occurring outside the United States. However, to the extent that part of an "act" of infringement occurs within this country, although such act be completed in a foreign jurisdiction, those who contributed to the act within the United States may be liable under U.S. copyright law.

P & D alleges that . . . the Film [was copied] in Florida at the behest of Cunard. . . . [S]uch an act would constitute an infringement under 17 U.S.C. §106. As P & D maintains, the subsequent performances of the Film on the Cunard cruise ships en route to the Island of St. Thomas would then simply be additional infringements of the Film. . . .

Because an infringing act is alleged to have occurred in the United States, this Court has subject matter over P & D's claims.

It doesn't take very much infringing activity in the United States to give District Courts subject matter jurisdiction, does it? In fact, it takes so little that by now, you should be wondering whether having subject matter jurisdiction empowers U.S. District Courts to *award damages* on account of *foreign* (as well as U.S.) activities. We'll get to that issue below. First, though, consider the following cases that tested just how little activity in the U.S. will give District Courts subject matter jurisdiction.

### iii. Activity in U.S. was *authorizing* activities abroad

### Subafilms, Ltd. v. MGM-Pathe Comm. Co.
### 24 F.3d 1088 (9th Cir.), cert. denied, 513 U.S. 1001 (1994)

Circuit Judge Dorothy Nelson:
In this case, we consider the "vexing question" of whether a claim for infringement can be brought under the Copyright Act . . . when the assertedly infringing conduct consists solely of the authorization within the territorial boundaries of the United States of acts that occur entirely abroad. We hold that such allegations do not state a claim for relief under the copyright laws of the United States.

*Factual and Procedural Background*

In 1966, the musical group The Beatles, through Subafilms, Ltd., entered into a joint venture with the Hearst Corporation to produce the animated motion picture entitled "Yellow Submarine" (the "Picture"). Over the next year, Hearst, acting on behalf of the joint venture (the "Producer"), negotiated an agreement with United Artists Corporation ("UA") to distribute and finance the film. Separate distribution and financing agreements were entered into in May, 1967. Pursuant to these agreements, UA distributed the Picture in  theaters beginning in 1968 and later on television.

In the early 1980s, with the advent of the home video market, UA entered into several licensing agreements to distribute a number of its films on videocassette. Although one company expressed interest in the Picture, UA refused to license "Yellow Submarine" because of uncertainty over whether home video rights had been granted by the 1967 agreements. Subsequently, in 1987, UA's successor company, MGM/UA Communications Co. ("MGM/UA"), over the Producer's objections, authorized its subsidiary MGM/UA Home Video, Inc. to distribute the Picture for the domestic home video market, and, pursuant to an earlier licensing agreement, notified Warner Bros., Inc. ("Warner") that the Picture had been cleared for international videocassette distribution. Warner, through its wholly owned subsidiary, Warner Home Video, Inc., in turn entered into agreements with third parties for distribution of the Picture on videocassette around the world.

In 1988, Subafilms and Hearst ("Appellees") brought suit against MGM/UA, Warner, and their respective subsidiaries (collectively the "Distributors" or "Appellants"), contending that the videocassette distribution of the Picture, both foreign and domestic, constituted copyright infringement and a breach of the 1967 agreements. The case was tried before a retired California Superior Court Judge acting as a special master. The special master found for Appellees on both claims. . . . Except for the award of prejudgment interest, which it reversed, the district court adopted all of the special master's factual findings and legal conclusions. Appellees were awarded $ 2,228,000.00 in compensatory damages, split evenly between the foreign and domestic home video distributions. In addition, Appellees received attorneys' fees and a permanent injunction that prohibited the Distributors from engaging in, or authorizing, any home video use of the Picture.

A panel of this circuit, in an unpublished disposition, affirmed the district court's judgment on the ground that both the domestic and foreign distribution of the Picture constituted infringement under the Copyright Act. . . . With respect to the foreign distribution of the Picture, the panel concluded that it was bound by this court's prior decision in *Peter Starr Prod. Co. v. Twin Continental Films, Inc.*, 783 F.2d 1440 (9th Cir. 1986), which it held to stand for the proposition that, although "'infringing actions that take place entirely outside the United States are not actionable' [under the Copyright Act, an] 'act of infringement within the United States' [properly is] alleged where the illegal authorization of international exhibitions takes place in the United States". . . . Because the Distributors had admitted that the initial authorization to distribute the Picture internationally occurred within the United States, the panel affirmed the district court's holding with respect to liability for extraterritorial home video distribution of the Picture.[3] [n3 At oral argument before this court Appellants' counsel conceded that the relevant authorization occurred within the United States. Counsel for Appellees, accepting this concession, additionally insisted that the authorization necessarily included the making of a copy of the negative of the Picture within the United States. Appellants' counsel responded that this contention was made before neither the special master nor the panel, and was not supported by the record. For the purposes of this decision, we assume, as apparently the panel did, that each of the defendants made a relevant "authorization" within the United States, and that the acts of authorization consisted solely of entering into licensing agreements.]

We granted Appellants' petition for rehearing en banc to consider whether the panel's interpretation of *Peter Starr* conflicted with our subsequent decision in *Lewis Galoob Toys, Inc. v. Nintendo of Am., Inc.*, 964 F.2d 965 (9th Cir. 1992), *cert. denied*, 113 S. Ct. 1582 (1993), which held that there could be no liability for authorizing a party to engage in an infringing act when the authorized "party's use of the work would not violate the Copyright Act". . . . Because we conclude that there can be no liability under the United States copyright laws for authorizing an act that itself could not constitute infringement of rights secured by those laws, and that wholly extraterritorial acts of infringement are not cognizable under the Copyright Act, we overrule *Peter Starr* insofar as it held that allegations of an authorization within the United States of infringing acts that take place entirely abroad state a claim for infringement under the Act. Accordingly, we vacate the panel's decision in part and return the case to the panel for further proceedings.

*Discussion*

I.   *The Mere Authorization of Extraterritorial Acts of Infringement does not State a Claim under the Copyright Act*

As the panel in this case correctly concluded, *Peter Starr* held that the authorization within the United States of entirely extraterritorial acts stated a cause of action under the "plain language" of the Copyright Act. . . . Observing that the Copyright Act grants a copyright owner "the exclusive rights to do and to authorize" any of the activities listed in 17 U.S.C. § 106(1)-(5), and that a violation of the "authorization" right constitutes infringement under section 501 of the Act, the *Peter Starr* court reasoned that allegations of an authorization within the United States of extraterritorial conduct that corresponded to the activities listed in section 106 "alleged an act of infringement within the United States". . . . Accordingly, the court determined that the district court erred "in concluding that 'Plaintiff alleged only infringing acts which took place outside of the United States,'" and reversed the district court's dismissal for lack of subject matter jurisdiction. . . .

The *Peter Starr* court accepted, as does this court, that the acts authorized from within the United States themselves could not have constituted infringement under the Copyright Act because "in general, United States copyright laws do not have extraterritorial effect," and therefore, "infringing actions that take place entirely outside the United States are not actionable.". . . The central premise of the *Peter Starr* court, then, was that a party could be held liable as an "infringer" under section 501 of the Act merely for authorizing a third party to engage in acts that, had they been committed within the United States, would have violated the exclusive rights granted to a copyright holder by section 106.

Since *Peter Starr*, however, we have recognized that, when a party authorizes an activity not proscribed by one of the five section 106 clauses, the authorizing party cannot be held liable as an infringer. . . .

As the Supreme Court noted in *Sony*, and this circuit acknowledged in *Peter Starr*, under the 1909 Act courts differed over the degree of involvement required to render a party liable as a contributory infringer. . . . Viewed with this background in mind, the addition of the words "to authorize" in the 1976 Act appears best understood as merely clarifying that the Act contemplates liability for contributory infringement, and that the bare act of "authorization" can suffice. . . . Consequently, we believe that "'to authorize' was simply a convenient peg on which Congress chose to hang the antecedent jurisprudence of third party liability." Although the *Peter Starr* court recognized that the addition of the authorization right in the 1976 Act "was intended to remove the confusion surrounding contributory . . . infringement," . . . it did not consider the applicability of an essential attribute of the doctrine identified above: that contributory infringement, even when triggered solely by an "authorization," is a form of third party liability that requires the authorized acts to constitute infringing ones. We believe that the *Peter Starr* court erred in not

298

applying this principle to the authorization of acts that cannot themselves be infringing because they take place entirely abroad. As Professor Nimmer has observed:

> Accepting the proposition that a direct infringement is a prerequisite to third party liability, the further question arises whether the direct infringement on which liability is premised must take place within the United States. Given the undisputed axiom that United States copyright law has no extraterritorial application, it would seem to follow necessarily that a primary activity outside the boundaries of the United States, not constituting an infringement cognizable under the Copyright Act, cannot serve as the basis for holding liable under the Copyright Act one who is merely related to that activity within the United States.

Appellees resist the force of this logic, and argue that liability in this case is appropriate because . . . the conduct authorized in this case was precisely that prohibited by section 106, and is only uncognizable because it occurred outside the United States. Moreover, they contend that the conduct authorized in this case would have been prohibited under the copyright laws of virtually every nation. . . .

Even assuming arguendo that the acts authorized in this case would have been illegal abroad, we do not believe the distinction offered by Appellees is a relevant one. Because the copyright laws do not apply extraterritorially, each of the rights conferred under the five section 106 categories must be read as extending "no farther than the [United States'] borders." . . . In light of our above conclusion that the "authorization" right refers to the doctrine of contributory infringement, which requires that the authorized act itself could violate one of the exclusive rights listed in section 106(1)-(5), we believe that "it is simply not possible to draw a principled distinction" between an act that does not violate a copyright because it is not the type of conduct proscribed by section 106, and one that does not violate section 106 because the illicit act occurs overseas. . . . In both cases, the authorized conduct could not violate the exclusive rights guaranteed by section 106. In both cases, therefore, there can be no liability for "authorizing" such conduct. . . .

To hold otherwise would produce the untenable anomaly, inconsistent with the general principles of third party liability, that a party could be held liable as an infringer for violating the "authorization" right when the party that it authorized could not be considered an infringer under the Copyright Act. Put otherwise, we do not think Congress intended to hold a party liable for merely "authorizing" conduct that, had the authorizing party chosen to engage in itself, would have resulted in no liability under the Act. . . .

Appellees rely heavily on the Second Circuit's doctrine that extraterritorial application of the copyright laws is permissible "when the type of infringement permits further reproduction abroad." *Update Art, Inc. v. Modiin Publishing, Ltd.*, 843 F.2d 67, 73 (2d Cir. 1988). Whatever the merits of the Second Circuit's rule, and we express no opinion on its validity in this circuit, it is premised on the theory that the copyright holder may recover damages that stem from a direct infringement of its exclusive rights that occurs within the United States. . . . In these cases, liability is not based on contributory infringement, but on the theory that the infringing use would have been actionable even if the subsequent foreign distribution that stemmed from that use never took place. . . .These cases, therefore, simply are inapplicable to a theory of liability based merely on the authorization of noninfringing acts.

Accordingly, accepting that wholly extraterritorial acts of infringement cannot support a claim under the Copyright Act, we believe that the *Peter Starr* court, and thus the panel in this case, erred in concluding that the mere authorization of such acts supports a claim for infringement under the Act.

## II. The Extraterritoriality of the Copyright Act

Appellees additionally contend that, if liability for "authorizing" acts of infringement depends on finding that the authorized acts themselves are cognizable under the Copyright Act, this court should find that the United States copyright laws do extend to extraterritorial acts of infringement when such acts "result in adverse effects within the United States." Appellees buttress this argument with the contention that failure to apply the copyright laws extraterritorially in this case will have a disastrous effect on the American film industry, and that other remedies, such as suits in foreign jurisdictions or the application of foreign copyright laws by American courts, are not realistic alternatives.

We are not persuaded by Appellees' parade of horribles. More fundamentally, however, we are unwilling to overturn over eighty years of consistent jurisprudence on the extraterritorial reach of the copyright laws without further guidance from Congress.

The Supreme Court recently reminded us that "it is a long-standing principle of American law 'that legislation of Congress, unless a contrary intent appears, is meant to apply only within the territorial jurisdiction of the United States.'" . . .

The "undisputed axiom" . . . that the United States' copyright laws have no application to extraterritorial infringement predates the 1909 Act, . . . and, as discussed above, the principle of territoriality consistently has been reaffirmed. . . . There is no clear expression of congressional intent in either the 1976 Act or other relevant enactments to alter the preexisting extraterritoriality doctrine. Indeed, the *Peter Starr* court itself recognized the continuing application of the principle that "infringing actions that take place entirely outside the United States are not actionable in United States federal courts." . . .

Furthermore, we note that Congress chose in 1976 to expand one specific "extraterritorial" application of the Act by declaring that the unauthorized importation of copyrighted works constitutes infringement even when the copies lawfully were made abroad. . . .Had Congress been inclined to overturn the preexisting doctrine that infringing acts that take place wholly outside the United States are not actionable under the Copyright Act, it knew how to do so.
. . .

. . . At the time that the international distribution of the videocassettes in this case took place, the United States was a member of the Universal Copyright Convention ("UCC"), and, in 1988, the United States acceded to the Berne Convention for the Protection of Literary and Artistic Works ("Berne Conv."). The central thrust of these multilateral treaties is the principle of "national treatment." A work of an American national first generated in America will receive the same protection in a foreign nation as that country accords to the works of its own nationals. . . . Although the treaties do not expressly discuss choice-of-law rules, . . . it is commonly acknowledged that the national treatment principle implicates a rule of territoriality. . . . Indeed, a recognition of this principle appears implicit in Congress's statements in acceding to Berne that "the primary mechanism for discouraging discriminatory treatment of foreign copyright claimants is the principle of national treatment," . . . and that adherence to Berne will require "careful due regard for the[ ] values" of other member nations.

. . . [W]e think it inappropriate for the courts to act in a manner that might disrupt Congress's efforts to secure a more stable international intellectual property regime unless Congress otherwise clearly has expressed its intent. The application of American copyright law to acts of infringement that occur entirely overseas clearly could have this effect. Extraterritorial application of American law would be contrary to the spirit of the Berne Convention, and might offend other member nations by effectively displacing their law in circumstances in which previously it was assumed to govern. Consequently, an extension of extraterritoriality might undermine Congress's objective of achieving "'effective and harmonious' copyright laws among all nations.'" . . . Indeed, it might well send the signal that the United States does not believe that the protection accorded by the laws of other member nations is adequate, which would undermine two other objectives of Congress in joining the convention: "strengthening the credibility of the U.S. position in trade negotiations with countries where piracy is not uncommon" and "raising the likelihood that other nations will enter the Convention.". . .

Moreover, although Appellees contend otherwise, we note that their theory might permit the application of American law to the distribution of protected materials in a foreign country conducted exclusively by citizens of that nation. . . . Of course, under the Berne Convention, all states must guarantee minimum rights, . . . and it is plausible that the application of American law would yield outcomes roughly equivalent to those called for by the application of foreign law in a number of instances. Nonetheless, extending the reach of American copyright law likely would produce difficult choice-of-law problems . . . , dilemmas that the federal courts' general adherence to the territoriality principle largely has obviated. . . .

Accordingly, because an extension of the extraterritorial reach of the Copyright Act by the courts would in all likelihood disrupt the international regime for protecting intellectual property that Congress so recently described as essential to furthering the goal of protecting the works of American authors abroad . . . , we reaffirm that the United States copyright laws do not reach acts of infringement that take place entirely abroad. It is for Congress, and not the courts, to take the initiative in this field.

*III. Other Arguments*

Appellees raise a number of additional arguments for why the district court's judgment should be affirmed. . . . Appellees maintain that they may recover damages for international distribution of the Picture based on the theory that an act of direct infringement, in the form of a reproduction of the negatives for the Picture, took place in the United States. Appellees also suggest that they may recover, under United States law, damages stemming from the international distribution on the theory that the distribution was part of a larger conspiracy to violate their copyright that included actionable infringement within the United States. In addition, they maintain that Appellants are liable for the international distribution under foreign copyright laws. . . .

We resolve none of these questions, but leave them for the panel, in its best judgment, to consider. . . .

*Conclusion*

We hold that the mere authorization of acts of infringement that are not cognizable under the United States copyright laws because they occur entirely outside of the United States does not state a claim for infringement under the Copyright Act. . . .

## Curb v. MCA Records Inc.
### 898 F. Supp. 586 (M.D.Tenn. 1995)

Thomas A. Wiseman, Jr., United States District Judge

This dispute between Mike Curb d/b/a Curb Music Co. and MCA Records, Inc., arises out of a joint venture between the parties gone sour. . . . Curb has moved for judgment on the pleadings or, in the alternative, summary judgment on MCA's counterclaim that Curb infringed MCA's copyrights in other sound recordings by sub-licensing them overseas. . . .

During the 1980s, Naomi and Wynonna Judd recorded 67 songs for RCA Records, Inc., as "The Judds." Many of these recordings were and are tremendously popular with country music audiences. That these parties have waged such protracted litigation is evidence enough of the recordings' continued commercial viability. . . .

Many of the salient facts underlying MCA's motion are undisputed by the parties.

In September 1983, Curb and MCA began a joint venture by entering into an Independent Production and License Agreement ("Venture Agreement"), under which the two companies have jointly produced record masters by a variety of artists. Under the Venture Agreement, MCA has sole right throughout the United States, Canada, and the United Kingdom to manufacture, advertise, publicize, sell, lease, license, or otherwise use or dispose of and exploit records and/or derivatives manufactured from the Masters . . . and to permit others to do so . . . or to refrain therefrom, subject to the terms of this Agreement, in MCA's sole discretion. . . .

Apart from the MCA venture, Curb produced Judds' records through most of the 1980s under a separate agreement with RCA Records (now BMG, Inc.). When that contract expired, Wynonna and Naomi signed a deal in June 1988 (the "Judds Addition Agreement"), making new Judds masters property of the Curb/MCA Joint Venture.

Curb and MCA have not been peaceable partners. Prompted in 1992 by other business concerns – the renegotiation of Curb's contract with venture artist Lyle Lovett and the negotiation for the rights to Lovett's and Wynonna Judd's recordings in a movie soundtrack – Curb and MCA began difficult and protracted negotiations to resolve their differences and enter into a new Venture Agreement.

Meanwhile, older Judds recordings continued to sell. Despite the Venture Agreement provision that previously recorded masters of Venture artists "will be deemed to have been recorded during the applicable Artist Term," Curb acted as though it held exclusive rights in the old Curb/BMG master recordings (the "Judds Masters"). . . .

Apart from the Joint Venture, MCA agreed in 1990 to license some of its master recordings ("the Licensing Agreement") by a variety of artists to Curb for distribution in the United States, Canada and the United Kingdom ("the Territory"). The licensing agreement, including a variety of older recordings by such diverse artists as Bing Crosby (including "White Christmas"), Gladys Knight, Debbie Reynolds, and Conway Twitty, permitted Curb to release the recordings in the Territory. The License Agreement, however, did not provide

Curb authority to release the recordings in any other country, except by permission of WEA (Warner/Elektra/Asylum), MCA's worldwide licensee.

In February 1991, Curb asked WEA for permission to sub-license some of the MCA recordings outside the Territory. A February 14, 1991, response from WEA indicated that its agreement with MCA expired in March 1991 and that any approval it might give would be irrelevant; the response referred Curb to MCA for approval. Subsequently, Curb entered into contracts to license recordings to sublicensees around the world, including Japan, Finland, Malaysia, Austria, South Africa, and Hong Kong.

MCA claims that some of the recordings included in the 1990 Licensing Agreement made its way onto tapes and albums overseas via Curb's contracts with its foreign sublicensees. Curb does not appear to challenge this assertion.

The only fact apparently in dispute is whether the Licensing Agreement required Curb to get *anyone's* approval for worldwide release of the recordings once WEA's agency with MCA expired in March 1991. Curb claims it needed no further authority. MCA claims that WEA put Curb on notice that a change was in the works in MCA's licensing agreements and that, in fact, BMG replaced WEA as MCA's worldwide licensee in 1991. MCA claims Curb needed BMG's approval to release the recordings outside the Territory.

. . . MCA has sued Curb under the Licensing Agreement alleging copyright infringement. . . .

Curb now moves for a judgment on the pleadings . . . or, in the alternative, summary judgment.

### B. The Extraterritorial Application of U.S. Copyright Law

Relying on a recent holding by the Ninth Circuit Court of Appeals, Curb argues that he is entitled to judgment on the pleadings because, he asserts, U.S. law does not apply to overseas acts that, if done in this country, would constitute infringement of a copyright owner's exclusive rights under 17 U.S.C. §106. . . .

### 2. Subafilms , authorization, and the Copyright Act

Curb argues that it did nothing more than sign contracts with entities abroad to distribute copies of sound recordings in which Curb held a license to reproduce. Curb's argument at law is this: Even assuming that such an action violated U.S. copyright law, such illegality is beyond the reach of this Court. There is recent precedent outside the Sixth Circuit that bears examination. In *Subafilms, Ltd. v. MGM-Pathe Communications Co.*, 24 F.3d 1088 (9th Cir. 1994), the Ninth Circuit addressed itself to the "vexing question of whether a claim for infringement . . . can be brought under the Copyright Act . . . when the assertedly infringing conduct consists solely of the authorization within the territorial boundaries of the United States of acts that occur entirely abroad." . . .

Early commentators suggest that *Subafilms* opens the door to massive foreign infringement of American cultural works, a devastating blow considering the worldwide popularity of U.S. films, books, videos and music. See generally, Michael W. Ballance, Note, Third-Party Innocence: Domestic Authorization of Foreign Copyright Infringement and Subafilms, Ltd. v. MGM-Pathe Communications Co., *20 N.C. J. Int'l L. & Com. Reg. 435 (1995)*. The key, however, to understanding Subafilms' applicability to this case is to break down what it stands for and what it does not.

First, Subafilms relies upon a peculiar interpretation of the scope and nature of the authorization right in 17 U.S.C. § 106. This interpretation, tying the authorization right solely to a claim of justiciable contributory infringement appears contrary both to well-reasoned precedent, statutory text, and legislative history.

Even if the Court accepted Subafilms' interpretation lashing the § 106 authorization right solely to claims of contributory infringement, however, a critical question remains: Is there any primary infringement? MCA argues there is. *Subafilms* emphasizes at several points that its holding goes only to the application of the Copyright Act against defendants who have committed no primary acts of infringement in the United States. . . . Therefore, in order for Curb to obtain summary judgment on this issue, it must show there is no issue as to this most material fact.

This threshold question may be called "localizing infringement." Paul E. Geller & Melville B. Nimmer, eds., 1 INTERNATIONAL COPYRIGHT LAW AND PRACTICE, *Intr.* § 3[b][i] (6th ed. 1994) ("Geller & Nimmer"). "More generally, in dealing with transborder conduct, it is advisable to analyze it down into discrete component acts country by country, before asking which law or laws should apply to which acts." . . . Simply put, the Court must determine whether an act of copyright infringement occurred within the boundaries of the United States. For if it did, even *Subafilms* concedes that further extraterritorial acts will not thwart a U.S. court's jurisdiction. . . .

In this case, MCA indisputably held copyrights in the sound recordings at issue. By the Licensing Agreement, MCA authorized Curb to reproduce and distribute copies of the recordings in the United States, Canada, and the United Kingdom.

MCA argues that when Curb expanded the market for these recordings to other countries, it infringed upon at least three of MCA's exclusive rights: reproduction, distribution, and authorization. If MCA can "present affirmative evidence" showing that genuine issues of material fact exist as to any of these allegations, it defeats Curb's motion.

The first question – one of reproduction – is precisely the question the *Subafilms* court avoided. . . .

MCA has produced copies of Curb's sublicensing agreements with entities in Hong Kong, Japan, and Australia. Each agreement required Curb to deliver duplicate master recordings to facilitate their reproduction. . . . Curb's unauthorized creation of duplicate master tapes for release into these countries would appear to amount to an infringement of MCA's reproduction right.

Curb responds that the Licensing Agreement permitted Curb to reproduce the recordings anyway. However, the Licensing Agreement clearly restricts Curb's rights to the United States, Canada, and the United Kingdom. If Curb's argument were valid, it could make as many copies of MCA's recordings as it wished, so long as the copies were not used for infringing purposes. While this argument sounds fine at first blush, it is undercut by its own faulty premise: Why would any copyright holder authorize reproduction for the domestic market when such a transfer could lead to unsanctionable reproduction for wholesale distribution in foreign markets?

Curb's reproduction of the masters, if it occurred (and it did unless Curb shipped its only copy in a circuit from foreign distributor to distributor), for distribution into unauthorized territory, therefore amounts to a primary infringement of MCA's exclusive rights. Curb has not shown that no genuine issue of material fact exists as to its reproduction; indeed, it appears even to concede it. . . .

Subafilms does, however, speak to the scope and extent of MCA's authorization right. Subafilms holds that § 106's authorization right is implicated only in cases of contributory infringement. . . . When no primary infringer is reachable by U.S. copyright law, either because the conduct falls short of infringement or because infringing conduct occurs outside the United States, the Ninth Circuit will not find the person who authorized the conduct liable. . . .

The Ninth Circuit rejected the argument that the 1978 addition of the words "to authorize" in § 106 created an independent right, just as the words "to do" do. Instead, *Subafilms* holds that "to authorize" merely codifies the doctrine of contributory infringement. Subafilms, thus, reads the authorization right out of the Act in cases of foreign infringement.

But piracy has changed since the Barbary days. Today, the raider need not grab the bounty with his own hands; he need only transmit his go-ahead by wire or telefax to start the presses in a distant land. *Subafilms* ignores this economic reality, and the economic incentives underpinning the Copyright Clause designed to encourage creation of new works, and transforms infringement of the authorization right into a requirement of domestic presence by a primary infringer. Under this view, a phone call to Nebraska results in liability; the same phone call to France results in riches. In a global marketplace, it is literally a distinction without a difference.

A better view, one supported by the text, the precedents, and, ironically enough, the legislative history to which the *Subafilms* court cited, would be to hold that domestic violation of the authorization right is an infringement, sanctionable under the Copyright Act, whenever the authorizee has committed an act that would violate the copyright owner's § 106 rights.

This was the approach taken by the court in *ITSI T.V. Productions v. California Authority of Racing Fairs,* 785 F.Supp. 854 (E.D.Cal. 1992). Faced with domestic authorization of infringing closed-circuit TV broadcasts in Mexico, the court found that sections 106 and 501 establish a direct cause of action for illegal authorizations under the Copyright Act. The court held that the location of the authorized act is irrelevant, so long as it is the sort of activity that infringes upon a copyright owner's exclusive 106 rights. Other courts agree. "There may be many reasons why a party may not be held accountable for its conduct in court. What is important is that contributory infringement be hinged upon an act of primary infringement, even if the primary infringer for some reason escapes judicial scrutiny." *Danjaq, S.A. v. MGM/UA Communications Co.,* 773 F.Supp. 194 (C.D.Cal. 1991). . . .

In this case, even taking Curb's argument that it lawfully acquired and reproduced copies of MCA's sound recordings as true, the act of authorizing the distribution of the recordings for sale to a worldwide public seems equally sanctionable under sections 106 and 501. That Curb authorized these sales does not appear to be in dispute. MCA's production of letters raising the overseas sales as issues with Curb executives are unchallenged by Curb's insistence upon *Subafilms* as its sole shield.

The Court is sensitive to the sovereignty and rule of law in other countries. Such sensitivity is only enhanced by the recognition of the United States' obligation under multilateral treaties such as the 1971 Geneva Phonograms Convention and the recently adopted TRIPS component of the General Agreement on Tariffs and Trade. However, a careful exercise of domestic jurisdiction is consistent with the approach of the leading treatise in the field of international copyright law:

> A U.S. court, for example, could grant injunctive remedies under U.S. law for acts that commence a course of infringing conduct in the United States, for example, acts of authorizing or copying, without regard for whether eventual exploitation is to take place at home or abroad. Such an injunction would be justifiable if it forestalled piracy, whether at home or abroad, but did not risk interfering with such relief as might be granted under foreign laws for exploitation abroad.

Because, therefore, issues of fact remain with regard to domestic infringement and authorization, the Court need not reach the question of whether domestic or foreign law may be applied to ultimately resolve the question of infringement. . . .Given the facts at hand and the law as it exists, *Subafilms* notwithstanding, the Court must deny Curb's motion for summary judgment.

A few years after *Curb* was decided, the issue arose yet again, in yet another Circuit. The defendant, an American company named Direct Line Cargo, had authorized *other* companies to use software *in Asia*, without the consent of the owner of the software's copyright. That copyright was owned by another American company named Expediters International, and it sued Direct Line for infringement, in federal District Court in New Jersey (the state in which Direct Line was incorporated). In response to Expediters's infringement lawsuit, Direct Line argued that the court did not have subject matter jurisdiction, citing the *Subafilms* decision. Expediters replied that the court did have subject matter jurisdiction, relying on *Curb*. The District Court decided that it did have subject matter jurisdiction for this reason:

### Expediters International v. Direct Line Cargo
### 995 F.Supp. 468, 476-77 (D.N.J. 1998)

Joel A. Pisano, U.S. Magistrate Judge: . . .

This Court agrees with *Curb*'s literal interpretation of Section 106, which clearly lends "the owner of a copyright . . . the exclusive rights to do and to authorize" the reproduction and distribution of copyrighted materials. Furthermore, the Court appreciates the policy observations set forth in *Curb*, which appear more closely adapted to our modern age of telefaxes, Internet communication, and electronic mail systems. The purpose behind the Copyright Act is to protect a copyright owner's right to be free from infringement in the United States. To allow an entity to curtail this right by merely directing its foreign agent to do its "dirty work" would be to hinder the deterrent effect of the statute and to thwart its underlying purpose. Because it is more closely aligned with the language, legislative history, and purpose of the statute, the Court adopts the *Curb* interpretation of Section 106 and finds that the mere authorization of infringing acts abroad constitutes direct infringement and is actionable under United States Copyright Law. . . .

So, for a while, it looked as though the judicial pendulum was swinging in the direction of finding that U.S. courts *do* have jurisdiction to hear claims that defendants authorized infringements abroad from within the United States. But then, the pendulum abruptly swung in the opposite direction again. In *Armstrong v. Virgin Records, Ltd.*, 91 F.Supp.2d 628, 634 (S.D.N.Y. 2000), a federal District Court in New York City rejected the reasoning and conclusions of *Curb* and *Expediters*, and agreed instead with *Subafilms* that U.S. courts do *not* have jurisdiction to hear claims that defendants authorized acts that are not themselves infringements under the U.S. Copyright Act. And a federal District Court in Chicago then held the same in *Seals v. Compendia Media Group*, 2003 U.S. Dist. LEXIS 2980 (N.D.Ill. 2003).

Do the decisions in *Curb* and *Expediters* necessarily *assume* that the activities the defendants authorized in other countries infringed the plaintiffs' rights under the copyright laws of *those countries*? Suppose that the activities the defendants authorized did *not* infringe the plaintiffs' rights under the copyright laws of the countries where those activities took place. Consider, for example, this hypothetical:

> Yankee Pictures and Aussie Pictures are movie production companies. Together, they co-produced the movie "A Yank in the Outback." Pursuant to their co-production agreement, Aussie owns the copyright to the movie in Australia, Canada, South Africa and the United Kingdom; and Yankee owns the movie's copyright in the rest of the world, including of course the United States. The Independent Film & Television Alliance sponsors an annual trade show in Santa Monica known as the American Film Market. Producers and distributors from all over the world attend the show. Producers attend in order to sell (i.e., license) distribution rights to distributors; and distributors attend in order to buy (i.e., license) distribution rights for the particular countries in which they do business.
>
> * If, during the American Film Market, Aussie Pictures issues licenses to Australian, Canadian, South African and British companies "authorizing" them to distribute that movie in Australia, Canada, South Africa and the UK, does Yankee have a valid claim under U.S. law because the "authorization" took place in the United States?
> * If, during the American Film Market, Aussie Pictures issues licenses to distribution companies from North Korea and Iran – two countries with which the United States does not have copyright treaties – "authorizing" them to distribute the movie in those countries, does Yankee have a valid claim under U.S. law because the "authorization" took place in the United States?

If you concluded that the answer to these questions is "no" (i.e., Yankee would not have a valid claim), then how should *Curb* and *Expediters* have been decided, *if* the uses authorized in those cases were uses that did *not* infringe copyright *under the copyright laws of those countries*? If you concluded that under those circumstances, *Curb* and *Expediters* should have been decided differently (i.e., no subject matter jurisdiction) that means (doesn't it?) that *Curb* and *Expediters* held, in effect, that it is an infringement under the U.S. Copyright Act to "authorize" in the United

States activity that takes place in other countries, *only if* that activity infringes the copyright laws of the other countries where that activity takes place. If so, wouldn't mean that in order for a U.S. District Court to decide whether it has subject matter jurisdiction, it first would have to decide the merits (or at least the probable merits) of the plaintiff's claim under the copyright law of the other country? Does this conclusion make sense?

*Subafilms* is binding precedent in the Ninth Circuit, and *Armstrong* and *Seals* are the opinions of two District Judges in the Second and Seventh Circuits where they aren't binding on other judges but are likely to be persuasive. *Curb* and *Expediters* are the opinions of two District Judges in the Sixth and Third Circuits, where they aren't binding on other judges but also are likely to be persuasive. How do you think judges in other circuits would decide the question of whether merely authorizing infringing activity abroad is sufficient to give them subject matter jurisdiction? The following hypothetical puts that question in context:

> Suppose that Freddie, working from his co-op apartment in Atlanta (in the Eleventh Circuit), begins to issue licenses to website operators in Europe, Asia and Africa, purporting to authorize them to post on their websites digital versions of motion pictures and music recordings whose copyrights are owned by American studios and record companies. Freddie isn't affiliated with any of these studios or record companies, and he isn't authorized to issue copyright licenses for the use of their works. Freddie is simply a fraud. He has been able to persuade website operators abroad that he is an authorized licensing agent for American studios and record companies. Taken in by his fraud, foreign website operators pay him license fees for authorization he has no power to grant. Assume that the movies and recordings are available on DVDs and CDs in the countries where these website operators are located, so Freddie doesn't even have to ship anything to them. He simply collects their license fees – which they pay through PayPal – and he sends them bogus license agreements as email attachments.

If the studios and record companies were to sue Freddie in federal District Court in Atlanta, do you suppose the court would have subject matter jurisdiction over their claims?

If not – that is, if the Eleventh Circuit were to follow *Subafilms, Armstrong* and *Seals* rather than *Curb* and *Expediters* – what could the studios and record companies do to prevent Freddie from continuing his fraud and to collect damages for what he has done already? (The answer to this question is addressed below, in the section on alternate grounds for subject matter jurisdiction.)

#### iv. Activity abroad resulted in infringing activities in U.S.

In *Subafilms, Curb, Expediters, Armstong* and *Seals*, the authorizations took place in the U.S. and the allegedly infringing activity took place abroad. Sometimes, though, activity takes place abroad that results in other allegedly infringing activity in the U.S. The issue in these kinds of cases is whether U.S. courts have subject matter jurisdiction over the acts that took place *abroad* (as well as the infringing activity that took place in the U.S.), or whether instead the foreign acts are beyond the reach of U.S. copyright law and thus beyond the jurisdiction of U.S. courts.

Suppose, for example, that a German company reproduced – in Germany – works whose copyrights were owned by someone *other than* the German company. Suppose too that the German company sold those works to a German wholesaler which resold them to an American retailer which sold them in the United States. U.S. District Courts would have subject matter jurisdiction to hear the copyright owner's infringement lawsuit against the hapless American retailer. But would U.S. District Courts also have subject matter jurisdiction against the German company on account of its actions that took place in Germany? (Of course, the U.S. court would have to have personal jurisdiction over the German company as well. That issue is considered next section of this chapter.)

### GB Marketing USA Inc. v. Gerolsteiner Brunnen GmbH & Co.
### 782 F.Supp. 763 (W.D.N.Y. 1991)

United States District Judge David G. Larimer: . . .

In 1988, plaintiff, GB Marketing USA Inc. ("GB"), a New York corporation, began distributing Gerolsteiner Sprudel ("the water") in the United States. The water was bottled in Germany by defendant Gerolsteiner Brunnen ("Gerolsteiner"), a German corporation, and exported to America by defendant Miller & Co. ("Miller"), also a German corporation. Miller in turn sold the water to GB in the United States for distribution. . . .

In an August 24, 1988 telex to Miller's President Jens Saggau ("Saggau"), Kenneth Gauntlett ("Gauntlett"), President of GB, expressed some dissatisfaction with the design of the label that was then being used on the bottles that were to be distributed in the United States. Gauntlett suggested that the label be replaced with one that he had "designed." . . .

In a fax on August 26, Saggau told Gauntlett that Miller would approve the new label. . . . Saggau also indicated that Gauntlett could copyright the label. . .
. .

On April 18, 1989, Gauntlett [GB's President] . . . submitted a registration form for the label to the United States Copyright Office (Registration Number TX 2 672 769). On the form, Gauntlett listed himself as the author. . . .

For reasons that are not altogether clear at this point, some problems arose in the relationship between GB and Miller. These problems eventually led to Miller's termination of the relationship in January 1991. Miller thereafter began using defendant Stockmeyer (North America) Inc. ("Stockmeyer"), a New Jersey corporation, as its American distributor.

GB commenced the instant action on April 5, 1991. The complaint . . . alleges that defendants have infringed its copyrights on the bottle label. . . . GB seeks an order permanently enjoining defendants from infringing the copyrights, and directing defendants to turn over all of plaintiff's copyrighted materials in defendants' possession. GB also requests damages for the infringement. . . .

Gerolsteiner . . . moves . . . for dismissal or summary judgment. . . .

Gerolsteiner alleges that the court lacks subject matter jurisdiction over the copyright claim as to Gerolsteiner because its alleged infringing activities all occurred outside the United States. Gerolsteiner notes that the complaint alleges that the labels are put on the bottles by Gerolsteiner in Germany.

GB agrees that there is no jurisdiction if the infringing actions occurred entirely outside the United States. GB argues, however, that defendants have distributed the water with the infringing labels in this country. GB contends that Gerolsteiner contributed to the infringement by affixing the labels, which were clearly designed for the American market, at Gerolsteiner's plant in Germany.

"It is well established that copyright laws generally do not have extraterritorial application." Where copyright infringement occurs both inside and outside the United States, the district court has jurisdiction, but only over the U.S. infringement.

An analysis of the copyright statute demonstrates that subject matter jurisdiction does exist in this case. Section 106 of Title 17 grants the owner of a copyright the exclusive rights "to do and to authorize" certain acts, among which are the reproduction and distribution of the copyrighted work. The distribution right includes the right to import copies of the work. 17 U.S.C. §602(a).

Congress's use of the phrase "to authorize" was intended to establish the liability of a "contributory infringer," which is a person "who, with knowledge of the infringing activity, induces, causes, or materially contributes to the infringing conduct of another."

Infringement, then, may be either direct (e.g., actual distribution of the work), or contributory. Title 17 U.S.C. §501 also makes this clear, since it defines a copyright "infringer" as "anyone who violates any of the exclusive rights of the copyright owner. . . ." Since one of those rights is the right to authorize importation, then, one who knowingly induces, causes, or contributes to the importation of a copyrighted work may be liable as a contributory infringer.

In the case at bar, Gerolsteiner's alleged activities include both direct and contributory infringement. Gerolsteiner's alleged labeling and sale of the bottles to Miller would (assuming the copyright to be valid) constitute a direct infringement of GB's reproduction and distribution rights. That act in itself would not confer subject matter jurisdiction over Gerolsteiner, however, because it occurred in Germany.

However, the court cannot ignore the fact that Gerolsteiner is alleged to have sold the bottles to Miller with the knowledge and intent that the water would then be exported to the United States and sold here. Gerolsteiner is also alleged to have specifically prepared the bottles for the American market in various ways, such as the manner in which they were packed for shipment. These allegations, if true, would support a claim of contributory infringement arising out of the importation of the water into this country.

I find that subject matter jurisdiction exists over Gerolsteiner. . . .

### v. Alternate grounds for subject matter jurisdiction

Congress has authorized U.S. District Courts to hear many kinds of cases, in addition to cases arising under the U.S. Copyright Act. Among the other kinds of cases that District Courts have been authorized to hear are those involving diversity of citizenship among the parties. This type of jurisdiction is called "diversity jurisdiction," and it is authorized by the following provision of federal law.

## United States Code, 28 U.S.C. §1332

(a) The district courts shall have original jurisdiction of all civil actions where the matter in controversy exceeds the sum or value of $75,000, exclusive of interest and costs, and is between –
  (1) citizens of different States;
  (2) citizens of a State and citizens or subjects of a foreign state. . . .

The question relevant to this course is whether U.S. District Courts may rely on diversity jurisdiction to hear and decide copyright cases arising out of infringements committed in other countries and thus under the laws of other countries.

## London Film Productions v. Intercontinental Communications
### 580 F.Supp. 47 (S.D.N.Y. 1984)

District Judge Carter:

This case presents a novel question of law. Plaintiff, London Film Productions, Ltd. ("London"), a British corporation, has sued Intercontinental Communications, Inc. ("ICI"), a New York corporation based in New York City, for infringements of plaintiff's British copyright. The alleged infringements occurred in Chile and other South American countries. In bringing the case before this Court, plaintiff has invoked the Court's diversity jurisdiction. 28 U.S.C. §1332(a)(2). Defendant has moved to dismiss plaintiff's complaint, arguing that the Court should abstain from exercising jurisdiction over this action.

*Background*

London produces feature motion pictures in Great Britain, which it then distributes throughout the world.[1] [Fn.1 These include: "The Private Life of Henry VIII", "Things To Come", and "Jungle Book", all of which are subjects of this suit.] ICI specializes in the licensing of motion pictures, produced by others, that it believes are in the public domain. London's copyright infringement claim is based mainly on license agreements between ICI and Dilatsa S.A., a buying agent for Chilean television stations. The agreements apparently granted the latter the right to distribute and exhibit certain of plaintiff's motion pictures on television in Chile. London also alleges that ICI has marketed several of its motion pictures in Venezuela, Peru, Equador, Costa Rica and Panama, as well as in Chile.

Plaintiff alleges that the films that are the subjects of the arrangements between Dilatsa S.A. and defendant are protected by copyright in Great Britain as well as in Chile and most other countries (but not in the United States) by virtue of the terms and provisions of the Berne Convention. The license agreements, it maintains, have unjustly enriched defendants and deprived plaintiff of the opportunity to market its motion pictures for television use.

Defendant questions this Court's jurisdiction because plaintiff has not alleged any acts of wrongdoing on defendant's part that constitute violations of United States law,[3] and, therefore, defendant claims that this Court lacks a vital interest in the suit. [Fn.3 The films named, although formerly subject to United States copyrights, are no longer so subject.] In addition, assuming

311

jurisdiction, defendant argues that because the Court would have to construe "alien treaty rights," with which it has no familiarity, the suit would violate, in principle, the doctrine of forum non conveniens. In further support of this contention, defendant maintains that the law would not only be foreign, but complex, since plaintiff's claims would have to be determined with reference to each of the South American states in which the alleged copyright infringements occurred.

*Determination*

There seems to be no dispute that plaintiff has stated a valid cause of action under the copyright laws of a foreign country. Also clear is the fact that this Court has personal jurisdiction over defendant; in fact, there is no showing that defendant may be subject to personal jurisdiction in another forum. Under these circumstances, one authority on copyright law has presented an argument pursuant to which this Court has jurisdiction to hear the matter before it. *Nimmer on Copyright.* It is based on the theory that copyright infringement constitutes a transitory cause of action, and hence may be adjudicated in the courts of a sovereign other than the one in which the cause of action arose. That theory appears sound in the absence of convincing objections by defendant to the contrary.

Although plaintiff has not alleged the violation of any laws of this country by defendant, this Court is not bereft of interest in this case. The Court has an obvious interest in securing compliance with this nation's laws by citizens of foreign nations who have dealings within this jurisdiction. A concern with the conduct of American citizens in foreign countries is merely the reciprocal of that interest. An unwillingness by this Court to hear a complaint against its own citizens with regard to a violation of foreign law will engender, it would seem, a similar unwillingness on the part of a foreign jurisdiction when the question arises concerning a violation of our laws by one of its citizens who has since left our jurisdiction. This Court's interest in adjudicating the controversy in this case may be indirect, but its importance is not thereby diminished.

Of course, not every violation of foreign law by a citizen of this country must be afforded a local tribunal, and defendants cite several cases in which, basically under general principles of comity, it would be inappropriate for this Court to exercise its jurisdiction. This is not one of those. The line of cases on which defendants rely can be distinguished on significant points. The Court in *Vanity Fair Mills, Inc. v. T. Eaton, Ltd.* (2d Cir.), cert. denied (1956), the principal case of those cited, found that the district court had not abused its discretion in declining to assume jurisdiction over a claim for acts of alleged trademark infringement and unfair competition arising in Canada under Canadian law. As defendant here has acknowledged, the complaint raised a "crucial issue" as to the validity of Canadian trademark law. This factor weighed heavily in the Court's decision.

We do not think it the province of United States district courts to determine the validity of trademarks which officials of foreign countries have seen fit to grant. To do so would be to welcome conflicts with the administrative and judicial officers of the Dominion Canada. But as Nimmer has noted, "[i]n adjudicating an infringement action under a foreign copyright law there is . . . no need to pass upon the validity of acts of foreign government officials," since foreign copyright laws, by and large, do not incorporate administrative formalities which must be satisfied to create or perfect a copyright.

The facts in this case confirm the logic of Nimmer's observation. The British films at issue here received copyright protection in Great Britain simply by virtue of publication there. Chile's adherence to the Berne Convention in

1970 automatically conferred copyright protection on these films in Chile. Therefore, no "act of state" is called into question here. Moreover, there is no danger that foreign courts will be forced to accept the inexpert determination of this Court, nor that this Court will create "an unseemly conflict with the judgment of another country." The litigation will determine only whether an American corporation has acted in violation of a foreign copyright, not whether such copyright exists, nor whether such copyright is valid.

With respect to defendant's forum non conveniens argument, it is true that this case will likely involve the construction of at least one, if not several foreign laws.[6] [Fn.6 Plaintiff has alleged infringements in Chile, Venezuela, Peru, Equador, Costa Rica and Panama. Since, under the Berne Convention, the applicable law is the copyright law of the state in which the infringement occurred, defendant seems correct in its assumption that the laws of several countries will be involved in the case.] However, the need to apply foreign law is not in itself reason to dismiss or transfer the case. Moreover, there is no foreign forum in which defendant is the subject of personal jurisdiction, and an available forum is necessary to validate dismissal of an action on the ground of forum non conveniens, for if there is no alternative forum "the plaintiff might find himself with a valid claim but nowhere to assert it."

While this Court might dismiss this action subject to conditions that would assure the plaintiff of a fair hearing, neither plaintiff nor defendant has demonstrated the relative advantage in convenience that another forum, compared to this one, would provide. The selection of a South American country as an alternative forum, although it would afford greater expertise in applying relevant legal principles, would seem to involve considerable hardship and inconvenience for both parties. A British forum might similarly provide some advantages in the construction of relevant law, however, it would impose additional hardships upon defendant, and would raise questions, as would the South American forum, regarding enforceability of a resulting judgment. Where the balance does not tip strongly in favor of an alternative forum it is well-established that the plaintiff's choice of forum should not be disturbed.

For all of the above reasons, the Court finds it has jurisdiction over the instant case and defendant's motion to dismiss is denied, as is its motion to have the Court abstain from exercising its jurisdiction here....

## ITSI T.V. Productions, Inc. v. California Authority of Racing Fairs
## 785 F.Supp. 854 (E.D.Cal. 1992)

Chief District Judge Emeritus Lawrence K. Karlton:

Defendant Hipodromo de Agua Caliente ("Caliente") moves to dismiss plaintiff ITSI T.V. Productions, Inc.'s ("ITSI") complaint for copyright infringement. Caliente asserts that this court lacks subject matter jurisdiction over ITSI's claims, because ITSI cannot show that Caliente is liable for an act of copyright infringement committed in the United States. For the reasons I explain herein, Caliente's motion to dismiss for lack of subject matter jurisdiction is granted.

*I.   Facts and Background*

Plaintiff ITSI T.V. Productions, Inc. is an Illinois corporation doing business in California. . . . Plaintiff alleges that defendant California Authority of Racing Fairs ("CARF"), a California joint powers authority, was created to serve as the agent of certain California fairs which conduct horse racing. . . . In 1983, prior to the 1984 horse racing season, ITSI contracted with CARF to provide closed-circuit television services to the tracks where horse races were being run.

From September 1986 to 1988, the CARF group broadcast plaintiff's television version of the horse races by satellite transmission to locations away from the track where the races were being run in order to facilitate off-track betting on the races. . . .The arrangement for some of the remote locations to receive the simulcast horse races was made by brokers or "disseminators" who "sold" the shows to the remote locations. Defendant Video Sports America ("VSA"), a Delaware corporation doing business in California, is alleged to be a disseminator of plaintiff's shows. . . .

Defendant Hipodromo de Agua Caliente, a Mexican corporation, operated its own horse racing track and twelve (12) off-track betting sites, or "remote locations," in Mexico. In August 1985, Caliente contracted with VSA to receive from VSA and distribute to Caliente's gaming establishments in Mexico "certain audio-visual signals of live horse racing programs, sporting events and related services."

Under the contract, VSA provided Caliente with a coded or scrambled signal of ITSI's shows, live satellite transmission of the shows, and the means and equipment to convert the signal into useable video images for viewing at sites in Mexico. . . .

In May 1988, Caliente began its efforts to contract directly with some California race tracks for the receipt of audio-visual signals. Defendant Los Angeles County Fair (LACF) executed contracts with Caliente on July 25, 1988, and August 16, 1989. CARF executed contracts with Caliente on June 22, 1988, and May 26, 1989. Each contract allows Caliente to "acquire the exclusive right to use, transmit, receive, and to provide for the dissemination of . . . audio-visual signals." Plaintiff alleges that CARF, various county and local fairs and tracks at which races were run, certain brokers or disseminators of the signal, and entities operating off-track betting locations infringed plaintiff's copyright in its "shows" of horse races by simultaneously broadcasting the shows to off-track betting locations without ITSI's authorization.

. . .

I turn now to analysis of the court's subject matter jurisdiction over plaintiff's claims for copyright infringement against defendant Caliente. [Judge Carter then did a lengthy and very sophisticated analysis of whether he had subject matter jurisdiction over the plaintiff's claim against Caliente under the United States Copyright Act; and he came to the following conclusion:]

Because plaintiff has failed to demonstrate that Caliente committed a direct act of copyright infringement in the United States . . . , the court lacks subject matter jurisdiction over plaintiff's claims against Caliente.

*VI. Application of Mexican Copyright Law*

Plaintiff suggests that if Caliente is not liable for an act of infringement which occurred in the United States, plaintiff should be given leave to amend its complaint to state a cause of action against Caliente under Mexican copyright laws for acts Caliente committed in Mexico. This position has gained some support among academics. See Goldstein, COPYRIGHT PRINCIPLES, LAW & PRACTICE ("subject to jurisdictional requirements, a copyright owner may sue an infringer in the United States courts even though the only alleged infringement occurred in another country"); NIMMER (it is "arguable that an action may be brought in [district] court for infringement of a foreign copyright law"). Although one district court has accepted jurisdiction over an action for foreign copyright infringement, see *London Film Productions, Ltd. v. Intercontinental Communications, Inc.*, I discern no clear authority for exercising such jurisdiction. See generally David R. Toraya, Note, "Federal Jurisdiction Over Foreign Copyright Actions – An Unsolicited Reply to Professor Nimmer," 70 *Cornell Law Rev.* 1165 (1985). Moreover, it appears to me that American courts should be reluctant to enter the bramble bush of ascertaining and applying foreign law without an urgent reason to do so.[20] [Fn.20 Even if subject matter jurisdiction did exist over plaintiff's claim for violation of Mexican copyright law, the court would decline to exercise jurisdiction on forum non conveniens grounds, as codified at 28 U.S.C. §1404(a), because exercise of jurisdiction over such a claim would work an extreme hardship on the court in discerning and applying Mexican law.] No such reason has been tendered in this case and, as a matter of common sense and judicial self-restraint, I think it appropriate to decline plaintiff's invitation.

For all the foregoing reasons, plaintiff's claims for copyright infringement against defendant Caliente are dismissed for lack of subject matter jurisdiction.

As powerful as United States District Courts are, they are courts of "limited jurisdiction." That is, their subject matter jurisdiction is limited to the particular types of cases that Congress – by statute – has authorized them to hear. As you have just read, they are authorized to hear copyright cases arising under the United States Copyright Act, and cases arising under other laws – including foreign copyright laws – *if* the parties are citizens of different states or are citizens of a state and another country.

Most *state* courts, by contrast, are courts of "general jurisdiction." This means they are authorized to hear cases of any type, except those types of cases that some other court has exclusive jurisdiction to hear. For example, California Superior Courts are courts of "general jurisdiction," because California law gives them the following authority.

### California Constitution, Article 6, Section 10

. . . Superior courts have original jurisdiction in all other causes [i.e., cases other than those seeking habeas corpus, mandamus, certiorari and prohibition, jurisdiction over which is asserted by the California Supreme Court or courts of appeal]. . . .

### California Code of Civil Procedure §410.10

A court of this state may exercise jurisdiction on any basis not inconsistent with the Constitution of this state or of the United States.

Recall (from the beginning of this chapter) that federal law gives federal District Courts the following authority to hear copyright cases:

### United States Judicial Code
### 28 U.S.C. §1338(a)

The district courts shall have original jurisdiction of any civil action arising under any Act of *Congress* relating to . . . copyrights . . . . Such jurisdiction shall be *exclusive* of the *courts of the states* in . . . copyright cases. [Emphasis added.]

Recall too (again, from the beginning of this chapter) your answer to this question:

1. In a purely *domestic* copyright infringement case – one in which an American alleges that its copyright was infringed by another American as a result of an unauthorized use of the plaintiff's work inside the United States – could the plaintiff's lawyer elect to file suit in, say, the Superior Court of the State of California, because (for example) the lawyer has a lot of experience in Superior Court (and with Superior Court juries) but none in federal court?

Now, consider California Constitution Article 6, California Code of Civil Procedure §410.10 and United States Judicial Code 28 U.S.C. §1338(a), and decide whether California Superior Courts have subject matter jurisdiction to hear claims of copyright infringement committed in other countries and thus under the copyright laws of other countries. In other words, if ITSI T.V. Productions had sued Hipodromo de Agua Caliente in California Superior Court in Fresno, instead of in the United States District Court for the Eastern District of California in Fresno, would the Superior Court have had subject matter jurisdiction to hear the case?

### b. Personal jurisdiction

In *addition to* subject matter jurisdiction, all courts (federal and state) also must have *personal* jurisdiction over defendants. You probably devoted a good deal of attention to the requirements of personal jurisdiction in your Civil Procedure course; and everything you learned there is pertinent here. Among other things, you'll recall that personal jurisdiction over a defendant is *always* necessary, and is *not* conferred by the *plaintiff's* residence in the district where suit is filed. So, an infringement committed abroad by a defendant that does not have the necessary contacts with the U.S. will *not* confer jurisdiction on an American court, even though the plaintiff is a U.S. national and its infringed work was created in U.S.

Because you've studied personal jurisdiction before, we can focus our inquiry into personal jurisdiction in the context of international copyright litigation on just two cases. They were decided within just a couple of years of one another; and both were decided by the Ninth Circuit Court of Appeals. Are they, however, consistent with one another? If not, which of the two decisions do you think reflects the better view concerning the circumstances under which American courts have personal jurisdiction over copyright defendants in other countries?

### Roth v. Garcia Marquez
### 942 F.2d 617 (9th Cir. 1991)

Circuit Judge Dorothy Nelson:

This case revolves around Richard Roth's and Richard Roth Productions' ("Roth") attempt to secure the movie rights to Gabriel Garcia Marquez' novel *Love in the Time of Cholera*. Roth appeals the district court's dismissal of his complaint for failure to state a claim and its denial of leave to amend. In addition, Garcia Marquez and agent Carmen Balcells appeal the district court's denial of their motion to dismiss for lack of personal jurisdiction. While none of these three issues is easily resolved, we initially affirm the district court's finding of personal jurisdiction. We also affirm the district court's dismissal for failure to state a claim and its denial of leave to amend. In sum, we are unwilling to grant through litigation what negotiation could not achieve.

## I.  Factual and Procedural Background

Appellant Richard Roth is a movie producer who lives in California and carries out his projects through Richard Roth Productions. Gabriel Garcia Marquez, an internationally renowned author who won the Nobel Prize for Literature in 1982, has written numerous bestselling novels. The film rights to his work *Love in the Time of Cholera* ("*Cholera*") are at issue in the present litigation. Garcia Marquez has resided in Mexico City for the last sixteen years. Carmen Balcells is the president of a literary agency headquartered in Barcelona, Spain. A resident of Barcelona, Balcells has been Garcia Marquez' literary agent for more than 25 years.

In late 1986, Roth contacted Garcia Marquez in Mexico City to express his interest in making a film based on *Cholera*. Roth flew to Havana, Cuba, to meet Garcia Marquez on this matter. Garcia Marquez told Roth that he would consider selling film rights under the following three conditions: 1) Roth would agree to pay him a large sum of money (later Balcells specified the sum of five million dollars); 2) Roth would agree to use a Latin American director; and 3) Roth would shoot the film in Colombia. Garcia Marquez later authorized Balcells to pursue negotiations with Roth.

Negotiations dragged on with disputes both about the price for the option and the identity of the possible director. Roth traveled a number of times to Barcelona and Mexico City to meet with Balcells and Garcia Marquez, and repeated calls, letters, and faxes passed between the parties. The only meetings that occurred in the United States were in May 1988, when Balcells traveled to California to attend an American Booksellers Association convention and met with Roth on the side, and in November 1988, when Garcia Marquez visited Los Angeles for four days at the social invitation of a friend. He met with Roth and agreed that Roth could shoot the film in Brazil, not Colombia, but he remained firm on the other two terms.

On November 17, 1988, the same day that Roth and Garcia Marquez met, Alan Schwartz, Roth's representative, faxed a letter to Balcells in Barcelona. The letter offered Garcia Marquez $200,000 for the grant of an option of two years on the film rights, the right to extend the option for another year for an additional $100,000, these monies to be applied against $1,250,000 to be paid when the option was exercised, $400,000 more on the release of the video, $350,000 more on the release of television showing, and 5% of the net profits of the film. On January 19, 1989, Schwartz telecopied another letter, which changed the first sum of $200,000 for the option to $400,000. The letter, which is the crux of this litigation, stated that the first paragraph of the November 17, 1988, letter was changed to the following:

> (a) A payment of $400,000 for an option of two years to acquire the motion picture and allied rights to this novel. The option shall commence upon signature by Gabriel Garcia Marquez to the formal agreement and the return of said signed agreement to me or Richard Roth, at which time the option payment shall be made to you as agent for Gabriel Garcia Marquez.

The letter also stated: "On behalf of Richard Roth and myself I am very happy to confirm the final agreement between Richard and Gabriel Garcia

Marquez . . ." and "Please convey to Garcia Marquez the excitement Richard and I feel in being able finally to get this project moving." Balcells countersigned the letter and faxed back the following the next day:

> Thank you for today's fax and I am happy that this deal is finally concluded. I had no time to tell Gabo [Marquez] about this conclusion. In any case, I am returning your letter duly signed. I shall await the formal agreement at your earliest convenience.

That same day, Roth wrote independently to Balcells thanking her "so much for concluding the deal" and telling her he was "putting the best champagne on ice so we can celebrate and drink it together."

In late February Schwartz transmitted the 25-page formal agreement to Balcells. Balcells objected to a number of points, particularly the omission of clauses about a Latin American director and the site of the shooting. Balcells communicated these objections, and weeks of renewed negotiations failed to produce an agreement. Garcia Marquez never signed the formal agreement, and the money was never paid him.

For personal jurisdiction analysis, Garcia Marquez lives in Mexico City and has never resided in California. He has visited the state four times for a total of twenty days. He met with Roth once in California, but entered the state for a social purpose. He has never owned property in the state, nor has he ever conducted business on a regular basis or authorized any resident of the state to do so on his behalf. He has maintained a checking account, not his principal one, in Los Angeles since 1988 for the purposes of having an account in dollars for certain transactions occurring outside of California.

Balcells lives in Barcelona. She has never lived in California, though she has visited twice. On one of those occasions, she met with Roth, though she was in the state for a convention. She has never owned property in California, has no office or telephone number there, and has never conducted business on a regular basis or authorized any resident of the state to do so for her.

In December 1989, Roth filed a complaint in district court seeking declaratory relief to determine the status of his rights to produce the film. Appellees filed a motion to dismiss, alleging both that the court lacked personal jurisdiction over each defendant and that because appellees had not entered into a binding contract, the complaint failed to state a claim upon which relief could be granted. The district court denied the motion to dismiss for lack of personal jurisdiction, but it granted the motion to dismiss for failure to state a claim. The district court also denied Roth's motion for leave to amend the complaint. Both sides now appeal the unfavorable ruling(s) against them.

## II. Personal Jurisdiction

Appellees cross-appeal the district court's denial of their motion to dismiss for lack of personal jurisdiction. Neither Balcells nor Garcia Marquez may be haled into court, they contend, without offending due process. . . .

The California long-arm statute provides that jurisdiction may be exercised over nonresident defendants "on any basis not inconsistent with the Constitution of this state or of the United States." Cal.Civ.Proc.Code §410.10. Since California's jurisdictional statute is coextensive with federal due process requirements, the jurisdictional inquiries under state law and federal due process merge into one analysis. The due process clause prohibits the exercise of jurisdiction over nonresident defendants unless those defendants have "minimum contacts" with the forum state so that the exercise of jurisdiction "does not offend traditional notions of fair play and substantial justice." *International Shoe Co. v. Washington*, 326 U.S. 310 (1945)

We have interpreted *International Shoe* and its progeny as allowing jurisdiction by California courts over a nonresident defendant if he has enough continuous contacts with California to subject him to the court's general jurisdiction or if the specific cause of action arises out of a defendant's more limited contacts with the state so that California may exercise limited or specific jurisdiction over him. Appellants concede that there is no general jurisdiction over appellees; the question, then, turns on whether the contacts in this case enable California to exercise limited jurisdiction over Balcells and Garcia Marquez. A three-part test has been articulated for limited jurisdiction: 1) the nonresident defendant must have purposefully availed himself of the privilege of conducting activities in the forum by some affirmative act or conduct; 2) plaintiff's claim must arise out of or result from the defendant's forum-related activities; and 3) exercise of jurisdiction must be reasonable.

A. *Purposeful Availment*

. . .

Appellees argue that because Roth initiated all the contacts and because he was the one who "reached out" to effect the contract, they should not be subject to California law. There was no solicitation of business by appellees, they maintain, that resulted in contract negotiations or the transaction of business. We have explained that "the purposeful availment analysis turns upon whether the defendant's contacts are attributable to 'actions by the defendant himself,' or conversely to the unilateral activity of another party."

Here, it seems clear that the predominant efforts were made by the appellant, not the appellees. Roth traveled to Havana, Barcelona, and Mexico City in his peripatetic effort to secure the movie rights. Garcia Marquez and Balcells were in Los Angeles for other purposes when each met individually with Roth. While we concede that negotiations did take place at that time, it should be borne in mind that "temporary physical presence" in the forum does not suffice to confer personal jurisdiction. Further, Roth and his agents placed over 100 calls and sent numerous faxes to the two appellees. "When a California business seeks out purchasers in other states . . . [and] deals with them by out-of-state agents or by interstate mail and telephone, it is not entitled to force the customer to come to California to defend an action on the contract."

Roth also contends that the phone lines were used in the other direction – i.e., appellees made calls and returned letters and faxes to him. As this court held in [in an earlier case], "[M]any transactions take place solely by mail or wire across state lines, obviating the need for physical presence. . . . Thus, the Court has held that the physical absence of the defendant and the transaction from the forum cannot defeat the exercise of personal jurisdiction." However, "both this court and the courts of California have concluded that ordinarily 'use of the mails, telephone, or other international communications simply do not qualify as purposeful activity invoking the benefits and protection of the [forum] state.'"

There are two facts, then, that marginally work in appellees' favor: their minimal physical presence in the forum and the fact that it was appellant who made the sedulous efforts of solicitation. While this is a very close call, a final and broader issue appears to swing the first prong for Roth, namely the future consequences of the contract. . . .

The point here is simply that the contract concerned a film, most of the work for which would have been performed in California. Though the shooting most likely would have taken place in Brazil, all of the editing, production work, and advertising would have occurred in California. This is not an instance where the contract was a one-shot deal that was merely negotiated and signed by one party in the forum; on the contrary, most of the future of the contract would have centered on the forum. The checks that Roth would have sent Garcia Marquez, which appellees attempt to minimize, would have depended upon activities in California and the United States. In looking at the "economic reality," it seems that the contract's subject would have continuing and extensive involvement with the forum.

Though neither side decisively triumphs under this analysis, it appears that there was enough purposeful availment here to compel a finding of jurisdiction on this prong.

### B. Arising Out of Forum-Related Activities

There is no dispute on this second prong, as appellees concede that appellant's claim arises out of the January 19 letter, which was negotiated and executed by a party who was in the forum at the time, namely Roth in Los Angeles.

### C. Reasonableness

The third prong asks whether the exercise of jurisdiction would be reasonable. We have set forth a congeries of factors to be considered in determining whether the exercise of jurisdiction over a nonresident defendant satisfies the reasonableness test: 1) the extent of the defendant's purposeful interjection into the forum state's affairs; 2) the burden on the defendant; 3) conflicts of law between the forum and defendant's home jurisdiction; 4) the forum's interest in adjudicating the dispute; 5) the most efficient judicial resolution of the dispute; 6) the plaintiff's interest in convenient and effective relief; and 7) the existence of an alternative forum. Since none of these factors is dispositive, we must balance the seven.

#### 1. Extent of Purposeful Interjection

In light of the first prong of purposeful availment, analysis of this first factor in the third prong would be redundant. As we have concluded, albeit narrowly, that appellees purposefully availed themselves of the privilege of conducting activities in California, there is no need to analyze this first factor separately.

#### 2. Burdens on Defendant

Appellees argue that because they are residents of foreign countries and speak different languages than English, requiring them to come defend a suit in California would impose a great burden. . . .

Roth argues that it would be no more burdensome for appellees to litigate here than for him to litigate in Mexico or Spain, and "this court 'must examine the burden on the defendant in light of the corresponding burden on the plaintiff.'" This seems to be in conflict with language from [an earlier case], which states that "[t]he primary concern is for the defendant's burden." At bottom, because Roth had no problems in his globe-trotting endeavors to persuade Balcells and Garcia Marquez to sell the film rights to him, he should not complain that litigation outside the United States would be particularly onerous for him. Appellees have shown no similar propensity for travel. Although this factor cuts in favor of appellees, "unless such inconvenience is so great as to constitute a deprivation of due process, it will not overcome clear justifications for the exercise of jurisdiction." An examination of the other factors is thus required.

#### 3. Extent of Conflict With Sovereignty of Foreign State

Appellees point the court to the language of [an earlier case]: "Great care and reserve should be exercised when extending our notions of personal jurisdiction into the international field." In addition, "a foreign nation presents a higher sovereignty barrier than another state within the United States." . . . This factor, then, must line up on appellees' side.

### 4. Forum State's Interest in Adjudication

Appellees argue that California has little interest in the outcome of a private contractual dispute. They distinguish torts, for which there is a strong public interest in redress of wrongs. Appellees even go so far as to say that assumption of jurisdiction where minimal contacts exist might have an adverse effect on commerce, since foreigners would be loathe to enter into contracts with Californians that might result in their being haled into foreign courts. Appellant states simply that any state has an interest in providing an effective means of redress for residents who have negotiated and executed contracts within the state. Of course, appellees remonstrate that their whole point is that this contract was neither negotiated − for the most part − nor executed in California.

. . . [T]his factor seems to be a toss-up, with perhaps a slight edge going to appellees.

### 5. Most Efficient Judicial Resolution

This category, too, holds no edge for either party. Appellees live outside the United States, while appellant lives in California. Witnesses to the meetings in Mexico City, Havana, and Barcelona obviously live in foreign countries, while Roth's agents live in California. Though the film would be financed in California and would employ other Californians, these persons' testimony would not be relevant to whether a contract was formed; they would not be witnesses in this trial. Other cases in this circuit provide no guidance because of differing fact patterns. This factor is a push.

### 6. Convenience and Effectiveness of Relief for Plaintiff

Appellees dare not argue that it would be more convenient for Roth to litigate outside the United States. Nevertheless, they posit that because Roth was willing and able to pursue Balcells and Garcia Marquez by flying to different countries, he cannot now complain that it would be too inconvenient for him to return to the site of his solicitations in order to seek by litigation what he failed to achieve by negotiation. . . . [N]o doctorate in astrophysics is required to deduce that trying a case where one lives is almost always a plaintiff's preference. . . . Here, Roth did display an ability to meet and work in foreign countries. In all, this factor goes to Roth, but not as decisively as in other cases.

### 7. Availability of an Alternative Forum

Alternative fora are Spain, where Balcells lives, and Mexico, where Garcia Marquez resides. While neither is decidedly a worse place than California to try the case, neither is demonstrably better. We have held that the plaintiff "bears the burden of proving the unavailability of an alternative forum." . . . Here, Roth has not shown that he could not litigate in Spain or Mexico. Doubtless he would prefer not to, but that is not the test. Chalk this one up for appellees.

### 8. Balancing the Seven Factors

Of the seven factors, then, the following two favor appellant: purposeful interjection and convenience for plaintiff. The following three tilt toward appellees: burden on defendant, conflict with sovereignty of another state, and availability of an alternative forum. Finally, two factors do not favor either side:

forum state's interest and efficient judicial resolution. This is, in sum, an extremely close question.

## D. Weighing the Three Prongs

Appellant has narrowly satisfied the first prong, namely that appellees purposefully availed themselves of the privilege of conducting activities in the forum. He has also passed the second prong in that the claim arises out of appellees' forum-related activities. Garcia Marquez and Balcells, on the other hand, can make a strong argument on the third prong, namely that the exercise of jurisdiction may be unreasonable. Their difficulty, though, is in surmounting the following standard: "Once purposeful availment has been established, the forum's exercise of jurisdiction is presumptively reasonable. To rebut that presumption, a defendant 'must present a compelling case' that the exercise of jurisdiction would, in fact, be unreasonable." Appellees may be able to show that the exercise of jurisdiction might be unreasonable, but the closeness of the question manifests that they cannot do so in a compelling fashion. Because in the end appellees' showing does not surmount their hurdle, we find that personal jurisdiction does exist. We affirm the district court's denial of appellees' motion to dismiss.

[However, the Ninth Circuit then went on to *affirm* the district court's *dismissal* of the case on the substantive ground that no contract existed between the parties!]

## Rano v. Sipa Press
### 987 F.2d 580 (9th Cir. 1993)

Melvin Brunetti, Circuit Judge:

*Overview*

This [is an] appeal from a dismissal for lack of personal jurisdiction . . . in a copyright infringement suit. . . .

*Facts and Proceedings Below*

The parties to this appeal include: Plaintiff-Appellant Kip Rano, a professional photographer and citizen of Great Britain who resides and has his principal place of business in California; and Defendants-Appellees Sipa Press, a French corporation, Sipa Press, Inc., a Delaware subsidiary corporation, and Sipa, Inc., a New York subsidiary corporation (collectively Sipa), and Goskin Sipahioglu, President and one of three owners of Sipa Press. Sipa is a photograph distribution syndicate.

In France, on or before 1978, the parties entered into an oral copyright license agreement whereby Rano granted to Sipa a non-exclusive license of unspecified duration to reproduce, distribute, sell, and authorize others to reproduce, distribute, and sell his photographs. In return, Sipa agreed to store and develop the negatives and to pay fifty percent of the net royalties generated from its sales and distributions.

The relationship went smoothly for about eight years. Pursuant to agreement, Rano submitted several thousand of his photographs to Sipa, which Sipa distributed and paid royalties for. In March of 1986, however, Rano sent a letter to Sipahioglu informing him that he was changing agencies and that he would no longer be sending his negatives to Sipa. He gave as his reasons Sipa's failure to timely pay royalties, low sales, poor photography assignments, and unwillingness to reimburse certain expenses. Starting in July of 1986, Rano made several requests that Sipa return all of the negatives he had sent to them. Finally, on March 12, 1987, Rano informed Sipahioglu that he "did not authorize Sipa to sell any more of [his] photographs."

In July of 1989, Rano sued Sipa and Sipahioglu alleging that Sipa infringed his copyright by: (1) failing to credit him for a photograph of the Duchess of York, the former Sara Ferguson; (2) failing to pay certain royalties; (3) continuing to distribute some of his photographs after he demanded their return and after he had attempted to terminate their licensing agreement; (4) failing to return some of his photographs upon demand; and (5) placing defective copyright notices on slide mounts for his photographs. . . . . . As a remedy for the copyright infringement claims, Rano sought an injunction against Sipa's further use of his photographs, the delivery of the photographs for impoundment, a declaratory judgment as to the rights to his photographs, compensatory and punitive damages, and costs of the suit and attorney's fees.

The district court . . . granted defendant Sipahioglu's motion to dismiss for lack of personal jurisdiction. . . .

*VI. Personal Jurisdiction Over Sipahioglu . . .*

The district court dismissed the claim against Sipahioglu because it found it lacked personal jurisdiction over him. Sipahioglu is a citizen of Turkey and a long-time resident of France. His ties to California include three short visits to California in the last seven years, totaling six days. None of Sipahioglu's visits to California involved Rano or his photographs.

There is no applicable federal statute governing personal jurisdiction in this matter, hence the law of the state in which the district court sits – California – applies. . . . California has adopted a typical "long-arm" statute, rendering jurisdiction coextensive with the outer limits of due process. . . . Cal. Code Civ. Pro. § 410.10.

A state may assert either general or specific jurisdiction over a nonresident defendant. If the defendant's activities in the state are "substantial" or "continuous and systematic," general jurisdiction may be asserted even if the claim is unrelated to the defendant's activities. . . .Rano does not argue that Sipahioglu is subject to general jurisdiction; instead, Rano relies on specific jurisdiction.

Under specific jurisdiction, a court may assert jurisdiction for a cause of action that arises out of the defendant's forum-related activities. In [an earlier case] we established a three-part test for determining when a court can exercise specific jurisdiction:

(1) the defendant must perform an act or consummate a transaction within the forum, purposefully availing himself of the privilege of conducting activities in the forum and invoking the benefits and protections of its laws;

(2) the claim must arise out of or result from the defendant's forum-related activities;

(3) exercise of jurisdiction must be reasonable. . . . Rano must show that all three prongs are satisfied for us to assert personal jurisdiction. . . .

Rano contends that Sipahioglu caused and profited from Sipa's grant of licenses of Rano's photographs to magazine publications that he knew would be distributed in California. This is enough, Rano argues, to satisfy the "purposeful availment" and "arising out of" requirements. . . .

We disagree. Sipahioglu could not have foreseen Rano's fortuitous move from Europe to California. . . . Further, there is no evidence that Sipahioglu invoked any of the benefits or protections of California's laws. Rano's argument, if accepted, would render Sipahioglu, and other foreign owners of art who sell their products to publications, amenable to personal jurisdiction in every state in which their art eventually is displayed. We have held that litigation against an alien defendant requires a higher jurisdictional barrier than litigation against a citizen from a sister state. . . .

We find that Rano has not satisfied the burden of establishing personal jurisdiction over Sipahioglu; hence we affirm the district court's dismissal of the claims against . . . Goskin Sipahioglu for lack of personal jurisdiction.

Although the text of the *Rano v. Sipa Press* opinion that you just read is tightly edited, that is *not* why you didn't see *Rano* cite to, let alone discuss, the court's then two-year old opinion in *Roth v. Garcia Marquez*. In deciding *Rano*, Judge Brunetti simply ignored Judge Nelson's opinion in *Roth*, as though *Roth* had never been decided at all. Taken together, what do the *Roth* and *Rano* opinions tell us about when courts in the Ninth Circuit have personal jurisdiction over parties in other countries? (If you become a civil litigator in Los Angeles – or elsewhere in the Ninth Circuit – this could become, for you, the most practical question asked in this entire book.)

Here's a concluding thought about *Roth v. Garcia Marquez* that may explain its outcome. If the Court of Appeals had held that the District Court did *not* have personal jurisdiction over Garcia Marquez, Roth could have refiled the lawsuit against Garcia Marquez in Mexico, couldn't he? However, because the Court of Appeals held that the District Court *did* have personal jurisdiction over him, *but no contract was ever entered into*, the case came to a complete end, with Garcia Marquez completely victorious, right? So, with respect to the personal jurisdiction issue, was Garcia Marquez better or worse off, as a result of the Court of Appeals' conclusion that the District Court did have personal jurisdiction over him? In other words, was a movie version of *Love in the Time of Cholera* finally made – by Stone Village Pictures and New Line Cinema, but *not* Richard Roth Productions – *because of*, or *in spite of*, the Court of Appeals' decision in *Roth v. Garcia Marquez*?

### c. Venue

Sometimes, even when courts *do* have personal jurisdiction over a defendant (as well as subject matter jurisdiction over the claim), defendants prefer that the case be heard in another court. Usually, the preferred court is one that is more convenient for the defendant than the court chosen by the plaintiff. Indeed, the legal doctrine that defendants use in those cases is the doctrine of "forum non conveniens" – Latin for "this forum isn't convenient." As you might suspect, the doctrine of forum non conveniens is often asserted in international cases, when a defendant from one country is sued in a court in the plaintiff's country.

The following case – *Boosey & Hawkes v. Disney* – nicely describes the doctrine of forum non conveniens and how it should be applied. The case is peculiar, though, in one respect: its fact pattern is the mirror image of cases in which the doctrine is most-often asserted. Boosey & Hawkes, a British company, sued Disney, an American company, in an American court in New York City where Disney has an office (and where its then Chairman of the Board had an apartment). Disney responded by asserting the doctrine of forum non conveniens; it argued – successfully, at first, though not in the end

– that Boosey & Hawkes should have filed the lawsuit in the court of another country – indeed, maybe in the courts of 18 other countries! Why do you suppose Disney argued that?

## Boosey & Hawkes Music Publishers, Ltd. v. Walt Disney Co.
## 145 F.3d 481 (2nd Cir. 1998)

Circuit Judge Pierre Leval:

Boosey & Hawkes Music Publishers Ltd., an English corporation and the assignee of Igor Stravinsky's copyrights for "The Rite of Spring," brought this action alleging that the Walt Disney Company's foreign distribution in video cassette and laser disc format ("video format") of the film "Fantasia," featuring Stravinsky's work, infringed Boosey's rights. In 1939 Stravinsky licensed Disney's distribution of The Rite of Spring in the motion picture. Boosey, which acquired Stravinsky's copyright in 1947, contends that the license does not authorize distribution in video format.

The district court (Duffy, J.) granted partial summary judgment to Boosey, declaring that Disney's video format release was not authorized by the license agreement. [Nevertheless] the court granted partial summary judgment to Disney, dismissing . . . Boosey's foreign copyright claims under the doctrine of forum non conveniens. Boosey appeals from [that ruling]. . . .

We . . . reverse the order dismissing for forum non conveniens. . . .

*I. Background*

During 1938, Disney sought Stravinsky's authorization to use The Rite of Spring (sometimes referred to as the "work" or the "composition") throughout the world in a motion picture. Because under United States law the work was in the public domain, Disney needed no authorization to record or distribute it in this country, but permission was required for distribution in countries where Stravinsky enjoyed copyright protection. In January 1939 the parties executed an agreement (the "1939 Agreement") giving Disney rights to use the work in a motion picture in consideration of a fee to Stravinsky of $6,000.

The 1939 Agreement provided that

> In consideration of the sum of Six Thousand ($6,000) Dollars, receipt of which is hereby acknowledged, [Stravinsky] does hereby give and grant unto Walt Disney Enterprises, a California corporation . . . the nonexclusive, irrevocable right, license, privilege and authority to record in any manner, medium or form, and to license the performance of, the musical composition hereinbelow set out . . .

Under "type of use" in ¶3, the Agreement specified that

> The music of said musical composition may be used in one motion picture throughout the length thereof or through such portion or portions thereof as the Purchaser shall desire. The said music may be used in whole or in part and may be adapted, changed, added to or subtracted from, all as shall appear desirable to the Purchaser in its uncontrolled discretion.
> . . . The title "Rites of Spring" or "Le Sacre de Printemps", or any other title, may be used as the title of said motion picture and the name of [Stravinsky] may be announced in or in connection with said motion picture.

The Agreement went on to specify in ¶4 that Disney's license to the work "is limited to the use of the musical composition in synchronism or timed-relation with the motion picture."

Paragraph Five of the Agreement provided that

> The right to record the musical composition as covered by this agreement is conditioned upon the performance of the musical work in theatres having valid licenses from the American Society of Composers, Authors and Publishers, or any other performing rights society having jurisdiction in the territory in which the said musical composition is performed.

We refer to this clause, which is of importance to the litigation, as "the ASCAP Condition."

Finally, ¶7 of the Agreement provided that "the licensor reserves to himself all rights and uses in and to the said musical composition not herein specifically granted" (the "reservation clause").

Disney released Fantasia, starring Mickey Mouse, in 1940. The film contains no dialogue. It matches a pantomime of animated beasts and fantastic creatures to passages of great classical music, creating what critics celebrated as a "partnership between fine music and animated film." The soundtrack uses compositions of Bach, Beethoven, Dukas, Schubert, Tchaikovsky, and Stravinsky, all performed by the Philadelphia Orchestra under the direction of Leopold Stokowski. As it appears in the film soundtrack, The Rite of Spring was shortened from its original 34 minutes to about 22.5; sections of the score were cut, while other sections were reordered. For more than five decades Disney exhibited The Rite of Spring in Fantasia under the 1939 license. The film has been re-released for theatrical distribution at least seven times since 1940, and although Fantasia has never appeared on television in its entirety, excerpts including portions of The Rite of Spring have been televised occasionally over the years. Neither Stravinsky nor Boosey has ever previously objected to any of the distributions.

In 1991 Disney first released Fantasia in video format. The video has been sold in foreign countries, as well as in the United States. To date, the Fantasia video release has generated more than $360 million in gross revenue for Disney.

Boosey brought this action in February 1993. The complaint sought (1) a declaration that the 1939 Agreement did not include a grant of rights to Disney to use the Stravinsky work in video format; [and] (2) damages for copyright infringement in at least 18 foreign countries. . . .

On cross-motions for summary judgment the district court made the rulings described above. In determining that the license did not cover the distribution of a video format, the district court found that while the broad language of the license gave Disney "the right to record [the work] on video tape and laser disc," the ASCAP Condition "prevents Disney from distributing video tapes or laser discs directly to consumers." . . . . The court therefore concluded that Disney's video format sales exceeded the scope of the license.

However, as noted, the district court invoked forum non conveniens to dismiss all of Boosey's claims of copyright infringement because they involved the application of foreign law. . . .

The decision below thus declared Disney an infringer, but granted Boosey no relief, leaving it to sue in the various countries under whose copyright laws it claims infringement. This appeal followed.

## II. Discussion

. . . . Disney challenges the summary judgment which declared that the 1939 Agreement does not authorize video distribution of The Rite of Spring. Boosey appeals . . . the dismissal for forum non conveniens. . . .

### A. Declaratory Judgment on the Scope of the License.

Boosey's request for declaratory judgment raises two issues of contract interpretation: whether the general grant of permission under the 1939 Agreement licensed Disney to use The Rite of Spring in the video format version of Fantasia (on which the district court found in Disney's favor); and, if so, whether the ASCAP Condition barred Disney from exploiting the work through video format (on which the district court found for Boosey).

#### 1. Whether the "motion picture" license covers video format.

. . . . [W]e hold that the district court properly applied [relevant Ninth Circuit doctrine] to find that the basic terms of Disney's license included the right to record and distribute Fantasia in video format.

#### 2. The ASCAP Condition.

Boosey further contends that distribution of Fantasia in video format violated the ASCAP Condition. The district court agreed. It granted summary judgment to Boosey declaring that the ASCAP Condition "prevents Disney from distributing video tapes and laser discs directly to consumers." . . .

Neither the plain terms of the 1939 Agreement nor the sparse and contradictory extrinsic evidence require the conclusion that Disney's license is limited to theatrical performance of the composition. Summary judgment is therefore inappropriate. We vacate the summary grant of declaratory judgment in Boosey's favor and remand for a trial to determine whether Disney's video format release violated the ASCAP Condition.

### B. Foreign Copyright Claims.

Invoking the doctrine of forum non conveniens, the district court dismissed Boosey's second cause of action, which sought damages for copyright infringement deriving from Disney's sales of videocassettes of Fantasia in at least eighteen foreign countries. The court below concluded that these claims should be tried "in each of the nations whose copyright laws are invoked." Boosey appeals, seeking remand to the district court for trial. . . . .

We recently explained that a motion to dismiss under forum non conveniens is decided in two steps. The district court first must determine whether there exists an alternative forum with jurisdiction to hear the case. If so, the court then weighs the factors set out in Gilbert, 330 U.S. at 508-09, 67 S. Ct. at 843 ("the Gilbert factors"), to decide which "forum . . . will be most convenient and will best serve the ends of justice."

The district court failed to consider whether there were alternative fora capable of adjudicating Boosey's copyright claims. It made no determination whether Disney was subject to jurisdiction in the various countries where the court anticipated that trial would occur and did not condition dismissal on Disney's consent to jurisdiction in those nations.

Furthermore, consideration of the Gilbert factors makes plain that forum non conveniens is inappropriate here. The district court must carefully weigh the private and public interests set forth in Gilbert and may grant the forum non conveniens motion only if these considerations strongly support dismissal. Relevant private interests of the litigants include access to proof, availability of witnesses and "all other practical problems that make trial of a case easy, expeditious and inexpensive."

The private interests of the litigants favor conducting the litigation in New York where the plaintiff brought suit. Disney does not allege that a New York forum is inconvenient. The necessary evidence and witnesses are available and ready for presentation. A trial here promises to begin and end sooner than elsewhere, and would allow the parties to sort out their rights and obligations in a single proceeding. This is not a circumstance where the plaintiff's choice of forum is motivated by harassment. Indeed, it seems rather more likely that Disney's motion seeks to split the suit into 18 parts in 18 nations, complicate the suit, delay it, and render it more expensive.

In dismissing the cases, the court relied on the "public interests" identified in Gilbert. It reasoned that the trial would require extensive application of foreign copyright and antitrust jurisprudence, bodies of law involving strong national interests best litigated "in their respective countries." The court concluded as well that these necessary inquiries into foreign law would place an undue burden on our judicial system."

While reluctance to apply foreign law is a valid factor favoring dismissal under Gilbert, standing alone it does not justify dismissal. District courts must weigh this factor along with the other relevant considerations. . . . Numerous countervailing considerations suggest that New York venue is proper: defendant is a U.S. corporation, the 1939 agreement was substantially negotiated and signed in New York, and the agreement is governed by New York law. The plaintiff has chosen New York and the trial is ready to proceed here. Everything before us suggests that trial would be more "easy, expeditious and inexpensive" in the district court than dispersed to 18 foreign nations. We therefore vacate the dismissal of the foreign copyright claims and remand for trial. . . .

The District Courts in the *Boosey & Hawkes* case and in the *ITSI T.V. Productions* case both expressed concern about the "undue burden" and "extreme hardship" that would be placed on them, if they were required to decide cases under the copyright laws of other countries. How do you suppose American judges would learn about the copyright laws of other countries, and how those laws should be applied to the particular facts in the cases before them? How did the judges in *Itar-Tass Russian News Agency v. Russian Kurier* (Chapter 4) determine what Russian law provides about copyright ownership?

## 2. In the courts of other nations

Notions of subject matter and personal jurisdiction are universal. They show up in the laws of all countries. The following decisions – all British – illustrate how similar the British doctrine of subject matter jurisdiction is to the U.S. doctrine, and how – because of the UK's membership in the European Union – British courts may have even more personal jurisdiction than do U.S. courts.

# Tyburn Productions Ltd. v. Conan Doyle
## [1990] 1 All E.R. 909, [1990] 3 WLR 167, [1990] RPC 185 (U.K. Chancery Div.)

J. Vinelott:

This is an application to strike out the statement of claim in this action. . . [i.e., what in the U.S. would be called a motion to dismiss for failure to state a claim].

The background to the action can be shortly stated and is not in dispute. The defendant, Lady Bromet, is the only surviving child of the late Sir Arthur Conan Doyle. She is commonly known as and is sued as Dame Jean Conan Doyle, though she was formerly married to the late Air Vice-Marshal Sir Geoffrey Bromet, who died in 1983. Lady Bromet, who was at one time Director of the Women's Royal Air Force, was created a Dame of the British Empire in 1963. She resides in England. Sir Arthur died in 1930 and accordingly United Kingdom copyright in all his works expired in 1980.

The plaintiff company, Tyburn Productions Ltd (Tyburn), was incorporated under United Kingdom Companies Acts. It carries on the business of producing and distributing cinematograph films and television programmes. In 1984 Tyburn produced a television film "The Masks of Death" which was made from a script written for Tyburn and based on a story also written for Tyburn. It is claimed and is not in dispute that the script and story were original in every respect save that they featured the characters Sherlock Holmes and Dr. Watson.

Tyburn sought to distribute the film in the United States of America through its distributor, Lorimar Distribution International Inc. (Lorimar). Before distribution had commenced in the United States of America Lorimar received a letter from the agents acting for Lady Bromet claiming that she was entitled to copyright in the characters of Sherlock Holmes and Dr. Watson and that distribution of the film in the United States of America would be an infringement.

By an agreement dated 10 July 1985 Lorimar agreed to pay Lady Bromet $30,000 in consideration of a waiver by Lady Bromet of her right to sue Tyburn and Lorimar for infringement under "copyright laws, unfair competition laws, trade mark laws or other laws relating to the protection of literary characters.". .

. .

Tyburn is now producing another television film, "The Abbot's Cry". The script and the book are again said to be based on original work commissioned by Tyburn save only that they feature the characters of Sherlock Holmes and Dr. Watson. Completion of the television film will involve Tyburn in considerable expense and it fears that it may not be able to recoup the expense unless it can distribute the film in the United States of America. A threat by Lady Bromet to take proceedings in the United States . . . would be likely to make it impossible to distribute the film in the United States unless a further payment satisfactory to Lady Bromet were made. *It is common ground also that Tyburn cannot obtain a declaration in the United States that the television film does not infringe any right of Lady Bromet.* . . . [Emphasis added.]

Tyburn thus finds itself in an unenviable position. If it completes the film it may be unable to distribute it in the United States if these claims are advanced again. At the same time there is no way in which Tyburn can compel Lady Bromet to initiate proceedings in which the existence of her claimed rights can be tested. The mere assertion of her rights may be enough to frustrate the distribution of the film in the United States.

It is in these circumstances that Tyburn seeks the assistance of the English courts. On 23 March 1989 Tyburn, having sought and having failed to obtain an assurance from Lady Bromet that she was not entitled to prevent it from making and distributing a film based on an original story and script but containing characters called Sherlock Holmes and Dr. Watson, issued the writ in this action with a statement of claim indorsed on it. The relief sought is, first, a declaration that Lady Bromet has no rights in the characters Sherlock Holmes and Dr. Watson under the copyright . . . laws of the United States of America such as would entitle her to prevent distribution in the United States of America of "The Abbot's Cry" or of any other cinematograph film or television programme which may hereafter be produced by Tyburn from an original story featuring the characters Sherlock Holmes or Dr. Watson and, second, an injunction restraining Lady Bromet from making to any third party any assertion to the effect that she is entitled to prevent the distribution in the United States of America of any such film or programme by reason of any interest or right claimed by her under the laws of the United States of America in those characters.

. . . As regards copyright law Lady Bromet has apparently been registered under provisions entitling the surviving child of an author to be registered as the person entitled to copyright in some of the late Sir Arthur Conan Doyle's work, the last 14 out of a total of some 60 [novels and short stories]. There is considerable dispute whether the claim that the characterisation of Sherlock Holmes and Dr. Watson if and so far as repeated in the later 14 works but derived from the earlier works attracts copyright protection. The claim if valid would seem to have the consequence of indirectly affording a measure of copyright protection to the earlier works in that they could not be reproduced without using those characters. It is not necessary and it would be wrong for me to form any opinion whether the claims by Lady Bromet are or are not well founded or as to the likelihood or otherwise that she could successfully assert them in . . . the United States of America. . . .

. . . [In] the recent decision of Sir Nicolas Browne-Wilkinson V-C in *Def Lepp Music v. Stuart-Brown* . . . one question was whether the plaintiffs could bring themselves within the "double actionability" rule which is stated in . . . in the following terms:

> As a general rule, an act done in a foreign country is a tort and actionable as such in England, only if it is both (a) actionable as a tort according to English law, or in other words is an act which, if done in England, would be a tort and (b) actionable according to the law of the foreign country where it was done. . . .

In the *Def Lepp* case the plaintiffs claimed to be the owners of the United Kingdom copyright in a tape recording. It was said that the sixth defendant, a company incorporated and resident in Luxembourg, had manufactured records from the recording and had sold them to the eighth defendant, a Dutch company, and that the eighth defendant in turn had sold them to the ninth defendant who had imported a number of them into the United Kingdom. Leave to serve the sixth and eighth defendants having been obtained ex parte they applied to set aside the order granting leave or alternatively to strike out the claim as against themselves. The evidence before the court was that the manufacture took place outside the United Kingdom and that the sales by the sixth defendant to the eighth defendant and by the eighth defendant to the ninth defendant took place outside the United Kingdom and that the eighth defendant had not imported the records into the United Kingdom. Sir Nicolas Browne-Wilkinson V-C accordingly treated the plaintiffs' primary claim as a claim for infringement of a United Kingdom copyright by acts done outside the United Kingdom. He held that that claim was bound to fail: ". . . only acts done in the United Kingdom constitute infringement either direct or indirect of such right." . . .

In my judgment . . . *Def Lepp Music v. Stuart-Brown* . . . is authority for the proposition that a claim that acts done outside the United Kingdom constitute an infringement of the copyright law of a foreign country is not justiciable in the English courts. . . .

In my judgment therefore the question whether Lady Bromet is entitled to copyright under the law of the United States of America . . . is not justiciable in the English courts. Counsel for Tyburn accepted, rightly, I think, that if this question is not justiciable in the English courts then . . . the claims for an injunction and a declaration must fail. . . .

In the instant case there is no evidence that if the validity of the rights claimed were justiciable in the English courts the decision of the English courts would be treated as binding on . . . [courts in] the United States of America and it would in my judgment be an exercise in futility to allow these claims, which raise complex issues which may require a survey by the English courts with the assistance of experts of the laws of . . . the United States of America, to continue.

In my judgment, therefore, this application succeeds. The statement of claim must be struck out in its entirety [and Tyburn's case was dismissed]. . . .

You noticed, didn't you, the following statement in the court's decision: "It is common ground also that Tyburn cannot obtain a declaration in the United States that the television film does not infringe any right of Lady Bromet. . . ." "Common ground" means that all parties agreed Tyburn could not obtain the declaration of non-infringement that it wanted "in the United States." Why do you supposed it couldn't? For substantive reasons, or jurisdictional reasons? If for jurisdictional reasons, what was missing: subject matter jurisdiction or personal jurisdictional?

The next cases rely on something called the "Brussels Convention." It is a treaty among countries that are members of the European Union (EU Official Journal C27, 26/01/1998)(available in Westlaw database "EU-ALL"). The Brussels Convention contains provisions similar to American "long-arm" statutes and the "Full Faith and Credit Clause" of the United States Constitution. For example, the Convention provides that a domiciliary of one EU country may be sued in "in matters of tort . . . in the courts for the place in which the harmful event occurred." It also provides that a "judgment given in a Contracting State shall be recognized in the other Contracting States without any special procedure being required." ("Contracting States" are EU countries.)

## ABKCO Music & Records Inc.
## v. Music Collection International Ltd.
### [1995] RPC 657, [1995] EMLR 449
### (UK Court of Appeal 1994)

Hoffmann LJ: The plaintiff ("ABKCO") claims the copyright in certain sound recordings made by Sam Cooke. The second defendant ("Charly") is a Danish company which claims to be entitled to the same copyright. On 26

February 1991 it granted a licence in writing to the first defendant ("Music Collection") to manufacture and sell copies of the sound recordings in the United Kingdom and Eire. Music Collection subsequently released compact discs of the recordings which purported to have been made under the licence.

The Copyright, Designs and Patents Act 1988 says:

> 16-(1) The owner of the copyright in a work has, in accordance with the following provisions of this Chapter, the exclusive right to do the following acts in the United Kingdom –
> (a) to copy the work . . .;
> (b) to issue copies of the work to the public . . .

and those acts are referred to in this Part as the "acts restricted by the copyright".

> (2) Copyright in a work is infringed by a person who without the licence of the copyright
> owner does, or authorises another to do, any of the acts restricted by the copyright.

On 4 November 1991 ABKCO issued a writ indorsed with statement of claim against Music Collection and Charly. It alleges that Music Collection had infringed its copyright by manufacturing and issuing to the public copies of the sound recordings and that Charly had done so by authorising or "directing counselling or procuring" the acts of Music Collection.

Music Collection is an English company. After being served with the writ it gave certain undertakings and the proceedings against it were stayed by consent pending a determination as between ABKCO and Charly on the question of who had title to the copyright.

Charly is domiciled in Denmark. It carries on no business in the United Kingdom. ABKCO served it under [the British long-arm statute] . . . on the ground that the English courts had jurisdiction under the Brussels Convention. The relevant Articles are 5(3) ("in matters relating to tort . . . the courts for the place where the harmful event occurred") and Article 6(1) ("where [the defendant] is one of a number of defendants, the courts for the place where any one of them is domiciled"). Charly does not dispute that ABKCO's case as pleaded falls within those Articles. But a defendant domiciled in another Contracting State cannot be impleaded unless the plaintiff's case satisfies the threshold requirement of disclosing a serious question to be tried. . . . Charly says that ABKCO's case fails this test. It therefore issued a summons . . . to set aside service. Mr Colin Rimer QC (sitting as a deputy High Court judge) dismissed the summons and Charly appeals.

. . . In *CBS Songs Ltd v Amstrad Consumer Electronics Plc* [1988] AC 1013, the House of Lords explained the meaning of "authorise" in section 1(2) of the Copyright Act 1956 which was in similar terms to section 16(2) of the 1988 Act. Lord Templeman said at page 1054:

> . . . an authorisation means a grant or purported grant, which may be expressed or implied, of the right to do the act complained of.

Mr Miller [Charly's barrister] accepts that if the licence of 26 February had been granted in the United Kingdom and upon its true construction it had purported to give Music Collections the right to manufacture and sell the records of which complaint is made, then Charly would be liable under section 16(2). But he says . . . that section 16(2) does not apply to a licence granted outside the United Kingdom. . . .

There is a striking contrast between section 16(1) which limits the acts restricted by the copyright to acts done in the United Kingdom, and section 16(2) which contains no territorial limit on where the doing of those acts may be authorised. Mr Miller however relied upon the general principle that, in the absence of express words or plain implication, United Kingdom statutes do not apply to the acts of foreigners outside the United Kingdom . . . . Mr Miller says that there are other infringement sections in the Act, such as section 23, which also contain no express territorial implication, but which are very unlikely to have been intended to have an extra-territorial application. Therefore, he says that no inference can be drawn from the express limitation of section 16(1) to acts done in the United Kingdom and the absence of such a limitation in section 16(2). The presumption against extra-territoriality should govern the latter subsection also. In principle the law of copyright is strictly territorial in its application. . . .

In my view, the reason why section 16(2) places no limit upon the place of authorisation is that the requirements of territoriality are satisfied by the need for the act authorised to have been done within the United Kingdom. It is true, as Mr Miller emphasised, that the doing of an act restricted by the copyright and its authorisation are separate torts. . . . But there is an overlap in the ingredients of the two torts in that "authorising" is a tort only if the act authorised is an act restricted by the copyright. . . . I do not think it is necessary for the purposes of jurisdiction that the link between the preliminary act and the consequence should have to be a causal one. It is I think sufficient that the definition of the tort requires an act and that that act is performed within the United Kingdom, however it may be linked to the preliminary act performed abroad.

As those are the rules of jurisdiction, I can see no reason why, on grounds of international comity or the principle of territoriality, it is necessary to construe the substantive provision creating such a tort so as to require the preliminary act to have taken place in the United Kingdom. I think that a territorial limitation on the act of authorising would lead to anomalies. Anyone contemplating the grant of a licence to do an act restricted by copyright would be able to avoid liability simply by having the document executed abroad. Mr Miller says that there are other anomalies created by the principle of territoriality in copyright and even more used to exist by virtue of the old requirement that a work had to be first published or performed in the United Kingdom. But these were the results of the express terms of the legislation. There seems to me no need to introduce anomalies by implication when this is not required by express language or general principles of international law. For those reasons, I would reject Mr Miller's point on extra-territoriality. . . .

In conclusion, therefore, I think that the judge was right and I would dismiss the appeal.

Neill LJ: I agree. I propose, however, to add a few words of my own on the question of the proper construction of section 16(2) of the Copyright, Designs and Patents Act 1988 ("the 1988 Act").

Chapter II of the 1988 Act is concerned with the rights of a copyright owner. Section 16(1) confers on the owner of the copyright in a work the exclusive right to do certain acts in relation to that work in the United Kingdom. These acts . . . are referred to in . . . the 1988 Act as "acts restricted by the copyright"....

It is clear that the rights conferred by section 16(1) are rights which protect the copyright only insofar as they are exercised in the United Kingdom. "Acts restricted by the copyright", if done without the licence of the owner of the copyright, constitute infringements. These infringements are confined within the same geographical limits as the owner's exclusive rights.

I turn therefore to section 16(2) which is in these terms:

> Copyright in a work is infringed by a person who without the licence of the copyright owner does, or authorises another to do, any of the acts restricted by the copyright.

It is plain that the "doer" of a restricted act will infringe the copyright if, but only if, he does that act within the United Kingdom. The act, if committed outside the United Kingdom, would not be a restricted act.

I can, however, see no satisfactory basis for placing a similar territorial limitation on the liability of a person who "authorises another to do" a restricted act. It is to be noted that authorising another to do a restricted act is not itself a restricted act.

. . . I have no doubt that, on its proper construction, an authorisation given outside the United Kingdom to another to do a restricted act in the United Kingdom is an authorisation to which section 16(2) extends. The scope of the tort has a sufficient territorial limitation because the restricted act which is authorised has to be done within the United Kingdom.

Some further support for this approach is to be found in Article 5 of the Brussels Convention itself, which provides:

> A person domiciled in a Contracting State may, in another Contracting State, be sued: . . . in matters relating to tort, delict or quasi-delict, in the courts for the place where the harmful event occurred. . . .

On the other matters referred to by Lord Justice Hoffmann in his judgment, I agree with him and have nothing to add. I would therefore dismiss the appeal.

In the *ABKCO Music* case which you just read, did the court rely on Brussels Convention to establish personal jurisdiction or subject matter jurisdiction or both? In the following case, did the court rely on the Brussels Convention to establish personal jurisdiction or subject matter jurisdiction or both?

### Pearce v. Ove Arup Partnership Ltd.
### [2000] Ch 403, [1999] 1 All ER 769, [2000] 3 WLR 332,
### [1999] FSR 525 (UK Court of Appeal 1999)

Roch LJ.

The plaintiff, Mr Pearce, is an architect. In 1986 he completed his diploma in architecture at the Architectural Association School of Architecture in London. Between December 1985 and June 1986, he undertook an architectural project for his diploma in which he produced drawings, detailed plans and paintings of a design for a town hall for the Docklands development in London. He claims . . . that he is the owner of United Kingdom and Dutch copyright in his Docklands plans.

Between 1990 and 1993, the City of Rotterdam, the fourth defendants, had constructed in Rotterdam a public building known as the Kunsthal. The first defendants, Ove Arup Partnership Ltd, were appointed as civil engineer for the construction of the Kunsthal. The third defendants and their director, Mr Koolhaas, the second defendant, were the architects who designed the building. In the autumn of 1992, Mr Pearce visited Rotterdam as a tourist. He saw the Kunsthal in the course of construction and believed that features of its design had been copied from his Docklands plans. In these proceedings, he claims that each of the defendants has infringed his United Kingdom or Dutch copyrights. It is accepted on his behalf that a damages claim for infringement of his United Kingdom copyright would be statute-barred, although the possibility of claiming an injunction is forensically retained. The main claim is for infringement of his Dutch copyright.

The first defendants are domiciled in the United Kingdom. Mr Koolhaas may be domiciled in the United Kingdom. The third and fourth defendants are domiciled in the Netherlands. Mr Pearce claims that the English courts have jurisdiction in relation to his claims against those defendants not domiciled in the United Kingdom under art 6(1) of the Convention on Jurisdiction and the Enforcement of Judgments in Civil and Commercial Matters 1968 . . . (the Brussels Convention). This provides that a person domiciled in a contracting state may be sued, where he is one of a number of defendants, in the courts for the place where any one of them is domiciled.

The plaintiff's writ and statement of claim were issued. . . . The . . . defendants served a defence. . . . Each of them denied infringement of the plaintiff's copyright. . . . [T]he . . . defendants [then] issued a notice of motion seeking to strike out those parts of the amended statement of claim which concerned alleged infringements of Dutch copyright on the ground that these were not acts which constitute torts actionable under English law. . . .[T]he plaintiff applied to strike out allegations in each of the defences which asserted that infringement of Dutch copyright is not actionable as a tort under English law.

These matters came before Lloyd J on 12 February 1997. In his judgment ([1997] 3 All ER 31, [1997] Ch 293) given on 7 March 1997 the judge declined to strike out the allegations of infringement of Dutch copyright on the ground that they were not justiciable under English law. But he upheld the defendants' submission that on the facts alleged the plaintiff's claim was bound to fail. He held that the degree of similarity between the plaintiff's Docklands design and the Kunsthal drawings was not sufficient to give rise to an inference of copying. He considered that the claim was based on speculation. He accordingly ordered the whole claim against each of the defendants to be struck out.

The plaintiff appeals. . . . The . . . defendants . . . contend that the judge's order should be affirmed on the additional ground that the alleged infringements of Dutch copyright against them are not actionable torts under English law. . . .

A judge at trial may conclude that . . . [the] similarities alleged by the plaintiff were coincidental. But we have all reached the clear conclusion, with the aid of the plaintiff's portfolio, that the plaintiff's allegations of similarity are not so fanciful that his claim as a whole should be regarded as speculative. . . . The plaintiff has, we think, pleaded a case of similarity which, with his evidence about access to his drawings, might be sufficient for an inference of graphic copying. Needless to say, we say nothing about the eventual strength of the parties' respective cases. Our present decision is, and only is, that the defendants do not establish that the plaintiff's claim is in this respect bound to fail.

. . . [W]e consider that there are sufficient basic coincidences of shapes, and a sufficient accumulation of other dimensional coincidence, such that this is a case which ought not to be struck out without full consideration of oral evidence, including expert opinion.

We consider, therefore, the judge's decision that the plaintiff's claim was bound to fail on the facts was wrong and should be reversed.

We turn, therefore, to the respondents' contention . . . that, nevertheless, the judge's order should be affirmed on the ground that the infringements of Dutch copyright alleged against the respondents are not actionable torts under English law.

In addressing this contention it is necessary to keep in mind that the acts alleged to be infringements of the plaintiff's Dutch copyright were done in Holland. There is no suggestion that, if the acts had been done anywhere other than in Holland, they would have constituted an infringement of the plaintiff's Dutch copyright; or, to put the point another way, that the rights conferred by the plaintiff's Dutch copyright extend to acts done outside Holland. Further, those acts, because they took place in Holland, could not constitute infringements of the plaintiff's United Kingdom copyright. Those acts are not actionable under English domestic law.

The relevant inquiry, therefore, is whether (assuming that the English court would otherwise have jurisdiction to hear proceedings against the relevant defendants) English law permits the English court, in the present context, to entertain a claim based on the infringement, by acts done in Holland, of a local right conferred in Holland by Dutch law. . . .

If the English court is permitted by English private international law rules to entertain a claim based on the infringement, by acts done in Holland, of a local right conferred in Holland by Dutch law, then it must follow as a necessary corollary that the same rules permit, or require, the English court to apply Dutch law in order to determine whether the claim is well-founded. There is no other law which the English court could sensibly apply for that purpose. To put the point another way, if there is some English conflict of laws rule which prevents the English court from applying Dutch law to determine whether the claim is well-founded, then that must be a powerful, if not conclusive, indication that the English court should not entertain the claim at all.

Subject to an argument based on the provisions of art 5(2) of the Berne Convention . . . , the respondents accept, as they must, that the English court has jurisdiction to hear an action against a defendant who is domiciled in England in respect of the infringement in Holland of a Dutch copyright. That must follow from the provisions in arts 2 and 16(4) of the Brussels Convention. The relevant provisions are:

> *Article 2* Subject to the provisions of this Convention, persons domiciled in a Contracting State shall, whatever their nationality, be sued in the courts of that State . . .

> *Article 16* The following courts shall have exclusive jurisdiction, regardless of domicile. . .

> (4) in proceedings concerned with the registration or validity of patents, trade marks, designs, or other similar rights required to be deposited or registered, the courts of the Contracting State in which the deposit or registration has been applied for, has taken place or is under the terms of an international convention deemed to have taken place. . . .

It is not suggested that the present proceedings (being proceedings in respect of copyright in which no question of deposit or registration arises) fall within art 16(4). It follows that the English court must accept jurisdiction in the proceedings against the first defendant (who is domiciled here) and, perhaps, also against the second defendant (who may be domiciled here) on the accession in 1978 of the United Kingdom to the Brussels Convention. Further, art 6(1) provides that a person domiciled in a contracting state may be sued, where he is one of a number of defendants, in the courts for the place where any one of them is domiciled. It is accepted that the third and fourth defendants – and also the second defendant, if not domiciled here – are domiciled in Holland. It follows that the English court must accept jurisdiction against those defendants also.

Nevertheless, it is submitted that jurisdiction is one thing; justiciability or actionability is another. It is not enough for the plaintiff to establish that he can bring proceedings against the defendants in the English court. Where the wrong of which he complains has been committed outside England, he must also establish that the English court, applying its own conflict of laws rules, will regard his complaint as giving rise to a cause of action that it will recognise and entertain.

The judge accepted that, but for the Brussels Convention, an action in the English courts which was founded on an alleged breach of Dutch copyright must be struck out as non-justiciable on one or both of two grounds. First, because . . . a claim for breach of a foreign statutory intellectual property right must be regarded as local and so could not be entertained by an English court; and, secondly, because such a claim could not satisfy the double-actionability rule. . . . But he was satisfied that to apply those rules in a case where the English court was given jurisdiction by arts 2 and 6 of the Brussels Convention would be inconsistent with, and would impair the effectiveness of, the convention; with the consequence that the English conflict of laws rules must be regarded as overridden by the convention in such a case and so inapplicable. . . .

The respondents place reliance on the decision of Vinelott J in *Tyburn Productions Ltd v Conan Doyle* [1990] 1 All ER 909, [1991] Ch 75. That is the only decision cited to us which could be said to provide direct support for the proposition that a claim for breach, outside England, of a foreign intellectual property right cannot be entertained by an English court. The plaintiff sought a declaration from the English court that the defendant (who claimed to be entitled to copyright in the works of her father, the late Sir Arthur Conan Doyle) had no rights under the copyright, unfair competition or trademark laws of the United States which would entitle her to prevent the distribution of a television film, produced by the plaintiff, which featured the characters 'Sherlock Holmes' and 'Dr Watson'. The defendant applied to strike out the proceedings on the ground that they disclosed no cause of action. Vinelott J acceded to the defendant's application. His reasoning is, we think, adequately summarised in the headnote ([1991] Ch 75):

> . . . the distinction between transitory and local actions which precluded English courts from entertaining questions as to the title, or of damages for trespass, to land abroad should be applied to intellectual property rights so that an action relating to the copyright laws of a foreign state was a local action, not justiciable in the English courts. . . .

Vinelott J . . . did not, of course, find it necessary to consider the Brussels Convention. The foreign state with which he was concerned (. . . the United States of America . . .) was not party to the convention.

We do not find it necessary to decide whether Vinelott J was correct to take the view (if he did) that an action for alleged infringement of a foreign

copyright by acts done outside the United Kingdom in a state not party to the Brussels Convention . . . was not justiciable in an English court. It is important to keep in mind that the question which he actually had to decide was whether to make a declaration that the defendant had no rights under the copyright . . . laws of the United States which would be infringed by what the plaintiff was proposing to do. He was invited to investigate the existence and validity of the rights claimed; not to decide whether there had been an infringement of rights the existence and validity of which were not in issue. He was, in our view, plainly correct to refuse to make the declaration sought.
. . .

We can derive little or no assistance from the decision in the *Tyburn Productions* case on the question whether an action for alleged infringement of a foreign copyright by acts done outside the United Kingdom, in a case where the existence and validity of the right is not in issue, is justiciable in an English court; and no assistance from that case where the question arises in the context of acts done in a contracting state. . . .

Encouraged, perhaps, by the reference made by this court in [another] case, the respondents contended that the provisions of the Brussels Convention are excluded, by art 57, from application to copyright infringement by the provisions of art 5(2) of the Berne Convention for the protection of literary and artistic works. Article 5(2) of the Berne Convention is in these terms:

> The enjoyment and exercise of these rights shall not be subject to any formality; such enjoyment and such exercise shall be independent of the existence of protection in the country of origin of the work. Consequently, apart from the provisions of this Convention the extent of protection, as well as the means of redress afforded to the author to protect his rights, shall be governed exclusively by the laws of the country where protection is claimed.

Article 57(1) of the Brussels Convention provides: "This Convention shall not affect any conventions to which the Contracting States are or will be parties and which in relation to particular matters, govern jurisdiction or the recognition or enforcement of judgments." . . . We think that there is good reason for that Article 5(2) of the Berne Convention does not purport to govern jurisdiction in relation to infringement of copyright. . . . [I]n relation to copyright, the question is not "in respect of which country is the protection claimed", but "where is the protection claimed". The protection is claimed in the country in which the proceedings are brought. Article 5(2) requires that the extent of the protection to be afforded is governed by the laws of that country. There is, of course, no reason to assume that the laws of that country do not include its own rules of private international law. What art 5(2) does, in our view, is to leave it to the courts of the country in which the proceedings are brought to decide whether the claim for protection should be upheld. It does not seek to confer jurisdiction on the courts of one country to the exclusion of any other.

We reject the submission that the Berne Convention excludes the application of the Brussels Convention to proceedings in respect of infringement of copyright. . . .

For the reasons which we have set out we are satisfied that the [law] does not require the English court to refuse to entertain a claim in respect of the alleged infringement of Dutch copyright; and that . . . the court is not required . . . to hold that the claim is bound to fail because the acts done in

Holland cannot amount to an infringement of United Kingdom copyright. It follows that we are not persuaded that the judge's order should be affirmed on the alternative ground advanced in the respondents' notice.

In those circumstances this appeal must be allowed.

Since the Brussels Convention is a treaty among members of the European Union, the United States of course is not a signatory (as the court pointedly noted in *Pearce v. Ove Arup*). Many other countries of the world too are not signatories to the Brussels Convention, even though their nationals are engaged in significant international business transactions.

As a result, in 2001, a Diplomatic Conference was held at the Hague to consider a proposed "Hague Convention" which would have made the *principles* found in the Brussels Convention available to signatory nations all around the world (not just in Europe). However, because many countries – including the United States – opposed the Hague Convention, it has not been adopted. Why do you suppose the U.S. opposed the treaty?

## B. Remedies

The questions of whether a U.S. court has subject matter jurisdiction over foreign infringements and personal jurisdiction over those who committed them are of course important. If the answer to either question is "no," the case comes to an immediate end (at least in that court). What clients care about, however, are remedies. So, as you read the following materials on remedies, *assume* that a U.S. court *does* have both subject matter and personal jurisdiction. The questions to be considered now are: how will recoverable damages be calculated, and how geographically broad an injunction may be granted? That is, may damages be awarded by the U.S. court based on infringements that occur abroad, as well as in the U.S.? And may an injunction prohibit further infringing conduct abroad, as well as in the U.S.?

### 1. Damages: geographic scope of measure of damages

#### Robert Stigwood Group, Ltd. v. O'Reilly
#### 530 F.2d 1096 (2d Cir. 1976), cert. denied, 429 U.S. 848 (1976)

Circuit Judge Gurfein:

"JESUS CHRIST SUPERSTAR" ("SUPERSTAR"), the successful rock opera, . . . was publicly performed by the defendants without permission. They have been found to be infringers. We are the first appellate court to be asked to decide how statutory damages are to be assessed when there have been multiple unauthorized performances of an opera, several copyrights of which were "infringed" at each performance. . . .

The joint plaintiffs, The Robert Stigwood Group Limited ("Stigwood"), Leeds Music Limited ("Leeds") and Leeds Music Corporation, own the United States copyrights in SUPERSTAR, and in separate musical compositions therein, as well as the performing stage rights. The defendants are Roman Catholic priests who performed SUPERSTAR without obtaining a license either from the plaintiffs or from the American Society of Composers, Authors and Publishers (ASCAP). The District Court found that these performances infringed the plaintiffs' copyrights, and issued a preliminary injunction enjoining the defendants from presenting any future performances of SUPERSTAR.[3] [Fn.3 The implied Robin Hood defense as justification for taking from the rich to give to the poor has not been accepted. And this court has already held that the contention that the performances fall within the religious works exemption of 17 U.S.C. §104 is frivolous. The question of damages comes to us at this stage, therefore, free from any possible differentiation based on the religious activities of the defendants. We say this because our rulings on the proper measure of damages should be taken to apply to any infringing producer with the same degree of wilful infringing activity.] On November 13, 1974, the District Court granted plaintiffs' motion for summary judgment, and awarded the plaintiffs $22,800 in damages and $4,700 for attorneys' fees. . . .

Neither side appeals from the conclusion that the defendants are liable. Each party appeals from the judgments on damages. . . .

In deciding the damage issue . . . Judge Zampano . . . [noted] that "[the] defendants concede that they performed the rock opera *at least* 50 times" (emphasis added), [and thus] he accepted "fifty" "as [the] baseline figure for the computation of damages." The court then reduced the "baseline figure of 50" to 38 by excluding twelve performances given in Canada. . . .

Plaintiffs-appellants contend that . . . the District Court should have . . . included the Canadian performances . . . . The defendants-appellants on their cross-appeal contend that . . . the Canadian performances are not infringements of the American copyrights. . . . The question[] for decision [is]: . . . Should the twelve Canadian performances be treated as infringements of United States copyrights and performing rights thereunder? . . .

It is agreed that there were twelve Canadian performances by the defendants, which Judge Zampano excluded in his calculations. The plaintiffs contend that the twelve performances in Canada should not have been excluded. They argue that in each instance the defendants assembled and arranged in the United States all the necessary elements for the performances in Canada, and then simply travelled to Canada to complete the performances. They urge that the acts in the United States constituted an "integral part of the Canadian performances" and that the defendants should, therefore, be made to respond in damages. They rely on *Sheldon v. Metro-Goldwyn Pictures Corp.* (2d Cir. 1939), aff'd, 309 U.S. 390 (1940), and *Famous Music Corp. v. Seeco Records, Inc.* (S.D.N.Y. 1961). Their reliance is misplaced. In *Sheldon*, the defendants made infringing negatives of the motion picture in the United States and thereafter exhibited the motion picture abroad. Judge Learned Hand did not hold that the manufacture of the negatives in the United States was an integral part of the exhibition abroad. He held, rather, that "exhibition is not the only act forbidden by the Copyright Act," that "negatives were 'records' from which the work could be 'reproduced,' and [that] it was a tort to make them in this country."[4] [Fn.4 The plaintiffs thus acquired an equitable interest in the negatives which entitled them to the profits made by the defendants from their exploitation, even when the negatives were exploited abroad. An ephemeral public performance on the stage is not like a film negative which can be reproduced.] . . .

In *Famous Music Corp.*, the defendant shipped tape recordings, made by him in the United States, containing renditions of plaintiffs' copyrighted musical compositions to persons in foreign countries where they were used to manufacture phonograph records. Judge Levet, in assessing a compulsory royalty, relied upon 17 U.S.C. §101(e) [of the 1909 Act], which makes "unauthorized manufacture" of such tapes an infringement of a musical copyright.

The steps taken by the defendants preliminary to the Canadian performances were certainly not the "manufacture" of anything, nor were the performances "records" from which the work could be "reproduced." It is only when the type of infringement permits further reproduction abroad that its exploitation abroad becomes the subject of a constructive trust. Judge Zampano properly excluded the Canadian performances. Copyright laws do not have extraterritorial operation. The Canadian performances, while they may have been torts in Canada, were not torts here. . . .

## Gaste v. Kaiserman
### 683 F.Supp. 63 (S.D.N.Y. 1988), aff'd 863 F.2d 1061 (2d Cir. 1988)

District Judge Conner:

In a jury verdict returned in this action on July 21 and 22, 1987 in favor of the plaintiffs, the jury found that the song "Feelings" infringed plaintiffs' copyright in the musical composition "Pour Toi" and awarded plaintiffs damages in excess of $500,000. A judgment was entered by this Court reflecting the verdict on July 27, 1987. Defendants Morris Kaiserman a/k/a Morris Albert ("Albert") and Fermata International Melodies, Inc. ("Fermata") have moved to alter or amend the judgment by . . . eliminating from the award all income earned by foreign performances on radio and television of recorded versions of "Feelings". . . .

In moving to reduce from the judgment all income earned by foreign performances, defendants rely on the Second Circuit Court of Appeals, decision in *Robert Stigwood Group Limited v. O'Reilly*. In that case, in addition to recovering profits from live performances of the infringing play in the United States, plaintiff sought recovery of profits from live performances of the play in Canada. The court excluded the award of damages stemming from the Canadian performances because the performances were live and could not be "reproduced." The Court held that it is only when the type of infringement permits further reproduction abroad that its exploitation abroad becomes the subject of a constructive trust.

Plaintiffs, in turn, maintain that the jury verdict properly included the foreign performances. To support their position, they rely on *Sheldon v. Metro-Goldwyn Pictures Corp.* (2d Cir. 1939), aff'd 309 U.S. 390 (1940), in which the Court of Appeals upheld a decision awarding plaintiff profits which defendant earned from exhibition of the infringing motion picture outside the United States. In his opinion for the Court, Judge Learned Hand noted:

> Section 1(d) [of the 1909 Copyright Act] gives to the author the exclusive right, not only to perform a dramatic work, but "to make . . . any transcription or record thereof . . . from which, in whole or in part, it may in any manner . . . be . . . reproduced." The Culver Company made the negatives in this country, or had them made here, and shipped them abroad, where the positives were produced and exhibited. The negatives were "records" from which the work could be "reproduced," and it was a tort to make them in this country. The plaintiffs acquired an equitable interest in them as soon as they were made, which attached to any profits from their exploitation, whether in the form of money remitted to the United States, or of increase in the value of shares of foreign companies held by the defendants. We need not decide whether the law of those countries where the negatives were exploited recognized the plaintiffs, equitable interest; we can assume arguendo that it did not, for, as soon as

any of the profits so realized took the form of property whose situs was in the United States, our law seized upon them with a constructive trust.

While it is certainly true that royalties from foreign performances are recoverable when the infringement in this country permits further exploitation abroad, plaintiffs presented no evidence at trial indicating that the foreign performances resulted from the reproduction of recordings originally made in the United States or any other recorded versions. It is clearly plaintiff's burden to show that the foreign performances resulted in a violation of the United States copyright. Because plaintiff failed to adduce any evidence to support that contention, the jury award must be reduced by whatever amount was awarded for foreign performances. . . .

For the reasons outlined above, defendants, motion to reduce the jury's damage award by that portion of the profits attributable to foreign performances is granted. . . .

## Update Art v. Modiin Publishing, Ltd.
### 843 F.2d 67 (2d Cir. 1988)

Circuit Judge Timbers: . . .

Appellants Modiin Publishing, Ltd. ("Modiin") and Maariv Promotions, Ltd. ("Promotions") appeal from a judgment entered October 1, 1987 in the Southern District of New York, Ruth V. Washington, Magistrate, . . . awarding Update Art, Inc. ("Update") summary judgment and $475,406 damages on its claim of copyright infringement with respect to its poster by appellants' newspaper.

On appeal, Modiin and Promotions contend that . . . the court lacked subject matter jurisdiction over part of the award since some of the infringing newspapers remained abroad. . . .

Appellee Update is a New York corporation engaged in the business of manufacturing and distributing graphic art designs imprinted on a variety of products, including posters, greeting cards, t-shirts and puzzles. Under a recorded license agreement dated October 10, 1985, Update owns the exclusive contract rights for worldwide publication and distribution of the art work known as "Ronbo." Update produced a "Ronbo" poster. The "Ronbo" poster is intended to mimic the character "Rambo" portrayed by Sylvester Stallone in several recent movies. "Ronbo" depicts President Reagan's head superimposed on a bare-chested muscular man's body wearing dog tags and carrying a machine-gun in a jungle setting.

Modiin is an Israeli corporation with annual gross revenues of $100 million. Promotions, a New York corporation, is a wholly owned subsidiary of Modiin. Modiin produces a number of publishing enterprises, including Maariv, a newspaper published in Hebrew. Maariv is the largest circulating daily newspaper in Israel. The weekend edition, which includes a magazine supplement, is distributed every Friday and sells approximately 250,000 copies in Israel. An international edition of the weekend edition is distributed in the United States through Promotions.

The grievance at issue arose when the February 28, 1986 weekend edition of Maariv contained an unauthorized full-page, full-color reproduction of the "Ronbo" poster in the magazine section to illustrate an article. On March 1, after discovering the infringement, Update notified Modiin and Promotions of the infringement and demanded that they cease and desist. They refused.

Update commenced the instant action on March 3 by filing a complaint against appellants and individually against certain managers, officers, employees and owners of Maariv alleging copyright infringement. . . .

. . .Trial on the merits was advanced and consolidated with the preliminary injunction hearing which was held on March 4. Appellants were found jointly and severally liable and were permanently enjoined from infringing the "Ronbo" copyright. Appellants were ordered to turn over the infringing negatives. The order provided that the magistrate would determine damages. . . .

What should have been a rather straightforward proceeding – presentation of evidence to the magistrate on the amount of damages – instead turned into a protracted dragging of feet on the part of appellants and their counsel. There were innumerable discovery conferences resulting in a series of court orders compelling appellants to respond to discovery requests. Appellants repeatedly failed to comply with the discovery orders, despite numerous extensions of time to respond which were granted. Appellants repeatedly were warned that sanctions would be imposed if they continued their noncompliance.

On March 31, 1987, these proceedings culminated with the magistrate imposing Rule 37 sanctions against appellants and their counsel. The magistrate concluded that appellants had acted in bad faith and their production was deficient. Moreover, the magistrate concluded that neither appellants' precise profits nor their alleged deductible expenses could be determined from their limited production. Accordingly, the magistrate granted summary judgment to Update on the issue of damages with respect to its claim of copyright infringement. She accepted Update's calculation of appellants' gross income of $475,406 from the infringement based on documentary evidence.[3] [Fn.3 This $475,406 figure was calculated as follows: 245,604 copies shipped x $1.50 income per copy = $368,406 total sales income + $107,000 advertising income from the weekend edition = $475,406.] She also accepted Update's calculation of its lost profits of $380,686. The magistrate awarded Update damages of $475,406 plus interest by adding to Update's lost profits of $380,686 that portion of appellants' income from the infringement that was not duplicative of Update's lost profits ($94,720). The magistrate also imposed $2,000 in sanctions against appellants' counsel of record for their part in the delay.

On April 28, 1987, the magistrate granted appellants' motion for reconsideration. At oral argument before the magistrate on May 14, 1987, appellants argued for the first time that Update's claim did not apply to the newspapers in Israel because American copyright laws had no extraterritorial application. In a memorandum decision and order dated September 16, 1987, the magistrate affirmed her prior decision in all respects except she vacated the sanction against appellants' counsel, on a finding that counsel was not to blame for appellants' contumacious conduct. The magistrate did not make findings as to appellants' extraterritoriality claim since she erroneously concluded that Judge Edelstein had ruled on this claim. . . .

This brings us to appellants' claim that the magistrate lacked subject matter jurisdiction over the infringing newspapers in Israel.

We are mindful, of course, that subject matter jurisdiction is a constitutional prerequisite to a federal court's power to act. Generally, unlike personal jurisdiction, the parties cannot waive lack of subject matter jurisdiction by consent, by conduct, or by estoppel. We also recognize that lack of subject matter jurisdiction may be raised for the first time on appeal.

We do not preclude appellants from raising a claim of lack of subject matter jurisdiction. Indeed, we have no power to do so. Rather, we hold that in light of the record before us, Update has stated a claim fully cognizable under the copyright laws.

It is well established that copyright laws generally do not have extraterritorial application. There is an exception – when the type of infringement permits further reproduction abroad – such as the unauthorized manufacture of copyrighted material in the United States.

Appellants concede the magistrate's jurisdiction over the newspapers distributed in the United States.[5] [Fn.5 This clearly is not a case, therefore, in which the magistrate would be completely divested of subject matter jurisdiction even were we to accept appellants' argument.] As the applicability of American copyright laws over the Israeli newspapers depends on the occurrence of a predicate act in the United States, the geographic location of the illegal reproduction is crucial. If the illegal reproduction of the poster occurred in the United States and then was exported to Israel, the magistrate properly could include damages accruing from the Israeli newspapers. If, as appellants assert, this predicate act occurred in Israel, American copyright laws would have no application to the Israeli newspapers. Since a large portion of the damage award accrued from the Israeli newspapers, our determination on this issue affects substantially the final judgment.

Update's complaint asserts that the acts complained of occurred in whole or in part in the United States. Update asserts that nowhere in the record do appellants definitively assert that the reproduction of the poster occurred in Israel. Appellants deny this assertion, relying on their response to one of Update's interrogatories. In their response, appellants stated that an editor of the magazine section observed the poster "on an office wall"; he thought the poster would be a good illustration for an article and had a photographer photograph it.

Nowhere do appellants state that the reproduction occurred in Israel. Nor is such a sworn statement to be found anywhere in the record. Indeed, even on appeal appellants have failed to present an affidavit from anyone with personal knowledge asserting that an authorized copy of the poster was reproduced in Israel. We further find it significant that Update, after receiving appellants' response to the question referred to above, complained of its insufficiency and specifically requested appellants to state where the wall was located, how a copy of the poster appeared on the wall, and whether that copy was authorized. Similar to their disregard of many other discovery requests, appellants never responded.

Appellants argue that, since their response referred to their magazine section staff reproducing the poster and the magazine section is produced in Israel, we should infer that the wall was located in Israel. In light of appellants' delaying tactics and bad faith conduct throughout the proceeding, resulting in a justified preclusion sanction, we decline appellants' invitation that we draw such an inference. Appellants' assertion that the predicate act of reproducing the poster occurred in Israel is not supported by the record. The poster was sold in the United States. Promotions is located in New York. Appellants at their own risk chose not to respond to discovery orders.

Accordingly, we hold that Update's claim was fully cognizable under American copyright laws. Damages accruing from the illegal infringement in the Israeli newspapers properly were awarded to Update. . . .

So, it now appears that a U.S. District Court may award a copyright owner money on account of infringements committed abroad, so long as those foreign infringements are the result of an earlier infringement committed within the United States. What, however, is the proper measure of the award for foreign infringements? The U.S. Copyright Act provides two measures:

## United States Copyright Act § 504(b)

Actual Damages and Profits. – The copyright owner is entitled to recover the actual damages suffered by him or her as a result of the infringement, and any profits of the infringer that are attributable to the infringement and are not taken into account in computing the actual damages.

In *Update Art v. Modiin Publishing*, the Magistrate Judge awarded the copyright owner the profits the infringer earned in Israel plus the actual damages the copyright owner suffered – presumably in Israel – as a result of the infringement there. The Magistrate reduced the infringer's profits by the amount of the copyright owner's actual damages from the infringement, as required by section 504(b); so the amount of the award was exactly equal to the infringer's profits in Israel. Thus the *Update Art* award may be viewed in either of two ways: (1) as an award of the copyright owner's actual damages *plus* the infringer's profits; or (2) as an award of the infringer's profits only. In the *Update Art* case, it didn't matter which way the award was viewed, because the copyright owner's actual damages were less than the infringer's profits.

However, in the following case – *Los Angeles News Service v. Reuters* – it did matter which way the award was viewed. It mattered because the infringer did not earn any profits from its foreign infringement, so naturally the copyright owner wanted to recover the actual damages it suffered as a result of that infringement. Thus, the question confronted in the next case was whether the copyright owner could recover the actual damages it suffered as a result of infringements abroad, or whether instead it could only recover only the amount of the infringer's profits abroad which was nothing. Before reading the case, ask yourself what you think the answer *should* be. No matter what you conclude, you can't be wrong. Though the case had a specific outcome, even the judges who decided it split 2-1 on what the answer "should" be.

## Los Angeles News Service v. Reuters
### 340 F.3d 926 (9th Cir. 2003), cert. denied, 124 S.Ct. 2158 (2004)

Circuit Judge Diarmuid F. O'Scannlain

We must decide whether a news organization may recover actual damages under the Copyright Act for acts of infringement that mostly occurred outside the United States.

*I*

The copyrighted works at issue here ("the works") are two video recordings, "The Beating of Reginald Denny" and "Beating of Man in White Panel Truck," which depict the infamous events at Florence Ave. and Normandie Blvd. during the 1992 Los Angeles riots. Los Angeles News Service ("LANS"), an independent news organization which produces video and audio tape recordings of newsworthy events and licenses them for profit, produced the works (and two other videotapes not at issue here) while filming the riots from its helicopter. LANS copyrighted the works and sold a license to rebroadcast them to, among others, the National Broadcasting Company ("NBC") network, which used them on the *Today Show.*

Visnews International (USA), Ltd. ("Visnews") is a joint venture among NBC, Reuters Television Ltd., and the British Broadcasting Company ("BBC"). Pursuant to a news supply agreement between NBC and Visnews, NBC transmitted the *Today Show* broadcast by fiber link to Visnews in New York; Visnews made a videotape copy of the works, which it then transmitted via satellite to its subscribers in Europe and Africa and via fiber link to the New York office of the European Broadcast Union ("EBU"), a joint venture of Visnews and Reuters. The EBU subsequently made another videotape copy of the works, and transmitted it to Reuters in London, which in turn distributed the works via video "feed" to its own subscribers.

LANS sued Reuters Television International, Inc., Reuters America Holdings, Inc., Reuters America, Inc. (collectively, "Reuters"), and Visnews for copyright infringement and certain other claims not relevant here. The district court subsequently granted Reuters and Visnews partial summary judgment on the issue of extraterritorial infringement, holding that no liability could arise under the Copyright Act for acts of infringement that occurred outside the United States. . . . However, the district court held that Visnews's act of copying the works in New York was a domestic act of infringement and rejected a claimed defense of fair use. . . .

The district court further concluded that LANS had failed to prove any actual damages arising domestically and that damages arising extraterritorially were unavailable under the Act, which meant that LANS was limited to statutory damages. . . . After a bench trial on the issue of statutory damages, the district court awarded LANS a total of $ 60,000. . . .

LANS appealed the district court's ruling on actual damages. . . . We subsequently reversed the district court's actual damages ruling, disagreeing with its interpretation of the Copyright Act's extraterritorial application. *L.A. News Serv. v. Reuters TV Int'l, Ltd. (Reuters III),* 149 F.3d 987, 992 (9th Cir. 1998). We concluded that although the district court was correct to hold that the Copyright Act does not apply extraterritorially, an exception may apply where an act of infringement is completed entirely within the United States and that such infringing act enabled further exploitation abroad. Relying on *Sheldon v. Metro-Goldwyn Pictures Corp.,* 106 F.2d 45 (2d Cir. 1939), aff'd, 309 U.S. 390, 84 L. Ed. 825, 60 S. Ct. 681 (1940), which held that profits from overseas infringement can be recovered on the theory that the infringer holds them in a constructive trust for the copyright owner, we reversed the grant of summary judgment. *Reuters III,* 149 F.3d at 991-92. We held that "LANS [was] entitled to recover damages flowing from exploitation abroad of the domestic acts of infringement committed by defendants." *Id. at 992.*

. . . After the Supreme Court denied certiorari . . . , the case returned to the district court, where Reuters and Visnews moved for summary adjudication of the claim for actual damages. They asserted that the *Reuters III* decision permitted LANS to recover only Defendants' profits attributable to extraterritorial infringement – not actual damages for injuries the infringements caused LANS overseas....

After a hearing, the district court agreed with Reuters and Visnews . . . and granted the motion. The court concluded that *Reuters III* had held only that LANS could recover any profits or unjust enrichment from domestic infringers, on the theory that the infringers held such profits in a constructive trust for LANS. "To permit [LANS] to recover damages other than Defendants' profits or unjust enrichment," the court stated, "would . . .

effectively permit [LANS] to recover damages for extraterritorial acts of infringement."

Having determined that LANS could recover only Defendants' profits, if any, the district court concluded that Reuters and Visnews had reaped no such profits from their infringement. The court held that LANS's "speculative" testimony about the competitive advantage that exclusive footage gives a subscription broadcaster was insufficient to create a factual dispute. It accordingly granted the motion for summary adjudication. In its order, the district court stated that LANS could elect to take the $60,000 in statutory damages awarded in *Reuters II* and affirmed in *Reuters III*. . . .

## II

LANS claims that the district court erred by disallowing recovery for actual damages. LANS, however, does not challenge the court's further conclusion that LANS had failed to show that Reuters and Visnews had earned any profits from the overseas infringement. Summary adjudication was therefore appropriate if the district court correctly concluded that LANS could not recover actual damages for overseas effects of Defendants' infringement.

### A

Both parties engage in detailed exegesis of our opinion in *Reuters III*. On LANS's reading, the *Reuters III* court's use of the term "damages" is dispositive. The statute uses "actual damages" and "profits" separately and distinctly, and provides that an infringer may recover both (in the ordinary case). LANS asserts therefore that the *Reuters III* court should be read as having meant what it said: "damages" means actual damages.

But LANS's interpretation does not fit with the context in which the *Reuters III* court discussed the recoverability of "damages." There, we relied on Judge Learned Hand's opinion in *Sheldon* and discussed damages entirely in the context of that case, which dealt exclusively with the recovery of the defendants' profits.

The *Sheldon* court had previously affirmed the defendants' liability for infringing the plaintiffs' copyright by incorporating their play into a movie. . . . After a remand, the defendants appealed the district court's decision to award the plaintiffs all the defendants' profits from exhibiting the motion picture. The Second Circuit, inter alia, determined that the profits traceable to overseas exhibition of the infringing movie should be included. Although "at first blush it [seemed] that [the overseas profits] should be excluded" because the overseas exhibition of the infringing movie was not tortious under American copyright law, the court nonetheless concluded that the plaintiffs could recover the overseas profits under a different theory, based on one defendant's having made the negatives in the U.S. The court elaborated:

> The negatives were "records" from which the work could be "reproduced," and it was a tort to make them in this country. The plaintiffs acquired an equitable interest in them as soon as they were made, which attached to any profits from their exploitation, whether in the form of money remitted to the United States, or of increase in the value of shares of foreign companies held by the defendants. . . . As soon as any of the profits so realized took the form of property whose situs was in the United States, our law seized upon them and impressed them with a constructive trust, whatever their form.

The *Sheldon* court relied exclusively on this rationale in holding that the plaintiffs could recover the defendants' profits from overseas exhibition.

As *Sheldon* considered only an award of profits, it is counter-intuitive that a court applying *Sheldon*'s rationale, but using the word "damages" as the *Reuters III* court did, was referring consciously to "actual damages" as opposed to "profits." Indeed our prior holding in *Reuters III*, based on the *Sheldon* constructive trust theory, demonstrates that we did not use the term "damages" in that formal sense. Rather, we used "damages" as a shorthand either for both the forms of relief that 17 U.S.C. § 504(b) makes available, *i.e.*, actual damages and defendants' profits, or only the recovery of defendants' profits. Understanding which applies requires closer analysis of *Sheldon* and its progeny.

### B

Of course, *Sheldon* did not explicitly deal with the issue of actual damages. But as LANS points out, there is some support in the Second Circuit's post-*Sheldon* case law for the recovery of extraterritorial actual damages once an act of domestic infringement is proven.

The most direct support for such position comes from *Update Art, Inc. v. Modiin Publ'g, Ltd.*, 843 F.2d 67 (2d Cir. 1988), in which the Second Circuit considered an Israeli newspaper's unauthorized reproduction of a poster copyrighted in the United States. *Update Art* held, albeit without much discussion, that the defendants had failed to make any showing that the initial copying of the poster had occurred abroad; thus . . . the court concluded that the "predicate act" of domestic infringement had occurred and that Update Art had stated a viable copyright. The court also affirmed the award of "damages accruing from the illegal infringement in the Israeli newspapers."

*Update Art*, however, is distinguishable from LANS's claim in a couple of important respects. First, several issues of the newspaper in which the infringing reproduction appeared were circulated in the United States. Second, and more importantly, the amount of damages awarded by the district court was based on defendants' profits. Finally, the panel did not even discuss the distinction between damages and profits, much less cite *Sheldon*. Rather, it merely concluded that the damages award could stand despite the extraterritoriality issue. . . .

### C

On the whole, we conclude that *Reuters III* adhered very closely to our decision in *Subafilms, Ltd. v. MGM-Pathe Communs. Co.*, 24 F.3d 1088 (9th Cir. 1994) (en banc). *Subafilms* reaffirmed that the copyright laws have no application beyond the U.S. border, and expressly took no position on the merits of the *Update Act* court's apparent willingness to award damages. LANS's appeal thus presents the precise question that *Subafilms* reserved, and as the prior panel recognized, such question should be resolved in light of the principles the en banc court laid down.

The import of such principles counsel a narrow application of the adoption in *Reuters III* of the *Sheldon* exception to the general rule. In particular, the *Sheldon* constructive trust rationale includes a territorial connection . . . that preserves consistency with Congress's decision to keep the copyright laws – presumably including § 504, which prescribes remedies – territorially confined. Moreover, no rational deterrent function is served by making an infringer whose domestic act of infringement – from which he earns no profit – . . . liable for the copyright owner's entire loss of value or profit from that overseas infringement, particularly if the overseas infringement is legal where it takes place. . . . Moreover, the resulting over-deterrence might chill the fair use of copyrighted works in close cases.

LANS counters that the assessment of damages based on a domestic act of infringement having had consequences in foreign territories is legitimate under "traditional tort principles." However, it offers no direct support for the proposition that those principles compel the extension of relief – legal or equitable – beyond the boundaries where Congress declared that liability stops. Its policy arguments to the contrary seem largely a complaint about the failure of Congress to make the copyright laws – those creating both rights and remedies – applicable extraterritorially.[9] [[9] See, e.g., Jane C. Ginsburg, *Extraterritoriality and Multiterritoriality in Copyright Infringement*, 37 Va. J. Int'l L. 587 at 598 (1997) (criticizing *Reuters III* for creating a parallel arbitrary distinction).]

*III*

Accordingly we read *Reuters III* to allow only a narrow exception for the recovery of the infringer's profits to *Subafilms*'s general rule against extraterritorial application. We conclude therefore that the Copyright Act does not provide LANS recovery for actual damages resulting from Reuters's and Visnews's infringement.

*Circuit Judge Barry G. Silverman, dissenting:*

In our previous decision, *L.A. News Serv. v. Reuters Television Int'l, Ltd. (Reuters III)*, we decided the very issue the majority now re-decides the other way. At that time, we identified the issue as whether "a plaintiff may recover actual damages accruing from the unauthorized exploitation abroad of copyrighted work infringed in the United States." We held that it could. Our mandate said, "We REVERSE the ruling barring the claim for extraterritorial damages and REMAND for a trial on actual damages, with directions that if LANS elects to recover actual damages, the award of statutory damages be vacated."

The majority now holds that when we said "actual damages," we didn't mean actual damages, but only whatever profits the infringer might have realized. This new holding is not only at odds with our previous holding, but it fails to take account of the fact that the Copyright Act itself specifically uses the terms "actual damages" and "profits" separately and distinctly. The district court should have allowed LANS to do what we said it could do – prove its actual damages. For that reason, I respectfully dissent.

At this stage of the case, the majority's reliance on *Sheldon v. Metro-Goldwyn Pictures Corp.*, 106 F.2d 45 (2d Cir. 1939), is puzzling. In *Sheldon*, the question of what constitutes "actual damages" wasn't an issue or even discussed. *Sheldon* was an appeal from an accounting. The sole question was whether the plaintiff could recover the profits earned by the defendant from its foreign exploitation of a motion picture that infringed the plaintiff's stage play, profits that were *discovered* during the accounting. The court held that the plaintiff could, on a constructive trust theory. "Actual damages" had nothing to do with the case.

*SubaFilms Ltd. v. MGM-Pathe Communs. Co.*, 24 F.3d 1088 (9th Cir. 1994), doesn't shed light on this problem, either. It merely holds that there is no recovery under American copyright law for infringements that do not occur within the United States. True enough, but as we previously held in *Reuters III*, "actual damages" *can* be recovered when the infringement occurs wholly within the United States. That's exactly what happened here, and why we reversed for a trial at which LANS would be allowed to prove its actual damages, if any. This is not a novel concept. . . .

There are any number of ways to compute actual damages. Neither the Copyright Act, nor our prior decision in *this* case, nor any *other* case, limits the calculation of actual damages to only the infringer's ill-gotten profits. LANS should have been allowed to put on its proof of its actual damages, as we previously held it could. I would remand for a trial on actual damages (just as we did *last* time) except *this* time, I would add that we really, really mean it.

## 2. Injunctive relief: geographic scope of injunction

Assume now that an American court has subject matter over a claim that infringements are being committed abroad, and personal jurisdiction over the person or company alleged to be committing them. Assume further that the foreign infringements are being committed as a direct result of an earlier infringement that occurred in the United States. (Imagine, for example, that CDs are being manufactured and sold abroad, using an unlicensed and infringing master recording that was made in the U.S.) May a U.S. District Court enjoin the infringer from continuing to commit infringements *abroad*? Surprisingly little has been said about this question. What, in a nutshell, does the following case say about it?

### Filmvideo Releasing Corp. v. Hastings
### 668 F.2d 91 (2d Cir. 1981)

Circuit Judge Van Graafeiland

. . . This is an appeal from a judgment of the United States District Court for the Southern District of New York, (Werker, J.), enjoining appellant from using, selling, or licensing certain Hopalong Cassidy motion pictures anywhere in the United States, directing appellant to transfer all of its prints, tapes and cassettes to appellees, and referring the computation of infringement damages and counsel fees to a magistrate. . . . Briefly, . . . the dispute is between the administrator . . . of the estate of Clarence Mulford and the trustees of several Mulford trusts, on the one hand, and the present holder of Hopalong Cassidy movie prints, on the other. The movies were made and copyrighted by Paramount Pictures, Inc., under a 1935 licensing agreement between Mulford, author of the Hopalong Cassidy books, and Prudential Studios Corporation. The copyrights in the books were renewed; the copyrights in the movies were not. Although all television, broadcasting, and radio rights were specifically reserved to Mulford in the 1935 agreement, appellant contended unsuccessfully below that it was entitled to make free and untrammeled use of the movie prints in all media. Judge Werker's rejection of this argument brings the matter to this Court. . . .

. . . Congress [intended] . . . to ensure that a failure of the derivative copyright would not diminish the statutory protection afforded the underlying copyright. Appellant Filmvideo, which had no rights under the 1935 licensing agreement, could not dispute appellees' claim to protection under the Mulford copyright.

We therefore affirm those portions of the district court's judgment which (1) enjoin the infringing use by the appellant and (2) direct the computation of damages. However, we reverse that portion of the judgment which directs appellant to deliver to appellees all negatives, prints, etc. in appellant's possession. As the district court implicitly recognized in the terms of its injunction, copyright laws do not have extraterritorial application. *Robert Stigwood Group Ltd. v. O'Reilly,* 530 F.2d 1096, 1101 (2d Cir.), cert. denied, 429 U.S. 848, 97 S. Ct. 135, 50 L. Ed. 2d 121 (1976). Appellant claims the right to show the Hopalong Cassidy films abroad, and the district court's injunction does not prevent it from so doing. In the absence of proof that appellant did not have legal possession of the films for his limited purpose, it was an abuse of discretion for the district court to direct that the films be turned over to appellees.

The judgment of the district court is affirmed, except as to that portion which directs delivery of films, prints, etc. to appellees. The portion of the judgment which directs such delivery is reversed. . . .

## C. Enforcement of foreign judgments

So far, this chapter has dealt with determining which court is the proper court to hear an international copyright case, and what remedies the court may award if the plaintiff proves an infringement took place. Consider, now, a case in which a proper court awarded the plaintiff a proper judgment against a defendant that has no assets in the country where the court is located. (This is an entirely possible scenario, because personal jurisdiction over a defendant does *not require* the defendant to have assets in the country where the case is filed.) Assume, though, that the defendant does have assets in some *other* country.

A judgment from the court of one country will not be sufficient, by itself, to enable the plaintiff to seize assets of the defendant that are located in another country. Rather, the plaintiff will have to enforce its judgment by filing a second lawsuit in the country where the defendant's assets are located, in order to get a judgment from a court in that country. However – and this is important – the second lawsuit will not involve a complete rehash of the merits of the infringement claim. Instead, it ought to be an almost *pro forma* lawsuit that simply converts the original "foreign" judgment into a "local" judgment that the plaintiff then can use to seize the defendant's local assets. For detailed guidance on how, exactly, this is done, see, Robert E. Lutz, A LAWYER'S HANDBOOK FOR ENFORCING FOREIGN JUDGMENTS IN THE UNITED STATES AND ABROAD (Cambridge Univ. Press 2007).

In *Sarl Louis Feraud International v. Viewfinder Inc.,* which is reproduced below, a French company obtained a judgment from a French court for the infringement, in France, of its French copyrights by an American company that has no assets in France but does have assets in the United States. In an effort to collect its judgment, the French company filed a second lawsuit against the American company, in an American court, seeking to convert its French judgment into an American judgment that could be used to seize the American company's assets in the U.S. To fully understand what the dispute was about in that case, it'll be helpful to know a bit about the French and American copyright laws that were at the heart of that dispute.

Here is the provision of French copyright law, on which the judgment in France was based:

## Copyright Code of France

http://www.wipo.int/clea/docs_new/en/fr/fr003en.html

*Art. L. 112-1.*

The provisions of this Code shall protect the rights of authors in all works of the mind, whatever their kind, form of expression, merit or purpose.

*Art. L. 112-2.*

The following, in particular, shall be considered works of the mind within the meaning of this Code:

. . .

14° Creations of the seasonal industries of dress and articles of fashion. Industries which, by reason of the demands of fashion, frequently renew the form of their products, particularly the making of dresses, furs, underwear, embroidery, hats, shoes, gloves, leather goods, the manufacture of fabrics of striking novelty or of special use in high fashion dressmaking, the products of manufacturers of articles of fashion and of footwear and the manufacture of fabrics for upholstery shall be deemed to be seasonal industries.

Here is an explanation of American copyright law on fashion design.

## Galiano v. Harrah's Operating Company, Inc.
### 416 F.3d 411 (5th Cir. 2005)

Jerry E. Smith, Circuit Judge: . . .

I.

Jane Galiano is the founder and owner of Gianna, Inc., which designs clothing and counsels various industries regarding their professional attire. In August 1995, Gianna and Harrah's entered into an agreement (the "Design Consulting Agreement") pursuant to which Gianna was to design uniforms for employees of various Harrah's casinos. Subsequent exchanges between the parties resulted in the creation of several proposed sketches.

Because Gianna did not have the capacity to produce patterns of the sketch designs or make the finished uniforms, it entered into a manufacturing agreement (the "Uniform Manufacturing Agreement") with Uniform Ideas, Inc., one of Harrah's' suppliers. That agreement stated that Uniform Ideas, Inc., would manufacture uniforms for Gianna during the period from September 1, 1995, to August 31, 1996. . . .

The design agreement between Gianna and Harrah's expired according to its terms on December 1, 1995. The parties entered into negotiations to extend the contract, but failed to do so and entered into an agreement purporting to settle all disputes in May 1996. Harrah's continued to order Gianna-designed costumes from its suppliers.

In October 1999 Gianna sought and received copyright protection for a collection of sketches entitled "Uniform and Costume Collection submitted to Harrah's Operating Company, Inc." The certificate identified the collection as "Artwork for Wearing Apparel" and classified the work as "2-dimensional artwork." Galiano is identified as the author of the copyrighted work. The collection includes more than fifty colored and numbered illustrations, including sketches of uniform style shirts, blouses, vests, jackets, pants, shorts, ensembles, elaborate masquerade-type costumes, and unique head gear and a dozen pages of silkscreen artwork.

Three months after obtaining the copyright protection, Gianna . . . sued in federal district court alleging that Harrah's had . . . committed copyright infringement by continuing to use and order Gianna-designed uniforms. . . .

## II.

. . .

We conclude that Gianna did not own a valid copyright in the clothing designs. . . .

## B.

This case involves the copyrightability of "pictorial, graphic, and sculptural works" ("PGS" works). These articles may be two- or three-dimensional and include works such as maps, fine or graphic art, diagrams, models, and technical drawings. 17 U.S.C. § 101. If an item qualifies as a "useful article" under the Act, however, it is entitled to copyright protection only to the extent that its artwork or creative design is separable from the utilitarian aspects of the work.

The applicable statute provides the following:

> Copyright protection subsists in original works of authorship fixed in any tangible medium of expression, now known or later developed, from which they can be perceived, reproduced, or otherwise communicated, either directly or with the aid of a machine or device. Works of authorship include pictorial, graphic, and sculptural works. . . .

17 U.S.C. § 102(a). The statute then defines what a PGS work is:

> Such works shall include works of artistic craftsmanship insofar as their form but not their mechanical or utilitarian aspects are concerned; the design of a useful article, as defined in this section, shall be considered a [PGS] work only if, and only to the extent that, such design incorporates [PGS] features that can be identified separately from, and are capable of existing independently of, the utilitarian aspects of the article.

17 U.S.C. § 101.

## C.

The test for whether Gianna can copyright the designs proceeds in two steps. First, we must determine whether the asset for which the creator seeks copyright protection is a "useful" article. If it is not, there is no PGS bar to copyright protection. If it is, the panel must determine whether the "design incorporates [PGS] features that can be identified separately from, and are capable of existing independently of, the utilitarian aspects of the article." *Id.* Answering the first question is easy; answering the second is not.

### 1.

There is little doubt that clothing possesses utilitarian and aesthetic value. . . . The hard questions involve the methodology for severing creative elements from industrial design features.

### 2. . . .

### b.

. . . [A] clothing design that is intended to be used on clothing is copyrightable only to the extent that its artistic qualities can be separated from the utilitarian nature of the garment. How to conduct the conceptual separation is, in turn, what continues to flummox federal courts. The leading treatise in the field, NIMMER ON COPYRIGHT, discusses conceptual separability extensively. It presents the conceptual separability test somewhat differently, and one standard reads as follows: "[I]t may be concluded that conceptual separability exists where there is substantial likelihood that even if the article had no utilitarian use it would still be marketable to some significant segment of the community simply because of its aesthetic qualities."

Nimmer's cogent discussion of the scope of copyright protection in design works breaks the subject into two categories: (1) fabric design and (2) dress design. Fabric designs include patterns or artistic features imprinted onto a fabric or that appear repeatedly throughout the dress fabric. Because one can generally separate the artistic elements of this design from the utility of the wearable garment, NIMMER ON COPYRIGHT states that fabric designs are generally entitled to copyright protection. On the other hand, dress designs, which graphically set forth the shape, style, cut, and dimensions for converting fabric into a finished dress or other clothing garment, generally do not have artistic elements that can be separated from the utilitarian use of the garment, and therefore typically do not qualify for copyright protection.[17] [[17] See Id. NIMMER ON COPYRIGHT does not conclude that clothing designs do not qualify for copyright protection *per se,* but it rather concludes that clothing designs rarely pass the "separability" test. This is an important distinction in light of existing case law, which can sometimes appear to implement a categorical approach. In *Whimsicality Inc. v. Rubie's Costume Co.,* 891 F.2d 452, 454 (2d Cir.1989), for example, the court concluded that "[c]lothing design is not copyrightable." As Gianna points out, this statement is *dictum,* because the holding was based on fraud of the Copyright Office, and no opinion of which we are aware creates any *per se* rule for clothing or any other type of design.]

The caselaw generally follows Nimmer's conceptual breakdown. Design of sweaters is usually classified as "fabric design" and is entitled to copyright protection. . . .

Cases dealing with the copyrightability of clothing designs do not exclude them from protection *per se;* they instead focus on the "separability" analysis. In *Poe v. Missing Persons,* 745 F.2d 1238 (9th Cir.1984), for example, the court awarded copyright protection to a swimsuit design.[19] [[19] In fact, the court *still* remanded the case to allow the jury to apply the separability test, concluding that "[n]othing in our legal training qualifies us to determine as a matter of law whether [the swimsuit design] can be worn as an article for swimming or any other utilitarian purpose."] *Poe* is quite enlightening, because it involved no ordinary swimsuit. The court found that there was little chance of this elaborately crafted swimsuit's ever being worn – it appeared that it was marketed as a work of art. . . .

The Second Circuit faced a similar situation dealing with belt buckles in *Kieselstein-Cord.* The court determined that "Winchester" and "Vaquero" belt buckles contained artistic elements that were conceptually separable despite the buckles' utilitarian functions. *See Kieselstein-Cord,* 632 F.2d at 993. This ruling was premised on the belief that the buckles could exist independently as a valuable artistic commodity. The court nonetheless determined that the belt buckle in question existed on the "razor's edge of copyright law." As with the court in *Poe,* the *Kieselstein/Cord* court's willingness to recognize the copyrightability of a useful article seems, at some elemental level, to turn on the capacity of the item to moonlight as a piece of marketable artwork.

c.

The caselaw on costume design is, to say the least, uneven. Generally speaking, however, it tends to reflect a direct relationship between a costume's copyrightability and its actual or potential market value as a stand-alone piece of artwork.[22] [[22] *See, e.g., Animal Fair Inc. v. Amfesco Indus.,* 620 F.Supp. 175 (D.C.Minn.1985), *aff'd mem.,* 794 F.2d 678 (8th Cir.1986) (holding that slipper depicting a bear's foot entitled to copyright protection because it was essentially a fanciful artistic rendition of a bear's foot); *National Theme Prod. v. Beck,* 696 F.Supp. 1348 (S.D.Cal.1988) (holding that masquerade costumes are entitled to copyright protection because their design and form have little to do with their suitability as wearing apparel – they were essentially a collection of accessories); *Whimsicality,* 891 F.2d at 456 (refusing to afford deference to registration of useful articles as "soft sculptures" where "Whimsicality knew full well that no reasonable observer could believe the costumes were soft sculpture.").]

Confusion regarding the copyrightability of costumes and questions from the garment industry led to a 1991 opinion from the United States Copyright Office, 56 FR 56530-02, 1991 WL 224879 (F.R.), which concluded that "[g]arment designs (excluding separately identified pictorial representations of designs imposed upon the garment) will not be registered even if they contain ornamental features, or are intended to be used as historical or period dress." *See id.*[23] [[23] The Office also concluded that "[f]anciful costumes will be treated as useful articles, and will be registered only upon a finding of separately identifiable pictorial and/or sculptural authorship." The Office added that masks were generally not useful articles, and generally would be entitled to copyright protection. *See* 56 FR 56530-02, 1991 WL 224879 (F.R.).] The garment industry had sought broader protections for elaborate garment designs; the Office answered that "[g]arments are useful articles, and the designs of useful articles are generally outside of the copyright law."[24] [[24] *Id.* The Office further concluded that "[p]arties wishing to modify this position must address their concerns to Congress."]

. . . We therefore adopt the likelihood-of-marketability standard *for garment design*". . . .

Gianna makes no showing that its designs are marketable independently of their utilitarian function as casino uniforms. Gianna correctly notes that there are costume museums and that they are replete with extravagant designs that might also have utilitarian qualities, but Gianna does not demonstrate that its designs describe such material. We therefore affirm the denial of summary judgment. . . .

Here now is the *Sarl Louis Feraud* decision, which deals with whether the French copyright judgment was enforceable in the United States.

## Sarl Louis Feraud International v. Viewfinder Inc.
### 489 F.3d 474 (2d Cir. 2007)

POOLER, Circuit Judge.

Plaintiffs-appellants Sarl Louis Feraud International ("Feraud") and S.A. Pierre Balmain ("Balmain") appeal from the . . . order of the United States District Court for the Southern District of New York (Lynch, J.) dismissing plaintiffs' action to enforce two judgments issued by the Tribunal de grande instance de Paris ("the French Judgments") against defendant-appellee Viewfinder, Inc. ("Viewfinder"). Plaintiffs challenge the district court's conclusion that enforcement of the French Judgments would be repugnant to the public policy of New York . . . because it would violate Viewfinder's First Amendment rights. Because the district court did not conduct the full analysis necessary to reach this conclusion, we vacate its order and remand for further proceedings consistent with this opinion.

## Background

. . . Feraud and Balmain are French corporations that design high-fashion clothing and other items for women. . . .Viewfinder is a Delaware corporation with a principal place of business in New York. Viewfinder operates a website called "firstView.com," on which it posts photographs of fashion shows held by designers around the world, including photographs of plaintiffs' fashion shows. Donald Ashby, the president of Viewfinder, is a professional fashion photographer. Viewfinder styles itself as an Internet fashion magazine akin to the online version of Vogue. The firstView website contains both photographs of the current season's fashions, which may be viewed only upon subscription and payment of a fee, and photographs of past collections, which are available for free. An annual subscription to firstView costs $999. *See http://www.firstview.com/subscribe_info.php* (last visited June 1, 2007). Users can also view the content for one hour for $5.95. *See http:// www.firstview.com/subscribe.php* (last visited June 1, 2007). Viewfinder does not sell clothing or designs.

In January 2001, Feraud and Balmain, along with several other design houses, each filed suit against Viewfinder in the Tribunal de grande instance de Paris seeking money damages from Viewfinder for alleged unauthorized use of their intellectual property and unfair competition. These civil actions stemmed from Viewfinder displaying photographs of the designers' fashion shows, which revealed designs from their upcoming collection, on the firstView.com website. Viewfinder was served in New York in accordance with the terms of the Hague Convention on the Service of Judicial and Extrajudicial Documents in Civil or Commercial Matters. Viewfinder failed to respond to the complaints, however, and therefore . . . the French court issued default judgment against Viewfinder. The French court found that plaintiffs' "ready-to-wear" and "haute couture" collections from 1996-2001 were available on the firstView .com website. The court further found that Viewfinder's posting of these photographs of plaintiffs' designs was "without the necessary authorization" and thus "constitute[d] counterfeit and violation of royalties pursuant to articles L 716-1 and L 122-4 of the Intellectual [P]roperty Code." The court also found with respect to each of the plaintiffs that Viewfinder had committed "parasitism" under French law because it had "take[n] advantage of plaintiff's reputation and commercial efforts creating confusion between the two companies." The French court ordered Viewfinder to remove the offending photographs, and awarded damages of 500,000 francs for each plaintiff, costs of the action, and a fine ("*astreinte* ") of 50,000 francs a day for each day Viewfinder failed to comply with the judgment.

. . . [P]laintiffs filed separate complaints in the United States District Court for the Southern District of New York to enforce the French Judgments. Plaintiffs sought enforcement under New York's Uniform Foreign Money Judgment Recognition Act, which provides that, subject to certain exceptions, foreign judgments that are "final, conclusive and enforceable" in the country where rendered are deemed conclusive between the parties and enforceable by U.S. courts. N.Y. C.P.L.R. §§ 5302, 5303. The district court consolidated these actions and also granted plaintiffs' request for an order of attachment. Federal jurisdiction is based on diversity of citizenship.

. . . Viewfinder filed a motion to dismiss or, in the alternative, a motion for summary judgment and a motion to vacate the attachment order. Viewfinder raised a variety of arguments in its motion papers, one of which was found meritorious by the district court. The district court found that enforcing the French Judgments would be repugnant to the public policy of New York because it would violate Viewfinder's First Amendment rights. *See Sarl Louis Feraud Int'l v. Viewfinder Inc.*, 406 F.Supp.2d 274, 281 (S.D.N.Y.2005). Specifically, the district court found that the fashion shows at issue were public events and Viewfinder had a First Amendment right to publish the photographs at issue. Thus, as the district court concluded, the "First Amendment simply does not permit plaintiffs to stage public events in which the general public has a considerable interest, and then control the way in which information about those events is disseminated in the mass media." The district court also stated that to the extent that plaintiffs' designs were protected by copyright, "the copyright law similarly provides, as a matter of First Amendment necessity, a 'fair use' exception for the publication of newsworthy matters." Based on its conclusion that enforcing the judgment would impinge upon Viewfinder's free speech rights, the district court dismissed the action and vacated the order of attachment. Plaintiffs filed a timely notice of appeal.

## *Discussion*

The question presented by this appeal is whether the district court properly found that the French Judgments were unenforceable under New York law. In order to address this question, we begin with the language of the relevant state statute: "A foreign country judgment need not be recognized if ... the *cause of action* on which the judgment is based is repugnant to the public policy of this state." N.Y. C.P.L.R. § 5304(b)(4) (emphasis added). . . . The default judgments issued by the French court explicitly state that Viewfinder's actions violated "articles L 716-1 and L 122-4 of the Intellectual Property Code." Article L 122-4 is in Book I, Title II, Chapter II of the French Intellectual Property Code, which are entitled "Copyright," "Authors' Rights," and "Patrimonial Rights," respectively. *See* Code de la propriete intellectuelle art. L 122-4(Fr.), *available at http://www.legifrance.gouv.fr.* Article L 122-4 provides: "Any complete or partial performance or reproduction made without the consent of the author or of his successors in title or assigns shall be unlawful." This is analogous to the United States Copyright Act, which defines a copyright infringer as one "who violates any of the exclusive rights of the copyright owner," including the rights of reproduction, performance, and public display. Under French copyright law, the "creations of the seasonal industries of dress and articles of fashion" are entitled to copyright protection. Code de la propriete intellectuelle art. L 112-2(Fr.), *available at http://www.legifrance.gouv.fr.* The French court found that Viewfinder's publication of numerous photographs depicting plaintiffs' design collections violated plaintiffs' copyrights. Furthermore, the French Judgments concluded that Viewfinder's reproduction and publication of plaintiffs' designs were "without the necessary authorization." Thus, it is apparent that the French Judgments were based in part on a finding of copyright infringement.

We cannot second-guess the French court's finding that Viewfinder's actions were "without the necessary authorization." Viewfinder had the opportunity to dispute the factual basis of plaintiffs' claims in the French court, but it chose not to respond to the complaint. . . ."By defaulting [in the foreign adjudication], a defendant ensures that a judgment will be entered against him, and assumes the risk that an irrevocable mistake of law or fact may underlie that judgment." Thus, for the purposes of this action, we must accept that Viewfinder's conduct constitutes an unauthorized reproduction or performance of plaintiffs' copyrighted work infringing on plaintiffs' intellectual property rights, and the only question to consider is whether a law that sanctions such conduct is repugnant to the public policy of New York.

The "public policy inquiry rarely results in refusal to enforce a judgment unless it is inherently vicious, wicked or immoral, and shocking to the prevailing moral sense.". . . "Under New York law [,] ... foreign decrees and proceedings will be given respect ... even if the result under the foreign proceeding would be different than under American law."[3] [Fn3 For this reason, we reject the argument advanced by Viewfinder and amici that holding Viewfinder liable under French copyright laws would be repugnant to public policy because plaintiffs' dress designs are not copyrightable in the United States. While it is true that United States law does not extend copyright protection to dress designs, Viewfinder presents no argument as to why this distinction would offend the public policy of New York. As the district court found in rejecting this argument below-which Viewfinder has not challenged on appeal-copyright laws are not "matters of strong moral principle" but rather represent "economic legislation based on policy decisions that assign rights based on assessments of what legal rules will produce the greatest economic good for society as a whole."] Thus, "[o]nly in clear-cut cases ought [the public policy exception] to avail defendant."

Laws that are antithetical to the First Amendment will create such a situation. Foreign judgments that impinge on First Amendment rights will be found to be "repugnant" to public policy. . . .The district court in this case reached the conclusion that the French Judgments were unenforceable because they impinged on Viewfinder's First Amendment rights. In doing so, however, it appears not to have conducted the full analysis for us to affirm its decision.

The district court's decision appears to rest on the assumption that if Viewfinder is a news magazine reporting on a public event, then it has an absolute First Amendment defense to any attempt to sanction such conduct. The First Amendment does not provide such categorical protection. Intellectual property laws co-exist with the First Amendment in this country, and the fact that an entity is a news publication engaging in speech activity does not, standing alone, relieve such entities of their obligation to obey intellectual property laws. While an entity's status as a news publication may be highly probative on certain relevant inquiries, such as whether that entity has a fair use defense to copyright infringement, it does not render that entity immune from liability under intellectual property laws. . . . Because the First Amendment does not provide news entities an exemption from compliance with intellectual property laws, the mere fact that Viewfinder may be characterized as a news magazine would not, standing alone, render the French Judgments repugnant to public policy.

Rather, because Section 5304(b) requires courts to examine the cause of action on which the foreign judgment was based, the district court should have analyzed whether the intellectual property regime upon which the French Judgments were based impinged on rights protected by the First Amendment. . . . In deciding whether the French Judgments are repugnant to the public policy of New York, the district court should first determine the level of First Amendment protection required by New York public policy when a news entity engages in the unauthorized use of intellectual property at issue here. Then, it should determine whether the French intellectual property regime provides comparable protections.

With regard to the protections provided by the First Amendment for the unauthorized use of copyrighted material, this court has held that absent extraordinary circumstances, "the fair use doctrine encompasses all claims of first amendment in the copyright field." . . . Because the fair use doctrine balances the competing interests of the copyright laws and the First Amendment, some analysis of that doctrine is generally needed before a court can conclude that a foreign copyright judgment is repugnant to public policy. . . .

In this case, the district court dispensed with the issue of fair use in a single sentence: "Similarly, even were plaintiffs' designs copyrightable, the copyright law similarly provides, as a matter of First Amendment necessity, a 'fair use' exception for the publication of newsworthy matters." To the extent the district court believed that Viewfinder's use was necessarily fair use because it was publishing "newsworthy matters," this was erroneous. . . . Whether the material is newsworthy is but one factor in the fair use analysis.

While both parties urge this court to resolve the issue of fair use, the record before us is insufficient to determine fair use as a matter of law. . . . For instance, the record is unclear as to the percentage of plaintiffs' designs that were posted on firstView.com. While the French Judgments do provide some information as to the number of photographs posted by Viewfinder, that information is both incomplete and unclear because it does not indicate what proportion of plaintiffs' designs were revealed by these photographs. Such factual findings are relevant in determining whether Viewfinder's use would constitute "fair use" under United States law. If the publication of photographs of copyrighted material in the same manner as Viewfinder has done in this case would not be fair use under United States law, then the French intellectual property regime sanctioning the same conduct certainly would not be repugnant to public policy. Similarly, if the sole reason that Viewfinder's conduct would be permitted under United States copyright law is that plaintiffs' dress designs are not copyrightable in the United States, the French Judgment would not appear to be repugnant. However, without further development of the record, we cannot reach any conclusions as to whether Viewfinder's conduct would fall within the protection of the fair use doctrine.

The record is similarly unclear as to the manner of protection afforded plaintiffs' fashion shows by French law as well as the protections afforded to alleged infringers generally, and photographers specifically, under French law. The minutes of the French criminal judgment contained in the record suggest that photographers may well enjoy some protection. These minutes indicate that the "Law covers a right to the benefit of the fashion designers that coexists with *that of the photographers.*" Memorandum from Jean-Marc Fedida to Don Ashby, June 17, 2005, at 3 (emphasis added). Moreover, Article L 122-5(3) of the French Intellectual Property Code permits unauthorized use of copyrighted material in limited circumstances similar to uses deemed "fair use" under United States law. *See* Code de la propriete intellectuelle art. L 122-5(3)(Fr.), *available at http:// www.legifrance.gouv.fr.* Whether such protections are sufficiently comparable to that required by the public policy of New York is a question best addressed in the first instance by the district court on a fully-developed record.

*Conclusion*

For the foregoing reasons, we vacate the judgment of the district court and remand for further proceedings consistent with this opinion. . . .

If enforcement of the French copyright judgment is barred by the First Amendment, is the U.S. Copyright Act unconstitutional *in toto*? If not, what would remain, after such a decision? For an argument that copyright law is perfectly constitutional in the United States, see Lionel S. Sobel, Copyright and the First Amendment: A Gathering Storm?, 19 ASCAP COPYRIGHT LAW SYMPOSIUM 43 (Columbia Univ. Press 1971), quoted in *Harper & Row, Publishers, Inc. v. Nation Enterprises*, 105 S.Ct. 2218, 2230 (1985).

Separate from the First Amendment issue, did you notice that the court said nothing at all about the fact that France and the United States both are members of the WTO and thus both are bound by TRIPs, or that both are adherents to the Berne Convention, or that both are adherents to the Universal Copyright Convention, or that the two countries entered into a bilateral copyright treaty with one another back in 1891? Even though the French company was in effect seeking to enforce its copyrights in the United States, the court correctly had no reason whatsoever to mention, let alone deal with, any of those treaties. Why? (If the answer doesn't come immediately to mind, look back at Chapter 4, especially sections A and B, concerning "national treatment.")

# Chapter 8

# International Copyright Licensing

As you know quite well by now, copyrighted works that originate in one country are entitled to protection in other countries, if certain requirements are satisfied. You have read about which country's law is applicable in cases involving cross-border uses of copyrighted works, and about which courts are proper for claiming the protection and remedies provided by copyright law.

While international copyright litigation is no longer uncommon – we've just devoted an entire chapter to procedural issues and remedies – choice of law issues are rarely difficult where the cross-border uses involve the public performance or reproduction of songs, movies or television programs, because the copyright laws of virtually all countries protect against the unauthorized performance or reproduction of these types of works. As a practical matter, this means that if copyrighted works are publicly performed or reproduced, those who do so are legally required to pay royalties to copyright owners, even if they are in other countries. And in fact, billions of dollars in royalties flow across national borders every year, to their rightful recipients, without litigation or even the threat of it. Those royalties flow, in other words, without any need to think about which court would be the proper court for a copyright owner to enforce its rights or seek its remedies. Administrative formalities may have to be complied with to obtain those royalties; but in many cases, copyright owners receive royalties from abroad by doing virtually nothing.

To explain how so much money flows so smoothly from one country to another, it is first necessary to distinguish between two types of royalties: (1) those that are paid as a result of individually negotiated voluntary licenses; and (2) those that are paid as a result of collectively administered or compulsory licenses.

## A. Individually negotiated voluntary licenses

Individually negotiated licenses would be used to authorize (for example):

- the foreign-language translation and publication abroad of a book written by an American author
- the performance of U.S.-authored play in London
- the theatrical exhibition abroad of a U.S.-produced movie
- television broadcasts in other countries of a U.S. program, and
- cable and satellite transmissions in other countries of original (as distinguished from retransmitted) programming, such as the programming carried on CNN, HBO and MTV.

These are just examples. Licenses to use other types of works in other ways are individually negotiated as well. What all of these types of works have in common is that the copyright laws of virtually all countries give copyright owners the right to license the use of these types of works, or withhold licenses, as copyright owners see fit. Licenses to use these types of works, in other words, are voluntary. And when licenses for their use are granted, they are granted as a result of individually negotiated, two-party licenses between the owner of the work's copyright and the company that wants to use it.

The terms of individually negotiated licenses authorizing the use of American copyrighted works abroad are almost identical to domestic license agreements. In other words, a license authorizing the performance in London or Milan of an American stage play would be almost identical to a license authorizing its performance in San Diego. Likewise, a license authorizing the performance in Los Angeles of a British or Italian play would be almost identical to a license authorizing its performance in Oxford or Florence.

International licenses may have special provisions dealing with such issues as:

- the approval of translations and other adaptations of the work, in order to "localize" it for the licensee's expected audience,
- ownership of the copyright to the translated version,
- choice of law, personal jurisdiction and service of process, should litigation become necessary,
- whether the licensee will be required to post a letter of credit to secure its payments to the copyright owner,
- payment of withholding taxes in the licensee's country, and
- currency conversion.

Special provisions like these may make international license agreements somewhat longer than purely domestic licenses. On the other hand, they may not. Cultural norms in the licensee's country may have a greater influence on the length of a license agreement than the fact that it's international. Japanese contracts, for example, are typically much shorter than American contracts; and for that reason, a license from an American copyright owner authorizing the use of its work in Japan may be shorter than a license from that same copyright owner authorizing the use of its work in New York.

Relations between copyright owners in one country and their licensees in another usually are about as cordial (or not) as relations between copyright owners and licensees in the same country. Where, however, a copyright owner is in one country and a licensee in another – and the license is voluntary and individually negotiated – the process of negotiating and documenting the license will be a significant one. The way in which international law enables the smooth flow of copyright royalties across national borders is more dramatically illustrated by the international operation of collectively administered or compulsory licenses.

## B. Collectively administered or compulsory licenses

Examples of collectively administered or compulsory licenses include licenses for:

- nondramatic public performances abroad of American musical compositions,

- the manufacture and sale of recordings of American musical compositions in other countries, and
- cable and satellite retransmissions abroad of American movies and television programs that are broadcast on conventional (over-the-air) television.

Again, these are just examples. Licenses to use other types of works in other ways are collectively administered or are handled by compulsory license too. What these types of works have in common is that the licensing practices or copyright laws of many countries, including the United States, use collective administration or compulsory licensing to authorize these uses of these works.

"Collective administration" is the term used to describe the issuance of licenses for certain types of uses of many separate works, and the collection of royalties from licensees, done by a single organization on behalf many separate copyright owners. In the United States especially there are sub-categories of collective administration that differ from one another slightly (though in ways that may be significant to those involved). But for present purposes, these distinctions may be disregarded.

Classic examples of collective administration in the United States are the licenses issued by ASCAP, BMI and SESAC to broadcasters and concert venues authorizing them to perform musical compositions nondramatically. (Dramatic musical performances – that is, performances during a musical stage play – are not licensed collectively; they are licensed individually.) These collectively administered licenses are referred to as "blanket licenses," because they authorize licensees to use, for a single fee, any or all of the songs represented by the licensing organization. The licensee is not required to identify in advance which songs will be performed. Nor is the licensee charged more if it chooses to perform popular songs, or less if it chooses to perform songs that are not well known.

In the United States, the law does not require songwriters and music publishers to use ASCAP, BMI or SESAC to issue public performances licenses. Legally, songwriters and music publishers may, if they wish, issue their own public performance licenses directly to broadcasters, concert venues and others. As a practical matter, however, songwriters and music publishers could not possibly issue their own licenses. There simply are too many music users to keep track of; there would be too much paper work to do; and the costs of doing so would exceed the license fees that could be charged or collected. For these practical reasons, songwriters and music publishers do appoint either ASCAP, BMI or SESAC to issue licenses and collect royalties on their behalves, even though American law does not require it.

"Compulsory licenses," also referred to as "statutory licenses," are those that are required by law – hence the names "compulsory" and "statutory." Copyright statutes around the world typically give copyright owners the "exclusive" right to do, or authorize others to do, certain things with their works. The word "exclusive" is misleading, however, because those same statutes typically contain other provisions that authorize certain types of uses of certain works, whether or not copyright owners like it. Of course, once certain uses are authorized – that is, licensed – by statute, the statute must provide a mechanism for establishing the license fee, as well as the procedure for collecting licensee fees from those that take advantage of this compulsory license, and for allocating and distributing to copyright owners the license fees that are collected.

In many (though not all) cases, collective rights organizations (like ASCAP, BMI and SESAC) participate in the process by which compulsory license fees are set; and in many (though not all) cases, compulsory license fees are paid or distributed to collective rights organizations for them to allocate among the copyright owners they represent.

The types of works and uses that are subject to compulsory licensing are determined by the copyright statutes of each country. The types of works and uses that are collectively administered are determined by the local practices of each country. Thus, to explain the international operation of collectively administered or compulsory licenses, it is necessary to consider them one type of use a time, one country at a time.

## 1. Nondramatic pubic performances

Royalties for nondramatic public performances (including broadcasts) of musical compositions are collected by performing rights organizations (often called "PROs" for short) in the countries where those performances take place. ASCAP, BMI and SESAC are the PROs that collect for performances in the U.S. Other PROs collect for performances in their own countries – SOCAN in Canada, SACEM in France, GEMA in Germany, JASRAC in Japan, and PRS in the U.K. (These are only examples; there are at least 85 separate PROs in the world.)

ASCAP, BMI and SESAC have entered into agreements with their counterparts around the world, pursuant to which:

- other PROs collect royalties in their countries on behalf of American songwriters and music publishers whose songs have been performed abroad, which royalties are then paid to ASCAP, BMI and SESAC for distribution to those entitled to them in the U.S.; and
- ASCAP, BMI and SESAC collect royalties in the U.S. for foreign songwriters and music publishers whose songs have been performed in the U.S., which royalties ASCAP, BMI and SESAC then pay to PROs in other countries for distribution to those entitled to them.

From the point of view of an individual songwriter or music publisher, the system is virtually seamless. All that is required is membership (or affiliation) with a local PRO; and if performances occur abroad, royalties from abroad will be received eventually.

Songwriters and publishers may have to satisfy some administrative formalities. If, for example, a songwriter composes a song that is in the soundtrack of a movie or television program that is broadcast in another country, cue-sheets must be submitted to that country's PRO so the song is properly credited to the songwriter and music publisher entitled to royalties on account of that broadcast. Likewise, if singer-songwriters go on tour in another country, they may have to submit "tour itineraries" and "set-lists" to that country's PRO so their songs can receive credit, and they can be paid royalties, for their performances of the songs they've written. But the same or similar administrative formalities would have to be complied with in order for them to receive credit for performances in their own countries, so little or no additional burdens are imposed on songwriters and publishers to collect their performance royalties internationally. That burden has been assumed for them by the PROs of the world, by means of a remarkably efficient network of international agreements for the reciprocal collective administration of music copyrights.

*Question:* You'll recall (from Chapter 2) that the Berne Convention provides (in Article 5(2)) that the "enjoyment and exercise of [the] rights [protected by national copyright laws] shall not be subject to any formality." Do PROs (that do business in countries that are Berne Convention members) violate the Berne Convention by requiring things like cue-sheets, tour itineraries and set lists in order for songwriters and music publishers to receive public performance royalties they are clearly entitled to receive, as a matter of national copyright law? If so, why are these requirements tolerated? If not, why not?

## 2. Manufacture and sale of music recordings

The copyright laws of all countries require those who record, manufacture and sell music recordings to obtain licenses from the owners of the copyrights to the songs on those recordings (that is, from music publishers or songwriters). This is so, because the law gives copyright owners the right to reproduce and distribute their works. Recording songs and manufacturing records results in the "reproduction" of the songs on the record; and the sale of recordings results in the "distribution" of those songs.

Though in the language of copyright law, record companies need "reproduction" and "distribution" licenses, those in the music business refer to these licenses as "mechanical licenses." (The reason is historic. Player piano rolls were the first "recordings." At the time, piano rolls were considered to be "mechanical" parts of pianos. Hence: "mechanical licenses.")

In the United States, many music publishers (or songwriters) issue mechanical licenses directly to record companies who request them. Most publishers, however, have appointed The Harry Fox Agency to handle mechanical licensing on their behalves. The Harry Fox Agency acts, literally, as the agent for its music publishing clients for this purpose. Publishers have a choice between doing it themselves using their own staff employees, or having The Harry Fox Agency do it for them in return for a fee.

United States copyright law contains a compulsory mechanical license that authorizes record companies to make new recordings of previously released songs, in return for the payment of a royalty of what is now (as of January 1, 2006) 9.1 cents per song for each recording sold. (The rate is adjusted periodically.) The compulsory mechanical license is a license of last resort, however, for most record companies, because most record companies try to make better deals for themselves through voluntary negotiations directly with music publishers.

Other countries handle mechanical licensing somewhat differently than does the U.S. In other countries, all mechanical licenses are issued – by local practice or law – by "mechanical rights societies." In some countries the mechanical rights society is the same organization that serves as that country's performing rights organization. GEMA for instance is both the PRO and mechanical rights society for Germany; and JASRAC is both the PRO and mechanical rights society for Japan. Mechanical and performing rights are legally distinct, however, and many countries have two separate organizations – one for each of these rights.

Moreover, in other countries, the mechanical license royalty is calculated differently than it is in the U.S. It's often a percentage of the wholesale price of the recording, divided equally among all the songs on the recording, regardless of how many or how few there are. In Germany, for example, the mechanical license royalty is 9.009% of the Published Price to Dealers (roughly, the wholesale price), regardless of the number of songs on the recording. Also, in other countries, record companies do not seek better deals through direct negotiations with music publishers. They don't, because all mechanical licenses are issued by mechanical rights societies; publishers in those countries do not issue mechanical licenses themselves.

If a song by an American songwriter is recorded abroad, The Harry Fox Agency will collect the royalties that are due from the mechanical rights society in that country, on behalf of the U.S. publisher of that song. The Harry Fox Agency will then send the collected royalty to the publisher, and the publisher in turn will pay the songwriter, in accordance with the contract between the publisher and the songwriter.

To collect foreign mechanicals this way, the U.S. publisher must affiliate with The Harry Fox Agency – must, in other words, appoint the Fox Agency its agent for making those collections – and the publisher must notify the Fox Agency which of its songs have been recorded, manufactured and sold abroad.

The Harry Fox Agency has "affiliation" agreements with some two dozen mechanical rights societies in other countries. Those agreements also authorize The Harry Fox Agency to issue mechanical licenses to record companies in the U.S. for songs written by songwriters from those countries.

Things are a bit more complicated for U.S. music publishers that don't use The Harry Fox Agency to collect foreign mechanical royalties, and for the collection of foreign mechanical royalties from countries whose mechanical rights societies are not affiliated with The Harry Fox Agency. In those cases, U.S. publishers must enter into sub-publishing agreements with music publishers in other countries; and foreign music publishers must enter into sub-publishing agreements with U.S. publishers. Sub-publishing agreements authorize music publishers to publish (in their own countries) songs that originated and were first published in other countries. In this fashion, sub-publishers collect mechanical royalties from the societies in their own countries, and then send those royalties (less their commissions) to the publishers in other countries with which they have entered into sub-publishing agreements.

Regardless of which technique is used – The Harry Fox Agency as intermediary, or sub-publishing agreements with foreign music publishers – American music publishers and songwriters are able to receive mechanical royalties from foreign record companies, without having to negotiate individual licenses, and without litigation. The same is true in reverse: songwriters and music publishers in other countries are able to receive mechanical royalties from U.S. record companies, without having to negotiate or litigate.

### 3. Cable and satellite retransmissions of broadcasts

The copyright laws of all countries now require cable systems and satellite television companies to pay royalties when they retransmit to their own subscribers the signals of over-the-air broadcasts. You read (in Chapter 5) how this came about in the European Union, as a result of the *Coditel* case and the EU Council Directive that followed.

These royalties are owed to the owners of the copyrights to the retransmitted programming. When cable and satellite companies transmit original programming (like CNN, HBO and MTV), they must pay royalties too; but that type of programming is licensed by voluntary direct negotiations with copyright owners (as you read near the beginning of this chapter). When cable and satellite companies retransmit over-the-air broadcasts, those retransmissions are licensed by statute or collective administration, somewhat differently in each country.

#### a. Europe

AGICOA (the Association for the International Collective Management of Audiovisual Works) is an organization whose members are *associations* of movie and TV program producers. U.S. producers are represented (within AGICOA) by the MPAA (for the "majors"), IFTA (for the "independents") and the American Public Television Producers Association.

AGICOA negotiates license fees with cable and satellite companies in those European countries whose laws do not contain compulsory or statutory broadcast retransmission license provisions. AGICOA also collects retransmission royalties from cable and satellite companies; and it distributes those royalties to its association members, which then distribute them to the producers those associations represent.

To receive retransmission royalties, programs that are broadcast in Europe must be registered with AGICOA, a process that can be done on behalf of U.S. producers by the associations to which they belong.

#### b. Canada

Cable and satellite companies in Canada pay retransmission royalties to several "copyright collective societies" representing movie and TV producers, sports leagues (that own copyrights to sports broadcasts), and music publishers and songwriters. To receive royalties, those entitled to them must affiliate with (or form) a copyright collective society. The society proposes a "tariff," which may be challenged by cable and satellite companies in proceedings before the Copyright Board of Canada. That Board "certifies" the tariff to be paid to each society. And the societies collect the tariffs and distribute them to those it represents.

American copyright owners are represented in Canada by several such societies:

- Border Broadcasters, Inc. (TV stations, for local programming the stations themselves produce)
- Canadian Retransmission Right Association (ABC, CBS, NBC)
- Copyright Collective of Canada (MPAA, IFTA)
- FWS Joint Sports Claimants (NFL, NBA, NHL)
- Major League Baseball Collective of Canada (Major League Baseball), and
- SOCAN (ASCAP, BMI)

### c. United States

Cable and satellite companies in the U.S. pay retransmission royalties as well, at rates established through proceedings administered by the U.S. Copyright Office. The royalties are paid to the Copyright Office, which then divides them among the owners of the copyrights to the retransmitted programs, in proportions determined by other proceedings administered by the Copyright Office.

When the signals of Canadian and Mexican television stations are retransmitted by cable and satellite companies in the U.S., the owners of the copyrights to those retransmitted programs are entitled to a share of the U.S. retransmission royalties. To get their shares, those Canadian and Mexican copyright owners participate in U.S. Copyright Office proceedings, side-by-side with American copyright owners.

### 4. Other royalties

Music performance royalties, mechanical royalties, and broadcast retransmission royalties are the most significant royalties paid as a result of collective administration or compulsory licensing, measured by the amount of money involved. There are, however, additional types of royalties, some of which are not required under U.S. law, but are required under the laws of other countries. Though these royalties are not required by the international copyright treaties to which the U.S. adheres, some countries pay these royalties to American copyright owners anyway – even though the U.S. does not reciprocate (because U.S. law does not require these royalties to be paid to anyone).

### a.  Private copying levies

Private copying levies (also known as blank tape and copier levies) are imposed by the laws of Austria, Belgium, Canada, Denmark, France, Germany, Netherlands, Spain and Switzerland. These levies are added to the price of blank tapes and copiers, and are then distributed to those whose works are likely to have been privately copied to blank media. American works are among those copied in the countries that impose these levies; and the Americans' share of these levies is collected on their behalf by the MPAA and IFTA (on behalf of movie and television producers) and ASCAP, BMI and SESAC (on behalf of music publishers and songwriters). (A narrow form of this levy exists in U.S. law, in the Audio Home Recording Act of 1992, about which more is said below.)

### b.  Video rental and lending levies

Video rental and lending levies are imposed by the laws of Germany, the Netherlands and Switzerland. The levy is collected by retail video stores from customers who rent or borrow videos, and it is distributed to those whose videos were rented or lent. American videos are among those rented and lent in those countries. And the Americans' share is collected on their behalf by the MPAA and AFMA from those organizations within Germany, the Netherlands and Switzerland that collect them from retail video stores there.

## 5.  American dissatisfaction

Though this system for collecting and distributing royalties across national borders works well, it is not entirely problem free, at least from the point of view of American copyright owners. Here is why some Americans are dissatisfied.

### a.  Royalties not paid to Americans

Some royalties are not paid to Americans even though they are paid to others. For example, royalties paid by European, Australian and Japanese radio stations on account of their broadcasts of music recordings by performers who are nationals of those countries are not paid for recordings by American performers released by American record companies. Similarly, royalties are paid to authors living in the European Economic Area on account of the loan of their books by libraries in the U.K. and Germany; but those royalties are not paid to authors living in the U.S., even when their books are lent by U.K. and German libraries.

There is of course a legal reason that these royalties are not paid to Americans, even though they are paid to others. The copyright treaties to which the United States adheres – such as the Berne Convention, the TRIPs Agreement, and the WIPO Copyright Treaty – do not require adhering countries to grant recording performance or library lending rights, and the

U.S. does not (except for very narrow digital performance rights). The Rome Convention *does* require adhering countries to pay royalties for broadcasts of recordings by nationals of adhering countries; but the United States has never adhered to Rome Convention, so American radio stations don't pay royalties to record companies or performers of any nationality – not even to Americans – for broadcasting their recordings.

### b. Royalties are paid, but not to "copyright owners"

Compulsory license royalties are not always paid to "copyright owners." The country where the royalty originates determines who is entitled to receive it. And in some countries, royalties are divided *by law* among authors, performers and producers – as defined by the laws of those countries – rather than being paid to copyright owners. In the United States entertainment industry, most works are created as "works made for hire," so that under U.S. law, production companies usually are the "authors" as well as the "copyright owners" of their works. Not so, elsewhere.

Of course, the concept of directing a portion of compulsory license royalties, by statute, to authors and performers, is no longer alien to American copyright owners. This very thing was done by the U.S. Congress in the Audio Home Recording Act of 1992 which statutorily allocates, by percentage, blank digital media and recorder royalties among featured recording artists, background vocalists, background musicians, record companies, songwriters and music publishers (Copyright Act §1006). The Act does not simply divide these royalties between record companies and music publishers, even though they are the copyright owners.

Congress did so again in the Digital Performance Right in Sound Recordings Act of 1995 which statutorily allocates, by percentage, digital public performance royalties among featured recording artists, backup vocalists, backup musicians, and recording companies (Copyright Act §114(g)(2)). The Act does not permit record companies (which are the copyright owners) to get all these royalties. As a result, when American copyright owners complain that other countries direct royalties away from copyright owners, that complaint is simply the international part of a broader complaint about something the U.S. does too.

### c. Foreign collecting organizations sometimes retain royalties

Royalties that might otherwise have been paid to Americans are sometimes retained by foreign collecting societies, for at least three reasons.

First, performing rights organizations sometimes have difficulty identifying songs that have been publicly performed in their countries. The public performance royalties earned by unidentified songs may be retained by PROs in a so-called "black box." These "black box" moneys are distributed eventually, but only to *local* music publishers, thus depriving American songwriters and publishers of their share.

Second, a portion of some collective and compulsory license royalties are diverted away from those who would otherwise receive them, and are used for local social and cultural purposes. In France, 25% of private copying royalties are used for French cultural purposes; and in Spain, 20% of private copying royalties are used for training and promoting young Spanish performers. French and Spanish recipients of these royalties get less than they otherwise would; the diversions are not just aimed at Americans. On the other hand, these diversions do benefit French and Spanish nationals, while they do not benefit Americans.

Third, a portion of some royalties are retained by local collecting organizations to fund health insurance, retirement programs, loans, grants and awards, and programs to promote live local performances. The royalties used for these purposes are retained from all that are collected – not merely from royalties collected for the use of American works. But again, these programs benefit only those who are members of the local collecting organizations; they do not benefit Americans.

Despite the complaints of Americans, the cross-border collection and distribution of royalties demonstrates that "international copyright law" is a body of law that actually works. What's more, given the distances involved, and the differences in language, culture and business practices among nations, it works remarkably well.

Made in the USA
Lexington, KY
28 February 2010